D0906565

BEHAVIOR IN EXCESS

BEHAVIOR IN EXCESS
An Examination of the Volitional Disorders

Edited by
S. Joseph Mulé

THE FREE PRESS
A Division of Macmillan Publishing Co., Inc.
NEW YORK

Collier Macmillan Publishers
LONDON

The Free Press
A Division of Macmillan Publishing Co., Inc.
866 Third Avenue, New York, N.Y. 10022

Collier Macmillan Canada, Ltd.

Library of Congress Catalog Card Number: 81-65506

Printed in the United States of America

printing number

1 2 3 4 5 6 7 8 9 10

Library of Congress Cataloging in Publication Data
Main entry under title:

Behavior in excess.

Includes index.
1. Obsessive-compulsive neurosis. 2. Drug abuse—
Psychological aspects. I. Mulé, S. J. II. Title:
Volitional disorders. [DNLM: 1. Behavior therapy.
2. Compulsive behavior. WM 176 B4195]
RC533.B44   616.85'227   81-65506
ISBN 0-02-922220-6   AACR2

Contents

Part III

Preface

At first glance, the volitional disorders described in this volume appear to be separate biomedical and psychological entities. However, closer examination reveals a commonality of properties, so that a comprehensive hypothesis appears feasible. Thus, overeating, drug abuse, compulsive gambling, excessive drinking and smoking, etc., are merely different reflections of the same underlying psychological dysfunction. This essentially obsessive-compulsive problem expresses itself differently in people, primarily as a result of the individual's genetic makeup and interaction with the environment.

Once the underlying, internal cause of these disorders is identified (irrespective of its behavioral expression), large-scale treatment or prevention becomes a reality. No longer will we need to tailor therapy to each and every case. By developing a basic therapeutic modality we may be able to attack the source of the disorder directly, ultimately eliminating it.

In this volume each disorder is discussed by experts who illuminate thoroughly the exaggerated behaviors. This approach of course does not lend itself to a homogenous presentation; however, every author was given an outline to help guide the writing of each chapter. Thus, an effort was made to synthesize the essential material: genesis, definitions, biological, psychological, behavioral, and sociological correlates.

I am extremely grateful to Philip Peck and D. Springer for their very thorough editorial assistance and helpful comments.

S. Joseph Mulé

About the Contributors

GEARY S. ALFORD received his Ph.D. from the University of Arizona in 1972. He completed his clinical internship at the University of Mississippi Medical Center and a two-year Career Medical Teacher Fellowship from the National Institute of Drug Abuse and the National Institute of Alcohol Abuse and Alcoholism. Dr. Alford is currently Associate Professor of Psychiatry and Human Behavior at the University of Mississippi Medical Center and holds joint appointments as Assistant Professor of Pharmacology and Toxicology and as Clinical Assistant Professor of Family Medicine.

GORDON G. BALL received his Ph.D. at Stanford University. Currently, he is a clinical Assistant Professor in the Department of Psychiatry at Cornell Medical School and an adjunct Assistant Professor at Rockefeller University, and he maintains a private practice in New York City. He has over 20 publications, in *Science* and other leading journals, in the area of the underlying neurophysiological mechanism involved in eating behavior.

ARTHUR ASA BERGER, Professor of Broadcast Communication Arts at San Francisco State University, has a Ph.D from the University of Minnesota in American studies. Among his books are *Pop Culture, The Comic-Stripped American, The TV-Guide American,* and *Television as an Instrument of Terror.* A Consulting and Contributing Editor of the *Journal of Communication* and Film and Television Review Editor of *Society,* he has written for *The Nation, Rolling Stone, Human Behavior,* and the *Journal of Popular Culture* and other publications in England and Italy.

JOHN L. FALK is presently Professor of Psychology, at Rutgers University, New Brunswick, New Jersey. After receiving his Ph.D. from the University of Illinois, he did postdoctoral research at the Department of Pharmacology, Harvard Medical School, and Department of Nutrition, Harvard School of Public Health. Currently, he is serving on National Research Council—Committee on Substance Abuse and Habitual Behavior and National Institute on Drug Abuse—Intramural Research Review Committee and is President-Elect (1980) of Division 28 (Psychopharmacology) of the American Psychological Association.

EMILE J. FARGE is Assistant Professor at Baylor College of Medicine. He received his doctorate in community health sciences at the University of Texas Health Science Center at Houston. He has published on topics of sports medicine in the *Journal of Gerontology, Medicine and Science Sports,* the *Journal of Personality Assessment, Preventive Medicine,* and popular journals as well.

JEROME D. GOODMAN, M.D., is presently Assistant Clinical Professor of Psychiatry, College of Physicians and Surgeons, Columbia University. He maintains a private practice office in Adult and Children Psychiatry in Saddle River, New Jersey, and has published numerous articles in child psychiatry and forensic psychiatry.

JOHN F. GREDEN, M.D., is currently Professor of Psychiatry, Director of the Clinical Studies Unit, and Scientific Associate of the Mental Health Research Institute, University of Michigan Medical Center in Ann Arbor. He has published numerous articles on caffeine.

JOËL A. GRINKER is presently Associate Professor in the Laboratory of Human Behavior and Metabolism at the Rockefeller University. She received her Ph.D. in experimental social psychology from New York University. A member of the American Society for Clinical Nutrition, Society for Neuroscience, New York Academy of Science, and the American Psychological Association, she is a frequent contributor to *Physiology and Behavior* and *Pharmacology, Biochemistry and Behavior.* Her most recent publications include "Behavioral and Metabolic Factors in Childhood Obesity" in *The Uncommon Child* (eds. Lewis and Rosenblum).

SANDRA HABER is Director of Psychological Services at Howard Shapiro Medical Associates, an interdisciplinary obesity treatment program based in New York City. She also maintains a private practice. She obtained her Ph.D. from the Graduate Center, City University of New York, and has published numerous articles in the area of obesity.

RICHARD C. W. HALL, M.D., is currently Professor of Psychiatry and Internal Medicine in the Department of Psychiatry at the Medical College of Wisconsin. In addition, he is Director of the General Hospital Psychiatry Division and Chief of Neuropsychiatry, Milwaukee County Medical Complex. Dr. Hall is author of over 120 scientific publications and of two books entitled *Psychiatry in Crisis* and *Psychiatry Presentations of Medical Illness.*

G. HARLEY HARTUNG, Assistant Professor of Medicine and Physical Medicine, Baylor College of Medicine, and Director of the Cardiac Rehabilitation Unit, The Methodist Hospital, Houston, received his Ph.D. from the University of Texas at Austin. He is Fellow of the American College of Sports Medicine and has published numerous research articles dealing with exercise physiology, coronary risk, and cardiac rehabilitation. Major publications have appeared in the *New England Journal of Medicine,* the *Journal of Gerontology, American Heart Journal, Preventive Medicine,* and the *Journal of Sports Medicine and Physical Fitness.*

REESE T. JONES, M.D., is Professor of Psychiatry at the Langley Porter Psychiatry Institute, University of California at San Francisco. He obtained his M.D. from the University of Michigan School of Medicine. His publications include "Tolerance and Disposition of Tetrahydrocannabinol in Man" in the *Journal of Pharmacology and Experimental Therapeutics* and approximately 40 other publications concerned with the human pharmacology of cannabis.

RONALD F. KOKES, currently Director of the Family and Sex Therapy Programs at the Veterans Administration Medical Center in Albuquerque, received his Ph.D. in clinical psychology from the University of Iowa. His clinical and research activities include behavioral treatment of psychologically disordered families, adolescents and adults, prognosis of mental illness, relationships of parent functioning to child behavior, and the effects of severe neurological and physical disability on instrumental roles of married couples. His publications have appeared in such journals as *Schizophrenia Bulletin, Archives of General Psychiatry,* and the *Journal of Abnormal Psychology.*

DANIEL C. MOORE, M.D., is Assistant Professor of Psychiatry, Yale University School of Medicine, and the Director of the Dana Psychiatric Clinic (outpatient) at Yale–New Haven Hospital, where he is involved in treatment of anorexia nervosa from both biological and family therapy perspectives. Dr. Moore is also Co-Director of the Yale Tardive Dyskinesia Clinic, where he does research into the cause and treatment of abnormal involuntary movement disorders. He received his M.D. from Boston University School of Medicine and his psychiatry residency training at the Yale University Department of Psychiatry.

WAYNE E. OATES is currently Professor of Psychiatry and Behavioral Sciences at the University of Louisville School of Medicine, where he is also the Director of the Program in Ethics and Pastoral Counseling. He is the author of over 35 books in the areas of pastoral counseling and workaholism.

MICHAEL K. POPKIN, M.D., is Associate Professor of Psychiatry and Medicine and the Director of the Consultation Psychiatry Service at the University of Minnesota Medical School in Minneapolis. He is a graduate of the University of Chicago Pritzker School of Medicine and received his psychiatric training at the Massachusetts General Hospital.

ROBERT M. POST, M.D., is currently the Chief, Section on Psychobiology, Biological Psychiatry Branch, National Institute of Mental Health. He received his M.D. from the University of Pennsylvania School of Medicine. The author of more than 150 articles on the psychopharmacology of manic-depressive illness, psychomotor stimulant administration, and seizures, he introduced the use of the anticonvulsant carbamazepine for the treatment of manic-depressive illness. Dr. Post received the A.E. Bennett Neuropsychiatric Research Award from the Society of Biological Psychiatry in 1973.

JACQUELYN ROGERS is currently the director of Smokenders and has personally analyzed over 15,000 case histories of smokers. She is the author of *You Can Stop.*

LEON SALZMAN, M.D., is currently Clinical Professor of Psychiatry at Georgetown University Medical School and is the past President of the American Academy of Psychoanalysis. He has published over 100 articles and two books: *Treatment of the Obsessive Personality* and *Developments in Psychoanalysis.*

CHARLES R. SCHUSTER, Professor of Psychiatry, Pharmacology, and Physiological Sciences at the University of Chicago, received his Ph.D. from the University of Maryland. He has published *Behavioral Pharmacology* (with T. Thompson) and *Drug Dependence* (with R.T. Harris and W.M. McIsaac).

FRANK A. SEIXAS, M.D., currently Medical Director of the Norwood Hospital Comprehensive Alcoholism Program, is on leave from the Cornell University Medical School, where he is Clinical Professor of Medicine. A member of the Executive Board of the American Medical Society on Alcoholism, he has published numerous articles, book reviews, and book chapters.

RALPH G. VICTOR, M.D., is currently Medical Director of the Fresno Community Hospital Mental Health Center and Clinical Assistant Professor of Psychiatry at the University of California at San Francisco. He has published numerous articles.

Introduction

S. Joseph Mulé

In viewing behavior as excessive, we might ask by what means or standard does one judge behavior abnormal or deviant? The direct approach would be to consult the American Psychiatric Association's third *Manual of Mental Disorders*. A more pragmatic approach would be simply to determine whether the behavior is harmful to the individual (medical deterioration), to society (violence, stealing, drunken driving, financial dependency), or to a combination of these. Once a consensus is achieved, the volitional disorder itself may be examined. What factors control the particular excessive behavior (drugs, food, gambling, sex, etc.)? Do environment, socioeconomic status, education, and/or genetics contribute to the disorder? Is the choice of activity conscious or unconscious? However chosen, the individual most certainly does not decide to become drug dependent or alcoholic or obese, etc., but in all probability over time and through continued reinforcement falls into the excess activity pattern, which culminates, at the very least, in a psychic dependency.

The question is whether a commonality of processes exists across the various forms of excessive behavior. If so, what are the shared properties and characteristics (etiological, biological, sociological, psychological) of the volitional disorders? If a common denominator runs through affected individuals, then one might expect the substitution of one substance for another (e.g., methadone for heroin); multiple substance abuse (simultaneous reliance, dependence, or excessive use of heroin, alcohol, tobacco, marijuana, and stimulants); or one disorder for another (overeating for smoking); or overlapping overactive behaviors (sexuality, work, drinking, eating, smoking). If in fact such convergence occurs, a general theory might be able to identify and explain the underlying cause of the exaggerated behaviors.

Volitional disorders then may simply be the end result of a conflict between internal and external forces, such as: *predisposition* (genotype, nutrition, sociocultural or socioeconomic milieu, temperament); *environment* (surroundings may enhance or inhibit the predisposing forces); *fortification* (behavior is reinforced through repetition and interactions of a pharmacological, biochemical, psychological, or sociological nature); *tolerance* (continued interaction of the substance or behavioral activity with the physiological system); *physiochemical change* (homeostatic mechanisms require continued substance use or excessive activity to prevent a negative adjustment in the system); *abstinence* (withdrawal symptoms occur when the level of substance use or activity is insufficient to maintain the dependent state); and *hypophoria* (negative feeling states are relieved by excessive behavior). The various components of the volitional disorders include an illusory conception of superiority (grandiosity), hypophoria, compulsivity, obsession, lack of control, depression, insecurity, anxiety, and frustration. Oftentimes, failure to control impulses and obsessional difficulties result in excessive behavior (e.g., drinking bouts and binge eating) that allows one for the moment to overcome personal inadequacies and enjoy illusory powers with the concomitant fulfillment of a fantasy life (grandiosity). If all control is lost, euphoric grandiosity may occur in the complete intoxicated state.

An example of how behavior in excess occurs might be provided by the socioeconomically deprived ghetto youngster who turns to heroin because of peer pressure and finds such use an acceptable means of alleviating negative personal feelings (anxiety, insecurity, hostility, frustration), allowing him to feel good about himself and his environment. On the other hand, a middle-class, Irish, Catholic white male may resort to excessive alcohol use as the preferred vehicle for alleviating his hypophoric state and capturing the same good feelings. It is not difficult to draw similar profiles of overeaters, heavy smokers, anorexics, compulsive gamblers, compulsive athletes, overworkers, and television addicts. If the etiology of volitional disorders as a class can be identified, then an effective therapeutic remedy can be found. The treatment must attack the psychic source of the disorder, extinguishing the outward behavioral expression as well as alter or eliminate socioeconomic and other external correlates.

Although some components of the volitional disorders may be described, this complex problem remains mysterious. An extensive, multifaceted effort (psychological, biochemical, pharmacological, economical, and sociological) is needed to gain full insight into the nature of these disorders, but the key to therapy is the inner dynamics of the compulsion (see Chapter 18).

A fascinating view of the generation and maintenance of excessive behaviors has promising implications for treatment (Chapter 17). Falk suggests that the environment triggers exaggerated behaviors. Therefore, alteration of the environment can eliminate the behavioral disorder. The difficulty here is matching theory with practical applications.

Certainly the need to alter excessive behavior through behavioral modification or therapy seem obvious. Chapter 19 demonstrates good results with individuals in well-designed multiple-component treatment programs that used contingency management, relaxation training, desensitization, covert sensitization, and self-control techniques. Successful treatment of this kind requires that the patient not exhibit chronic psychopathology.

Behavioral therapy is particularly useful in the development of skills necessary for life management outside the treatment setting.

One hopes that the future will bring a regimen that prevents the development of behaviors in excess. At present, the reader can gain insight into the psychodynamics of these behaviors and from this knowlege a real benefit in managing his or her life.

PART
ONE

1
Opiates

Charles R. Schuster

This chapter selectively reviews aspects of the pharmacology of opiates that are relevant to their nonmedical self-administration. I discuss phenomena such as tolerance to and physical dependence upon opiates only as they relate to opiate drug-seeking behavior. Major emphasis is placed on studies demonstrating the pharmacological, organismic, and environmental variables affecting this behavior. A secondary purpose of this chapter is to describe both the common and the unique characteristics of opiate drug-seeking behavior compared to behaviors maintained by the delivery of other drugs, food, or water.

The behavioral aspects of opiate dependence can be fruitfully analyzed within the conceptual framework of the experimental analysis of behavior, which utilizes the principles of both operant and classical conditioning. Behavior controlled by its consequences is called "operant behavior" and the controlling consequence is designated a "reinforcer." The process through which behavior is strengthened (i.e., the probability of its occurrence is increased) by a reinforcer is termed "reinforcement." In this context opiate drug-seeking behavior is viewed as operant behavior maintained by the administration of the opiate, which serves as the "positive reinforcer." By viewing drugs as reinforcers, we can use the vast body of data generated by experimental psychologists in the study of more traditional reinforcers (e.g., food, water, sex) as a guide to the variables that affect the rate, pattern, and persistence of drug-seeking behavior. This approach has already begun to generate a literature demonstrating the similarity between drug reinforced behaviors and responses maintained by other stimuli in terms of variables that control performance (1, 2, 37, 134). Under certain circumstances drug injections may be avoided or terminated. When behavior is strengthened by the avoidance or termination of an event we refer to that event as a "negative reinforcer." Although this drug avoidance-escape behavior has only begun to be studied, it appears that the same variables control this behavior as control avoidance or escape from events such as electric shock.

For a complete understanding of the behavioral aspects of opiate dependence, it is also necessary to analyze those aspects of the behavior that are classically conditioned. Classical conditioning involves the pairing of an unconditioned stimulus (UCS), which elicits some unconditioned behavioral response (UCR), with a neutral stimulus. After a number of pairings of these two stimuli, the neutral stimulus (CS) acquires the ability to produce a response, called the "conditioned response." A variety of responses to drugs can be conditioned and have been shown to be important in a range of problems including opiate tolerance and relapse to drug use (4, 5).

This chapter is concerned primarily with analyzing laboratory research, usually conducted in animals, to understand the persistent, self-destructive, socially costly phenomenon of opiate abuse by humans. The use of animals in the investigation of drug-seeking behavior has clear ethical and practical advantages. As stated over a decade ago, the most important advantage is that the use of animals forces investigators to divest themselves of simplistic preconceptions regarding personality and/or social factors in opiate dependence (6). The laboratory scientist approaches the problem empirically in order to determine the operationally definable manipulations that alter an organism's propensity to self-administer opiates (in recent years laboratory studies in humans modeled on animal drug self-administration experiments have begun (7-9).

Pharmacological Variables in the Self-administration of Opiates

Nature of the Drug

Morphine can serve as a reinforcer in a variety of species and under diverse environmental circumstances. Table 1-1 lists other opiate agonist drugs that also can serve as reinforcers. Although many opiate agonists remain to be investigated, the data obtained to date seem to justify the conclusion that the ability to serve as a reinforcer for operant behavior is a general property of this class of drugs.

Within this class of drugs, the physical and chemical properties of the various opiate agonists apparently influence their reinforcing efficacy. Heroin, for instance, is highly lipophilic and penetrates the brain faster than morphine (10). It has long been a popular conception that the preference for heroin over morphine is determined, at least in part, by its more rapid onset of action. Unfortunately, there have been no direct investigations of the acquisition and maintenance of opiate reinforced behavior when a time delay has been imposed between the drug-seeking behavior and the delivery of the drug reinforcer. Investigations using non-

TABLE 1–1.
Opiate Agonists
That Serve as Reinforcers

l-Alpha-acetylmethadol
Azidomorphine
Codeine
Etonitazine
Etorphine
Fentanyl
Heroin
Ketobemidone
Levomethorphan
Levorphanol
Meperidine
Methadone
Morphine
Oxymorphone
d-Propoxyphene (hydrochloride)
d-Propoxyphene (napsylate)
Tilidine

drug reinforcers have demonstrated that both acquisition and maintenance of behavior are weakened as a direct function of reinforcement delay (11). In one study using intravenous cocaine as the reinforcer, monkeys were allowed to choose between completing response requirement for the drug on one of two levers. Completion of the response requirements on one of the levers produced an immediate injection of cocaine, whereas completion of the ratio on the other lever resulted in the illumination of a red light and the injection of cocaine 15 seconds later. Surprisingly, monkeys showed a clear preference for the delayed cocaine option (12). Whether this experiment uncovered a unique difference between cocaine as a reinforcer or a more general property distinguishing drugs from food remains to be resolved. Regardless, physical and chemical factors influencing extent and rate of drug penetration into the brain seem to affect a drug's reinforcing efficacy.

Although we can generalize about the reinforcing action of opiate agonists of the morphine type, the situation with mixed agonist-antagonist compounds is more complex. These compounds appear to vary in their reinforcing actions probably depending on the relative proportion of their agonistic and antagonistic action and also on whether the test subjects are physically dependent upon an opiate agonist. Descriptions of the opiate withdrawal syndrome in humans emphasize the suffering and general aversiveness of the condition. This is particularly true when the withdrawal syndrome is brought on abruptly by the administration of an opiate antagonist. It is not surprising, therefore, that compounds with antagonistic properties are avoided by animals physically dependent on an opiate.

Goldberg and colleagues demonstrated that rhesus monkeys physically dependent upon morphine would lever-press to terminate either a stimulus associated with naloxone or nalorphine infusions (avoidance) or infusion of the antagonist itself (escape) (13). In subsequent experiments, similar results were obtained with pentazocine and propiram. However, pentazocine and propiram would not maintain responses that terminated a stimulus associated with these agents in animals not physically dependent upon morphine (14). Nalorphine and cyclazocine, on the other hand, have been shown to generate and maintain avoidance-escape responses in rhesus monkeys with no history of opiate dependence; however, the dose required is much higher than in morphine dependent animals (15). Furthermore, naloxone will maintain escape responses in opiate-naive monkeys but again only at dose levels much higher than those necessary to maintain avoidance-escape behavior in rhesus monkeys physically dependent upon morphine (40).

Three important points emerge from this somewhat confusing picture. First, both antagonist (naloxone) and mixed agonist-antagonist (pentazocine, propiram, nalorphine) compounds will serve as negative reinforcers in morphine dependent rhesus monkeys. Second, certain of these compounds (nalorphine, naloxone, cyclazocine) will serve as negative reinforcers in opiate-naive monkeys but only at dose levels markedly higher than those that maintain avoidance-escape responses in physically dependent animals. Finally, certain of these drugs (propiram, pentazocine) will serve as positive reinforcers in opiate-naive animals but as negative reinforcers in monkeys physically dependent upon an opiate.

The research demonstrating that drugs function as negative reinforcers supports the observation that performance maintained by drugs is similar to behavior maintained by other events. Drugs such as naloxone can control responses in a manner similar to that found with electric shock. Animals will avoid or escape both these stimuli under a variety of schedules; the characteristics of the response are the same regardless of the maintaining event (16). Furthermore, under certain environmental conditions, animals will administer rather than avoid both electric shock and naloxone (17, 40), which again points to the functional similarity between drugs and other types of reinforcers.

Route of Administration

The majority of studies of opiate self-administration have used intravenous administration. The intravenous route has several advantages, including precise control over the dose delivered, rapidity of onset of the drug effect, and avoidance of taste and olfactory factors, which may influence the oral consumption of drugs. However, orally delivered opiates also can serve as reinforcers in rats and monkeys (18–22). Many studies have demonstrated that animals will drink solutions of various opiates in sufficient quantities to produce obvious pharmacological effects including physical dependence. But because of the opiates' bitter taste, animals must often be severely deprived of water in order to induce them initially to consume a solution containing an opiate. An intermittent food delivery schedule that produces polydipsia is one way to induce animals to consume large quantities of a solution containing an opiate (23, 24). Alternatively, consumption has been increased by adding to the solution either salt or saccharin (25, 26). These studies do *not* demonstrate that the drug is serving as a positive reinforcer. A drug can be considered such only if an animal's consumption of the drug solution is significantly greater than its consumption of a control solution or if animals show a preference for the drug in a choice situation.

In addition to intravenous and oral delivery, other routes of administration have been used. For instance, morphine given intragastrically has served as a reinforcer for lever-pressing in both rats and monkeys (27, 3). Finally, Goldberg and associates have shown that behavior can be maintained in rhesus monkeys by an intramuscular injection of morphine (28). The response rate for intramuscular morphine, however, is significantly lower than that maintained by the intravenous administration. As stated previously, the greater efficacy of the intravenous route of administration rests on a more rapid onset of action, minimizing reinforcement delay.

Dosage

The effects of drug dose have been systematically investigated in self-administration procedures delivering drugs through venous catheters. Changing dose per infusion in the context of drug self-administration studies can be viewed as manipulating magnitude of reinforcement. Psychologists have studied magnitude of reinforcement using a variety of other reinforcers including food and water. Generally, the larger the magnitude, the greater the strength of the behavior (29). In drug self-administration studies, the relationship between rate of responding and magnitude of the reinforcer varies with the drug class. These differences may reflect the development of tolerance to and physical dependence on some classes of self-administered drugs (e.g., opiates and barbiturates) but not others (e.g., psychomotor stimulants). With opiates (e.g., morphine, methadone, propoxyphene, codeine), experiments using both rats and rhesus monkeys have found an inverse relationship between rate of responding maintained under a fixed-ratio schedule (drug delivery for every nth response) and dose of the drug reinforcer (30–34). Tolerance to the opiates shifts this function to the right and lessens the steepness of the slope (35).

These studies suggest that higher doses of an opiate are less reinforcing than lower doses since less behavior is maintained. This seemingly paradoxical outcome is explained by the fact that under fixed-ratio schedules of reinforcement, the frequency of injection is related directly to the rate of responding so that animals cumulate morphine by repeated injections during each session. Inspection of cumulative response records of fixed-ratio paradigms examining opiates reveals a marked negative acceleration over the session. As has been discussed in detail elsewhere, reinforcing drugs possess other pharmacological properties that also alter the rate of responding (36, 37). A drug that serves as a positive reinforcer will increase responding leading to its delivery. This effect on rate is dependent upon the contingency relationship between responding and reinforcement delivery. The drug, however, has effects on behavior regardless of the event maintaining it. Opiate drugs in general decrease the response rate for all reinforcers delivered under a fixed-ratio schedule (38, 39, 150–153). Thus, the rate of response under a fixed-ratio schedule is not an appropriate measure of the relationship between the magnitude of a drug reinforcer and the strength of the behavior it maintains.

A variety of experimental procedures have been developed to obtain a more specific measure of a drug's reinforcing efficacy (36, 37). Briefly, these procedures include schedules such as fixed-interval, concurrent, second-order, progressive-ratio, and choice (41–45). Only a few of these procedures have been used to investigate the relation of dose of an opiate drug to its efficacy as a reinforcer. For instance, the rate disrupting effects of opiates can be minimized by conditions in which the drug is administered infrequently. Goldberg and Tang used a second-order schedule in which animals (squirrel and rhesus monkeys) received an intravenous injection of morphine for the completion of a fixed-ratio 30 (FR-30) requirement only after 60 minutes had elapsed (46). Prior to this, a brief stimulus correlated with the morphine infusion had been presented following each FR-30 (a fuller descripton of such second-order schedules appears in a later section). After the animals' response rate stabilized under this schedule at 1.5 mg/kg (squirrel monkeys) or 1.0 mg/kg (rhesus monkeys) of intravenous morphine, the dose of morphine was systematically varied. Response rate was related directly to dose at levels below the training dose but was asymptotic at higher levels.

One method that has been used extensively to compare the reinforcing efficacy of different drugs, as well as various doses of the same drug, is the progressive-ratio procedure (44, 47–49). In this procedure, the ratio requirements for the drug reinforcer are progressively increased and the "breaking point" (i.e., the highest ratio completed before the animal fails to complete a ratio within some period of time) is obtained. Using this general method, researchers found that breaking point increased as a direct function of dose for heroin and codeine. In contrast, an inverted U-shaped function was obtained between dose and breaking point for pentazocine and propoxyphene, suggesting that at higher dose levels these drugs may indeed have some aversive effects (49).

Drug preference procedures have also been used to investigate the relationship between the dose of a drug and its strength as a reinforcer (36, 45). With psychomotor stimulant drugs (which share with opiates an inverse relationship between dose and response rate under fixed-ratio schedules) drug preference is a direct function of dose. Unfortunately, these methods have not been used to study drug dose preferences with opiates. However, the evidence presented suggests a direct relationship (up to some asymptotic level) between the dose of the opiate reinforcer and response strength, which can be easily demonstrated using a variety of the procedures described. These procedures should be used in the future to determine how factors such as tolerance specifically modify the reinforcing property of opiates.

Tolerance

It has long been recognized that tolerance develops to many of the actions of opiates (50). Cross-tolerance between morphine and other drugs is in fact one of the criteria for designating a drug a member of the opiate class. A variety of biochemical theories seek to explain tolerance to opiates (51-53). In general terms, these theories suggest that opiates alter the release of certain neurotransmitters in the central nervous system. As a consequence of this alteration, compensatory mechanisms (e.g., activation of alternative pathways, proliferation of new receptors, and/or increases in the affinity of such receptors for a "blocked" neurotransmitter) are set in motion. These compensatory mechanisms are assumed to be a simple response to the presence of the drug at certain sites within the central nervous system and are often referred to as "receptor tolerance." Recently, however, exciting discoveries have been made that indicate the tremendous importance of environmental variables in the development of opiate tolerance. In a series of classic experiments, Siegel demonstrated that tolerance to opiates is mediated, at least in part, by classically conditioned responses (4). Pavlov first noted that drug administration procedures contain all of the elements necessary for the conditioning of a drug response (54). The drug can be viewed as an unconditioned stimulus that elicits certain unconditioned responses from the organism. Stimuli associated with the injection procedure can acquire the ability to produce a response because of their temporal association with the unconditioned stimulus (the drug). Such conditioning would be expected if animals received repeated injections under the same environmental circumstances, and this kind of conditioning has been demonstrated with a wide variety of psychoactive drugs (4).

One controversy surrounding this area of research, however, has to do with the nature of the conditioned response. When drugs are used as the UCS, some studies (but not all) have found that the conditioned response is opposite in direction to the unconditioned one. For example, if a stimulus is paired with atropine injections, the conditioned response is excessive salivation rather than decreased salivation, which is the response produced by atropine itself (55–59). Similarly, although morphine produces brady-cardia, hyperthermia, and analgesia, some investigators have reported that conditioned stimuli associated with morphine produce conditioned responses that are opposite in direction (i.e., tachycardia, hypothermia, and hyperalgesia), which is termed an "opponent process" (60).

Siegel argued that tolerance to opiates occurs because of the interaction between conditioned and unconditioned responses to the drug. He suggested that the gradual development of tolerance is a reflection of the gradual increase in magnitude of the conditioned response, which in effect opposes the unconditioned response. These two responses sum algebraically so that over time, with the increase in the magnitude of the conditioned response, the observed response diminishes. Supporting this hypothesis is a series of experiments by Mitchell and his colleagues demonstrating the situational specificity of tolerance to the analgesic effects of morphine in both animals and humans (61–72). These experiments found that tolerance to the analgesic effects of morphine was greatest in test situations in which the animal or human had been tested repetitively. In contrast, when tolerant animals or humans were given a novel test for analgesia, they showed far less tolerance. Thus, the degree of tolerance was not·a simple function of drug exposure but rather the result of an interaction between drug and test situation.

Siegel has confirmed and extended this work by demonstrating a conditioned response to stimuli associated with daily administration of morphine; he also has shown that tolerance, because it is a conditioned response, can be extinguished (4). In his study, rats were treated daily with morphine and tested for analgesia. Progressive tolerance was observed to the analgesic effects of morphine. When these tolerant animals were administered a placebo and tested, they showed a significant hyperalgesia. This finding was interpreted as a conditioned response to the stimuli associated with the injection of morphine. Siegel reasoned that if this response were conditioned, it should be possible to extinguish it. To test this hypothesis he treated two groups of rats daily with 5 mg/kg of morphine and tested them on a hot plate for analgesia. As expected, three consecutive days of injections produced significant tolerance to morphine's analgesic effect. Furthermore, in one group (REST), which was left undisturbed for nine days, significant residual tolerance was found when morphine was again given and the animals were retested for analgesia. During the nine-day period, the second group (EXT) of animals received daily sessions on the hot plate but got placebo (saline) injections. This group showed significantly less tolerance than the REST group when tested with morphine on the tenth day. Although both groups of animals had identical pharmacological histories, they differed in terms of their experience during the nine-day period between the induction of tolerance and test for residual tolerance. The EXT group had been repetitively exposed to the conditioned stimuli (i.e., environmental stimuli associated with the drug injection, as well as the testing apparatus) but without any association with the unconditioned stimulus (i.e., the morphine injection). This is, of course, the operation for extinguishing a conditioned response. This extinction of the conditioned response (i.e., hyperalgesia) resulted in the loss of tolerance to the analgesic effect of morphine. This loss of tolerance through extinction was replicated by Siegel using a paw-press analgesiometer with rats (4).

These experiments by Mitchell and colleagues and Siegel found that tolerance to at least certain actions of opiates is mediated by the classical conditoning caused by association of environmental stimuli with injections of the opiate. Clearly, such a mechanism cannot explain all aspects of opiate tolerance (e.g., tolerance engendered by the subcutaneous implantation of a slow-release pellet of morphine); however, this mechanism does point to a new set of variables pharmacologists and clinicians must consider when repetitively administering opiates.

Since it is well established that tolerance develops to many opiate effects, it is noteworthy that no investigations have been reported demonstrating tolerance to the reinforcing action of opiates. Though under fixed-ratio schedules, the response rate for morphine increases for the first 4 to 6 weeks of continuous access to the drug (73), this pattern most likely represents tolerance to the rate limiting, depressant effect of the drug, with the consequence that more injections can be administered. In an experiment designed to determine the role of drug histories, Hoffmeister and Schlichting substituted various opiate drugs as reinforcers in rhesus monkeys previously trained to self-administer either codeine or cocaine (152). Animals previously using codeine showed higher rates of responding for all the opiate agonists tested. This finding would suggest that prior exposure to codeine rendered the animals tolerant to the depressant action of opiates. However, responses for both codeine and morphine were maintained at lower dose levels (codeine 10 times lower; morphine 100 times lower) in animals trained with codeine as opposed to those trained with cocaine. Clearly, a history of opiate self-administration made the monkeys more sensitive to opiate reinforcers as judged by the threshold dose able to maintain response. This suggests that the pharmacological history of the organism is not the only historical factor affecting rate of self-administration. Examining this possibility, Weeks and Collins found that postdependent rats previously trained to maintain their physical dependence by pressing a lever to produce intravenous injections of morphine responded at higher rates and received more morphine under a schedule of intravenous morphine injections than postdependent rats that previously had been made physically dependent by noncontingent morphine injections but trained to press a lever for water (74). However, this latter group responded at higher rates and received more morphine than rats previously trained to lever-press for morphine but never physically dependent on it. Thus, both pharmacological and behavioral history are important. It remains to be seen how far either of these factors, or both, contribute to individual differences among humans in terms of the opiates' ability to serve as positive reinforcers.

Physical Dependence

The investigation of the role of physical dependence in opiate self-administration is concerned with two questions: (1) is physical dependence necessary before opiates can serve as reinforcers; (2) does physical dependence influence the reinforcing efficacy of opiates?

In this context physical dependence is important because it sensitizes the organism to drug deprivation as well as to the administration of opiate antagonists. Both of these manipulations produce a withdrawal syndrome that (as will be demonstrated) enhances the reinforcing efficacy of opiates in the same way that deprivation influences the reinforcing efficacy of food, water, or sex.

Many of the early animal studies concluded that physical dependence upon morphine is necessary for the drug to act as a reinforcer (75, 76). Descriptions of an abstinence induced withdrawal syndrome in both animals and humans stressed the aversive quality of this condition. Since these aversive effects could be terminated by an injection of morphine, behavior leading to morphine injections could be characterized as escape behavior. This concept was readily accepted since it fit into the drive reduction models of reinforcement, prevalent in American psychology during the 1940s and fifties.

Beach was the first to provide data questioning the adequacy of the drive reduction model of morphine reinforcement (77). In his experiment, Beach made rats physically dependent upon morphine; then he conducted tests in a Y-maze to determine which goal box each animal preferred. Next, animals undergoing mild withdrawal were given saline injections and placed in the preferred goal box for an hour. Following this experience the animals were given an injection of morphine to terminate their withdrawal syndrome and immediately placed into the nonpreferred goal box for one hour. After several days of exposure to these pairings, animals were again tested for their preferences and overwhelmingly chose the goal box associated with the morphine injection (i.e., the initially nonpreferred box).

This experiment would, of course, support the hypothesis that morphine reinforcement is based upon the drug's ability to terminate the aversive aspects of the withdrawal syndrome. However, Beach also demonstrated that animals placed in the originally nonpreferred goal box one hour after a morphine injection also switched their preference to this goal box. He argued that morphine reinforcement responsible for the development of the goal box preference in this group of rats could not have been based on withdrawal syndrome relief, since that would have occurred before the introduction of these animals into the goal box. Beach concluded that morphine acts as a reinforcer both by reducing the aversive properties of withdrawal and by its long-lasting euphoric effects. Subsequently, different investigations have shown that various opiate drugs can serve as reinforcers at dose levels or under conditions of intermittency that preclude the development of demonstrable physical dependence (78–80). Furthermore, we know that substantial amounts of drug-seeking behavior are maintained even when a sufficient quantity of an opiate is being concurrently infused to prevent any signs of withdrawal (81, 82).

This evidence justifies the conclusion that physical dependence, with the consequent cyclical withdrawal state, is not a necessary condition for opiates to serve as reinforcers. On the other hand, there is no question that physical dependence does amplify the reinforcing efficacy of opiates. Operationally, one can view the withdrawal state as a deprivaton condition. Research with food and water has shown that low to moderate levels of deprivation increase the reinforcing efficacy of these items as judged by response rates or preference measures (29). It is now well established that this pattern also describes opiate reinforcement. Thompson and Schuster, for example, found that increasing the morphine deprivation of monkeys from 6 to 24 hours produced a large increase in response rate maintained by morphine on a chained fixed-interval–fixed-ratio schedule (83). They also found that withdrawal initiated by the administration of the opiate antagonist nalorphine produced comparable increases in response rate. Similarly, Weeks and Weeks and Collins reported that nalorphine given to rats self-administering morphine under a fixed-ratio schedule produced response rate increments that were comparable to those produced by morphine deprivation (30, 31). Goldberg and colleagues found a biphasic action of nalorphine in physically dependent rhesus monkeys responding under a fixed-ratio schedule for morphine reinforcement (84). Dose related increases in response rates were observed in doses of nalorphine up to .3 mg/kg. Higher doses produced a suppression of responding, probably the result of incapacity engendered by the intense withdrawal syndrome. These data support the general conclusion that physical dependence, although not a necessary condition for opiates to function as reinforcers, can markedly influence their reinforcing efficacy. Furthermore, physical dependence apparently produces an organismic state comparable to that of hunger or thirst. This correspondence again suggests that variables that modify performance maintained by drugs are similar to those that control performance maintained by other events.

Manipulating the Reinforcing Efficacy of Opiates

In discussing physical dependence, I reviewed data on the effects of non-contingent administration of opiate antagonists on behavior maintained by opiate reinforcement. In this section we will look at some of the same studies, as well as others, in the context of the development of a drug for treatment of opiate addiction. If a drug could be found that significantly reduced the reinforcing efficacy of heroin, this compound might be useful in treatment.

The attempt to find a pharmacological solution to the problem of opiate dependence has a long history. In the late nineteenth century, Freud treated a patient with cocaine for opiate addiction (85). Indeed, even heroin, when it was first synthesized, was advocated as a cure for morphine addiction (86). More recently a variety of drugs including methadone, naltrexone, haloperidol, and clonidine have been advocated for treatment (87–90).

At the present time, methadone maintenance is the most successful drug therapy for heroin addiction. However, its behavioral and/or pharmacological mechanism of action is not entirely understood. Possibly methadone prevents heroin seeking behavior by producing either satiation or cross-tolerance, by preventing the occurrence of opiate withdrawal, or by some combination of all three actions. Thus far, results from experimental investigations of the effects of methadone on opiate reinforced behavior do not always differentiate among these possibilities. Jones and Prada studied the effects of methadone on drug reinforced behavior in humans and dogs (80, 81). In their human experiment, subjects were required to ride a stationary bicycle in order to receive an intravenous injection of hydromorphone. The drug reinforced behavior was studied prior to and during a period of methadone maintenance in which the dose was gradually raised from 5 to 100 mg per day orally. Under these circumstances, subjects obtained virtually all of the available hydromorphone under the baseline condition and continued to perform a substantial amount of bicycle riding while receiving daily doses of methadone up to 50 mg. At 100 mg of daily methadone, however, most subjects stopped bicycle riding. At the higher doses of methadone the speed of subjects who continued to bicycle ride was significantly decreased, suggesting some degree of drug induced physical handicap. Subjects indicated verbally, however, that they stopped taking the hydromorphone not because of physical incapacitation but because they could no longer "feel" it. This report suggests that methadone reduced the reinforcing efficacy of hydromorphone through its ability to produce cross-tolerance—as satiation can decrease food maintained responses. However, unlike with food satiation, it is possible that if subjects could have obtained more hydromorphone they would have continued to work for the drug since they would have been able to exceed their level of tolerance and thereby achieve a reinforcing effect.

A subsequent experiment in which dogs were allowed to self-administer unlimited quantities of intravenous morphine was designed to differentiate between satiation and cross-tolerance. This experiment investigated the effects of noncontingent infusions of morphine and methadone. Initially, animals were allowed a seven-day period of morphine self-administration to determine baseline levels of intake. For the next two weeks, methadone or morphine was given noncontingently as a continuous intravenous infusion. The dose of methadone or morphine infused was equal to (morphine) or equipotent to (methadone) the average daily amount of morphine that each animal had worked for during the baseline period. When methadone was infused, the animals' rate of responding for morphine was markedly suppressed on the first few days but subsequently showed a gradual increase back to baseline levels. Thus, where an unlimited amount of morphine could be obtained, the effects of methadone on the animals' work output for morphine was only transitory. A similar result was obtained with noncontingent infusions of morphine. These data suggest that methadone exerts its effects by cross-tolerance rather than satiation.

In a further study of the effects of noncontingent opiates, Griffiths and associates used an elegant discrete-trial choice procedure in which baboons were allowed to choose between food and heroin injections (91). The dosage of heroin was selected so that under baseline conditions animals chose it on approximately 25 percent of the trials. When naloxone was administered, the percentage of trials in which heroin was chosen showed a dose related increase, suggesting that the animals were physically dependent upon heroin. Infusions of methadone over a 12-day period produced a consistent and significant decrease in the number of times heroin was chosen over food. A subsequent experiment showed a similar decrease in choices for heroin during periods of noncontingent morphine infusion (92). These data suggest that noncontingent methadone and morphine administration had produced satiation and thereby decreased the number of trials in which the animal selected heroin over food. This was a complex procedure, however, in which the selection of heroin resulted in the loss of opportunity to obtain food for another three hours.

This study may indicate that methadone maintenance programs would be most successful under conditions where choosing to work for illicit drugs meant giving up the opportunity to work for another type of reinforcer. On the other hand, the investigation by Jones and Prada suggests that when conditions prevail such that a drug is available in unlimited supply and no negative consequences are associated with drug-seeking behavior, methadone maintenance might be relatively ineffective (82). Note, however, that the dose levels self-administered by the dogs were extremely high—far beyond the range generally available to heroin addicts in the United States. Therefore, even though it may be possible to exceed the level of tolerance by the self-administration of very high doses, this amount of heroin could hardly be obtained on a regular basis.

Although methadone's effectiveness in the previous studies perhaps rested on its ability to produce cross-tolerance or satiation, another important action of the drug discourages opiate seeking behavior. Methadone satisfies the organism's physical "need" for an opiate and prevents the occurrence of withdrawal. Since the reinforcing efficacy of opiates is enhanced by withdrawal, methadone may in this manner indirectly decrease the reinforcing efficacy of opiates. Other nonopiate drugs may also be effective via this mechanism. Several recent reports have indicated that clonidine (an antihypertensive that presumably acts on adrenergic receptors) blocks many of the physiological and behavioral manifestations of opiate withdrawal. In animals, clonidine has been shown to antagonize naloxone induced disruption of food reinforced operant behavior and weight loss in morphine dependent rats (93). Gold and colleagues demonstrated that humans may be detoxified from methadone relatively "painlessly" by substituting clonidine, which is then gradually withdrawn (94). Clonidine may prove to be a very useful adjunct in the treatment of opiate addiction since it can block the withdrawal syndrome, which enhances the reinforcing efficacy of opiates.

Drugs that prevent physiological events associated with food deprivation (i.e., the physiological concomitants of hunger) may in a similar manner decrease the reinforcing efficacy of food. Recently, for instance, Della-Fera and Baile showed that cholecystokinin caused a relatively specific decrease in the amount of food eaten by goats when they had been deprived of food for a period approximating their normal intermeal interval (95). Even more striking is a recent report on a newly isolated factor in human blood (satietin) that decreased the eating behavior of rats deprived of food for 72 hours; of major importance, no other physiological or behavioral measures were altered by satietin (96). All these investigations were seeking a pharmacological agent that specifically reverses the effects of deprivation (food or drug) and thereby prevents the usual deprivation induced enhancement of the reinforcing action of food or drug. Whether this reversal is achieved by preventing withdrawal through giving an opiate (methadone) or by some other mechanism (e.g., clonidine), the net result is the same.

One of the mechanisms responsible for methadone's efficacy, as previously discussed, is that it produces sufficient cross-tolerance so that the usual dose of heroin self-administered is not reinforcing. This is the so-called blocking action of methadone (87). Opiate antagonists also can be used to block the reinforcing action of opiates but in a different manner: antagonists block the actions of heroin by occupying the opiate receptor mediating the drug's effects. Thus, although the mechanism of action is different for methadone and antagonists, the net effect may be the same—prevention of opiate reinforcement. Martin and his colleagues suggested that the blocking property of opiate antagonists (at that time cyclazocine) could be used in the treatment of opiate addiction (97). They reasoned that heroin addicts could be detoxified and then given an opiate antagonist on a daily basis. The opiate antagonist, by occupying the receptor, would block the reinforcing effect of any opiate consumed and thus would extinguish the drug-seeking behavior. Despite this intuitively appealing analysis, few data demonstrate antagonist produced extinction of behavior maintained by an opiate reinforcer. The results that would be expected if extinction were occurring are an initial increase followed by a gradual decline in drug taking (98).

Some preliminary evidence that opiate antagonists may produce extinction has been provided by studies in which these agents were administered acutely. In these investigations, low and moderate doses of opiate antagonists generally gave rise to a dose related *increase* in rate of responding or, in a choice procedure, an increase in preference for the opiate alternative (31, 83, 84, 91). This may be comparable to the initial rate increase ("extinction burst") produced when any reinforcer is withheld. In studies that chronically administered an antagonist, this initial increase was not always noted. For instance, in experiments using human subjects treated with antagonists, requests for heroin ceased immediately (99). Apparently, the subjects simply discriminated the antagonist treatment as a condition under which heroin reinforcement was unavailable and therefore engaged in minimal drug-seeking behavior. Thus, there was no opportunity for the drug-seeking behavior to be extinguished.

Perhaps a better criterion for demonstrating an antagonist's blocking action is failure to initiate drug taking. For instance, when naltrexone was continuously infused into rhesus monkeys given the opportunity to self-administer morphine, the animals did not show any increase in responding over that seen for saline. In contrast, when methamphetamine was made available in the presence of naltrexone, the response rate increased markedly, indicating that opiate seeking behavior was not suppressed nonspecifically (100). Although other animal experiments have yielded some data suggesting that chronic treatment with an antagonist causes complete extinction of heroin reinforced behavior (101), another interpretation is possible: opiates administered in the presence of a narcotic antagonist may be aversive. Woods and co-workers showed that a combination of naloxone and codeine produced a rapid and long-lasting suppression of fixed-ratio responding, which led to a delivery of the compound more indicative of punishment than extinction (102). Possibly, antagonists such as naloxone and naltrexone do block the reinforcing action of opiates, but not all other actions. Some of these other actions are aversive, yet normally are not seen because of the dominant reinforcing property of the drug. When the subject is treated with an antagonist and allowed to self-administer an opiate, the behavior may be suppressed by the aversive property of the drug mixture before extinction can take place. Martin hypothesized the existence of three types of opiate receptors; mu, kappa, and sigma (103). Presumably, the reinforcing action of opiate agonists is mediated by mu receptors, whereas the aversive property would be mediated by sigma and/or kappa receptors. If the antagonist has greater affinity for the mu receptor than for either the sigma or the kappa, this agent could convert an ordinarily reinforcing drug into an aversive one. Clearly, more research is needed to substantiate this hypothesis.

Another means of blocking the reinforcing action of opiate drugs is active or passive immunization. Monkeys can be either actively or passively immunized, which condition modifies their self-administration of heroin or morphine (104, 105). In the active immunization experiment, a monkey was allowed to self-administer cocaine or heroin on alternate days. Daily drug sessions lasted two hours, during which period heroin or cocaine was available under a fixed-ratio 10 schedule of reinforcement. Colored stimulus lights signaled to the animal which drug was available. After the behavior had stabilized, saline was substituted for heroin in several sessions in order to observe the rates and patterns of extinction responding. Subsequently, the monkey was treated with a morphine-protein conjugate previously demonstrated to produce antibodies that bind both morphine and heroin but not cocaine (106, 107). After 20 weeks the serum binding capacity for morphine stabilized at approximately 100 pmol/ml. At this point the animal was again allowed to self-administer cocaine and heroin on alternate days. The response rate maintained by heroin administration was markedly lower than that seen prior to immunization, whereas cocaine self-administration levels were unchanged. When the dose per infusion of heroin was increased sixteenfold, the antibody blockade was finally overcome, as evidenced by increased response rates for heroin. In a second experiment, two rhesus monkeys were passively immunized by the infusion of whole antiserum obtained from monkeys immunized with the antigen previously described (105). Self-administration rates for heroin initially increased markedly, then showed a progressive decline over days that was correlated with the blood level of the antibody. Passive immunization did not affect cocaine self-administration. The changes in heroin self-administration were comparable to those produced by the administration of low doses of naloxone. The fact that active immunization decreased heroin maintained fixed-ratio responding whereas passive immunization increased such responding most likely attributable to the lower level of antibody generated by passive immunization (50 pmol versus 100 pmol/ml). Partial blockade of heroin's reinforcing effect would be expected to increase the self-administration rate in the same manner that low doses of naloxone do.

These experiments point to the possibility of immunizing people against the effects of heroin as a prophylactic measure in heroin addiction. Several practical (not to mention ethical) obstacles discourage this procedure: first, immunization requires a lengthy series of injections in order to generate a high blood titer of antibody; second, the antibodies developed are specific to opiates with a chemical structure similar to that of morphine and would therefore be ineffective against other opiates (107); third, the blockade can be overcome by increasing the dose of self-administered opiate, thereby saturating the binding capacity of the morphine antibody; finally, toxic consequences (e.g., kidney damage) may result if morphine or heroin is administered to humans immunized against these drugs.

Both antagonist therapy and immunization seek to prevent the reinforcing effect of opiates. One of the major problems with antagonist therapy is patient noncompliance and dropout from treatment (a problem likely with immunization, too, which would require periodic booster shots to maintain high levels of antibody). Methadone is slightly more successful in keeping patients in treatment, presumably because oral methadone itself (unlike antagonists) has reinforcing efficacy (108). Bigelow and co-workers demonstrated the importance of using drugs with some reinforcing action to maintain patient compliance to behavioral therapies for obesity (109). In this study, patients given *d* amphetamine stayed with a weight control program longer and lost more weight than those given placebo; patients given fenfluramine (an amphetamine analogue not self-administered by animals) stopped treatment more quickly than those in the placebo group and also lost less weight. It would appear, therefore, that the use of psychotropic drugs with some reinforcing efficacy in the treatment of both obesity and heroin addiction may produce better patient compliance and afford an opportunity for more effective treatment.

Organismic Variables in the Self-administration of Opiates

In a previous review of the behavioral analysis of opiate dependence, I discussed the available studies investigating the importance of organismic variables in opiate drug-seeking behavior (110). There has been little subsequent research in this area. Since most of these data were fully reviewed elsewhere, only a brief summary will be given here.

Species

Most studies of opiate self-administration have used rats or rhesus monkeys as subjects. Intravenously delivered opiate drugs have been found to serve as reinforcers in both species and no reports have noted significant individual differences in either species regarding the acquisition or maintenance of opiate drug-seeking behavior. One study found similar results with cats (143). However, a large percentage of dogs tested did not self-administer morphine when initially given the opportunity (111). Nevertheless, dogs will learn to lever-press for intravenous morphine after being made physically dependent and will even "relapse" to drug-taking after being drug-free one to six months. The significance of these individual differences in dogs remains to be elucidated. It would be of great interest to determine whether similar individual differences would be observed in dogs allowed to self-administer a wide variety of other psychotropic drugs.

Age

It is commonly reported that heroin addicts tend to stop drug taking after the age of 35—the so-called maturing out phenomenon. This suggests that the reinforcing efficacy of opiates decreases with age. In support of this observation, Nichols found that the intake of morphine in rats declined with age (18). Although similar experimental studies have not been conducted with other drugs, Parry and colleagues showed that drug preferences do change with age (112). For instance, amphetamines are more likely to be taken by young people; benzodiazepines, by older adults. These findings must be interpreted with caution since a variety of other personal characteristics are correlated with age, e.g., socioeconomic status and access to legal drugs. Whether these factors are relevant to the phenomenon of maturing out is not clear.

Sex

One recent study compared the ingestion of morphine by rats of both sexes and found that female rats drank significantly greater quantities of the morphine solution than did males (113). In contrast, studies in the United States have shown that heroin addiction occurs predominantly in males. This sex related difference in addiction rate probably implicates social rather than endocrine factors. We need systematic animal studies in this area, especially with primates, whose endocrine system is similar to that in humans.

Genotype

Although all humans can be made physically dependent upon opiates, only certain individuals search out and self-administer these drugs illicitly. Whether genetically determined differences are important in individual variations in drug-seeking behavior is not known, although a genetic explanation is highly appealing. Several early animal studies have suggested that genetic differences may play a role. Nichols and Hsiao were able to breed rats that were either susceptible or resistant to drinking morphine solutions. Susceptible animals also drank more alcohol (114). Cross-fostering studies ruled out differences in maternal care as a variable. Furthermore, susceptible rats were not found to be more emotional in open-field studies; however, they made fewer errors in maze learning. More recently, Horowitz and co-workers showed that C57BL6J mice will drink large quantities of morphine when it is dissolved in a saccharin solution (115). The drug was serving as a reinforcer because these mice showed a distinct preference for the saccharin solution with the drug compared to a straight saccharin solution. In contrast, mice of the DBA/25 strain avoided the morphine solution. This difference in drug taking was, however, paralleled by differential response in the two strains to taste factors. The strain that drank the morphine solution (C57BL6J) also drank more of other bitter solutions.

Psychopathology

Individual tendencies toward illicit opiate use could also be a result of personality. Clinicians generally acknowledge that drug abusers have some form of psychopathology (116). And recent studies have demonstrated a high frequency of mental depressison in heroin addicts (117–120). Many of these studies assumed that depression is a preexisting condition that enhances the reinforcing efficacy of opiates. Schuster and colleagues reviewed this literature and suggested an alternate interpretation of the observed correlation between depression and heroin addiction (121). Looking at animal studies of drug-seeking behavior, they argued that were it not for countervailing societal influences, heroin use might be the norm rather than an aberration. Psychopathology (especially depression) may prevent the development or weaken psychological checks on unregulated drug use. Thus, depression may increase the probability of heroin use because normal societal restraints on this behavior are ineffective. It is also likely that illicit drug use (directly through pharmacologic actions of the drug or indirectly because of the addict's lifestyle) produces depression. Regardless of the interpretation, however, a substantial literature shows a correlation between depression and heroin addiction. Accordingly, effective therapy for heroin addicts should include therapy for depression as appropriate.

Environmental Variables in the
Self-administration of Opiates

Conditioned Drug Effects

Opiates can serve other stimulus functions besides providing reinforcement. For instance, Holtzman, Woods, and their colleagues demonstrated that opiate agonist, mixed agonist, and even antagonists can function as discriminative stimuli signaling the availability of a reinforcer (122, 123, 139). Opiates also have been shown to function as unconditioned stimuli in classical conditioning paradigms. In this section, I review data demonstrating that under certain circumstances, environmental stimuli associated with morphine administration can acquire the ability to elicit morphinelike effects.

Lynch and his colleagues recently reviewed the classical conditioning of a variety of opiate effects (125, 126). Pavlov himself showed that stimuli associated with morphine acquired the ability to produce the signs of morphine administration, including nausea, vomiting, salivation, and sleep. More recently, Lal and his colleagues reviewed a number of experiments conducted by their group demonstrating the classical conditioning of a variety of morphine actions, including hyperthermia, hyperglycemia, and increased levels of striatal homovanillic acid, as well as the reversal of certain physiological and behavioral signs of the opiate withdrawal syndrome (127). Thompson and Schuster also demonstrated that the abstinence induced disruption of food reinforced and shock avoidance behavior in morphine dependent rhesus monkeys could be temporarily reversed by stimuli normally associated with morphine administration (83). Tye and Iversen confirmed these findings in a study in which the disruption of operant behavior in rats caused by morphine abstinence was reversed by the presentation of morphine associated stimuli (128). However, these same stimuli were ineffective in reversing the withdrawal induced behavioral disruption produced by the administration of naloxone.

The neurochemical mechanisms underlying classical conditioning of morphinelike effects are unknown. Lal and colleagues reported that naloxone (a relatively pure opiate antagonist) can block the ability of the conditioned stimulus to produce the morphine response (127). Since naloxone is known to antagonize the actions of endorphine, this finding implies some involvement of endorphine in the mediation of classical conditioning of morphine effects. However, in a more recent study by Eikelboom and

Stewart, naloxone failed to block a conditioned morphine response (129). Since their methods were different from those employed by Lal and his colleagues we cannot reach any conclusions about the discrepancy at this time. Clearly, more parametric research is needed to determine whether and under what conditions naloxone can block the elicitation of conditioned morphine effects. If this phenomenon is elucidated, it may be possible to determine the mechanism mediating the conditioning of opiate effects.

Some investigators have reported that the conditioned response obtained by associating morphine with a bell or tone is opposite in direction to that produced by morphine itself. Therefore, investigators who are able to condition morphinelike responses (e.g., hyperthermia) are at odds with those who obtain a conditioned response opposite to that produced by the UCS morphine (i.e., hypothermia). A recent report by Eikelboom and Stewart indicated that this situation is even more complicated (129). In their study, the body temperature of rats was obtained under three conditions: home cage, preinjection environment, and postinjection environment. The preinjection and postinjection environments differed in lighting, noise level, and temperature. After a number of morphine injections two types of conditioned effects were observed: hypothermia, which occurred in the preinjection environment, and hyperthermia, which was manifested in the postinjection environment. Thus, in this study both morphinelike and responses opposite in direction to morphine's effects were conditioned in the same animals. Whether these findings can help to resolve the conflicts in this area of research remains to be seen. Clearly, we need more methodological research on the circumstances determining the outcome of conditioning experiments using morphine as the UCS before explaining other phenomena by such conditioned responses.

One of the other phenomena that may be based upon the classical conditioning of morphinelike effects is that stimuli associated with opiate administration acquire conditioned reinforcing properties. Such stimuli actually may serve simultaneously (1) as a conditioned stimulus for respondent behavior, (2) as a discriminative stimulus signaling the availability of the drug, and (3) as a conditioned reinforcer. Many studies purporting to analyze the conditioned reinforcing effects of a drug have failed to recognize the possibility of these additional functions. Regardless, such stimuli do have profound effects upon the rate and patterning of drug reinforced behavior.

Conditioned reinforcers have been studied under three principal conditions: extinction, second-order schedules, and acquisition of a new response. In the extinction procedure, the drug reinforcer is no longer administered and the ability of the stimulus previously associated with its delivery to delay extinction or temporarily to reinstate responding is determined. Using such a procedure Schuster and Woods demonstrated that the response contingent presentation of stimuli previously associated with the delivery of an intravenous morphine reinforcer increased response rate during extinction in rhesus monkeys (130). Furthermore, they demonstrated that such stimuli increased response rate even after a two-week drug-free period, suggesting that physical dependence was not a necessary condition for the stimuli to serve as a conditioned reinforcer. Similarly, Wikler and associates demonstrated that anise flavoring became a conditioned reinforcer by virtue of its association by rats with the oral ingestion of a morphine solution (131). The anise flavoring continued to exert behavioral effects for over 200 days after termination of its presentation with morphine. Finally, Davis and Smith showed that the strength of the conditioned reinforcing effect was a direct function of the dose of morphine with which it was paired (132). In the same study, these investigators found that pretreatment with naloxone did not block the conditioned reinforcing effects of stimuli already associated with morphine reinforcement. This finding is of importance because it differentiates between a drug's ability to serve as a CS for morphinelike effects and its ability to act as a conditioned reinforcer. As mentioned previously, Lal and associates reported that naloxone blocked the evocation of a morphinelike response by a conditioned stimulus (127). If this pattern characterizes all classically conditioned morphine responses, the finding that naloxone does not block conditioned reinforcement implies that these two stimulus functions are independent.

Another experimental paradigm used to demonstrate the conditioned reinforcing effect of drugs is the second-order schedule. Behavior (e.g., lever-pressing) of squirrel and rhesus monkeys can be maintained under complex schedules in which drug injections occur only after the completion of several successive actions. Each action is terminated by the brief presentation of a stimulus that is paired with the injection of the reinforcing drug. Such complex programs of reinforcement are called "second-order schedules." For example, in a study by Goldberg and Tang, rhesus and squirrel monkeys were studied under a second-order schedule in which responding was maintained by injections of morphine under a fixed-interval schedule with fixed-ratio units (46). Completion of each 30 response fixed-ratio unit was followed by the presentation of a brief light; the first fixed-ratio unit completed after 60 minutes elicited both the light and an intravenous dose of morphine. Using such a schedule, one study recently demonstrated that response rates are significantly higher if the brief stimulus presented at the completion of the fixed-ratio is paired with the terminal drug reinforcer; furthermore, rates decline markedly when no brief stimuli are presented (133). These data suggest that stimuli associated with opiate reinforcement become conditioned reinforcers that can maintain long sequences of behavior that are only intermittently reinforced with a drug. Spealman and Goldberg have discussed the use and importance of such second-order schedules (134).

The third procedure, and perhaps the one unequivocally to demonstrate that a stimulus is serving as a conditioned reinforcer, involves the acquisition of some new response that is reinforced solely by the stimulus previously paired with a drug. An experiment by Beach (previously described) illustrates this phenomenon (77). In this experiment rats were injected with morphine and then placed in a nonpreferred goal box of a Y-maze. The animals were retested after several stimuli pairings for their goal box preference. As predicted, the rats favored the goal box associated with morphine, indicating that the stimuli in this box had become conditioned reinforcers. A subsequent experiment by Kumar confirmed this finding (135). In both these experiments a new response, going to a particular goal box, was acquired solely because it produced stimuli previously linked to morphine.

In summary, a number of experiments using various approaches have demonstrated that drug associated stimuli can acquire conditioned reinforcing efficacy. In most instances, the conditioned reinforcers were paired only with the actual drug injection, i.e., their onset was relatively simultaneous. It has been demonstrated under a chain schedule that a discriminative stimulus which signals response contingent food availability can function as a conditioned reinforcer in the preceding component. The discriminative stimulus associated with this component can then function as a conditioned reinforcer in an even earlier component. In this manner long chains of behavior have been acquired (136). Although this pattern has not been reported for drug reinforcers, it is extremely likely. Indeed, such chains of behavior leading to drug reinforcement are probably involved in the street addict's daily hustling. Failure to extinguish stimulus complexes that have become conditioned reinforcers may in part explain relapse after detoxification.

Conditioned Withdrawal

I have already reviewed data demonstrating that physical dependence is neither a necessary nor a sufficient condition to cause drug-seeking behavior. However, once drug-seeking behavior is established, physical dependence produces a state in which drug deprivation markedly strengthens the reinforcing efficacy of opiates. I suggested earlier that this strengthening occurs because drug deprivation leads to a variety of aversive symptoms that can be eased by administration drug (a form of pharmacological escape). Wikler noted that addicts often report the recurrence of certain withdrawal signs after long periods of complete abstinence from opiates (137, 138). He suggested that such withdrawal signs and symptoms become classically conditioned through repeated association of a specific environment with the opiate withdrawal syndrome. He cautioned that the appearance of such classically conditioned withdrawal signs in postdependent subjects could encourage relapse into drug-seeking behavior. That behavior enters the addict's behavioral repertoire through operant conditioning based upon the reinforcement provided by the drug, which reduces withdrawal distress (5). Thus, Wikler's theory uses both classical and operant conditioning in explaining relapse by postdependent opiate addicts.

The first suggestion that the opiate withdrawal syndrome could be classically conditioned came from Irwin and Seevers (140). While physically dependent upon a variety of opiates (morphine, ketobemidone, racemorphan, and methadone), rhesus monkeys repeatedly underwent nalorphine induced withdrawal. After one or two months' abstinence, certain monkeys continued to show withdrawal signs when administered nalorphine. More important, these monkeys also initially showed the same response to an injection of saline, which response disappeared after repeated injections. In rats, one of the withdrawal signs is "wet-dog shakes" (19, 141, 142). Wikler demonstrated that this withdrawal sign occurs when postdependent rats are returned to cages in which they had undergone withdrawal (19, 142). More recently, Goldberg and colleagues have reported on experiments investigating the classical conditioning of physiological and behavioral signs of the opiate withdrawal syndrome in rhesus monkeys. This work has been summarized elsewhere (143, 149). The initial study demonstrated that a tone repeatedly paired with nalorphine could elicit both physiological (bradycardia, salivation, and emesis) and behavioral (suppression of lever-pressing maintained by food delivery) signs of withdrawal (144). Subsequently, this finding was replicated and shown to persist in postdependent rhesus monkeys (145). This effect was extinguished, however, by daily presentation of the tone and an injection of saline. In a further study, Goldberg and co-workers investigated the effects of conditioned withdrawal on responses maintained by morphine: nalorphine at certain doses caused a large increase in morphine maintained responses; after repeated administration of nalorphine, injections of saline produced an increased rate of responding for morphine as well (146). Thus, the conditioned withdrawal syndrome apparently has the same potentiating effect on morphine's reinforcing efficacy as actual withdrawal.

As mentioned previously, several clinical reports have suggested that postdependent opiate addicts experience certain withdrawal signs when they return to an environment in which they had been previously addicted. These withdrawal signs are relieved by the administration of an opiate (147). O'Brien and his colleagues investigated this phenomenon in a series of experiments and found that auditory and olfactory stimuli associated with naloxone induced withdrawal could produce certain signs and symptoms of the withdrawal syndrome (148). The conditioned withdrawal syndrome was indistinguishable by the subjects from the abstinence response elicited by naloxone.

Recently, Meyer and Mirin described a program of research analyzing the variables affecting heroin reinforced behavior in humans in a controlled ward setting (99). Their data suggest that craving for heroin occurs when the drug is available, a condition often signaled by the stimulus feedback from the injection of the drug itself. They termed the stimulus complex associated with heroin availability the "heroin stimulus"; this is the stimulus that leads to actual drug taking. They did not note any conditioned withdrawal signs antecedent to drug taking.

Although a substantial body of data shows that certain aspects of the opiate withdrawal syndrome can be classically conditioned, the importance of this in the heroin relapses of postaddicts remains to be elucidated.

Conclusions

One of the major purposes of this book is to determine commonalities among various forms of substance abuse. This chapter suggests that this search should be approached by looking for functional similarities in the variables controlling the diverse behaviors. I reviewed evidence demonstrating the importance of pharmacological, organismic, and environmental variables in the generation and maintenance of opiate drug-seeking behavior. Unfortunately, relatively few studies have systematically manipulated such controlling variables to determine whether they have similar effects on behaviors reinforced by other drugs and by food. Yet the available research points to functional similarities. Only further systematic research can determine whether there are common variables that give rise to the excessive quality of behavior that characterizes substance abuse. The success to date in demonstrating commonalities among behaviors maintained by various reinforcing events gives promise that such research may be fruitful.

I would like to acknowledge the support of the National Institute on Drug Abuse career scientist award, DA-00024. I would also like to thank Dr. Chris-Ellyn Johanson for her contributions to this chapter.

References

1. Morse, W. H., Introduction: the control of behavior by consequent drug injections, *Pharm. Rev. 27,* 301–305 (1975).
2. Kelleher, R. T., and Goldberg, S. R., Control of drug-taking behavior by schedules of reinforcement, *Pharml. Rev. 27,* 291–299 (1975).
3. Altshuler, H., Weaver, S., and Phillips, P., Intragastric self-administration of psychoactive drugs by the rhesus monkey, *Life Sci. 17,* 883–890 (1975).
4. Siegel, S., A Pavlovian conditioning analysis of morphine tolerance, in

Behavioral Tolerance: Research and Treatment Implications (NIDA Research Monograph No. 18), N. Krasnegor, ed., GPO, Washington, D.C., 1978, pp. 27–53.

5. Wikler, A., Conditioning factors in opiate addiction and relapse, in *Narcotics,* D. M. Wilner and G. G. Kassebaum, eds., McGraw-Hill, New York, 1965.

6. Schuster, C. R., and Villarreal, J. E., The experimental analysis of opioid dependence, in *Psychopharmacology: A Review of Progress, 1957–67,* D. Efron, ed., American College of Neuropsychopharmacology, 1968, pp. 811–828.

7. Johanson, C. E., and Uhlenhuth, E. H., Drug self-administration in humans, in *Self-administration of Abused Substances: Methods for Study* (NIDA Research Monograph No. 20), N. Krasnegor, ed., GPO, Washington, D. C., 1978, pp. 68–85.

8. Griffiths, R. R., Bigelow, G., and Liebson, I., Experimental human drug self-administration: generality of relationships across species and type of drug, in *Self-administration of Abused Substances: Methods for Study* (NIDA Research Monograph No. 20), N. Krasnegor, ed., GPO, Washington, D.C., 1978, pp. 24–43.

9. Griffiths, R. R., Bigelow, G. E., and Henningfield, J. E., Similarities in animal and human drug taking behavior, in *Advances in Substance Abuse: Behavioral and Biological Research,* N. K. Mello, ed., Jai Press, Greenwich, 1980.

10. Oldendorf, W. H., Hyman S., Braun, L., and Oldendorf, S. Z., Blood-brain barrier penetration of morphine, codeine, heroin, and methadone after carotid injection, *Science 178,* 984–986 (1971).

11. Skinner, B. F., *The Behavior of Organisms,* Appleton-Century-Crofts, New York, 1938.

12. Johanson, C. E., Pharmacological and environmental variables affecting drug preference in rhesus monkeys, *Pharml. Rev. 27,* 343–355 (1975).

13. Goldberg, S. R., Hoffmeister, F., Schlichting, U. U., and Wuttke, W., Aversive properties of nalophine and naloxone in morphine-dependent rhesus monkeys, *J. Pharml. Exp. Ther. 179,* 268–276 (1971).

14. Goldberg, S. R., Hoffmeister, F., and Schlichting, U. U., Morphine antagonists' modification of behavioral effects by morphine dependence, in *Drug Addiction I: Experimental Pharmacology,* J. M. Singh, L. Miller, and H. Lal, eds., Futura Press, Mount Kisco, 1972, pp. 31–48.

15. Hoffmeister, F., and Wuttke, W., Negative reinforcing properties of morphine-antagonists in naive rhesus monkeys, *Psychopharmacologia 33,* 247–258 (1973).

16. Downs, D. A., and Woods, J. H., Fixed-ratio escape and avoidance-escape from naloxone in morphine-dependent monkeys: effects of naloxone dose and morphine pretreatment, *J. Exp. Anal. Beh. 23,* 415–427 (1975).

17. McKearney, J. W., Maintenance of responding under a fixed-interval schedule of electric shock presentation, *Science 160,* 1249–1251 (1968).

18. Nichols, J. R., How opiates change behavior, *Sci. Amer. 212,* 80–88 (1965).

19. Wikler, A., Martin, W. R., Pescor, F. T., and Eades, C. G., Factors regulating oral consumption of an opioid (etonitazene) by morphine-addicted rats, *Psychopharmacologia 5,* 55–76 (1963).

20. Kumar, R., Steinberg, H., and Stolerman, I. P., Inducing a preference for morphine in rats without premedication, *Nature 218,* 564–565 (1968).

21. Meisch, R. A., and Stark L. J., Establishment of etonitazene as a reinforcer for rats by use of schedule-induced drinking, *Pharml. Biochem. Beh. 7,* 195–203 (1977).

22. Carroll, M. E., and Meisch, R. A., Etonitazene as a reinforcer: oral intake of etonitazene by rhesus monkeys, *Psychopharmacology 59,* 225–229 (1978).

23. McMillan, D. E., and Leander, J. D., Schedule-induced oral self-administration of etonitazene, *Pharm. Biochem. Beh. 4,* 137–141 (1976).

24. Leander, J. D., McMillan, D. E., and Harris, L. S., Effects of narcotic agonists and antagonists on schedule-induced water and morphine ingestion, *J. Pharm. Exp. Ther. 195,* 271–278 (1975).

25. Leander, J. D., McMillan, D. E., and Harris, L. S., Schedule-induced oral narcotic self-administration: acute and chronic effects, *J. Pharm. Exp. Ther. 195,* 279–287 (1975).

26. Hill, S. Y., and Powell, B. J., Acquired preference for morphine but not d-amphetamine as a result of saccharine adulteration, *Psychopharmacology 50,* 309–312 (1976).

27. Trojuar, W., Cytawa, J., Frydrychowski, A. and Luszanska, D., Intragastric self-administration of morphine as a measure of addiction, *Psychopharmacologia 37,* 359–364 (1974).

28. Goldberg, S. R., Morse, W. H., and Goldberg, D. M., Behavior maintained under a second-order schedule by intramuscular injection of morphine or cocaine in rhesus monkeys, *J. Pharm. Exp. Ther. 199,* 278–286 (1976).

29. Mackintosh, N. J., *The Psychology of Animal Learning,* Academic, New York, 1974.

30. Weeks, J. R., Experimental morphine addiction: method for automatic intravenous injections in unrestrained rats, *Science 138,* 143–144 (1962).

31. Weeks, J. R., and Collins, R. J., Factors affecting voluntary morphine intake in self-maintained addicted rats, *Psychopharmacologia 6,* 267–279 (1964).

32. Weeks, J. R., and Collins, R. J., Self-administration of morphine in the rat: relative influence of fixed-ratio and time-out, *Pharm. Biochem. Beh. 9,* 703–704 (1978).

33. Werner, T. E., Smith, S. G., and Davis, W., A dose-response comparison between methadone and morphine self-administration, *Psychopharmacology 47,* 209–211 (1976).

34. Schuster, C. R., and Balster, R. L., Self-administration of agonists, in *Agonist and Antagonist Actions of Narcotic Analgesic Drugs,* H. W. Kosterlitz, H. O. J. Collier, and J. E. Villarreal, eds., Macmillan, New York, 1973, pp. 243–254.

35. Schuster, C. R., Variables affecting the self-administration of drugs by rhesus monkeys, in *The Use of Non-human Primates in Drug Evaluation,* H. Vagtborg, ed., University of Texas Press, Austin, 1968, pp. 283–299.

36. Johanson, C. E., and Schuster, C. R., Procedures for the preclinical assessment of abuse potential of psychotropic drugs in animals, in *Predicting Dependence Liability of Stimulant and Depressant Drugs*, T. Thompson and K. R. Unna, eds., University Park Press, Baltimore, 1977, pp. 203–229.

37. Johanson, C. E., Drugs as reinforcers, in *Contemporary Research in Behavioral Pharmacology*, D. E. Blackman and D. J. Sanger, eds., Plenum, New York, 1978, pp. 325–390.

38. Woods, J. H., and Schuster, C. R., Opiates as reinforcing stimuli, in *Stimulus Properties of Drugs*, T. Thompson and R. Pickens, eds., Appleton-Century-Crofts, New York, 1971, pp. 163–175.

39. Leander, J. D., and McMillan, D. E., Meperidine effects on schedule-controlled responding, J. *Pharm. Exp. Ther. 201*, 434–443 (1977).

40. Downs, D. A., and Woods, J. H., Naloxone as a negative reinforcer in rhesus monkeys: effects of dose, schedule, and narcotic regimen, *Pharm. Rev. 27*, 397–406 (1975).

41. Balster, R. L., and Schuster, C. R., Fixed-interval schedule of cocaine reinforcement: effect of dose and infusion duration, J. *Exp. Anal. Beh. 20*, 119–129 (1973).

42. Iglauer, C., and Woods, J. H., Concurrent performances: reinforcement by different doses of intravenous cocaine in rhesus monkeys, J. *Exp. Anal. Beh. 22*, 179–196 (1974).

43. Goldberg, S. R., Comparable behavior maintained under fixed-ratio and second-order schedules of food presentation, cocaine injection, or d-amphetamine injection in the squirrel monkey, J. *Pharm. Exp. Ther. 186*, 18–30 (1973).

44. Griffiths, R. R., Findley, J. D., Brady, J. V., Dolan-Gutcher, K., and Robinson, W. W., Comparison of progressive-ratio performance maintained by cocaine, methylphenidate, and secobarbital, *Psychopharmacologia 43*, 81–83 (1975).

45. Johanson, C. E., and Schuster, C. R., A choice procedure for drug reinforcers: cocaine and methylphenidate in the rhesus monkey, J. *Pharm. Exp. Ther. 193*, 676–688 (1975).

46. Goldberg, S. R., and Tang, A. H., Behavior maintained under second-order schedules of intravenous morphine injection in squirrel and rhesus monkeys, *Psychopharmacology 51*, 235–242 (1977).

47. Yanagita, T., An experimental framework for evaluation of dependence liability in various types of drugs in monkeys, *Bull. Narc. 1*, 25–57 (1973).

48. Griffiths, R. R., Brady, J. V., and Snell, J. D., Progressive-ratio performance maintained by drug infusions: comparison of cocaine, diethylpropion, chlorphetnermine, and fenfluramine, *Psychopharmacology 56*, 5–13 (1978).

49. Hoffmeister, F., Progressive-ratio performance in the rhesus monkey maintained by opiate infusions, *Psychopharmacology 62*, 181–186 (1979)

50. Jaffe, J. H., Narcotic analgesics, in *The Pharmacological Basis of Therapeutics*, L. S. Goodman and A. Gilman, eds., Macmillan, New York, 1970.

51. Collier, H. O. J., Tolerance, physical dependence, and receptors, in *Advances in Drug Research,* vol. 3, N. J. Harper and A. B. Simmonds, eds., Academic, New York, 1966, pp. 171–188.

52. Jaffe, J. H., and Sharpless, S. K., Pharmacological denervation supersensitivity in the central nervous system: a theory of physical dependence, *Proc. Ass'n. Res. Nerv. Ment. Dis. 46,* 226–246 (1968).

53. Martin, W. R., Physiological redundancy as an adaptive mechanism in the central nervous system, *Fed. Proc. 29,* 13–18 (1970).

54. Pavlov, I. P., *Conditioned Reflexes,* Oxford University Press, New York, 1927.

55. Korol, B., Sletten, I. W., and Brown, M. L., Conditioned physiological adaptation to anticholinergic drugs, *Amer. J. Physiol. 211,* 911–914 (1966).

56. Lang, W. J., Brown, M. L., Gershon, S., and Korol, B., Classical and physiologic adaptive conditioned responses to anticholinergic drugs in conscious dogs, *Inter'l. J. Neuropharm. 5,* 311–315 (1966).

57. Lang, W. J., Rush, M. L., and Pearson, L., Pharmacological investigation of the mechanism of conditional salivation in dogs induced by atropine and morphine, *Eur. J. Pharm. 5,* 191–195 (1969).

58. Mulinos, M. G., and Lieb, C. C., Pharmacology of learning, *Amer. J. Physiol. 90,* 456–457 (1929) (abstract).

59. Wikler, A., Recent progress in research on the neurophysiologic basis of morphine addiction, *Amer. J. Psychiat. 105,* 329–338 (1948).

60. Solomon, R. L., and Corbit, J. D., An opponent-process theory of motivation, *Psych. Rev. 81,* 119–145 (1974).

61. Adams, W. H., Yeh, S. Y., Woods, L. A., and Mitchell, C. L., Drug-test interaction as a factor in the development of tolerance to the analgesic effect of morphine, *J. Pharm. Exp. Ther. 168,* 257 (1969).

62. Ferguson, R. K., Adams, W. J., and Mitchell, C. L., Studies of tolerance development to morphine analgesia in rats tested on the hot plate, *Eur. J. Pharm. 8,* 83–92 (1969).

63. Gebhart, G. F., and Mitchell, C. L., Further studies on the development of tolerance to the analgesic effect of morphine: the role played by the cylinder in the hot plate testing procedure, *Arch. Inter'l. Pharmacodyn. Ther. 191,* 96–103 (1971).

64. Gebhart, G. F., and Mitchell, C. L., The relative contributions of the testing cylinder and the heated plate in the hot plate procedure to the development of tolerance to morphine in rats, *Eur. J. Pharm. 18,* 56–62 (1972).

65. Gebhart, G. F., Sherman, A. D., and Mitchell, C. L., The influence of learning on morphine analgesia and tolerance development in rats tested on the hot plate, *Psychopharmacologia 22,* 295–304 (1971).

66. Gebhart, G. F., Sherman, A. D., and Mitchell, C. L., The influence of stress on tolerance development to morphine in rats tested on the hot plate, *Arch. Inter'l. Pharmacodyn. Ther. 197,* 328–337 (1972).

67. Kayan, S., Ferguson, R. K., and Mitchell, C. L., An investigation of the pharmacologic and behavioral tolerance to morphine in rats, *J. Pharm. Exp. Ther. 185,* 300–306 (1973).

68. Kayan, S., and Mitchell, C. L., Further studies on the development of tolerance to the analgesic effect of morphine, *Arch. Inter'l. Pharmacodyn. Ther. 182,* 257–268 (1969).

69. Kayan, S., and Mitchell, C. L., Studies on tolerance development to morphine: effect of the dose-interval on the development of single dose tolerance, *Arch. Inter'l. Pharmacodyn. Ther. 199,* 407–414 (1972).

70. Kayan, S., Woods, L. A., and Mitchell, C. L., Experience as a factor in the development of tolerance to the analgesic effect of morphine, *Eur. J. Pharm. 6,* 333–339 (1969).

71. Kayan, S., Woods, L. A., and Mitchell, C. L., Morphine-induced hyperalgesia in rats tested on the hot plate, *J. Pharm. Exp. Ther. 177,* 509–513 (1971).

72. Ferguson, R. K., and Mitchell, C. L., Pain as a factor in the development of tolerance to morphine analgesia in man, *Clin. Pharm. Ther. 10,* 372–382 (1969).

73. Deneau, G. E., Yanagita, T., and Seevers, M. H., Self-administration of psychoactive substances by the monkey: a measure of psychological dependence, *Psychopharmacologia 16,* 30–48 (1969).

74. Weeks, J. R., and Collins, R. J., Patterns of intravenous self-injection by morphine addicted rats, in *The Addictive States,* A. Wikler, ed., Williams and Wilkins, Baltimore, 1968.

75. Spragg, S. D. S., Morphine addiction in chimpanzees, *Comp. Psych. Monog. 15,* 1–172 (1940).

76. Nichols, J. R., Morphine as a reinforcing agent: laboratory studies of its capacity to change behavior, in *The Addictive States,* A. Wikler, ed., Williams and Wilkins, Baltimore, 1968.

77. Beach, H. B., Morphine addiction in rats, *Can. J. Psych. 11,* 104–112 (1957).

78. Woods, J. H., and Schuster, C. R., Reinforcement properties of morphine, cocaine, and SPA as a function of unit dose, *Inter'l. J. Addict. 3,* 231–236 (1968).

79. Weeks, J. R., and Collins, R. J., Dose and physical dependence as factors in the self-administration of morphine by rats, *Psychopharmacology 65,* 171–177 (1979).

80. Sanchez-Ramos, J. R., and Schuster, C. R., Second-order schedule of intravenous drug self-administration in rhesus monkeys, *Pharm. Biochem. Beh. 1,* 443–450 (1977).

81. Jones, B. E., and Prada, J. A., Drug-seeking behavior during methadone maintenance, *Psychopharmacologia 41,* 7–10 (1975).

82. Jones, B. E., and Prada, J. A., Effects of methadone and morphine maintenance on drug-seeking behavior in the dog, *Psychopharmacology 54,* 109–112 (1977).

83. Thompson, T., and Schuster, C. R., Morphine self-administration and food-reinforced and avoidance behaviors in rhesus monkeys, *Psychopharmacologia 5,* 87–94 (1964).

84. Goldberg, S. R., Woods, J. H., and Schuster, C. R., Nalorphine-induced

changes in morphine self-administration in rhesus monkeys, *J. Pharm. Exp. Ther.* *176,* 464–471 (1971).

85. Byck, R., *Cocaine Papers: Sigmund Freud,* Stonehill, New York, 1975.
86. Musto, D., *The American Disease: Origins of Narcotic Control,* Yale University Press, New Haven, 1973.
87. Dole, V. P., Nyswander, M. E., and Kreek, M. J., Narcotic blockade, *Arch. Int. Med. 118,* 304–309 (1966).
88. Martin, W. R., Jasinski, D. R., and Mansky, P. A., Naltrexone: an antagonist for the treatment of heroin dependence, *Arch. Gen. Psychiat. 28,* 784–791 (1973).
89. Karkalas, J., and Lal, H., A comparison of haloperidol with methadone in blocking heroin-withdrawal symptoms, *Inter'l. Pharmacopsychiat. 8,* 248–251 (1973).
90. Gold, M. S., Redmond, D. E., Jr., and Kleber, H. D., Clonidine in opiate withdrawal, Lancet *1,* 929–930 (1978).
91. Griffiths, R. R., Wurster, R. M., and Brady, J. V., Discrete-trial choice procedure: effects of naloxone and methadone on choice between food and heroin, *Pharm. Rev. 27,* 357–365 (1975).
92. Wurster, R. M., Griffiths, R. R., Findley, J. D., and Brady, J. V., Reduction of heroin self-administration in baboons by manipulation of behavioral and pharmacological conditions, *Pharm. Biochem. Beh. 7,* 519–528 (1977).
93. Sparber, S. B., and Meyer, D. R., Clonidine antagonizes naloxone-induced suppression of conditioned behavior and body weight loss in morphine dependent rats, *Pharm. Biochem. Beh. 9,* 319–325 (1978).
94. Gold, M. S., Pottash, A. C., Sweeney, D. R., and Kleber, H. D., Opiate withdrawal using clonidine, *JAMA 243,* 343–364 (1980).
95. Della-Fera, M. A., and Baile, C. A., Cholecystokinin octapeptide: continuous picamole injections into the cerebral ventricles of sheep suppress feeding, *Science 206,* 471–473 (1979).
96. Knoll, J., Satietin: a highly potent anorexigenic substance in human serum, *Pharm. Biochem. Beh. 23,* 497–502 (1979).
97. Martin, W. R., Gorodetzky, C. W., and McClane, T. K., An experimental study in the treatment of narcotic addicts with cyclazocine, *Clin. Pharm. Ther. 7,* 455–465 (1966).
98. Ferster, C. B., and Skinner, B. F., *Schedules of Reinforcement,* Appleton-Century-Crofts, New York, 1957.
99. Meyer, R. E., and Mirin, S. M., *The Heroin Stimulus: Implications for a Theory of Addiction,* Plenum, New York, 1979.
100. Harrigan, S. E., and Downs, D. A., Continuous intravenous naltrexone effects on morphine self-administration in rhesus monkeys, *J. Pharm. Exp. Ther. 204,* 481–486 (1978).
101. Killian, A. K., Bonese, K., and Schuster, C. R., The effects of naloxone on behavior maintained by cocaine and heroin injections in the rhesus monkey, *Drug and Alc. Depend. 3,* 245–251 (1978).

102. Woods, J. H., Down, D. A., and Villarreal, J. E., Changes in operant behavior during deprivation-/ and antagonist-/induced withdrawal states, *Bayer Symposium IV: Psychic Dependence,* 114–121 (1973).

103. Martin, W. R., History and development of mixed opioid agonists, partial agonists, and antagonists, *Brit. J. Clin. Pharm. 7,* 3 (1979)

104. Bonese, K. F., Wainer, B. H., Fitch, F. W., Rothberg, R. M., and Schuster, C. R., Changes in heroin self-administration by a rhesus monkey after morphine immunization, *Nature 252,* 708–710 (1974).

105. Killian, A., Bonese, K., Rothberg, R. M., Wainer, B. H., and Schuster, C. R., Effects of passive immunization against morphine on heroin self-administration, *Pharm. Biochem. Beh. 9,* 347–352 (1978).

106. Wainer, B. H., Fitch, F. W., Rothberg, R. M., and Fried, J., Morphine-3-succinyl-bovine serum albumin: an immunogenic hapten-protein conjugate, *Science 176,* 1143–1144 (1972).

107. Wainer, B. H., Fitch, F. W., Fried, J., and Rothberg, R. M., A measurement of the specificities of antibodies to morphine-6-succinyl BSA by competitive inhibition of [14] C-morphine binding, *J. Immun. 110,* 667–673 (1973).

108. Schuster, C. R., Smith, B., and Jaffe, J. H., Drug abuse in heroin users, *Arch. Gen. Psychiat. 24,* 359–362 (1971).

109. Bigelow, G., Liebson, I., Kaliszak, J., and Griffiths, R. R., Therapeutic self-medication as a context for drug abuse research, in *Self-administration of Abused Substances: Methods for Study* (NIDA Research Monograph No. 20), N. Krasnegor, ed., GPO, Washington, D.C., 1978, pp. 44–58.

110. Schuster, C. R., and Johanson, C. E., Behavioral analysis of opiate dependence, in *Opiate Addiction: Origins and Treatment,* S. Fisher and A. M. Freedman, eds., Winston, New York, 1973, pp. 77–92.

111. Jones, B. E., and Prada, J. A., Relapse to morphine use in the dog, *Psychopharmacologia 30,* 1–12 (1973).

112. Parry, H. J., Balter, M. B., Mellinger, G. D., Cisin, I. H., and Manheimer, D. I., National patterns of psychotherapeutic drug use, *Arch. Gen. Psychiat. 28,* 769–783 (1973).

113. Alexander, B. K., Coombs, R. B., and Hadaway, P. F., The effect of housing and gender on morphine self-administration in rats, *Psychopharmacology 58,* 175–179 (1978).

114. Nichols, J. R., and Hsiao, S., Addictive liability of albino rats: breeding for quantitative differences in morphine drinking, *Science 157,* 561–563 (1967).

115. Horowitz, G. P., Whitney, G., Smith, J. C., and Stephan, F. K., Morphine ingestion: genetic control in mice, *Psychopharmacology 52,* 119–122 (1977).

116. Khantzian, E. J., Opiate addiction: a critique of theory and some implications for treatment, *Amer. J. Psychother. 28,* 59–70 (1974).

117. Frederick, C. J., Resnick, H. L. P., and Wittlin, B. J., Self-destructive aspects of hard core addiction, *Arch. Gen. Psychiat. 28,* 579–585 (1973).

118. Robins, P. R., Depression and drug addicton, *Psych. Q. 48,* 375–388 (1974).

119. Weissman, M. M., Slobetz, F., Prusoff, B., Mezvitz, M., and Howard, P., Clinical depression among narcotic addicts maintained on methadone in the community, *Amer. J. Psych. 133,* 1434–1438 (1976).

120. Woody, G. E., O'Brien, C. P., and Rickels, K., Depression and anxiety in heroin addicts: a placebo-controlled study of doxepin in combination with methadone, *Amer. J. Psych. 132,* 447–450 (1975).

121. Schuster, C. R., Renault, P. E., and Blaine, J., An analysis of the relationship of psychopathology to non-medical drug use, in *Psychiatric Factors in Drug Abuse,* R. Pickens and L. L. Heston, eds., Grune & Stratton, New York, 1979, pp. 1–19.

122. Holtzman, S., and Shannon, H., Further evaluation of the discriminative effects of morphine in the rat, *J. Pharm. Exp. Ther. 201,* 55–66 (1977).

123. Woods, J. H., Hein, D., Valentino, R. J., and Herling, S., Narcotic drug discrimination in rhesus monkeys and pigeons (in press).

125. Lynch, J. J., Fertziger, A. P., Teitelbaum, H. A., Cullen, J. W., and Gantt, W. H., Pavlovian conditioning of drug reactions: some implications for problems of drug addiction, *Cond. Reflex 8,* 211–223 (1973).

126. Lynch, J. J., Stein, E. A., and Fertziger, A. P., An analysis of seventy years of morphine classical conditioning: implications for clinical treatment of narcotic addiction, *J. Nerv. Ment. Dis. 163,* 47–58 (1976).

127. Lal, H., Miksic, S., Drawbaugh, R., Numan, R., and Smith, N., Alleviation of narcotic withdrawal syndrome by conditional stimuli, *Pav. J. Biol. Sci., 11,* 251–262 (1976).

128. Tye, N. C., and Iversen, S. D., Some behavioral signs of morphine withdrawal blocked by conditional stimuli, *Nature 255,* 416–418 (1975).

129. Eikelboom, R., and Stewart, J., Conditioned temperature effects using morphine as the unconditioned stimulus, *Psychopharmacology 61,* 31–38 (1979).

130. Schuster, C. R., and Woods, J. H., The conditioned reinforcing effects of stimuli associated with morphine reinforcement, *Inter'l. J. Addict. 3,* 223–230 (1968).

131. Wikler, A., Pescor, F. T., Miller, D., and Norrell, H., Persistent potency of a secondary (conditioned) reinforcer following withdrawal of morphine from physically dependent rats, *Psychopharmacologia 20,* 103–117 (1971).

132. Davis, W. M., and Smith, S. G., Role of conditioned reinforcers in the initiation, maintenance, and extinction of drug-seeking behavior, *Pav. J. Biol. Sci. 11,* 222–236 (1976).

133. Goldberg, S. R., Spealman, R. D., and Kelleher, R. T., Enhancement of drug-seeking behavior by environmental stimuli associated with cocaine or morphine injections, *Neuropharm.* (in press).

134. Spealman, R. D., and Goldberg, S. R., Drug self-administration by laboratory animals: control by schedules of reinforcement, *Ann. Rev. Pharm. Tox. 18,* 313–339 (1978).

135. Kumar, R., Morphine dependence in rats: secondary reinforcement from environmental stimuli, *Psychopharmacologia 25,* 332–338 (1972).

136. Findley, J., An experimental outline for building and exploring multioperant behavior repertoires, *J. Exp. Anal. Beh. 5,* 113–166 (1962).

137. Wikler, A., A psychodynamic study of a patient during experimental self-regulated re-addiction to morphine, *Psychiat. Q. 26,* 270–293 (1952).

138. Wikler, A., On the nature of addiction and habituation, *Brit. J. Addict. 57,* 73–79 (1961).

139. Shannon, H., and Holtzman, S., The evaluation of the discriminative effects of morphine in the rat, *J. Pharm. Exp. Ther. 198,* 54–65 (1976).

140. Irwin, S., and Seevers, M. H., Comparative study of regular and n-allylnormorphine induced withdrawal in monkeys addicted to morphine, 6-methylhydromorphine, dromoran, methadone, and ketobemidone, *J. Pharm. Exp. Ther. 106,* 397 (1952).

141. Martin, W. R., Wikler, A., Eades, C. G., and Pescor, F. T., Tolerance to and physical dependence on morphine in rats, *Psychopharmacologia 4,* 247–260 (1963).

142. Wikler, A., and Pescor, F. T., Classical conditioning of a morpine abstinence phenomenon, reinforcement of opioid-drinking behavior, and "relapse" in morphine-addicted rats, *Psychopharmacologia 10,* 255–284 (1967).

143. Goldberg, S. R., Relapse to opioid dependence: the role of conditioning, in *Advances in Mental Science II: Drug Dependence,* R. T. Harris, W. M. McIsaac, and C. R., Schuster, eds., University of Texas Press, Austin, 1970, pp. 170–197.

144. Goldberg, S. R., and Schuster, C. R., Conditioned suppression by a stimulus associated with nalorphine in morphine-dependent monkeys, *J. Exp. Anal. Beh. 10,* 235–242 (1967).

145. Goldberg, S. R., and Schuster, C. R., Conditioned nalorphine-induced abstinence changes: persistence in post-dependent monkeys, *J. Exp. Anal. Beh. 14,* 33–46 (1970).

146. Goldberg, S. R., Woods, J. H., and Schuster, C. R., Morphine: conditioned increases in self-administration in rhesus monkeys, *Science 166,* 1306–1307 (1969).

147. O'Brien, C. P., O'Brien, T. J., Mintz, J., and Brady, J. P., Conditioning of narcotic abstinence symptoms in human subjects, *Drug and Alc. Depend. 1,* 115–123 (1975).

148. O'Brien, C. P., Testa, T., O'Brien, T. J., Brady, J. P., and Wells, B., Conditioned narcotic withdrawal in humans, *Science 195,* 1000–1002 (1977).

149. Goldberg, S. R., Conditioned behavioral and physiological changes associated with injections of a narcotic antagonist in morphine-dependent monkeys, *Pav. J. Biol. Sci. 11,* 203–221 (1976).

150. Wilson, M. C., and Schuster, C. R., The effects of stimulants and depressants on cocaine self-administration behavior in the rhesus monkey, *Psychopharmacologia 31,* 291–304 (1973).

151. Hoffmeister, F., and Schlichting, U. U., Reinforcing properties of some opiates and opioids in rhesus monkeys with histories of cocaine and codeine self-administration, *Psychopharmacologia 23,* 55–74 (1972).

152. Downs, D. A., and Woods, J. H., Morphine, pentazocine, and naloxone effects on responding under a multiple schedule of reinforcement in rhesus monkeys and pigeons, *J. Pharm. Exp. Ther. 196,* 298–306 (1976).

153. Goldberg, S. R., Morse, W. H., and Goldberg, D. M., Some behavioral effects of morphine, naloxone, and nalorphine in the squirrel monkey and the pigeon, *J. Pharm. Exp. Ther. 196,* 625–636 (1976).

2

Sedatives, Hypnotics, and Minor Tranquilizers

Geary S. Alford

Pharmacology

Drugs classified as hypnotics, sedatives, and minor tranquilizers are so labeled because their administration typically results in decreased arousal and motor activity, sedation, sleep induction, and—in progressively larger doses—general anesthesia, coma, and medullary depression causing death. Although the so-called minor tranquilizers are often considered apart from hypnotic-sedatives, they exhibit fundamental common properties. All drugs of this class are central nervous system (CNS) depressants, have similar behavioral-pharmacologic effects, can induce tolerance and physical addiction, and, where tolerance or addiction has developed, result in similar withdrawal syndromes upon abrupt cessation of use (15, 26, 55). There are, however, significant differences among these compounds in potency, duration of action, rate of tolerance and addiction induction, and certain behavioral effects. Table 2–1 lists the most common drugs in this pharmacologic class according to chemical structure and behavioral effects.

The prototypic hypnotic-sedatives are the barbiturates, a group of drugs derived from barbituric acid and initially synthesized for medical use in the first decade of the twentieth century. Since that time numerous barbiturate derivatives have been produced and are in current clinical use. The major differences among barbiturates are potency and duration of action. The CNS is exquisitely sensitive to these drug depressant effects, although technically the barbiturates can, in sufficiently high doses, produce depression in all excitable body tissue. Within the range of usual clinical doses, very little effect on skeletal, cardiac, or smooth muscle tissue occurs (26). Although once widely used in psychiatry in the treatment of anxiety, hyperarousal, and extreme agitation, barbiturates currently are employed as anticonvulsant or sleep inducing agents; they are also used to induce hypnosis (e.g., Amytal interview) or rapid sedation and to achieve detoxification. Some physicians continue to prescribe barbiturates for anxiety

39

TABLE 2-1.
The Most Common Hypnotics, Sedatives, and Minor Tranquilizers

Barbiturates	
Amobarbital (Amytal)[a]	Primidone (Mysoline)
Hexobarbital (Sombucaps)	Secobarbital (Seconal)
Pentobarbital (Nembutal)	Thiamylal (Surital)

Carbamates and Dicarbamates	
Carisoprodol (Soma, Rela)	Meprobamate (Equanil, Miltown)
Ethinamate (Valmid)	Methocarbamol (Robaxin)
Mebutamate (Capla)	Tybamate (Solacon, Tybatran)

Benzodiazepines and Methaqualone	
Chlorazepate (Tranxene)	Lorazepam (Ativan)
Chlordiazepoxide (Librium)	Oxazepam (Serax)
Diazepam (Valium)	Prazepam (Verstran)
Flurazepam (Dalmane)	Methaqualone (Quaalude, Sopor)

Alcohols	
Chloral Hydrate	Ethchlorvynol (Placidyl)
Ethanol	Phenaglycodol (Ultran)

[a] Trade names given for identification purposes only.

and related complaints, but this practice is contra-indicated and is becoming increasingly uncommon.

In the 1950s, barbiturates were replaced in the management of schizophrenia by neuroleptics and in the treatment of neurosis and other anxiety related dysfunctions by meprobamate (Equanil, Miltown). Over the past two decades, meprobamate has gone out of vogue and been replaced by benzodiazepines (e.g., Librium, Valium, Serax, Ativan, Tranxene). During this time meprobamate, benzodiazepines, and related compounds were given the label "minor tranquilizers" or "anxiolytics" (antianxiety agents), which unfortunately obscures the fact that these drugs share most of the pharmacological properties of barbiturates, including addictive potential. Nevertheless, there are important differences. For example, studies of experimental neuroses in animals have repeatedly found differential effects on avoidance and escape behavior from benzodiazepines as compared with barbiturates. While both barbiturates and minor tranquilizers will decrease both avoidance and escape responding, anxiolytics, particularly benzodiazepines, have a much greater effect on avoidance than on escape behavior (31–33). Operant behaviors acquired through positive reinforcement procedures (e.g., food reinforced lever-pressing) but subsequently depressed via punishment (e.g., approach-avoidance training) display significant reinstatement of responding after animals are administered benzodiazepines. In contrast, neuroleptics (so-called major tranquilizers) or stimulants (amphetamines) usually either produce no changes in punishment depressed responding or further reduce response rates (31). Perhaps even more interesting, Kelleher and Morse showed that most anxiolytics given in low, nonsedating doses will increase the frequency of both previously unpunished and previously punished behaviors in animals that have undergone punishment or avoidance training (33). All hypnotic-sedatives and anxiolytics do share the behavioral-pharmacologic property of inducing state dependent learning (48). That is, behaviors acquired in the drug state partly or wholly fail to transfer to the nondrug state but will exhibit significant reinstatement of response upon reintoxication. This phenomenon has been demonstrated with barbiturates (48), meprobamate (48), benzodiazepines (5), and ethyl alcohol (27). It has been suggested that alcohol induced blackouts are partially a function of the state dependent properties of ethyl alcohol. Although little systematic documentation is available, such dissociative phenomena are sometimes observed or reported with other hypnotic-sedatives.

The exact mechanisms of action of the different CNS depressants are still not known. A growing body of evidence suggests that barbiturates exert their effect at the synapse, rather than on neuronal conduction (26, 47), by decreasing the amount of transmitter released (47). Benzodiazepines may exert similar effects by reducing the turnover rate of probable transmitters such as noradrenaline and 5-hydroxytryptamine, (31, 57) and/or by stimulating the release of gamma-amino butyric acid (GABA), thus increasing its inhibitory effect (31). Although currently available evidence suggests probable mechanisms for a wide variety of depressant effects on molar behavior such as wakefulness, arousability, or sedation, the mechanisms for the antianxiety effects are still elusive (1, 26, 32). Most models implicate the limbic system as the most probable principal locus, but limbic structures are suggested more on the basis of what *is* known about their role in various emotional or emotionally mediated behaviors than on direct evidence of selective action of these drugs. A more extensive review of these theories and their supporting evidence is beyond the scope or purpose of this chapter but may be found elsewhere (1, 26, 31, 32, 39, 47, 57).

The CNS depressants, then, share many properties and probable mechanisms of action; however, the different subclasses of hypnotics, sedatives, and anxiolytics may entail somewhat diverse specificity of action on various CNS structures and systems, thus generating their different behavioral effects (26, 31). Anxiolytics are generally less sedating, have a significantly higher margin of safety (i.e., LD_{50}), are slower to induce tolerance, and exhibit greater antianxiety effects with less sedation than do barbiturates; these features contribute to their popularity among physicians treating anxiety, tension, agitation, and other manifestations of aversive autonomic arousal. Anxiolytics are frequently used in the treatment of essentially every form of neurosis, many personality disorders, depression where anxiety and agitation are present, conversion reactions, situational adjustment reactions, alcoholism and chemical dependency, and (at least as implied by one drug company advertisement to physicians) women who get tense doing household chores they dislike. Over 60 million prescriptions for diazepam (Valium) alone are written each year and almost that many for chlordiazepoxide (Librium) (2). Hypnotics, sedatives, and minor tranquilizers account for approximately 70 percent of all prescriptions written for psychoactive drugs (52). Furthermore, although anxiolytics can be extremely valuable on a time limited basis to instate or enhance conditions for and otherwise facilitate specific therapeutic procedures aimed at anxiety, tension, and aversive autonomic arousal related disorders (6), their use over protracted periods is rarely necessary for such conditions if appropriate and effective forms of psychologic intervention are utilized. In fact, however, many patients are maintained over extended periods of time on anxiolytics, sometimes combined with other hypnotic-sedatives or anxiolytics (e.g., 5 mg diazepam three times a day and 15 mg flurazepam at bedtime, often combined by patients with their usual alcohol intake, and sometimes prescribed for relatively minor complaints (15, 52, 55). Some practitioners deny that anxiolytic misuse and addiction are significant problems and even argue that adverse publicity about the abuse potential of anxiolytics has been exaggerated and is "detrimental to the medical profession and the doctor-patient relationship" (12). Because minor tranquilizers are so widely available and broadly used, reliable representative data on their abuse are difficult to obtain. However, a growing body of evidence on the incidence and complications of hypnotic–sedative–minor tranquilizer misuse, dependency, and physical addiction indicates that these problems are widespread and similar in nature and effects to alcoholism (15, 55).

Use, Misuse, and Addiction

Several factors contribute to the misuse and abuse potential of hypnotics, sedatives, and minor tranquilizers. They are relatively easy to obtain, induce some very pleasurable, desirable, positively reinforcing sensory-perceptual effects, and generally have minimal unpleasant side effects in the early stages of misuse.

In general, hypnotic-sedative compounds and particularly the anxiolytics have psychological and behavioral effects similar in nature to those of ethyl alcohol, with which they are almost perfectly cross-tolerant (and which, incidentally, is also a CNS depressant and technically falls within the pharmacologic class of hypnotic-sedatives). The most common effects with administration of nonhypnotic doses of these substances are enhanced feelings of relaxation or tranquility; decreased sensations of tension, anxiety, or apprehension; and a sense of well-being or even euphoria. In many instances, effects are manifested by transient disinhibition of desired behavior, such as social skills performance and sexual responsivity, and a state of intoxication similar in many ways to alcohol intoxication. Somewhat larger oral doses (relative to the specific compound) induce sleep.

Of course, not all of the sensations of acute intoxication are pleasurable. Like alcohol, hypnotics, sedatives, and minor tranquilizers can precipitate a release phenomenon in which the individual may suddenly become quite internally and externally disinhibited (26, 55). At times the individual may experience and express extreme anger, rage, anxiety, or depression or may become very emotionally volatile, overreactive, or impulsive—more stimulated than sedated. However, although these kinds of reactions are *sometimes* experienced by the user as unpleasant, overt behavioral manifestations are commonly perceived by everyone else as offensive. Indeed, many users rather enjoy these emotional upheavals and most certainly feel justified in having them. In short, use and misuse of these drugs produces a variety of acute pleasurable, pleasant, and desirable effects but very few acute aversive sensations.

One of the recurring myths in the field of addictive behaviors is that such positive effects occur only in individuals who are unusually tense, anxious, or neurotic to begin with. While it may be true that the contrast from nondrug to drug state may be greater in individuals who are experiencing aversive emotional arousal, it does not follow that a preintoxication state of arousal is *necessary* for the pleasurable sensations of drug intoxication to be detected (32, 48). One need not be an alcoholic, a neurotic or even mildly tense to experience the effects of a cocktail. Nevertheless, the preintoxication condition is a major contributing variable to the matrix of effects a given compound will produce (32, 52). To the extent that drug effects are not only positively reinforcing in generating pleasurable sensations but also negatively reinforcing in decreasing, removing, or avoiding aversive sensations, the reinforcement potential of drug effects is significantly enhanced (32, 45, 60).

Mild, transient, intermittent sensations of stress, tension, or anxiety are so common in modern society as to be almost universal. In addition, many individuals have developed behavior or personality patterns of cognitive-emotional overreactivity in which objectively minor events elicit unpleasant and overt emotional reactions (18, 41). Furthermore, a variety of clinically significant behavioral disorders, such as severe phobias and neuroses, entail disruptively high levels of aversive emotional arousal. Hypnotics, sedatives, or tranquilizers taken under such conditions will generate marked state changes, and the negative reinforcing effects will be most profound. Added to this population are individuals who begin taking this class of drugs primarily for a high. That is, there may be initially very little negative reinforcement effect involved; the drugs are taken for their primarily positive consequences. Most major aversive effects, as I discuss later, rarely occur or are experienced in the initial stages of chemical use and misuse.

In sum, some individuals use or misuse a compound because they enjoy the pleasurable effects (appetitive use). Others enjoy the pleasurable sensations arising from the intoxication but also experience relief from unpleasant sensations (escape-avoidance use). In addition, a wide variety of external and internal antecedent stimuli can set the scene for drug usage. These elicitory events may be associated with primarily appetitive behavior or predominantly avoidance-escape behavior. For example, a fight with one's spouse, anticipation of anxiety during an upcoming meeting, or depressing thoughts and feelings may each evoke chemical usage. On the other hand, not all antecedent conditions can be considered negative or aversive. Many causative events are associated with appetitive use of chemicals. Social gatherings, festive occasions, as well as a wide range of common stimuli prompt appetitive chemical use (in our culture the chemical of choice is ethyl alcohol, followed by marijuana and other drugs). In sum, the antecedent conditions for chemical use may be internal or external and may be associated with appetitive or escape-avoidance tendencies or both.

Initial sampling or use of chemicals may result from one or more sources of influence: for example, peer and other social pressure, modeling, or medical treatment (52). Whatever the initial motivation, most individuals taking a given drug experience similar effects (e.g., sedatives tranquilize, amphetamines stimulate, and analgesics reduce pain). How reinforcing these effects may be for various individuals is determined by how enjoyable and desirable the positive effects are, as well as by the desired reduction of aversive sensations. For as yet unestablished reasons, many individuals independently either control (i.e., do not accelerate) their usage or discontinue use of, or experimentation with, drugs. Of course, many people avoid chemical use in the first place. Such avoidance most probably occurs in individuals who fear addiction, anticipate significant aversive consequences of use or misuse, or have other strong reservations against chemical use. The focus of this chapter, however, is individuals who do find the psychopharmacologic effects of chemicals more reinforcing (positively and/or negatively) than neutral or punishing and thus maintain or accelerate chemical intake.

Where use (misuse) continues over time, tolerance begins to develop so that an increasingly higher dose becomes necessary for the user to experience the desired drug effects. This is commonly accomplished by increasing the frequency of administration and/or the dosage per administration (e.g., taking two tablets four times a day instead of one three times daily), by switching to a more potent drug, or by combining drugs (e.g.,

Valium plus cocktails). Increasing tolerance is associated with the development of withdrawal symptoms as drug levels fall within the person. At first these symptoms rarely include the complete, clinically identifiable hypnotic-sedative withdrawal syndrome, with noticeable tremor, profuse sweating, disorientation, or convulsions. Rather, the initial symptoms in these cases include generally increasing tension, tremulousness, anxiety, irritability, emotional overreactivity, with a marked return of conditioned emotional reactions and conditioned avoidance responses. In short, this subclinical withdrawal syndrome entails many of the very sensations and behaviors as so aversive to the user in the first place. Relief is gained by rapid reintoxication. Again, one must recognize that the same withdrawal effects occur in users who may not have experienced a significant degree of such aversive feelings *prior* to their use of and subsequent induced tolerance to these chemical agents. That is, for example, an otherwise emotionally stable, psychologically healthy individual who began taking a minor tranquilizer to facilitate sleep induction, "occasionally" resorted to taking one or so pills during the day to help him or her relax, and finally accelerated to a dose schedule sufficient to induce at least some degree of tolerance may during withdrawal intervals experience feelings of tension and anxiety at a theretofore unknown level and in situations in which he or she had never previously felt much discomfort. At this point, these users are similar to those individuals whose chemical usage serves both to avoid or escape negative sensations and to instill positive, pleasurable effects. That is, as tolerance develops, reintoxication will have significant negative reinforcing as well as positive reinforcing components in *any* user. As the response pattern develops, a wide variety of internal cues (such as an increasing sense of tension, anxiety, or discomfort) or allied external situations (having an argument, facing a stressful social interaction, or perhaps just time of day) set the occasion for drug usage. As tolerance progresses, acceleration of drug intake must keep pace, eventually resulting in dependence and physical addiction.

It is not primarily the dependence or the physical addiction per se that makes chemical misuse such a devastating personal and social problem. Rather, it is the constellation of undesirable, disruptive consequences that stem from the toxic effects of chronic misuse. As noted earlier, during periods of acute intoxication the user may internally experience a largely positive set of sensations yet be very offensive to others. However, paradoxical effects may occur that are experienced by the intoxicated user as aversive; such consequences rarely outweigh the positive sensations. These aversive effects include increased excitability, violent mood swings, emotional overreactivity, and overt expression of depression, anxiety, anger, or rage. To an extent, some of the aversive effects of intoxication are paradoxically similar to certain sensations experienced during drug withdrawal and likewise to some of the aversive sensations many users sought to diminish by using drugs in the first place. When these paradoxical effects occur during phases of intoxication, they typically trigger more drug taking.

In addition to the sensations experienced by the user, a number of other adverse intrapersonal and interpersonal consequences result from CNS depressant misuse. In general, mild to moderate intoxication resembles intoxication with ethyl alcohol. Behavioral manifestations include general sluggishness, impaired judgment, decreased memory, decreased reaction time and coordination, emotional lability and impulsivity, sometimes hostility, quarrelsomeness, moroseness, and signs of depression, and occasionally paranoid ideation and homicidal or suicidal acts (14, 15, 26, 52, 55). Once a degree of tolerance is attained, some of these effects will occur during mild abstinence and will particularly include anxiety, agitation, tension, irritability, and general emotional excitability (55). The effects, of course, contribute to a wide range of undesirable overt behavior patterns such as marital and family arguments and conflict, inappropriate social behavior offensive to others, decreased or impaired vocational skill and job performance, and even civil or criminal offenses related to inappropriate behavior in public, automobile accidents while intoxicated, and illegal procurement of drugs. Eventually, such behaviors result in separation and divorce, loss of friends, loss of jobs and income. Further economic cost results from the expense of the drugs themselves, legal fees associated with civil or criminal litigation, and the cost of treatment for chemical dependency.

As we have seen, use and abuse of hypnotics, sedatives, and minor tranquilizers have a variety of internal and external consequences. Many of these effects are extremely pleasurable. Alternately, many consequences are aversive, painful, and punishing. Were it possible to place simultaneously in the cognitive-emotional perceptual balance all the positive and negative effects of substance misuse, the negative would appear to outweigh the positive: the punishment would be greater than the reinforcement, and little chemical misuse would ever occur (e.g., if painful tumors developed minutes after lighting a cigarette, few individuals would have any desire to continue the behavior and smoking would not become an addictive habit; however, after years of habitual smoking, even cancer may not be sufficiently aversive in some cases to reduce or eliminate the behavior).

To understand how addictive behavior develops and is maintained as a volitional disorder, it is necessary to examine some relationship variables between the pattern of drug use and its differential effects.

Latency of Consequences

The time is quite short between the ingestion of drugs and their desired effects on sensation and perception. For drugs injected or inhaled, drug action onset occurs in seconds. While chemicals administered intramuscularly or orally have a somewhat longer latency of onset, this interval is usually a matter of only minutes. Within seconds to minutes of using a chemical, the individual begins to experience (depending on the compound) relaxation, tranquilization, stimulation, euphoria, and/or a decrease in aversive sensations such as pain, tension, or anxiety. Thus, there is temporal contiguity between drug intake and the pleasurable reinforcing consequences, consistent with both classical and operant learning principles (8, 44, 45, 60). With the relatively uncommon exception of such drug reactions, as anaphylaxis or bad trips, aversive consequences of misuse rarely occur with drug ingestion; indeed, most serious and perceptually aversive psychological, medical, and environmental consequences require months to years to occur (e.g., chronic organic brain syndromes, liver disease, or emphysema and lung cancer). Even physical addiction itself may require many months to develop with certain drugs. In short, the pleasurable, positively reinforcing effects of chemical use and abuse are *immediate,* while the negative ones are delayed.

Onset and Detectability of Consequences

Just as the pleasurable consequences of drug intoxication come very soon after drug ingestion, they also attain their peak effect rather quickly. That is, after (or during) ingestion, there is a relatively rapid acceleration of drug effects resulting in the desirable state of intoxication and a clear contrast between drug and nondrug states. The user unequivocally detects the pleasurable drug induced changes. In contrast, many of the adverse consequences of misuse come on very gradually. Changes in behavior patterns (personality); diminished memory and cognitive capacity; verbal, motor, and social skills deterioration; decreased job performance; increased marital conflict; and physical disease processes usually have a relatively slow course. Adverse changes are often so gradual that they go undetected by both the user and, in the short run, close observers (spouses, friends, etc.). Often, untoward changes in the nature and level of behavioral function are apparent only after several months of use.

Probability of Consequences

Although both pleasurable and aversive consequences of chemical misuse have an empirically established high probability of occurring, probability *as experienced* is quite another thing. An individual's assessment of the probability of a given outcome derives from personal experience, incidental education (e.g., vicarious experience), and formal education (in this case knowledge of behavioral pharmacology)—commonly in that order. Just as the positively reinforcing drug effects occur immediately upon use and have a relatively rapid acceleration to peak levels, and thus are detectable, so the pleasurable effects are highly probable. That is, they occur essentially every time the user engages in chemical misuse: the user thus knows from experience that the high will occur with almost 100 percent probability. The aversive consequences, on the other hand, occur sporadically; indeed, some may never occur. Therefore, the user concludes that negative effects have a very low probability of occurring. In addition, as we shall see subsequently, some adverse consequences of drug abuse are frequently *not attributed* to the drug.

Moreover, while many users may have intermittent exposure to addicts who have suffered the most salient and profound adverse consequences of chemical misuse, the majority of their drug using acquaintances are at roughly their own level of function. Users who have suffered catastrophic consequences usually have dropped out of sight by gravitating to a lower subculture (e.g., skid row), by incarceration in legal and/or treatment institutions, or by death. Thus, vicarious experience tends to confirm the low probability rate of adverse consequences based on the user's history. When exposed to obvious deterioration, users usually invoke alleged differences in health, personality, situation, and/or use pattern between themselves and those in whom they have witnessed the devastating consequences. Idiosyncratic differences in dose response curves with respect to the negative consequences' timing, rate, sequence, and specific nature contribute to these distorted perceptions.

Finally, formal education on drug effects has little impact. Such information is most often discounted as exaggerated and biased. For example, films on alcoholism and drug addiction generally include scenes of skid row, delirium tremens, or narcotic withdrawal. For the individual in the early phases of chemical dependency, such effects are contrary to their own experience and to that of the vast majority of their drug using friends. The weight of the acceptable evidence suggests relatively low probability that they personally will suffer devastating effects.

Attribution of Consequences

The preceding differential relationships between abuse pattern and positive versus negative effects contribute to one of the most important phenomena in chemical dependency: misattribution. As we have seen, since pleasurable effects occur along with drug intake, produce a clearly detectable drug state, and have a high probability, positive consequences of misuse are directly associated with drug ingestion. Because the aversive consequences are delayed and "improbable," even when they do occur in subjectively detectable magnitude, users often fail to attribute them to chemical abuse. By the time serious negative consequences are noted, partial to full tolerance and physical addiction often have developed, enhancing the negative reinforcing properties of drug use. Paradoxically, when aversive consequences are detected by the user, they are often identical to the external and internal stimuli that occasion additional drug taking. A simple but clear example exists when a spouse gets drunk in reaction to a marital fight over drinking.

In addition, many adverse events in fact associated with the effects of drug use are ascribed to nondrug causes. For example, a late-night automobile accident may be attributed by the driver to sleepiness rather than to heavy drinking; increased tension and irritability during falling drug levels may be perceived as a reaction to primarily external events; deteriorating personal relationships may be viewed by the user as a result of personality changes in others; and decreased performance and loss of job may be explained by employers' prejudice. Thus, many drug related events are "safely" ascribed to factors ostensibly unconnected to the individual's addictive behavior.

Further complicating and obscuring the relationship between chemical misuse and negative consequences is the phenomenon of "denial." Variously defined as an unconscious defense mechanism by which aspects of reality are distorted or rejected or as conscious, outright lying, denial is considered by most sophisticated researchers to play a significant role in addictive behavior and to constitute a major problem in treatment (13, 34). Denial probably entails elements of both definitional extremes. Ample evidence indicates that human beings selectively attend to stimuli (7, 11, 17, 49) and selectively remember events (7, 20), that aversively conditioned stimuli can even, via cognitive mediation, selectively motivate forgetting (22), and that various cognitive strategies (rationalization, cognitive dissonance reduction) can be employed to avoid acknowledging unpleasant realities (20, 41). The differential empirical relationships between drug misuse and positive versus negative consequences provide ample opportunity for subtle and sophisticated forms of denial: failure to detect adverse chemical effects, failure to perceive or believe the actual probability of adverse effects, and failure to attribute such effects to addictive behavior patterns are all examples of this mechanism. Thus, potential intraorganismic mediation between behavior and its adverse consequences is disrupted, further reducing the punishing effects that such consequences might otherwise exert on chemical misuse behavior.

Treatment

Treatment approaches for hypnotic, sedative, and minor tranquilizer misuse and addiction are in general very similar to those employed for other drugs of abuse, including the CNS depressant ethyl alcohol. Because the fundamental processes of addictive behavior are shared by the various forms of chemical dependency, this discussion, although focused on CNS sedatives and minor tranquilizers, addresses addictive behavior in general.

Diverse therapeutic procedures reflect the particular conceptual models of addiction to which therapists, programs, and institutions adhere. That various treatments for chemical dependency have had limited success is broadly acknowledged (13, 34, 45, 46, 50). Although much political as well as scientific controversy surrounds addiction treatment research, examination of some current and traditional treatment concepts in light of the foregoing discussion may help elucidate principal issues and problems.

Detoxification

Although no current model of addiction considers detoxification per se sufficient to modify addictive behavior, analysis of major reasons why detoxification alone does not work may help clarify the critical issues and at least set the stage for subsequent analysis of the more complex treatment models. In the first place, that detoxification *alone* has little sustained impact on the vast majority of chemical abusers should strongly suggest that models of addictive behavior that conceptualize chronic drug abuse as primarily an avoidance of withdrawal or abstinence are wrong. Since appropriate detoxification precludes the withdrawal syndrome, the detoxified user cannot be reinstituting drug use to avoid such symptoms. Further evidence for this conclusion is that a significant proportion, perhaps the majority, of addicts placed on drug substitution therapy (e.g., methadone maintenance) continue to "chip" heroin or other drugs, including extra doses of methadone. This occurs in patients who are, in fact, being maintained in a relative state of intoxication as well as avoiding withdrawal symptoms. Detoxification reduces only some of the internal stimulus events that evoke drug use. That is, it greatly reduces only the possiblity of the withdrawal syndrome; it does not affect many similar aversive sensations resulting from intraorganismic and environmental stimuli that also occasion chemical misuse. More important, detoxification itself has no impact on the history of positive conditioning that has resulted in the high probability and high evaluation of pleasurable drug use effects. Finally, detoxification itself does not instill more adaptive, alternative behaviors for reducing aversive sensations and for acquiring positive, pleasurable ones through nonchemical means. For any therapeutic approach to be successful, it must effectively address all of these issues.

Psychodynamic Models

Even though subtle variations exist, most psychodynamic models of addictive behavior are predicted on the assumption that drug and alcohol abuse derives from underlying psychologic disturbances (orality, passive-dependence, etc.) or other psychologic disorders (e.g., anxiety neurosis) (16, 30, 35, 42, 51). Hence, the addictive behavior tends to be viewed as *symptomatic* and not as the behavioral disorder in itself. Treatment, then, focuses on identifying the underlying problem, which when resolved presumably will ameliorate the chemical dependency. This view is supported by a mass of soft-core personality studies on alcoholics and drug addicts and their psychopathology. More sophisticated and detailed presentations of this theoretical position are available (16, 35, 51, 54).

Although the efficacy of traditional psychodynamic therapies even for personality and neurotic disorders per se has yet to be empirically documented, there are a number of problems with such approaches. Although several well-done studies have found evidence of psychopathology (e.g., symptoms of personality disorders, neuroses, or psychoses) in alcoholic and drug dependent populations (14, 16, 21, 34, 54), they have not provided ante hoc empirical documentation that such symptoms or conditions were present to any significant or abnormal extent *prior* to the development of the addictive behavior. Indeed, several careful investigations failed to demonstrate differential personality traits between alcoholic and nonalcoholic populations (44, 46). In one of the very few controlled predictive studies in which comprehensive psychological and medical examinations of nonalcoholic youngsters were compared, McCord and McCord found no significant differences between subjects who later became alcoholics and those who did not in regard to metabolic, glandular, or general physical functioning; feelings of inferiority or anxiety; oral tendencies; or other personality characteristics prior to the onset of abusive drinking (40). These findings seriously compromise models of addictive behavior that postulate underlying disorders as the primary etiological factors in excessive substance use.

To be sure, as will be discussed later, preexisting cognitive, emotional, and overt behavior patterns most probably do contribute to the development of addictive behavior, but available empirical evidence does not indicate that they are either necessary or sufficient for the development of chemical dependency. Finally, regardless of the exact role preexisting personality factors play in addictive behavior, the powerful reinforcement history of the chemical abuse pattern is not eradicated by psychotherapeutically removing part of the supposed original motivation for misuse.

Biological Models

At least since the late nineteenth century, alcoholism and drug addiction have been conceptualized by many as a hereditary, now a genetically transmitted, disorder (28, 29). What confounds this view, of course, is the potency of environmental influence, particularly modeling (8, 53). Speaking poor English, taste for certain foods, and even selection of occupations also tend to run in families. Even where biological factors have been separated from social-familial influences, results have not been clear-cut. Goodwin and his associates, in one of the best large-scale genetic studies of addictive behavior, compared adopted and nonadopted children of alcoholics and concluded that genetic inheritance was more significantly related to subsequent alcoholism than were various environmental factors (28, 29). Close examination of these statistics, however, reveals that while significant, these correlations were far from perfect. Many children who had one or more alcoholic biological parents did not evidence abusive drinking or alcoholism; yet many offspring of nonalcoholic parents did subsequently develop alcoholism. What's more, this same group of researchers found little correlation in other drug abuses. Like preexisting personality or cognitive-emotional behavior patterns, genetic factors probably can increase the susceptibility of individuals to develop chemically dependent behavior. Again, however, such factors do not appear to be either necessary or sufficient.

We have no model of how genetic factors contribute to addictive behavior. Clearly, such factors do not transmit the entire, highly complex cognitive, emotional, and overt behavior repertoire involved in chemical dependency. Rather, they most probably exert their influence via individual reactivity to environmental stimuli and/or idiosyncratic reactivity to drug effects. In addition, changes in neuronal receptor sensitivity to endogenous as well as exogenous compounds from repeated drug use may have similar effects (23, 24). That is, if neurophyisologic adaptation to the presence of certain compounds in fact occurs, then the consequent protracted, residual, drug abstinent conditions (as contrasted with the abstinence syndrome per se) following detoxification may leave the individual in a state of subnormally low tolerance to pain, anxiety, etc., which in turn would contribute to the negative reinforcing effects of intoxication.

Social-Psychological Models

Perhaps the central feature of social-psychological models of chemical dependency is the theory that addictive behaviors result primarily from direct social influence (9, 38, 52). Such approaches share with the psychodynamic models an emphasis on internal conflict, emotional pain and discomfort, and other variations of aversive arousal as contributory events in chemical abuse. However, rather than attribute these internal conditions to distal, early life events such as traumas in psychosexual development, sociological models attribute them to observable environmental stimuli: pressures of ghetto life, with its overcrowding, poverty, hunger, unemployment, high crime rate, etc., or (in attempts to account for middle- and upper-class addiction) job pressure, disrupted family life, generation gap, alienation, etc. Unfortunately, such sociological models also share with psychodynamic models the difficulty in accounting for, on the one hand, the substantial percentage of chemical misusers who have no unusual or abnormal amount of environmental pressure and, on the other, the very large percentage of individuals under apparently extreme socioenvironmental pressure who do not become chemically dependent. After the fact arguments that people who have become addicted must have been experiencing great internal and external pressure and that nonaddicts cannot have been equally stressed or have healthier, stronger egos are circular, theoretically meaningless, and pragmatically useless. But the influence of social pressure, modeling, and social learning should not be discounted vis-à-vis the acquisition, maintenance, and modification of behavior (8, 45, 52, 53).

Modern American society is a drug oriented society. Not only are pushers on the street attempting to persuade potential clients to try new, more powerful and expensive drugs, but also our television sets tell us that failure to fall soundly asleep within 15 seconds after going to bed is pathological. Headaches, we are told, are not only undesirable, uncomfortable, and mildly disruptive but also unfair. The answer, of course, is to take a pill. Drug using models are abundant in the natural environment and most certainly exert a major influence on many individuals. Still, were it not for the nature of the drug action and its diverse consequences, chemical dependency would not develop. That is, sociocultural factors such as grossly disrupted family life, the pressures of certain jobs, and the acute stresses of poverty, overcrowding, and unemployment may encourage drug taking, but such factors do not in themselves, *cause* drug addiction, nor are they the central process of behavior change by which addiction develops. Finally, while noting many important contributory factors, socio-pyschological models fail sufficiently to recognize that whatever motivated initial drug use, drug abuse, once developed, generates a powerful, resistant pattern that is almost always functionally autonomous of its roots.

Theoretical models have value to the extent that they yield verifiable hypotheses, predict and control specific dependent variables in the laboratory, and generate efficacious treatment procedures in the clinic. The preceding models have not been very successful in empirically documenting their value. Although, as noted, they do call attention to important contributory factors in addictive behavior, objective support for treatment tactics based on these models has not been forthcoming. For example, I am distressed to see conventional psychotherapy widely recommended in texts as the core treatment for chemical dependency (30, 36, 56); not only has psychodynamic therapy not been shown effective for addictive behavior, but also we lack objective evidence that this modality is better than placebos or passage of time in ameliorating most psychologic disorders (10, 19, 21, 25). Furthermore, some aspects of traditional models may have deleterious effects in treating chemically dependent persons. The notion that underlying conflicts, anxiety, feelings of inferiority, etc., are causative in addiction (16, 30, 35, 51) leads many physicians to prescribe drugs in an attempt to decrease deep-seated pyschic tensions. In practice, this often translates into rather long-term anxiolytic pharmacotherapy, ostensibly as an adjunct to psychotherapy. Alcoholics, for example, are commonly placed on benzodiazepines (after detoxification) during the course of psychotherapy. Since benzodiazepines are intoxicating, addicting, and almost perfectly cross-tolerant with alcohol, this practice is functionally equivalent to methadone maintenance for opiate dependent patients. What's more, long-term administration of anxiolytics (or any other phar-macotherapy) is not necessary in the treatment of the vast majority of per-sonality disorders and neuroses (6, 8), even if the empirical evidence demonstrated that such conditions are ubiquitous in chemically dependent patients, which of course it does not. In that minority of addicts exhibiting major thought disorders or affective psychoses (as distinguished from acute drug induced psychoses) that contribute to drug misuse, long-term phar-macotherapy with appropriate neuroleptics, lithium carbonate, etc., is ac-ceptable.

To be sure, the foregoing survey of psychodynamic, sociological, and biological factors in chemical dependency oversimplified each approach; more sophisticated arguments in their favor are provided elsewhere (9, 16, 28, 29, 38). However, some of the central features were identified with respect to their contribution to understanding chemical dependency. I do not suggest that preexisting traits, personality or behavior patterns, behavioral dysfunctions, biological factors, or sociocultural and other en-vironmental influences do not contribute to chemical dependency. Ample post hoc evidence, incidental and anecdotal, and even some empirical find-ings suggest that these factors play a role in the etiology and maintenance of addictions. The point is that while such factors may be contributory, they are neither necessary nor causative.

Behavioral Models

As with the preceding models, behavioral models vary, though they all rely on empirically derived principles from experimental psychology as their theoretical foundation (44–46, 60). In essence, behavioral models assume that addictions are learned in the same way that other complex behaviors are acquired, that is, through classical and operant conditioning and social learning principles (8, 60). Although early behavioral treatment models were too simplistic, current procedures for modifying addictive behavior have a number of positive features. One of the most important is the emphasis on controlled empirical research in the laboratory or clinic and in outcome studies. Unlike the models in the preceding sections, behavioral treatment models are less concerned about etiology per se, concentrating on current behavior patterns, their relevant setting events, and consequences for the individual user (reinforcing and punishing stimuli). In addition to modifying elicitory stimulus conditions and reactions with such techniques as desensitization, biofeedback, and social skills training (44–46), behavioral procedures attempt critically to modify the long history of chemical misuse by aversively conditioning the stimuli directly associated with drug abuse. Essentially, this involves pairing systematically the relevant stimulus cues (liquor bottles, smell and taste of alcohol, syringes, etc.) with aversive stimuli (aversive electrical shock, noxious odors, temporary paralysis, aversive images). In other words, negative stimuli are presented along with cues eliciting drug abuse. Finally, relevant environmental (family-social) problems are addressed. Depending on the specific behavioral excesses or deficiencies of the patient, assertive drug refusal and social skills are taught, and behavior patterns considered incompatible with chemical misuse (e.g., involvement in health oriented activities) are encouraged. While behavior therapeutic research with alcoholics has provided some impressive documentation of success (44–46, 50), a sufficient number of studies applying this model to other forms of drug abuse have not yet been completed.

In spite of its relatively solid foundation in empirically derived laws of behavior and its impressive record thus far of therapeutic efficacy, the behavioral model has potential weak points. There is a general tendency in behavior therapy to view an individual's different forms or patterns of behavior as more functionally independent and unrelated than they might in fact be. Such a view resulted in part as a reaction to traditional psychodynamic theory, which considers almost every behavioral response a manifestation of rather global underlying personality traits or dynamics (43). Just as the psychodynamic model may overemphasize the role of preexisting patterns of cognitive, emotional, and overt behavior (personality and/or psychologic dysfunction), behavioral models may not pay sufficient attention to the sometimes critical role personality factors play in addiction. In addition, behavioral approaches may at times rely too heavily on laboratory models and data in analyzing chemical misuse as well as in measuring treatment efficacy. For example, in an outcome study of Alcoholics Anonymous (AA)–treated alcoholics, incidental evidence revealed that almost all spouses of married alcoholics said they could definitely tell when their mates had been drinking heavily; a substantial percentage associated various behavior changes in their alcoholic spouses with only one or two drinks (these informal data usually took the form of "his [or her] whole personality seems to change after just one or two drinks''). Some behavioral researchers have argued that such signs are not apparent in controlled laboratory conditions. It is somewhat paradoxical that behavioral researchers, who have so appropriately noted the liabilities of self-report, fail to recognize that to a large extent human behavior displayed in the simulated natural setting of a laboratory, under the scrutiny of professional observers, *is* a form of self-reporting. If the abusive parent fails to beat his or her children in the playroom laboratory (even prior to treatment), this does not reveal very much about the patient's behavior in the natural environment. This is not to diminish the value of laboratory studies; they are essential and can be critically revealing, but they do have limitations (58). Finally, behavioral models have yet to tackle sufficiently the problem of motivation in chemically dependent persons who resist treatment (this is a problem shared by psychodynamic and sociological approaches). That is, treatment models tend to describe their therapies in reference to patients who are actively seeking help. In fact, the vast majority of chemical abusers are *not* actively seeking treatment and resist giving up their addictive behavior. Even when social or legal pressures force users into treatment, denial and resistance are highly common (13, 34, 37).

However, current limitations of behavioral models are not fundamental. Rather, they exist principally in relation to the *range* of behavior often associated with addiction and its treatment. Unlike previous models, the behavioral approach is based more on empirically derived functional relationships than on demographic data or traditional psychiatric theory. In addition, this model relies heavily on controlled empirical research to verify findings on specific treatment components and overall therapeutic efficacy. With respect to the chemical effects and relationship variables described earlier, behavioral models address all the components suggested as essential in treating addicts (manipulating stimulus conditions, modifying effects of earlier reinforcement history, and developing alternative, more adaptive behavior patterns).

Alcoholics Anonymous Model

AA is the oldest, largest, and best-known self-help program for alcoholics; in many ways this organization is the progenitor of most of the newer such programs. Very little formal theory is explicit in the AA model aside from the disease paradigm of chemical dependency and the conceptual implications of the 12-step program for recovery (2, 37, 59). Among the fundamental assumptions of the AA approach to chemical dependency, the disease model is probably central. In this view, chemical dependency is a progressive disease about which the individual can do little except to abstain from mood altering drugs, which precipitate the florid symptomatology of the disease. Paradoxically, the AA model shares with psychodynamic models the notion that chemical misuse and behavioral consequences result from an underlying pathology (i.e., the disease) but shares with behavioral models the view that the addictive disorder is the real problem. In fact, AA counselors tend to relate almost every undesirable dysfunctional element in the alcoholic's life to chemical dependency and are generally reluctant to acknowledge that neurotic or even psychotic behavior patterns may be independent of chemical craving. Accordingly, in many AA settings it is often difficult to maintain on neuroleptics a chronic schizophrenic who is also alcoholic since not only are neuroleptics generally considered mood altering drugs (though, of course, they are not addictive or particularly pleasant to be on and are rarely abused), but many AA counselors privately admit that when dealing with cases of chemical misuse they assume all "crazy" behavior to be a consequence of the dependency until absolutely proven otherwise, regardless of the user's psychiatric history. AA is partially supported in this view because many addicted individuals are misdiagnosed and treated for an "underlying psychologic disorder" while the chemical dependency is functionally ignored (since it should disappear when the *real* problems are resolved.

Behavioral researchers have argued that the disease model tends to take the responsibility for change away from the user since addicts can claim, "How can I do anything? I've got a disease" (44). Aside from the fact that this is a curious charge from a human psychology model in which behavior is considered not truly volitional but the product of environmental conditioning, it misses the point of AA's position. Besides providing some conceptual framework for the organization's beliefs, the disease model functions, intentionally or not, to convince individual users that they cannot (or will not) control their chemical misuse, its consequences on their behavior, or its results on the environment. More generally, the disease concept has tempered the moralizing and the sometimes irrational legal reactions to alcoholics and drug addicts, in addition to stressing the point that such disorders are potentially treatable. In fact, the AA model emphasizes individual responsibility for behavior and, with regard to the disease model, in essence says, "You've got a disease. It's up to you to do something about it with our help" (2, 59).

Too much is probably made of the disease model both inside and outside AA. Many writers confuse a set of events with the consequences of that set. For example, while evidence indicating a hereditary (genetic) susceptibility to alcoholism comes close to providing some basis for a disease model, it does not account for those alcohol dependent persons with no such identifiable family history. However, the fact that excessive use of chemicals often leads to tissue damage (e.g., hepatic pathology) does *not* contribute to a disease model. Playing high school football often results in a number of physical injuries for many teenagers, but this does not mean that playing high school football is a disease. The mere fact that certain behaviors result in physical injuries or serious medical conditions does not make those behaviors into diseases.

Examination of AA treatment procedures reveals a number of interesting components. Kissin suggested that AA is probably the most effective approach to attacking patients' resistance and denial (34). This is accomplished primarily by confronting the patient with other people's observations of his or her behavior. Spouses, children, parents, employers, friends, clergy, etc., are brought in and encouraged to confront the patient with his or her alcohol use and associated behaviors. Peer group therapy and evaluation further clarify the patient's current behavior as well as present evidence on how alcohol use has adversely affected other people. Lectures, films, reading material, and individual counseling also educate the patient to drug effects. Thus, while behavioral models use systematic aversion therapy to attack established patterns, AA employs emotionally loaded personal events and vicarious education in the form of other people's harrowing stories. Also like the behavioral model, AA is much less concerned with the etiology of chemical misuse than with the current dependency and its treatment.

AA has received general criticism from various researchers for failure to document empirically its claims of efficacy (34, 45, 46). However, a number of studies bearing on AA and a two-year follow-up study of AA treated alcoholics have been published (3, 37). An as yet unpublished small-scale pilot study found that 8 of 13 drug addicted patients who completed AA inpatient treatment were employed, socially stable, and chemically abstinent at 6 and 12 months after discharge; 6 of these 13 met these criteria at a two-year follow-up (4). However, because AA lacks an explicit, coherent scientific theory and does not generally encourage critical empirical research, it may be less responsive to discoveries and treatment innovations that could enhance the program's effectiveness. Nevertheless, the AA model of treatment does address the psychological components and processes central to chemical dependency and implicitly incorporates into its therapeutic program procedures that mediate cognitively-emotionally between chemical use and its various adverse consequences. Furthermore, AA tactics attack denial and other cognitive strategies (e.g., rationalization) that obscure the addictive behavior pattern and its relation to elicitory stimuli and consequences. Finally, AA provides models of "healthy," chemically free lifestyles and socially reinforces such behavior among its members.

Conclusion

In briefly reviewing the major current conceptual and treatment models, I made no attempt to provide a comprehensive evaluation. Rather, this review identified some of the central elements in each system. Each model tends to focus on particular aspects of addictive behavior and its treatment. Curiously, etiologic notions within each theoretical system provide mechanisms for denying individual responsibility for addictive behavior. It is not only the disease model that incurs this liability. Biological models provide a genetic basis; psychodynamic models posit an underlying "mental illness" basis; sociological and behavioral models suggest an environmental basis. While such formulations may be important both in analyzing the processes by which chemical dependency develops and in designing effective preventive programs, too much retrospective focus on etiology within the context of treating patients may be useless or even countertherapeutic because this emphasis tends to remove the locus of control from the individual who is displaying the behavior and place control in external or historical factors. Therapy cannot change the history (or genetics) of an addicted patient but can modify the effects, though only when the patient perceives the locus of control to be internal. Responsibility for his or her behavior and behavior change always rests with the patient.

External stimuli do not cause behavior, but only create conditions under which an organism "perceives" (by history or anticipatory expectancy) one course of action as more rewarding and/or less punishing than another; and this is probably as much or more a function of motivation, or emotion, or autonomic-subcortical processes as it is of conscious cognitive, intellectual, cerebral probability estimation and decision making.

Chemically dependent patients do not change their addictive behavior because they discover how it was developed, nor because they intellectually realize its adverse effects. They begin to seek alternative behaviors when the constellation of adverse effects becomes more potent and punishing than the sensory-perceptual or cognitive-emotional reinforcement of pleasurable effects. Put another way, for treatment to be effective, it must mitigate the reinforcement history of chemical use. This goal can be accomplished in part by reducing the aversive antecedent conditions and the individual's internal reaction to these stimulus events, thereby reducing the negatively reinforcing value of intoxication as well as the number of stimulus conditions that trigger chemical use. This approach, however, is not enough. Most drugs of abuse have very powerful positively reinforcing properties; these effects, combined with the history of use, give the stimuli associated with misuse a high positive valence. Reduction of this positive valence usually requires some form of aversion training. Behavioral models attack this therapeutically by aversive conditioning (44, 45, 46, 50). AA, in a surprisingly similar fashion, attacks this component by repeatedly pairing descriptions of the user's addictive behavior with a wide range of emotionally loaded adverse consequences, as well as by vicarious exposure to the devastating effects of alcoholism.

Behavioral approaches also systematically train addicts in alternative behaviors inconsistent with chemical use. Likewise, AA provides both healthy, drug-free models (e.g., former users) and substantial social support and verbal reinforcement for staying abstinent (3, 37). Finally, AA type programs offer extended (essentially lifelong) follow-up contact; lengthy follow-up is also encouraged and supported by behavioral, psychodynamic, and other models.

In the future, careful examination of various theoretical and treatment models, along with studies of their efficacy, may result in diverse approaches integrating effective stratagems and components from each model. Continued systematic analysis of specific treatment procedures, is essential, as is documenting efficacy through empirical outcome studies. Future investigations of predisposing factors need to be more carefully designed and executed and perhaps should attempt empirically to identify biological, environmental, and individual behavior patterns that appear to encourage or discourage chemical dependency. Finally, comparative analyses of diverse forms of behavioral excess may yield valuable clues about common contributing factors, components, and processes in such disorders.

References

1. Abel, E. L., *Drugs and Behavior: A Primer in Neuropsychopharmacology,* Wiley, New York, 1974.

2. Alcoholics Anonymous World Services, *Alcoholics Anonymous,* New York, 1976.

3. Alford, G. S., Alcoholics Anonymous: an empirical outcome study, *Addict. Beh. 5,* 359–370 (1980).

4. Alford, G. S., Alcoholics Anonymous inpatient treatments of drug addicted abusive drinkers: a small-scale outcome study, unpublished manuscript, available in limited supply from the author).

5. Alford, G. S., and Alford, H., Benzodiazepine induced state-dependent learning: a correlary of abuse potential? *Addict. Beh. 1,* 261–267 (1976).

6. Alford, G. S., and Williams, J. G., The role and uses of psychopharmacologic agents in behavior therapy, in *Progress in Behavior Modification,* M. Hersen, R. M. Eisler, and P. M. Miller, eds., (in press).

7. Allport, G. W., and Post, L. H., *The Basic Psychology of Rumor,* Holt, New York, 1947.

8. Bandura, A., *Principles of Behavior Modification,* Holt, New York, 1969.

9. Beigel, A., and Ghertner, S., Toward a social model: an assessment of social factors which influence problem drinking and its treatment, in *The Biology of Alcoholism V: Treatment and Rehabilitation of the Chronic Alcoholic,* B. Kissin and H. Begleiter, eds., Plenum, New York, 1977.

10. Bergin, A. E., Some implications of psychotherapy research for therapeutic practice, *J. Abnorm. Psych. 71,* 235–246 (1966).

11. Bruner, J. S., On perceptual readiness, *Psych. Rev. 64,* 123–152 (1957).
12. Carranza, J., Long-term use and abuse of benzodiazepines, *Pharmacopsychiatric* (in press).
13. Chafetz, M. E., Alcoholism and alcoholic processes, in *Comprehensive Textbook of Psychiatry,* vol. 2, A. M. Freedman, H. I. Kaplan, and B. J. Sadock, eds., Williams & Wilkins, Baltimore, 1975.
14. Cole, J. O., and Davis, J. M., Minor tranquilizers, sedatives, and hypnotics, in *Comprehensive Textbook of Psychiatry,* vol. 2, A. M. Freedman, H. I. Kaplan, and B. J. Sadock, eds., Williams & Wilkins, Baltimore, 1975.
15. Cooper, J. R., *Sedative-Hypnotic Drugs: Risks and Benefits,* GPO, Washington, D. C., 1978.
16. deVito, R. A., Flaherty, L. A., and Mozdzierz, G. J., Toward a psychodynamic theory of alcoholism, *Dis. Nerv. Syst. 31,* 43–49 (1970).
17. Egeth, H., Selective attention, *Psych. Bull. 67,* 41–57 (1967).
18. Ellis, A., *The Essence of Rational Psychotherapy: A Comprehensive Approach to Treatment,* Institute for Rational Living, New York, 1970.
19. Eysenck, H. J., The outcome problems in psychotherapy: a reply, *Psychotherapy 1,* 97–100 (1964).
20. Festinger, L., *A Theory of Cognitive Dissonance,* Harper, New York, 1957.
21. Franks, C. M., Alcoholism, in *Symptoms of Psychopathology,* C. G. Costello, ed., Wiley, New York, 1970.
22. Glucksberg, S., and Ling, L. J., Motivated forgetting mediated by implicit verbal chaining: a laboratory analog of repression, *Science 158,* 517–519 (1967).
23. Goldstein, A., Opiate receptors and opioid peptides: a ten-year overview, in *Psychopharmacology: A Generation of Progress,* M. A. Lipton, A. DiMascio, and K. F. Killam, eds, Raven, New York, 1978.
24. Goldstein, A., Recent advances in basic research relevant to drug abuse, in *Handbook on Drug Abuse,* R. I. DuPont, A. Goldstein, and J. O'Donnell, eds., GPO, Washington, D. C., 1979.
25. Goldstein, A. P., and Dean, S. J., *The Investigation of Psychotherapy,* Wiley, New York, 1966.
26. Goodman, L. S., and Gilman, A., *The Pharmacological Basis of Therapeutics,* Macmillan, New York, 1975.
27. Goodwin, D. W., Powell, B., Hoine, H., and Stern, J., Alcohol and recall: state-dependent effects in man, *Science 163,* 1350–1360 (1969).
28. Goodwin, D. W., Schulsinger, F., Hermanson, L., Guze, S. B., and Winokur, G., Alcohol problems in adoptees raised apart from alcoholic biological parents, *Arch. Gen. Psychiat. 28,* 238 (1973).
29. Goodwin, D. W., Schulsinger, F., Moller, N., Hermanson, L., Winokur, G., and Guze, S., Drinking problems in adopted and non-adopted sons of alcoholics, *Arch. Gen. Psychiat. 31,* 164–169 (1974).
30. Grinspoon, L., Drug dependence: nonnarcotic agents, in *Comprehensive Textbook of Psychiatry,* vol. 2, A. M. Freedman, H. I. Kaplan, and B. J. Sadock, eds., Williams & Wilkins, Baltimore, 1975.

31. Haefly, W. E., Behavioral and neuropharmacological aspects of drugs in anxiety and related states, in *Psychopharmacology: A Generation of Progress,* M. A. Lipton, A. DiMascio, and K. F. Killam, eds., Raven, New York, 1978.

32. Iverson, S. D., and Iverson, L. L., *Behavioral Pharmacology,* Oxford University Press, New York, 1975.

33. Kelleher, R. T., and Morse, W. H., Escape behavior and punishment behavior, *Fed. Proc. 23,* 808–817 (1964).

34. Kissin, B., Theory and practice in the treatment of alcoholics, in *The Biology of Alcoholism V: Treatment and Rehabilitation of the Chronic Alcoholic,* B. Kissin and H. Begleiter, eds., Plenum, New York, 1977.

35. Knight, R. P., Psychodynamics of chronic alcoholism, *J. Nerv. and Ment. Dis. 86,* 538 (1937).

36. Kolb, L. C., *Modern Clinical Psychiatry,* Saunders, Philadelphia, 1973.

37. Leach, B., and Norris, J. L., The development of Alcoholics Anonymous, in *Biology of Alcoholism V: Treatment and Rehabilitation of the Chronic Alcoholic,* B. Kissin and H. Begleiter, eds., Plenum, New York, 1977.

38. Lemert, E., *Human Deviance, Social Problems, and Social Control,* Prentice-Hall, Englewood Cliffs, 1967.

39. Lipton, M. A., DiMascio, A., and Killam, K. F., *Psychopharmacology: A Generation of Progress,* Raven, New York, 1978.

40. McCord, W., and McCord, J., *Origins of Alcoholism,* Stanford University Press, Stanford, 1960.

41. Meichenbaum, D., *Cognitive-Behavior Modification: An Integrative Approach,* Plenum, New York, 1977.

42. Menninger, K. A., *Man against Himself,* Harcourt, New York, 1938.

43. Michel, W., *Personality and Assessment,* Wiley, New York, 1968.

44. Miller, P. M., *Behavioral Treatment of Alcoholism,* Pergamon, New York, 1976.

45. Miller, P. M., and Eisler, R. M., Alcohol and drug abuse, in *Behavior Modification: Principles, Issues, and Applications,* W. E. Craighead, A. E. Kazdin, and M. J. Mahoney, eds., Houghton Mifflin, Boston, 1976.

46. Nathan, P. M., Alcoholism, in *Handbook of Behavior Modification and Behavior Therapy,* H. Leitenberg, ed., Prentice-Hall, Englewood Cliffs, 1976.

47. Nicoll, R., Selective actions of barbiturates in synaptic transmission, in *Psychopharmacology: A Generation of Progress,* M. A. Lipton, A. DiMascio, and K. F. Killam, eds., Raven, New York, 1978.

48. Overton, D. A., State-dependent learning produced by addicting drugs, in *Opiate Addiction: Origins and Treatment,* S. Fisher and A. M. Freedman, eds., Winston, Washington, D. C., 1973.

49. Pustell, T. E., The experimental induction of perceptual vigilance and defense, *J. Percep. 25,* 425–438 (1957).

50. Rachman, S., and Teasdale, J., *Aversion Therapy and Behavior Disorders: An Analysis,* University of Miami Press, Miami, 1969.

51. Rado, S., The psychoanalysis of pharmacothymia, *Psychoanal. Q. 2,* 1 (1933).

52. Ray, O., *Drugs, Society, and Human Behavior,* Mosby, St. Louis, 1978.
53. Rosenthal, T. L., and Zimmerman, B. J., *Social Learning and Cognition,* Academic, New York, 1978.
54. Sherfey, M. J., Psychopathology and character structure in chronic alcoholism, in *Etiology of Alcoholism,* O. Diethelm, ed., Thomas, Springfield, 1955.
55. Smith, D. E., Wesson, D. R., and Seymour, R. B., The abuse of barbiturates and other sedative-hypnotics, in *Handbook on Drug Abuse,* R. I. DuPont, A. Goldstein, and J. O'Donnell, eds., GPO, Washington, D. C., 1979.
56. Solomon, P., and Patch, V. D., *Handbook of Psychiatry,* Lange Medical Publications, Los Altos, 1974.
57. Stein, L. S., Wise, C. D., and Berger, B. D., Antianxiety action of benzodiazepines: decrease in activity of serotonin neuroses in the punishment system, in *The Benzodiazepines,* S. Garattini, E. Mussini, and L. O. Randall, eds., Raven, New York, 1973.
58. Strickler, D. P., Dobbs, S. D., and Maxwell, W. A., The influence of setting on drinking behaviors: the laboratory vs. the barroom, *Addict. Beh. 4,* 339–344 (1979).
59. Alcoholics Anonymous World Services, *Twelve Steps and Twelve Traditions,* New York, 1979.
60. Wikler, A., Interaction of physical dependence and classical and operant conditioning in the genesis of relapse, in *The Addictive States,* A. Wikler, ed., Williams & Wilkins, Baltimore, 1968.

3

Psychomotor Stimulants as Activators of Normal and Pathological Behavior: Implications for the Excesses in Mania

Robert M. Post

Psychomotor stimulants should play a central role in a discussion of behavior in excess since this is their prototypic effect. By definition they are stimulants of psychic and motor activity. The psychomotor stimulants as a class are unique compounds in the discussion of behavior in excess not only because their self-administration can become compulsive but also because their behavioral effects can become repetitious and compulsive. Thus, in contrast to the opiatelike compounds, where drug administration can be compulsive but the resulting behavior is often tuned down, restricted, the abuser "nodding out" and withdrawing, the amphetaminelike psychomotor stimulants can produce both excessive use and marked behavioral activation. Many of the behaviors associated with acute low doses, appear to be within the normal range of experience. However, with chronic and/or higher doses behavior becomes increasingly frenetic, compulsive, bizarre, and, at times, clearly psychotic.

Thus, the psychomotor stimulants may be a useful model for a variety of psychiatric syndromes involving behavioral excess. In particular, many of the signs and symptoms associated with psychomotor stimulant abuse are also associated with the endogenous psychosis of mania. In both instances, normal behaviors become excessive. There is excess motor and verbal behavior and ideation, along with mood changes, primarily euphoria but also mood lability and irritability, and, in severe drug intoxication or severe mania, aggressive, destructive, and psychotic trends as well.

Chronic amphetamine and cocaine use has been examined in detail as a model for paranoid and schizophreniform psychoses (1–5). The schizophreniform state induced by the psychomotor stimulants will not be discussed in this chapter: primary focus will be on the parallel between the psychomotor stimulant effect and mania since both involve classical excesses of behavior that are more familiar to a general audience.

Some of the variables involved in determining degree of behavioral excess in response to the psychomotor stimulants may shed light on variables involved in the manic process. For example, dose, duration, and interval of psychomotor stimulant administration are critical to the ultimate behavioral output. In a similar fashion, the degree, duration, and continuity of activation of normal brain chemical systems could be related to the degree of behavioral excess and pathology in mania. Thus, the psychomotor stimulants may affect basic mechanisms normally involved in motivation, memory, and stress activation that can be driven to excess. Dissection of the important variables related to stimulant administration may thus help clarify mechanisms underlying the evolution of pathological behavior (Figure 3-1) and its treatment.

This chapter treats the psychomotor stimulants as a class, but discussion centers on amphetamine and cocaine, the best-known drugs of this

FIGURE 3-1.
Interaction of Dose and Duration
in Cocaine Induced Psychopathology

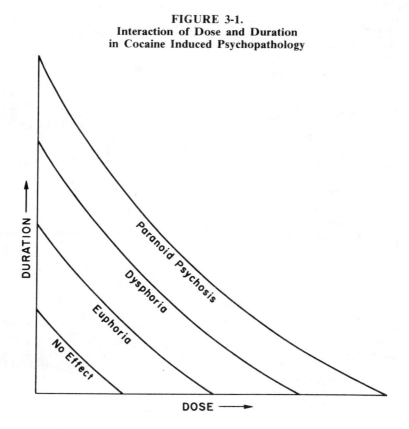

category. However, methylphenidate (Ritalin), a great many amphetaminelike compounds, and a variety of other related drugs all appear to have psychomotor stimulant properties in adults. Each appears to differ slightly in behavioral and biochemical effects, but the commonalities across drugs appear far to exceed the minor differences (Table 3–1). They all seem to act, at least in part, through neuronal mechanisms normally involved in

TABLE 3–1
Behavioral and Biochemical Similarities between
Amphetamine and Cocaine

Behavioral and Biochemical Aspects[a]	Degree of Similarity	Differences
Behavioral		
Activation and mood effect in man	+	
Cocaine-amphetamine not discriminated by man	+	
Confusional-toxic psychosis	+	
Cue generalization in animals	+	
Self-administration	+	
Increased self-stimulation reward	+	
Effects blocked by neuroleptics	+	
Dyskinesias	+	
Behavioral sensitization to activity stereotypy	+	More head nodding (cocaine)
End-stage behaviors	+	Slight differences
Paranoid psychosis in man	+	Poorly documented (cocaine)
Environment (context) dependency	+	Cocaine > amphetamine
Cross-sensitization	+	Amphetamine $\nleftrightarrow$ cocaine
Behavioral depression on withdrawal	−	Amphetamine > > cocaine
Biochemical		
Block norepinephrine, dopamine, reuptake	+	
Increased release of norepinephrine, dopamine	+	Amphetamine > > cocaine
Local anesthetic	−	Cocaine > > amphetamine
Convulsant	−	Cocaine > > amphetamine
Chronic Effects		
Increased ß-receptor binding	+	
Neuroleptic sensitivity	+	
Catecholamine depletion	+	Amphetamine > cocaine
AMPT sensitivity	−	Amphetamine > > cocaine
Reserpine sensitivity	−	Cocaine > > amphetamine
Increased tyrosine hydroxylase	−	Cocaine only

[a] All effects were found in animal studies unless otherwise stated.

motivation and central reward. They affect a class of chemical transmitters in the brain called catecholamines, in particular dopamine and norepinephrine. The stimulants enhance the effects of catecholamines by increasing their release (amphetamine) and inhibiting inactivation by blocking reuptake in nerves (amphetamine and cocaine (6–9) (Figure 3–2). They also affect a variety of other chemical systems in the brain including serotonin, but their effects on the catecholamines, especially dopamine, appear most closely related to their stimulant properties.

Several lines of evidence indicate that potentiation of the noradrenergic and dopaminergic systems accounts for many of the psychological and behavioral effects of the psychomotor stimulants. If these systems are blocked with the major tranquilizers (which rather specifically block dopamine receptors and less specifically, norepinephrine systems), most of the behavioral effects of amphetamine or cocaine are inhibited (8). Depletion of the chemical neurotransmitters dopamine and norepinephrine either with a toxic drug called 6-hydroxydopamine or with reserpine will also block many of the behavioral effects of the psychomotor stimulants.

FIGURE 3-2.
Schema of Psychotropic Drug Effects
on Biosynthetic and Receptor Mechanisms

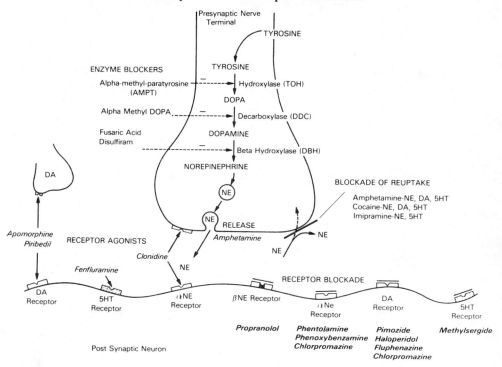

Similarly, inhibition of the synthesis of the catecholamines with a drug called AMPT will inhibit psychomotor stimulant effects (Figure 3–3). Several recent reviews discuss the pharmacology of these compounds in detail (8–11).

Psychomotor Effects of Amphetamine and Cocaine in Animals and Man

Acute doses of amphetamine or cocaine result in marked increases in locomotor hyperactivity in a variety of experimental animals. More chronic administration or use of higher doses produces repetitive movements and fragmentary behavioral sequences called stereotypy (Figure 3–4). Effects on motor activity are thought to be mediated largely by dopamine in a part of the limbic system called the nucleus accumbens. Stereotypy is likewise thought to involve dopamine effects, but more specifically in a part of the brain affected in Parkinson's disease—the striatum (12–15). In man, increases in gross locomotor activity are not always observed, though marked

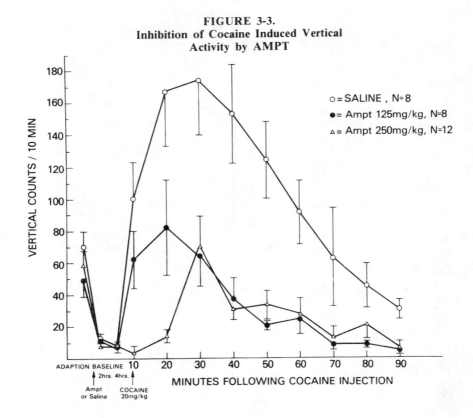

FIGURE 3-3.
Inhibition of Cocaine Induced Vertical
Activity by AMPT

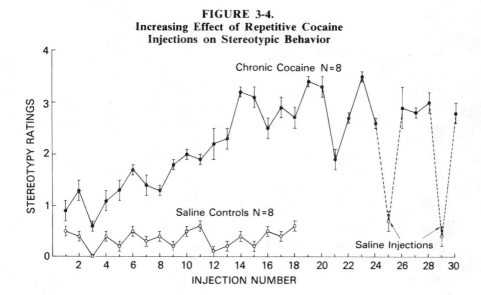

FIGURE 3-4.
Increasing Effect of Repetitive Cocaine
Injections on Stereotypic Behavior

increases in pressure of speech and flight of ideas often accompany acute psychomotor stimulant administration (Table 3-2). One can only speculate whether the ideation hyperactivity in man is analogous to motor hyperactivity in animals. Nauta and collaborators suggested that there is a notable dopaminergic enervation of the cerebral cortex, which could form the parallel anatomical substrate for ideational hyperactivity in man to that of motor activity in experimental animals mediated by subcortical dopaminergic systems (16).

Accompanying this psychomotor stimulation is a potent effect on mood. In many cases the psychomotor stimulants produce a pure and boundless euphoria. Intravenous use may cause an orgasmiclike rush. One description suggests, "When you shoot coke (cocaine) in the mainline there is a rush of pure pleasure to the head. Ten minutes later you want another shot. Intravenous C is electricity through the brain, activating cocaine pleasure connections. There is no withdrawal syndrome with C. It is a need of the brain alone" (17). However, with more chronic administration and higher doses, increases in mood lability, irritability, anger or aggression, or dysphoria often emerge (8, 9, 18).

The mood elevating and energizing properties of the psychomotor stimulants have long been known. For centuries the Indians of the Peruvian Andes have chewed coca leaves to increase their endurance while decreasing the appetite. Early note of an ecstatic experience induced by cocaine was made by Paolo Mantegazza in 1859: "Borne on the wings of two coca leaves, I flew about in the spaces of 77,438 worlds, one more splendid than another. I prefer a life of ten years with coca to one of a hundred

TABLE 3.2
Stimulant Induced Excesses in Man[a]

MILD TO MODERATE	SEVERE
Mood amplification, both euphoria and dysphoria	Irritability, withdrawal, hostility, anguish, fear
Energy	Boundless energy, utter exhaustion
Alertness, arousal, vigilance	Distractibility, hyperstartle, extreme paranoia
Sleep disturbance, Insomnia	Total insomnia
Motor hyperactivity	Frequent motor sequences, catatonic-like inhibition
Verbal hyperactivity and pressure of speech	Rambling incoherence
Ideational hyperactivity	Disjointed flight of ideas
Increased sexual interest	Decreased sexual interest
Anger and verbal aggression	Extreme violence
Compulsive motor rituals	Sterotypies, dyskinesias
Excessive undereating, anorexia	Total anorexia
Inflated self-esteem	Grandiose delusions, loss of self boundaries

[a] Effects depend on many variables of drug administration, including dose, duration, and environmental context, such that opposite effects on behavior can at times be manifest in contrast to those listed in the table.

thousand without it. It seemed to me that I was separated from the whole world, and I beheld the strangest images most beautiful in color and in form than can be imagined'' (19).

Freud remarked on the mood elevating property of cocaine as well as on its possible energizing effect, caused predominantly by increasing motivation:

After a short time [10–20 minutes], he feels as though he had been raised to the full height of intellectual and bodily vigor, in a state of euphoria, which is distinguished from the euphoria after consumption of alcohol by the absence of any feeling of alteration. . . . one can perform mental and physical work with great endurance, and the otherwise urgent needs of rest, food, and sleep are thrust aside, as it were. During the first hours after cocaine, it is even impossible to fall asleep. This effect of the alkaloid gradually fades away after the aforesaid time, and is not followed by any depression. . . . I could not fail to note, however, that the individual disposition plays a major role in the effects of cocaine, perhaps a more important role than with other alkaloids. The subjective phenomena after ingestion of coca differ from person to person, and only few persons experience, like myself, a pure euphoria without alteration. Others already experience slight intoxication, hyperkinesia, and talkativeness after the same amount of cocaine, while still others have no subjective symptoms of the effects of coca at all (20).

It is noteworthy that Freud recognized that the psychomotor stimulants appear to exert their effects through a motivation pathway rather than increase strength directly. The psychomotor stimulants likewise seem to produce excessive conceptions of the self. Mild inflations of self-esteem with acute low doses of amphetamine or cocaine can give way to a delusional grandiosity in which any feat, no matter how difficult, is not to be ruled out. More recent descriptions of the cocaine high appear in the autobiography of Malcolm X: "It was when I got back into that familiar snow feeling that I began to want to talk. Cocaine produces, for those who sniff its powdery white crystals, an illusion of supreme well-being, and a soaring overconfidence in both physical and mental ability. You think that you could whip the heavyweight champion; and that you are smarter than everybody" (21).

While the psychomotor stimulant cocaine has achieved a special place in both the folk literature and the modern drug culture (22), recent studies have suggested that even an experienced user cannot typically differentiate the amphetamine and the cocaine experience (23). Fischman and co-workers and Martin and collaborators noted that most of the energizing and mood altering properties of the psychomotor stimulants are essentially indistinguishable (23, 24). Moreover, animals trained to respond only in the presence of cocaine (the drug is acting as a cue) show generalization of the cocaine cue to amphetamine and other psychomotor stimulants (25, 26).

Three of the main effects of the psychomotor stimulants—increases in motor activity, increases in ideational activity, and increases in mood intensity (if not consistently euphoria)—form the cornerstone of the diagnosis of manic illness. Mania perhaps epitomizes behavior in excess. Particularly in hypomania there is increased motor activity, pressure of speech, and flight of ideas with consistent alterations in mood, usually euphoria (Figure 3–5 and Table 3–3). The patient experiences boundless energy and is able to go for prolonged periods with no or few hours of sleep with minimal fatigue. However, as mania increases in severity, behavior becomes more excessive, disorganized, and dysfunctional (See stages II and III in Table 3–3). Both psychic and motor activity becomes increasingly frenetic, with speech pressured to the point of rambling incoherence. Insomnia may be total. Reality functions may be impaired. A feeling of robust self-esteem may sequentially give way to delusional beliefs in one's omnipotence and even to the view of the self as God. Hallucinations, confusion, aggression, and extreme regressive behavior may supervene.

A similar transition can occur following excessive use of psychomotor

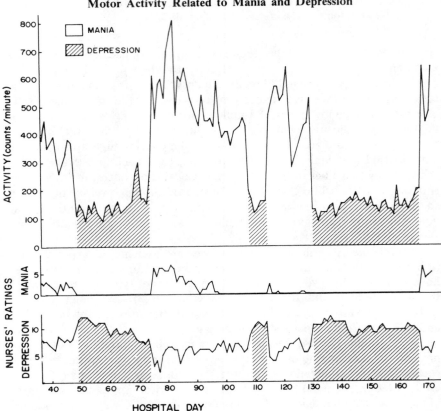

FIGURE 3-5.
Motor Activity Related to Mania and Depression

stimulants. Mild psychomotor stimulant induced effects are easy to recognize by the college student who uses amphetamine for cramming prior to an examination. Not only is there increased energy and a tolerance for sleeplessness, but there is also increased productivity in terms of written output in the next day's examination. Though this may be useful at times, many students have had the disillusioning experience that while they felt they had performed wondrously on the examination, their performance was not highly regarded. More excessive states of amphetamine use may be characterized by increased writing output, or hypergraphia, that is disorganized and disjointed. Again, this condition is a frequent accompaniment of hypomania and mania (Figure 3-6).

As documented in the clinical literature as well as in the experimental laboratory under more controlled circumstances, increasing amphetamine use is associated with behavioral excesses that become increasingly dysfunctional. For example, the amphetamine abuser may be endlessly preoccupied

TABLE 3.3
A Continuum of Manic Symptoms

	HYPOMANIA STAGE I	MANIA STAGE II	EXTREME MANIC PSYCHOSIS STAGE III
Global rating	2–3	4–8	8–15
Sleep	Mild decrease	Hyposomnia	Insomnia
Mood	Euphoria→	Lability → (dysphoria/euphoria)	Dysphoria
Self-reference	Increased self-esteem → overconfidence	Paranoid and grandiose ideation → religiosity →	Delusional beliefs (self as animal, inert object, God), paranoia, Shneiderian, Positive ideas of influence
Activation			
Motor	Mild hyperactivity → hypergraphia →	Severe hyperactivity, stereotypies	Extreme excitement, stereotypies, immobility
Verbal	Pressure of speech →	Clanging	Incoherent shouting and screaming
Thought	Racing thoughts →	Flight of ideas	Incoherence
Cognitive-attentional	Heightened awareness, distractibility	Cognitive distortion	Full-blown auditory and visual hallucinations

(continued)

TABLE 3.3
A Continuum of Manic Symptoms

	HYPOMANIA STAGE I	MANIA STAGE II	EXTREME MANIC PSYCHOSIS STAGE III
Energy	Increased	Boundless	Exhaustion
Aggression	Verbal aggression	Explosiveness and assaultiveness	Extreme physical violence
Interpersonal sensitivity	Loss of social cues	Intrusiveness	Confusional psychosis, delirius mania
Response to limit setting	Reasonable	Rare	None
Social function	Mildly enhanced to mildly inappropriate	Disorganized, poor judgment	Psychotic regression, incontinence, eating and smearing feces
Clinical pharmacology	Lithium	Lithium, neuroleptics, carbamazepine[a]	Neuroleptics, lithium and neuroleptics, carbamazepine,[a] ECT

→ indicates presence in more severe stages.
[a] An experimental treatment strategy (76, 77)

FIGURE 3-6.
Hypergraphia during Mania

with useless tasks such as taking apart electrical equipment, investigating parts and connections over and over, but usually failing ever to rebuild the apparatus (7, 29, 30). Psychic energizing effects may lead to increased arousal and complete insomnia. Increased vigilence may turn into paranoia (8, 9, 27):

I imagined every one was looking at me and watching me; even when locked in my own room, I could not persuade myself there were not watchers outside, with their eyes glued to imaginary peepholes. If I ventured into the street I thought I was followed and that the passers-by made remarks about me; I thought my vice was known to all, and on all sides I could hear the widespread word 'Cocaine . . .'. It is curious that directly after the effect of cocaine had passed away all the suspicions and delusions vanished instantly. I could see the absurdity and impossibility of the idea that a whole town was watching and talking about one obscure individual. I realized the folly of thinking that spies were in the room above, watching me through holes pierced in the ceiling. Yet, the overpowering desire to repeat the dose would overtake me, and almost instantly after taking it all delusions would return in full force, and no reasoning would banish them (28).

Lewin noted that

mental weakness, accompanied by irritability, erroneous conclusions, suspicion, bitterness towards his environment, a false interpretation of things, groundless jealousy, etc. bring about in the individual, now suffering from insomnia, illusions of the senses while fully conscious. Hallucinations of vision, hearing, smell and taste, disturbances in the sexual sphere and the general condition master those who are severely affected. In many cocaineomaniacs confusional insanity preceded by general mental disorders, vacancy of mind as in delirium tremens, extreme alarm due to false impressions, set in. A cocainist who had snuffed 3.25 gr. cocaine armed himself for protection against imaginary enemies; another in an attack of acute mania jumped overboard into the water; another broke the furniture and crockery into pieces and attacked a friend (31).

Variables Affecting Behavioral Excess

Interval Between Drug Administrations

Under some circumstances of chronic administration, behavioral effects of the psychomotor stimulants can develop progressively over time (the user shows behavioral sensitization) as opposed to the development of tolerance, or decreased reactivity. As illustrated in Figures 3–4, 3–7, and 3–8, with repeated injections of cocaine, both hyperactivity and stereotypies can show progressive increases following daily administration. However, the interval between drug administration appears to be one important determinant of whether tolerance or sensitization is manifest. Several studies have indicated that chronic, more continuous administration is associated with tolerance, while once daily or intermittent administration may lead to behavioral sensitization (32, 33).

Thus, it would appear that under some defined circumstances ex-

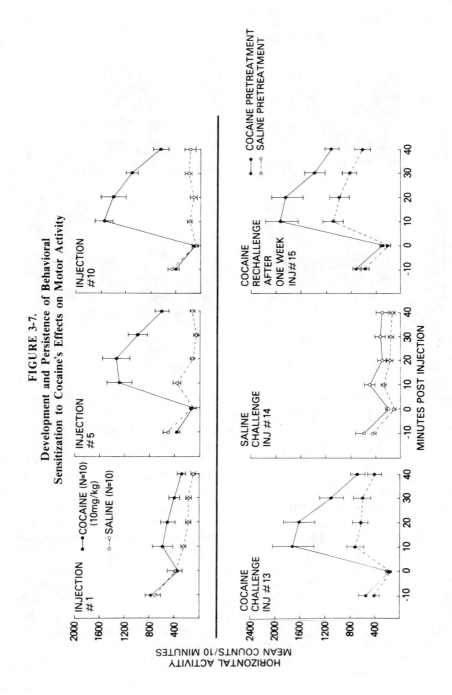

FIGURE 3-7.
Development and Persistence of Behavioral
Sensitization to Cocaine's Effects on Motor Activity

FIGURE 3-8.
Visual Tracking Behavior
with Chronic Cocaine Administration

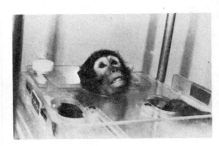

cessive behavior associated with psychomotor stimulant administration may in itself with repeated administration lead to greater excesses of behavior; certain neuroregulatory systems seem to work in a positive feedback system producing progressively greater excesses rather than adaptation and tolerance (Table 3-4). Nelson and Ellison demonstrated the effect of the interval between drug administration in producing tolerance or sensitization (32). They showed that repeated injections of amphetamine on an intermittent basis produced increasing behavioral pathology (sensitization) while chronic administration through an implanted pellet, which delivered equivalent amounts of drug but much more slowly and continuously, tended to produce adaptation and tolerance. This variable of timing between injections may be of particular clinical importance as the typical pattern of intravenous use of amphetamine and cocaine appears to be one of rapidly repeated injections over short intervals. Since the "high," or "rush," is brief, in an effort to sustain the euphoria an abuser may exhaust his or her entire drug supply in a matter of hours, even if a large amount is on hand. In this fashion, relatively massive doses of amphetamine and cocaine may be injected, presumably associated with the development of acute tolerance. However, in other instances extreme toxicity, convulsions, and death have been reported following small doses.

TABLE 3-4
Psychomotor Stimulant Effects Generally Reported to
Develop Tolerance or Sensitization

	TOLERANCE	SENSITIZATION
Anorexia	+ +	−
Hypothermia	+ +	−
Response suppressing effects	+ +	±
Hypertension	+ +	−
Tachycardia	+ +	−
Tachypnea	+ +	−
Discriminative stimulus properties	+	−
EEG arousal	+ +	+
Hyperthermia	?	+
Activity	±	+ +
Stereotypy	±	+ +
Dyskinesias	−	+ +
Convulsions	±	+ +
Lethality	+ +	+ +
Catalepsy	−	+ +

Genetic Predisposition

Genetic predisposition can lead to marked differences in the degree of behavioral, biochemical, and physiological reaction to the psychomotor stimulants. Following amphetamine administration one genetic subtype of mice shows hyporeactivity, hypothermia, and decreases in the dopamine metabolite HVA in the brain; another genetic subtype shows marked hyperactivity, hyperthermia, and increases in HVA in the brain (34). Recently, Nurnberger and collaborators found that identical twins have a more similar amphetamine response than can be attributed to chance and suggested that genetic variables are important in amphetamine response in man (35). Thus, some genetically and biochemically predisposed individuals may be particularly susceptible to excessive activation, euphoria or dysphoria, and psychosis associated with psychomotor stimulant administration.

Previous Exposure: Relation to Psychic Induction

Environmental and experiential variables are also important determinants of the degree of behavioral activation and excess. A variety of studies have

shown that animals reared in isolation or under stress have increases in amphetamine induced repetitive or stereotypic behavior (36). Likewise, as
discussed previously, prior exposure to amphetamine or cocaine appears to
increase susceptibility to pathological reactions to amphetamine. Kramer
and colleagues suggested that once stimulant-induced paranoia occurs, it is
more easily reactivated and occurs earlier during subsequent periods of
stimulant use (28, 37). This phenomenon may be analogous to the more
rapid onset of motor hyperactivity and stereotypies in animals repeatedly
exposed to cocaine or amphetamine (38–41). In this regard it is of interest
that many experimental studies of chronic high dose amphetamine administration have used experienced addict-volunteers. Thus, the estimate of
how easy it is to induce dysphoric and psychotogenic effects in normal,
drug-naive subjects possibly was skewed by the selection process in these
studies. Perhaps the psychotic reactions develop from the interaction of
stimulants and either genetically or experientially susceptible individuals (in
part self-selected by their previous amphetamine abuse). Nevertheless, the
literature suggests strongly that given enough stimulants for a long enough
period of time, most people eventually will develop behavioral aberrations
if not psychosis.

Environmental Context and Conditioning

Two of the most interesting aspects of excessive behavior associated with
psychomotor stimulants are its conditional components and context
dependency. That is, environmental activity at the time of administration
appears to be a key determinant of associated behavioral effects. Ellinwood
and Kilbey noted that cats receiving amphetamine while in contact with ex-
perimenters developed behavioral rituals and stereotypic responses involving the laboratory personnel (42). In a rat social colony, subordinate
animals withdrew and acted defensively while dominant animals were
oblivious to others following chronic amphetamine (43). Stevens and colleagues noted decreases in amphetamine induced stereotypic head
movements in blindfolded cats, suggesting that sensory feedback from the
environment is important in maintaining some aspects of stimulant induced
behavior (44).

     Other investigators also have noted that excessive behaviors under
psychomotor stimulants are produced in part by the environmental context
(7, 42, 44–47). For example, Figure 3–9 illustrates that rats treated with cocaine in one environment appeared to be much more reactive when tested in
that same environment compared to rats receiving the same amount of
cocaine in a different environment (and experiencing cocaine for the first

FIGURE 3-9.
Effect of Prior Behavior Context and Environment
on Cocaine Induced Activity

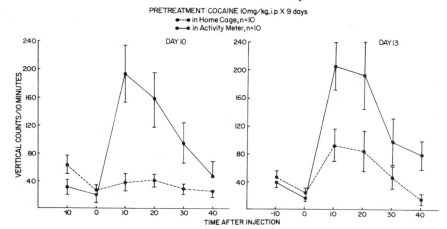

time in a novel situation). Another interesting example of the role of environmental context and contingencies in the development of behavior in excess comes from Woolverton and associates (48). They gave cocaine either before or after an animal engaged in bar-pressing for a sweet-milk reward. When cocaine was given before each bar-pressing session, the animal developed tolerance to the appetite suppressing effect of the drug. In contrast, when cocaine was given after each bar-pressing session, sensitization (or suppression of milk intake) occurred.

A very dramatic illustration of this effect has been observed by Collins and Lesse (50). They trained both rats and cats either to press a bar or to inhibit bar-pressing depending on the activation or silence of a tone signal. The animals learned this discrimination quite well. When cocaine was administered with the signal activated, indicating bar-pressing would produce a reward, behavior was markedly enhanced. However, when cocaine was administered with the signal off and animals were not rewarded for bar-pressing, cocaine was associated with inhibition of bar-pressing activity.

In sum, these results indicate that psychomotor stimulant induced behaviors can be significantly affected by the stimulus cues and the environmental context available to the subject, i.e. conditioning variables. These observations suggest that the psychomotor stimulants affect motivationally relevant systems and are capable of amplifying ongoing behavior, which under different circumstances might result in either enhancement or suppression of a particular behavior.

Internal State

In our work with psychomotor stimulant administration in depressed patients we observed that amphetamine and cocaine markedly enhanced dysphoric responses in some individuals (51–53). Patients almost universally showed evidence of activation of psychic processes, motor systems, and affective responsivity. As noted in Table 3–5, they talked more, were more animated, and were more emotionally involved.

Most interesting, however, mood responses were not uniformly positive. Some depressed patients experienced intensification of their preex-

TABLE 3–5
Proportion of Change (≥ 2 Units) in Subjects on Scale Items Following Placebo and Amphetamine Infusions (53)

CHANGE	% PLACEBO	% AMPHETAMINE	P
Physician's BPRS[a]			
Decreased withdrawal-retardation cluster	17	94	< .001
Decreased anxiety-depression cluster	6	67	< .01
Decreased paranoid disturbance cluster	0	56	< .01
Decreased withdrawal	11	56	< .01
Decreased depression	0	50	< .01
Decreased blunted affect	11	50	< .05
Decreased retardation	0	44	< .05
Decreased hostility	0	33	< .05
Decreased tension	0	33	< .05
Decreased anxiety	22	50	NS
Decreased suspicion	6	39	NS
Decreased noncooperation	0	22	NS
Increased grandiosity	0	22	NS
Increased somatic concern	6	22	NS
Decreased guilt	0	17	NS
Decreased thought disturbance cluster	0	11	NS
Increased disorganization	0	11	NS
Increased posturing	6	11	NS
Increased hallucination	0	0	NS
Increased odd thoughts	0	0	NS
Physician's Ratings			
Increased emotional recall	22	83	< .01
Increased elation	6	61	< .01

[a] BPRS = Brief Psychiatric Rating Scale.

isting dysphoria and hopelessness, supporting the widely accepted notion that the stimulants are not generally useful antidepressants. An intriguing symmetry exists: proven mood elevators (stimulants) in normal individuals are not necessarily antidepressants and, conversely, the useful antidepressants are not mood elevators in normal individuals. These data highlight the importance of underlying clinical and biological states in determining responsivity to stimulants. Very different effects may occur depending on this internal state, or biological substrate (54). Animals and people also appear differentially responsive to the activating and toxic effects of stimulants depending on the time of day that administration occurs.

Superficially, these considerations of state dependent drug effects might explain the apparently paradoxical calming effect of amphetamine (Ritalin), and related stimulants on hyperactive and inattentive children suffering from the hyperkinetic syndrome or minimal cerebral dysfunction (MCD). However, recent studies by Rapoport and collaborators have indicated that normal, nonhyperactive children also become more calm, move less, attend more, and learn better, as do hyperactive children, when given stimulants (55). Though the mechanisms at work in these responses to stimulants remain to be elucidated, these findings reemphasize the complicated nature of stimulant induced behavior.

Relation of Stimulant Induced States to Normal Behavior and Stress

The data reviewed in the preceding section support the notion that the psychomotor stimulants can amplify a wide range of behavior. The psychomotor stimulants may potentiate ongoing behaviors just the way brain stimulation has been shown to do this depending on environmental context. For example, Valenstein documented that stimulation of the hypothalamus increased drinking behavior in animals when water was available; however, when water was removed and food was substituted, animals eventually increased their eating behavior with stimulation of the same electrode and at the same current (Figure 3-10) (56). This indicates that stimulation of specific neuronal pathways in the motivationally relevant hypothalamus does not produce a specific behavior but amplifies ongoing behavior, which is determined by the environment.

Several other lines of evidence point to the nonspecificity of stimulant induced activation. The stimulants appear to act through pathways responsible for normal behavioral and affective arousal. Antelman, Eichler, and associates showed that a variety of stresses cross-sensitize to amphetamine effects and vice versa (57–59). That is, animals subject to the stress of hunger, tail pinch, or mild shock are more reactive than controls to a subse-

FIGURE 3-10.
Valenstein Effect

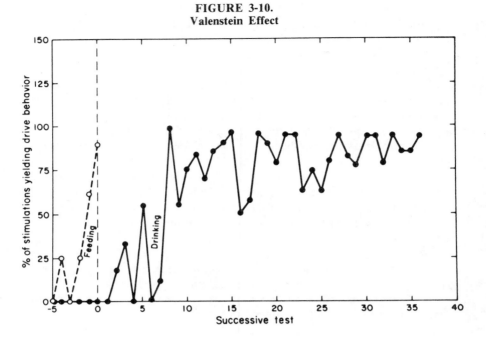

quent challenge with amphetamine. Another example of the cross-reactivity of the stimulant and stress comes from a study by Marshall and colleagues in which animals were made less active and less responsive by damaging discrete portions of the brain (usually involving damage to dopamine cells) (60). Animals having this brain damage move slowly, if at all, will not eat or drink, and usually die if not force-fed. Amphetamine will transiently reverse these deficits, as will a variety of stresses, including forced swimming or running, mild foot shock, or cold water immersion.

These data regarding the interaction of stimulants and stress are consistent with the hypothesis that amphetamine works through brain pathways involved in drug-free behavior. The excitement of an anticipated event and its completion have made most of us experience an increased sense of energy, tirelessness, giddy hyperactivity, pressure of speech, mood elevation, increased alertness and memory, and decreased need for sleep, etc.— the classical acute, low dose stimulant syndrome. These observations likewise are consistent with the current view that dopamine and norepinephrine (the chemical messengers most affected by the stimulants) are also involved in and mediate activation, motivation, memory, and learning. The stimulants influence these general systems rather than produce a given behavioral sequence or repertoire.

The Effects of Pyschomotor Stimulants on Learning and Memory

Recent studies in both animals and man have suggested that stimulants enhance specific aspects of learning and memory. As illustrated in Figure 3–11, Reus and associates demonstrated that amphetamine administration increases free recall for deeply processed and encoded or meaningful stimuli (61). These findings in depressed subjects have subsequently been replicated in normal adults, as well as in both normal and hyperactive children. All these studies suggest that the psychomotor stimulants, through their effects on catecholamine mechanisms, may be associated with alterations in the memory process. Weingartner and co-workers showed in animals and man that the degree of arousal or motivation associated with a given task may be directly relevant to how well the task is learned (62). This variable can be altered either through psychosocial manipulations, such as stress or anxiety, or through psychomotor stimulants, such as amphetamine or cocaine. These data in relation to learning and memory indicate further that amphetamine works rather like normal mechanisms of motivation and arousal.

In our studies, memory improved most in subjects with low baseline measures of norepinephrine and least in those with already high norepine-

FIGURE 3-11.
Effect of Amphetamine on Verbal Recall

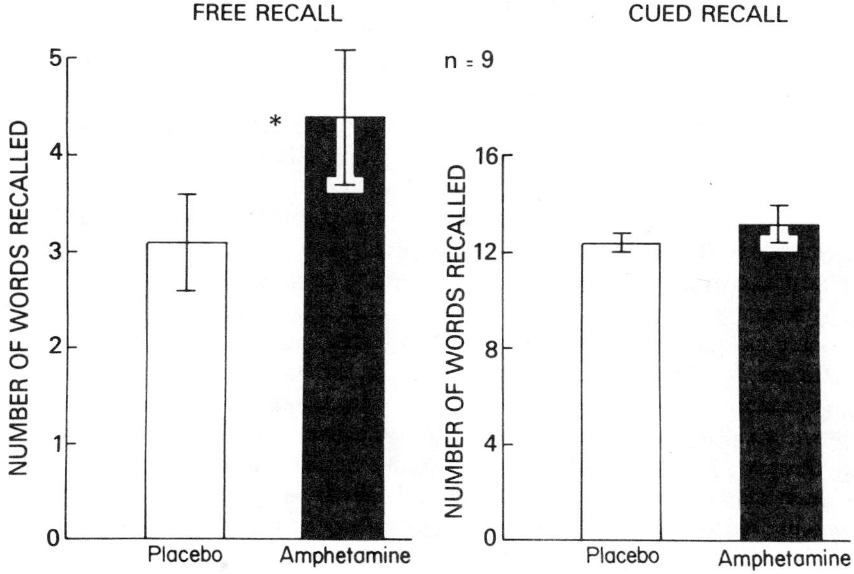

phrine (61), suggesting that a small amphetamine induced increase in norepinephrine might be helpful only if one were not already overstressed. Kornetsky and Mirsky speculated that schizophrenic patients may already be overstimulated and that increases in natural arousal or amphetamine induced activation might lead to further deterioration (63). A little anxiety may help us study, learn, integrate new concepts, but an excess might be disorganizing.

Self-administration of Stimulants

Olds noted that animals will work endlessly for the privilege of electrically stimulating certain areas of their own brains (again, those closely associated with the catecholamines norepinephrine and dopamine) (64). Not surprisingly, amphetamine and cocaine increase bar-pressing for this brain stimulation reward (65, 66). This is perhaps further evidence that the stimulants act on brain centers involved in reinforcement and reward behaviors and perhaps even pleasure. Animals prefer higher doses of cocaine over lower doses and rhesus monkeys will accept shock punishments in order to self-administer cocaine (70, 71). It is noteworthy that the monkeys showed less suppression by shock of self-administration of cocaine than of morphine or pentobarbital self-administration, suggesting that cocaine is even more reinforcing and rewarding than some opiates or sedatives (72).

If given the opportunity, animals will engage in brain self-stimulation to the point of exhaustion even without the aid of stimulants. Likewise, animals allowed free access to cocaine will self-administer it to the point of severe toxicity or even death (67). They may stop lever-pressing for stimulants only because they are physically incapacitated; when they recover adequately, they may resume this compulsive overdosing (68, 69).

It is interesting to speculate on what the rat or monkey might see in the recreational use of such drugs. Perhaps, "amping" to the point of frenzied stereotypies, incoordination, convulsions, or death beats the boredom of eating, drinking, sleeping, and other routines in the laboratory cage. Without anthropomorphizing unduly, compulsive stimulant intake in animals probably has human parallels in obliviousness to or disregard of consequences, inability to stop, etc. For whatever the reason, self-preservation—among the most basic of drives—may be set aside under stimulant administration. Perhaps the stimulants act strongly enough on systems mediating euphoria and self-pleasure to overpower usual self-maintenance behavior. It is also possible that the stimulants energize and activate systems directly involved in self-maintenance to the point that they become dysfunctional, with potentially lethal consequences.

Treatment of Psychomotor Stimulant and Associated Behavioral Excesses

As noted earlier, a number of drugs that interfere with catecholamine mechanisms tend to block stimulant effects in animals and man. Again, there is a notable correspondence between the drugs useful in treating acute psychomotor stimulant effects and those useful in the treatment of acute mania. The major tranquilizers (neuroleptics, drugs that act by blocking dopamine receptors) are particularly effective in blocking psychomotor stimulant effects in man (4, 8). Drugs in this category, such as Thorazine (chlorpromazine), Mellaril (thioridazine), Haldol (haloperidol), and Pimozide, are often used alone or in combination with lithium carbonate to treat the behavioral excesses of mania (Figure 3–12). These same drugs are also useful in the treatment of schizophrenia and related psychotic syndromes. Although they are effective in the detoxification phase, they may not be useful as maintenance or prophylactic treatment of stimulant abuse,

FIGURE 3-12.
Time Course of Antimanic Response to
Pimozide and Lithium

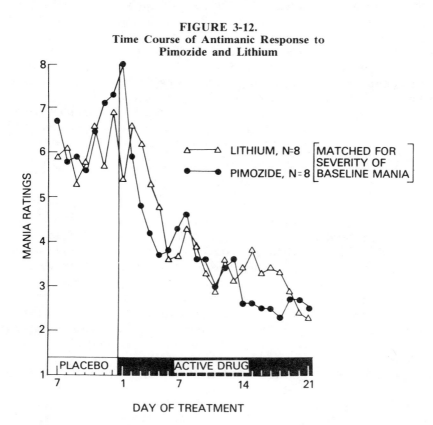

in part because of their efficacy in blocking the euphoria and other positive aspects of the high.

It is noteworthy that AMPT, which inhibits synthesis of dopamine and norepinephrine, blocks psychomotor stimulant effects in animals (Figure 3–3) as well as in man (73). AMPT blocks effects of amphetamine even better than those of cocaine (in contrast, reserpine—which depletes neurotransmitter amines—blocks cocaine effects better than those of amphetamine). AMPT has been reported to have antimanic effects in a small number of patients (74, 75). Similarly, lithium carbonate, the drug of choice in treating the behavioral excesses associated with mania, is of some utility in blocking amphetamine induced alterations in patients (77). The long-term clinical utility of lithium carbonate as a maintenance treatment to prevent the recurrence of psychomotor stimulant abuse remains essentially untested. We are currently testing whether the anticonvulsant Tegretol (carbamazepine), which we have found useful in treating the motor and affective excesses of mania and depression, affects stimulant-induced behavior in animals (76, 77). As noted by Gay and Inaba, treatment of the acute and chronic toxicology of psychomotor stimulant abuse may be quite different from treatment of the patient in the drug-free state (78). Specific approaches to the underlying personality, mood, and biological variables may be indicated. For example, if psychomotor stimulant abuse is secondary to an underlying depressive reaction, treatment of that mood disorder with antidepressants in combination with psychotherapy may be of value. Several authorities have emphasized the importance of a supportive individual or group psychotherapeutic relationship during the stimulant detoxification and treatment phases.

Conclusion

During mild intoxication the psychomotor stimulants often produce a classical syndrome of behavior in excess. Many of these signs and symptoms are closely paralleled by those in hypomania. They may include motor, verbal, and ideational hyperactivity, increased social and sexual interest, increased productivity, and memory and mood alterations, including euphoria. With higher dose and chronic psychomotor stimulant use, the syndrome can be associated with delusional grandiosity, increasing dysphoria, and evolving behavioral aberrations that may closely resemble those seen in severe mania and even in paranoid schizophrenia.

Psychomotor stimulants, though of interest in their own right in a discussion of behavior in excess, also carry unusual theoretical implications for endogenous disturbances associated with behavior in excess, such as mania or in some instances schizophrenia. The effects of these agents are produced by complex interactions among a number of variables, including dose, duration, route, and rapidity of administration; environmental context and conditioning; ongoing behavior; history of use; as well as genetic and experiential predisposing variables. Depending on the presence or absence of these variables, psychomotor stimulant use might lead to either euphoria or dysphoria, hyperactivity or inhibition. Careful analysis of clinical and experimental studies of psychomotor stimulants in animals and man may help elucidate the basic mechanisms involved in normal and pathological states of behavior in excess.

NOTE: *This activity will not involve the use of government-financed time, supplies, or services of other government employees.*

References

1. Connell, P. H., *Amphetamine Psychoses,* Oxford University Press, New York, 1958.
2. Angrist, B., and Gershon, S., The phenomenology of experimentally induced amphetamine psychosis: preliminary observations, *Biol. Psychiat. 2,* 95–107 (1970).
3. Griffith, J. D., Cavanaugh, J. H., Held, J., and Oates, J. A., Experimental psychosis induced by the administration of d-amphetamine, in *International Symposium on Amphetamines and Related Compounds,* E. Costa and S. Garattini, eds., Raven, New York, 1970, pp. 897–904.
4. Gunne, L. M., Anggard, E., and Jönsson, L. E., Clinical trials with amphetamine blocking drugs, *Psychiat. Neuro. Neurochem. 75,* 225–226 (1972).
5. Bell, D. S., The experimental reproduction of amphetamine psychosis, *Arch. Gen. Psychiat. 29,* 35–40 (1973).
6. Hertig, L., Axelrod, J., and Whitby, L. G., Effect of drugs on the uptake and metabolism of H^3 norepinephrine, *J. Pharm. Exp. Ther. 134,* 146–153 (1961).
7. Scheel-Kruger, J., Braestrup, C., Nielson, M., Golembrowska, K., and Mogilnicka, E., Cocaine: discussion on the role of dopamine in the biochemical mechanism of action, in *Advances in Behavioral Biology XXI: Cocaine and Other Stimulants,* E. H. Ellinwood, Jr., and M. M. Kilbey, eds., Plenum, New York, 1977, pp. 373–408.
8. Snyder, S. H., Banerjee, S. P., Yamamura, H. I., and Greenberg, D., Drugs, neurotransmitters, and schizophrenia, *Science 184,* 1243–1254 (1974).
9. Randrup, A., and Munkvad, I., Biochemical, anatomical, and psychological investigations of stereotyped behavior induced by amphetamines, in *International Symposium on Amphetamines and Related Compounds,* E. Costa and S. Garattini, eds., Raven, New York, 1970, pp. 695–713.
10. Costa, E., and Garattini, S., *International Symposium on Amphetamines and Related Compounds,* Raven, New York, 1970.
11. Ellinwood, E. H., Jr., and Kilbey, M. M., *Advances in Behavioral Biology XXI: Cocaine and Other Stimulants,* Plenum, New York, 1977.

12. Costall, B., and Naylor, R. J., Mesolimbic and extrapyramidal sites for the mediation of stereotyped behavior patterns and hyperactivity by amphetamine and apomorphine in the rat, in *Advances in Behavioral Biology XXI: Cocaine and Other Stimulants,* E. H. Ellinwood, Jr., and M. M. Kilbey, eds, Plenum, New York, 1977, pp. 47–76.

13. Costall, B., and Naylor, R. J., The site and mode of action of ET-495 for the mediation of stereotyped behavior in the rat, *Naunyn-Schmiedebergs Arch. Pharm. 278,* 117–133 (1973).

14. Ljungberg, T., and Ungerstedt, U., Classification of neuroleptic drugs according to their ability to inhibit apomorphine-induced locomotion and gnawing: evidence for two different mechanisms of action, *Psychopharmacology 56,* 239–247 (1978).

15. Kelly, P. H., and Iversen, S. D., Selective 6-OHDA-induced destruction of mesolimbic dopamine neurons: abolition of psychostimulant-induced locomotor activity in rats, *Eur. J. Pharm. 40,* 45–56 (1975).

16. Nauta, J. H., and Domesick, V. B., Crossroads of limbic and striatal circuitry: hypothalamic-nigral connections, in *Limbic Mechanisms: The Continuing Evolution of the Limbic System Concept,* K. Livingston and O. Hornykiewicz, eds., Plenum, New York, 1978, pp. 75–93.

17. Burroughs, W., *Naked Lunch,* Grove, New York, 1966.

18. Post, R. M., Cocaine psychoses: a continuum model, *Amer. J. Psychiat. 132,* 627–634 (1975).

19. Musto, D. F., A study in cocaine: Sherlock Holmes and Sigmund Freud, *JAMA 204,* 125–130 (1968).

20. Freud S., *The Cocaine Papers,* Dunquin, New York, 1963.

21. Haley, A., and Malcolm X, *The Autobiography of Malcolm X,* Grove, New York, 1966.

22. Gay, G. R., Sheppard, C. W., Inaba, D. S., and Newmeyer, J. A., Cocaine in Perspective: "Gift from the Sun God" to "The Rich Man's Drug". Drug Forum *2,* 409–430 (1973).

23. Fischman, M. W., Schuster, C. R., and Krasnegor, A., Physiological and behavioral effects of intravenous cocaine in man, in *Advances in Behavioral Biology XXI: Cocaine and Other Stimulants,* Plenum, New York, 1977, pp. 647–664.

24. Martin, W. R., Sloan, J. W., Sapira, J. D., and Jasinski, D. R., Physiological, subjective, and behavioral effects of amphetamine, methamphetamine, ephedrine, phenmetrazine, and methylphenidate in man, *Clin. Pharm. Ther. 12,* 245–258 (1971).

25. Colpaert, F. C., Niemegeers, C. J. E., and Janssen, P. A. J., Cocaine cue in rats as it relates to subjective drug effects: a preliminary report, *Eur. J. Pharm. 40,* 195–199 (1976).

26. Colpaert, F. C., Niemegeers, C. J. E., and Janssen, P. A. J., Neuroleptic interference with the cocaine cue: internal stimulus control of behavior and psychosis, *Psychopharmacology 58,* 247–255 (1978).

27. Ellinwood, E. H., Jr., Amphetamine psychosis I: description of the individuals and process, *J. Nerv. Ment. Dis. 144,* 273–283 (1967).

28. Woods, J. H., and Downs, D. A., Drug use in America: problem in perspective, *Patterns and Consequences of Drug Use,* GPO, Washington, D. C., 1973, p. 116.

29. Schiorring, E., Changes in individual and social behavior induced by amphetamine and related compounds in monkeys and man, in *Advances in Behavioral Biology XXI: Cocaine and Other Stimulants,* E. H. Ellinwood, Jr., and M. M. Kilbey, eds., Plenum, New York, 1977, pp. 481–521.

30. Rylander, G., Psychoses and the punding and choreiform syndromes in addiction to central stimulant drugs, *Psychiat. Neuro. Neurochem. 75,* 203–213 (1972).

31. Lewin, L., in *Phantastica, Narcotic and Stimulating Drugs: Their Use and Abuse,* P. H. A. Wirth, ed., Dutton, New York, 1931, pp. 75–88.

32. Nelson, L. R., and Ellison G., Enhanced stereotypies after repeated injections but not continuous amphetamines, *Neuropharmacology 17,* 1081–1084 (1978).

33. Post, R. M., Central stimulants: clinical and experimental evidence on tolerance and stimulation, in *Research Advances in Alcohol and Drug Problems,* Y. Israel, F. Glaser, H. Kalant, R. E. Popham, W. Schmidt, and R. Smart, eds., Plenum, New York, in press.

34. Jori, A., and Garattini, S., Catecholamine metabolism and amphetamine effects on sensitive and insensitive mice, in *Frontiers in Catecholamine Research,* E. Usdin and S. H. Snyder, eds., Pergamon, New York, 1973, pp. 939–942.

35. Nurnberger, J. I., Gershon, E. S., Jimerson, D. C., Buchsbaum, M. S., Gold, P. W., Brown, G. L., and Ebert, M., Pharmacogenetics of d-amphetamine response in man, in *Genetic Strategies in Psychobiology and Psychiatry,* E. S., Gershon, S. Matthysse, X. O. Breakefield, and R. D. Ciaranello, eds., Boxwood Press, Calif., in press.

36. Sahakian, B. J., Robbins, T. W., Morgan, M. J., and Iversen, S. D., The effects of psychomotor stimulants on stereotypy and locomotor activity in socially-deprived and control rats, *Brain Res. 84,* 195–205 (1975).

37. Kramer, J. C., Fischman, V. S., and Littlefield, D. C., Amphetamine abuse: pattern and effects of high doses taken intravenously, *JAMA 201,* 89–93 (1967).

38. Post, R. M., and Rose, H., Increasing effects of repetitive cocaine administration in the rat, *Nature 260,* 731–732 (1976).

39. Kilbey, M. M., and Ellinwood, E. H., Jr., Reverse tolerance to stimulant-induced abnormal behavior, *Life Sci. 20,* 1063–1076 (1977).

40. Segal, D. S., Behavioral and neurochemical correlates of repeated d-amphetamine administration, in *Advances in Biochemical Psychopharmacology XIII: Neurobiological Mechanisms of Adaptation and Behavior,* A. J. Mandell, ed., Raven, New York, 1975, pp. 247–262.

41. Klawans, H. L., and Margolin, D. I., Amphetamine-induced dopaminergic sensitivity in guinea pigs, *Arch. Gen. Psychiat. 32,* 725–732 (1975).

42. Ellinwood, E. H., Jr., and Kilbey, M. M., Amphetamine stereotypy: the influence of environmental factors and prepotent behavioral patterns on its topography and development, *Biol. Psychiat. 10,* 2–16 (1975).

43. Gambill, J. D., and Kornetsky, C., Effects of chronic d-amphetamine on social

behavior of the rat: implications for an animal model of paranoid schizophrenia, *Psychopharmacology 50,* 215–223 (1976).

44. Stevens, J., Livermore, A., and Cronan, J., Effects of deafening and blind-folding on amphetamine induced stereotypy in the cat, *Physiol. Beh. 18,* 809–812 (1977).

45. Post, R. M., Lockfeld, A., Squillace, K. M., and Conbel, N. R., Drug-environment interaction: context dependency of cocaine-induced behavioral sensitization, *Life Sci. 28,* 755–760 (1981).

46. Schiff, S. R., and Bridger, W. H., The behavioral effects of chronic administration of d-amphetamine and apomorphine and the development of conditioned stereotypy, *Soc'y Neuro. Sci. Abstr. 2,* 488 (1977).

47. Tilson, H. A., and Rech, R. H., Conditioned drug effects and absence of tolerance to d-amphetamine induced motor activity, *Pharm. Biochem. Beh. 1,* 149–153 (1973).

48. Woolverton, W. L., Kandel, D., and Schuster, C. R., Tolerance and cross-tolerance to cocaine and d-amphetamine, *J. Pharm. Exp. Ther. 205,* 525–535 (1978).

49. Marriott, A. S., The effects of amphetamine, caffeine, and methylplenidite on the locomotor activity of rats in an unfamiliar environment, *Inter'l. J. Neuropharm. 7,* 487–491 (1968).

50. Collins, J. P., and Lesse, H., Cocaine-induced stereotyped behavior: ongoing responses determine drug effects, paper presented to the 9th annual meeting of the Society for Neuroscience, Atlanta, 1979.

51. Post, R. M., Progressive changes in behavior and seizures following chronic co-caine administration: relationship to kindling and psychosis, in *Advances in Behavioral Biology XXI: Cocaine and Other Stimulants,* E. H. Ellinwood, Jr., and M. M. Kilbey, eds., Plenum, New York, 1977, pp. 353–372.

52. Jimerson, D. C., Post, R. M., Reus, V. I., vanKammen, D. P., Docherty, J., Gillin, J. C., Buchsbaum, M., and Bunney, W. E., Jr., Predictors of am-phetamine response on depression, paper presented to the 130th annual meeting of the American Psychiatric Association, Toronto, 1977.

53. Silberman, E. K., Reus, V. I., Jimerson, D. C., Hynott, A. M., and Post, R. M., Types of amphetamine response in an endogenously depressed population, *Amer. J. Psychiat.* (in press).

54. Reus, V. I., Weingartner, H., and Post, R. M., Clinical implications of state learning, *Amer. J. Psychiat. 136,* 927–931 (1979).

55. Rapoport, J. L., Buchsbaum, N. B., Zahn, T. P., Weingartner, H., Ludlow, C., and Mikkelsen, E. J., Dextroamphetamine: cognitive and behavioral effects in normal prepubertal boys, *Science 199,* 560 (1978).

56. Valenstein, E. S., Behavior elicited by hypothalamic stimulation, *Brain Beh. Evol. 2,* 295–316 (1969).

57. Antelman, S. M., and Eichler, A. J., Persistent effects of stress on dopamine-related behaviors: clinical implications, in *Program and Abstracts of the Fourth International Catecholamine Symposium,* cited in *Catecholamines: Basic and*

Clinical Frontiers, vol. II, E. Usdin, I. J. Kopin, and J. Barchas; eds; Pergamon, New York, 1979, pp. 1759–1761.

58. Antelman, S. M., Eichler, A. J., Black, C. A., and Kocan, D., Interchangeability of stress and amphetamine in sensitization, *Science 207,* 329–331 (1980).

59. Rowland, N., Eichler, A. J., Antelman, S. M., Shipley, J., Kocan, D., and DeGiovanni, L., Amphetamine sensitization: stress to genetic hypertension, *Neurosci. Abstr. 5,* 660 (1979).

60. Marshall, J. F., Levitan, D., and Stricker, E. M., Activation-induced restoration of sensorimotor functions in rats with dopamine-depleting brain lesions, *J. Comp. Physiol. Psych. 90,* 536–546 (1976).

61. Reus, V. I., Silberman, E. K., Post, R. M., Weingartner, H., d-Amphetamine: effects on memory in a depressed population, *Biol. Psychiat. 14,* 345–356 (1979).

62. Weingartner, H., Sitaram, N., and Gillin, J. C., Role of catecholamines in memory consolidation, unpublished data.

63. Kornetsky, C., and Mirsky, A. P., On certain psychopharmacological and physiological differences between schizophrenic and normal persons, *Psychopharmacologia 8,* 309–318 (1966).

64. Olds, J., Behavioral studies of hypothalamic functions: drives and reinforcements, in *Biological Foundations of Psychiatry, vol. 1,* R. G. Grenell and S. Gabay, eds., Raven, New York, 1976, pp. 321–447.

65. Crow, T. J., Enhancement by cocaine of intracranial self-stimulation in the rat, *Life Sci. 9,* 375–381 (1970).

66. Esposito, R. U., Allen, H. D., Kornetsky, M., and Kornetsky, C., Cocaine: acute effects on reinforcement thresholds for self-stimulation behavior to the medial forebrain bundle, *Pharm. Biochem. Beh. 8,* 437–439 (1978).

67. Deneau, G., Yangita, T., and Seevers, M. H., Self-administration of psychoactive substances by the monkey, *Psychopharmacologia 16,* 30–40 (1969).

68. Thompson, T., and Pickens, R., Stimulant self-administration by animals: some comparisons with opiate self-administration, Fed. Proc. *29,* 6–12 (1970).

69. Brady, J. V., and Griffiths, R. R., Drug-maintained performance and the analysis of stimulant reinforcing effects, in *Advances in Behavioral Biology XXI: Cocaine and Other Stimulants,* E. H. Ellinwood, Jr., and M. M. Kilbey, eds., Plenum, New York, 1977, pp. 599–613.

70. Johanson, C. E., and Schuster, C. R., A comparison of cocaine and diethylpropion under two different schedules of drug presentation, in *Advances in Behavioral Biology XXI: Cocaine and Other Stimulants,* E. H. Ellinwood, Jr., and M. M. Kilbey, eds., Plenum, New York, 1977, pp. 545–570.

71. Balster, R. L., and Schuster, C. R., A preference procedure that compares efficacy of different intravenous drug reinforcers in the rhesus monkey, in *Advances in Behavioral Biology XXI: Cocaine and Other Stimulants,* E. H. Ellinwood, Jr., and M. M. Kilbey, eds., Plenum, New York, 1977, pp. 571–584.

72. McLendon, D. M., and Harris, R. T., The effects of response contingent and non-contingent shock on drug self-administration in rhesus monkeys, in *Ad-*

vances in Behavioral Biology XXI: Cocaine and Other Stimulants, E. H. Ellinwood, Jr., and M. M. Kilbey, eds., Plenum, New York, 1977, pp. 585–598.

73. Bunney, W. E., Brodie, H. K. H., Murphy, D. L., and Goodwin, F. K., Studies of alpha-methyl-para-tyrosine, L-dopa, and L-tryptophan in depression and mania, *Amer. J. Psychiat. 127,* 872–881 (1971).

74. Brodie, H. K. H. Murphy, D. L., Goodwin, F. K., and Bunney, W. E., Catecholamine and mania: the effect of alpha-methyl-para-tyrosine on manic behavior and catecholamine metabolism, *Clin. Pharm. Ther. 12,* 218–224 (1971).

75. Van Kammen, D. P., and Murphy, D. L., Attenuation of the euphoriant and activating effects of d-amphetamine by lithium carbonate treatment, *Psychopharmacologia 44,* 215–224 (1975).

76. Ballenger, J. C., and Post, R. M., Therapeutic effects of carbamazepine in affective illness: a preliminary report. *Comm. in Psychopharm. 2,* 159–175 (1978).

77. Ballenger, J. C., and Post, R. M., Carbamazepine (Tegretol) in manic-depressive illness: a new treatment. *Amer. J. Psychiat. 137,* 782–790 (1980).

78. Gay, G. R., and Inaba, D. S., Acute and chronic toxicology of cocaine abuse: current sociology, treatment, and rehabilitation, in *Cocaine: Chemical, Biological, Clinical, Social, and Treatment Aspects,* S. J. Mulé, ed., CRC Press, Cleveland, 1976, pp. 243–252.

4

Hallucinogens: A Chemical Trip to Wonderland

Richard C. W. Hall
Michael K. Popkin

Albert Hoffman's discovery of the hallucinogenic properties of LSD did more to influence society's thinking about the effects of drugs on the mind than anything previous in our history (1). The widespread acceptance of hallucinogenic agents by adolescents and young adults is testimony to a desire on the part of many to alter their consciousness or to disrupt their normal cognitive function. The use and abuse of hallucinogens is the subject of this chapter.

Hallucinogens Defined

Various terms have been used to describe hallucinogens— psychotomimetics, hallucinogenics, dysleptics, psychedelics, psycholytics, and consciousness altering drugs. All of these terms suggest a potential for the induction of a dreamlike, psychotic, or dysphoric state in the user, and in fact the hallucinogens can produce changes in perception, mood, and thought in the absence of changes in conscious awareness such as are produced by the deliriants. Whereas the latter cloud the sensorium and diminish awareness, hallucinogens predominantly alter perception and the processing of sensory experiences. Nevertheless, these categories of drug overlap, particularly with the belladonna alkaloid group.

This chapter follows Hoffer and Osmond, who defined a hallucinogen as a substance of plant or synthetic origin "which in nontoxic doses produces changes in perception, in thought, and in mood, but which seldom produces mental confusion, memory loss, or disorientation for person, place, and time. These latter changes are characteristic of organic mental disorders emerging due to intoxications with alcohol, anesthetics and other drugs (1).

The hallucinogens have another interesting and unusual property. The circumstances attending their administration dramatically affect the user's responses. To understand the psychological and physiological reactions of individuals who take hallucinogens, one must understand the where, how, how much, by whom, and with whom dimensions of the experience (2).

Among the substances defined as hallucinogens are d-lysergic acid diethylamide (LSD), mescaline, psilocybin, dimethyltryptamine (DMT), and, in sufficient doses, cannabis. All of these agents are of plant origin and occur in natural states. The synthetic hallucinogens include diethyltryptamine, PCP, and STP.

A Historical Perspective

Although medical interest in the widespread use of hallucinogens is relatively recent, they have age-old religious and sociological importance. Mescaline, which is derived from the peyote cactus, and psilocybin, which is derived from "magic mushrooms," are both used by Indians of Mexico and Central America in religious ceremonies. Hashish has long been known to the natives of India. Cohoba, a snuff made from seeds containing dimethyltryptamine, was apparently used by indigenous Haitians during the time of Columbus. West African and Congolese peoples have for centuries chewed ibogaine to "release the gods," the latter effect caused by the root's high tryptamine content. And in countless civilizations the power of healers has been predicated in part on their ability to provide other members of the tribe with supernatural experiences triggered by the administration of hallucinogens.

Current scientific interest in the hallucinogens dates to the 1880s, when Louis Lewin, a German pharmacologist, described the reactions of Indians in the American Southwest to peyote ingestion. His early reports led to extensive investigations into the sociological and psychological forces determining the use of hallucinogenic substances. Many investigators concluded that the psychological state produced by the hallucinogenic cactus resembles a psychotic state. Lewin, writing in 1924, suggested that an understanding of the hallucinogens would be of fundamental importance in explaining the etiology of mental illness (2).

A step toward this understanding was taken in 1943, when Albert Hoffman, a chemist at Hoffman-LaRoche, accidentally ingested a minute quantity of LSD. The first person to experience the drug's adverse hallucinogenic effects, Hoffman was also the first to suggest its dangers (3). From 1943 to 1955, more than 80 scientific papers were published on the biochemical properties of LSD. Limited human experimentation began during this time, prompting a warning of the drug's exquisite danger. Elkes and Mayer-Gross concluded that subjects taking LSD under controlled conditions could become dangerous to themselves and others and that latent psychiatric conditions could be exacerbated by minute doses (4).

Worldwide reports of hallucinogenically induced "model psychoses" encouraged further work with LSD and mescaline and stimulated research into the "mind expanding" and distorting effects of other drugs that likewise might help bridge the gap between chemically induced and naturally occurring mental illnesses. Throughout the 1950s and 1960s, extensive research on the biochemical, psychological, and therapeutic uses of hallucinogens took place throughout the world (5, 13, 14, 19). Concurrently, nonmedical investigators began to express interest in hallucinogens as a means to obtain religious insight. Timothy Leary and his League for Spiritual Discovery fostered major religious movements based on mind expansion via LSD (6). These new so-called religions promised transcendental insights into both the self and the universe and touched off a craze of self-administration of hallucinogens on college campuses.

Since LSD and other new hallucinogens were easy to produce chemically, they rapidly found their way into the illicit drug market. Despite widespread government and media reports on severe reactions to these drugs (e.g., homicide, suicide, acute panic attacks, the self-enucleation of eyes), their use continued to grow. The counterculture generation of the sixties no longer believed the establishment and cited earlier government publications, such as "Marijuana: The Killer Weed," as reasons to dismiss current warnings. The drug subculture crested, finding solutions to individual and societal ills through chemical insights and mind expansion. As the number of reported medical and psychiatric casualties grew, the medical community urged that legislative action be taken to restrict traffic in these substances. By 1966, the use of LSD was so widespread that its distribution was totally curtailed by Hoffman-LaRoche, even to legitimate scientific investigators; Hoffman-LaRoche turned over its entire stock of LSD to the National Institutes of Mental Health. To this day, in both the United States and Great Britain, the government controls the distribution of LSD for research purposes (7).

During the early 1970s, street use of LSD began to decline, following credible reports of genetic damage (8). "Acid" was replaced on street corners by a new group of drugs that included PCP, DMT, and STP. Since the mid-seventies the use of all hallucinogens, particularly LSD and DMT, has declined significantly. Emergency room visits prompted by ingestion of these agents have become less frequent, with one exception. Phencyclidine (PCP, or angel dust) abuse continues to increase. PCP users are currently the most likely drug abusers to be seen in emergency rooms or to be apprehended by police because of unpredictable or violent behavior (9).

Classification

We can classify the hallucinogens by effect and chemical structure. Besides a miscellaneous category, there are the phenylethylamines and the tryptamine related hallucinogens.

Epinephrine Related Hallucinogens:
The Phenylethylamines

The hallucinogens of this group are related to epinephrine, which has no hallucinogenic activity of its own but is a neurotransmitter that modulates nerve impulses in both the central and the peripheral nervous system. Many drugs in this group are chemically related to the amphetamines. Some of the synthetic street hallucinogens are direct amphetamine derivatives. These drugs include TMA (trimethoxyamphetamine), MDA (methylenedioxyamphetamine), DMA (2,5-di-methyoxyamphetamine), DOM (2,5-dimethoxy-4-methylamphetamine), which is also known as STP, DOET (2,5-dimethoxy-4-ethylamphetamine), DMMDA (2,5-dimethoxy-3,4-methylenedioxyamphetamine), and MMDA (3-methoxy-4,5-methyl-enedioxyamphetamine).

Other drugs of this group include mescaline, a derivative of peyote; myristicin, derived from *Myristica fragrans* (nutmeg); and the tetrahydrocannabinols, of which delta-9-tetrahydrocannabinol (THC) is the most widely known (found in marijuana and other hemp products, particularly hashish). The amphetamines and marijuana are discussed in Chapters 3 and 4. Let us turn our attention here to the properties of three prototypes of the phenylethylamine group of hallucinogens: mescaline, STP, and myristicin.

Mescaline

Mescaline derives its name from the Mescalero Apaches, who developed the peyote cult. The Native American Church uses peyote during religious ceremonies. Trimethoxyphenylethylamine, the major active ingredient, is present in the buttons of the cactus *Lophophora williamsii;* a German chemist named Heffter determined its formula in 1896, and chemists can synthesize this ingredient with little difficulty.

The fact that mescaline is structurally related to epinephrine has stimulated research into the role of altered central catecholamine metabolism in various forms of mental illness. Many question mescaline's direct hallucinogenic effect and suspect that since it must be consumed in such large quantities (200–500 mg) compared to other hallucinogens, some intermediate metabolite is responsible for mescaline's hallucinogenic properties. Under any form of administration, nausea and vomiting usually occur within one hour, followed by palpitations, subjective sensations of temperature change, anxiety, and motor restlessness. The physiological and psychological symptoms produced by the drug usually peak within 1–3 hours following ingestion and then disappear gradually over the next 24 hours. Clinical effects are similar to those associated with LSD. Mescaline, however, has a longer duration of action, a stronger autonomic nervous system effect, and supposedly a more sensual and peaceful experience than LSD. Tolerance occurs more slowly with mescaline than with LSD. In addition to the often colorful visual hallucinations that the drug produces, depersonalization, disorientation, and time distortion frequently occur.

In 1928 Kluver reported that mescaline affects perception of color brightness and generates elaborate colored visions, succeeded by colored forms and form combinations (10). Most subjects report brilliant geometric patterns, transparent colored objects, and cobweblike forms. Auditory hallucinations often accompany the color visions and are associated with a peculiar type of time disorganization, which may involve visualizing environmental experiences out of normal time sequence or misperceiving the duration of an event by a considerable margin. Time during the mescaline experience is greatly lengthened, so subjects perceive the unfolding of an event over several minutes, while an observer would note an almost instantaneous occurrence. The hallucinatory effects of the drug notwithstanding, the subjects' consciousness remains clear, so they are able to remember large portions of the drug episode when it is over (11).

Attempts to correlate the symptoms produced by mescaline (and other hallucinogens) with naturally occurring psychiatric symptoms reveal that the drug's effects are determined largely by the personality configuration and dynamics of the user, as well as by the physical and social setting in which the drug is ingested. The dosage and the presence of other individuals during the experience also influence the responses (11).

Mescaline and the other hallucinogens are not addictive in the sense that individuals develop physical dependence and exhibit withdrawal symptoms upon termination of usage. A very small minority of users, however, do become psychologically dependent on these agents (12).

The most serious late occurring side effects are persistence of the drug state or its reappearance days or weeks following the last ingestion, i.e., flashbacks. In addition, episodes of emotional lability and the sudden emergence of severe psychiatric symptoms, such as hallucinations, delusions, or paranoid ideation, may occur. The latter are most frequently reported in emotionally disturbed users.

STP

STP, or 2,5-dimethoxy-4-methylamphetamine (also called DOM), was the product of a research and development effort designed to find a new antipsychotic drug. STP remains a widely used hallucinogen, particularly in urban centers.

The drug produces effects within one to two hours following ingestion. Subjects report an initial euphoria, which peaks between three and five hours and subsides by seven to eight hours. Perceptual distortions and hallucinations occur between one and five hours. The effects of the drug in low to moderate doses last 7–10 hours. Many subjects report that after sleeping they have mild, alternating bouts of euphoria and depression. At high doses, STP produces an LSD-like experience, which one subject described as follows:

> The first effect came during lunch [two hours after administration of the drug] when I started staring at the orange sherbet, which was beautiful, brilliant orange, falling disorganizedly like a whirlpool. . . . later [five hours after ingesting the drug] I began shrinking and water in the glass on the table was getting bigger and moving towards me, coming to envelop me. . . . I was really scared. . . . I saw a witchdoctor and then a horse on the wall . . . then the ceiling started moving up and down and was purple and yellow. . . . I felt I was losing control (13).

Twenty percent of STP is excreted unchanged in the urine during a 24-hour period. An excretory peak occurs three to six hours after ingestion, suggesting that STP is slowly absorbed into the circulation and that behavioral changes are related to peak plasma concentrations of the unmetabolized drug. Physical signs that occur three to four hours following ingestion may include pupillary dilation; increased pulse rate and systolic blood pressure; a one or two degree temperature elevation; nausea; paresthesia; sweating; and tremor. Plasma free fatty acid levels double within four hours postingestion.

The psychological changes produced by STP include feelings of euphoria, loss of control over thoughts, and sensations that thoughts are independently generated. Subjects report difficulty expressing inner sensations and being flooded by thoughts. On occasion, their minds "go totally blank." The majority report increased distractibility. Visual blurring; the vibration of solid objects; and multiple, brightly colored visual hallucinations characterized by distorted shapes that fluctuate with clearly defined and enhanced images are typical. Time is slowed and distorted. In spite of these sensations, most STP users recall the drug experience quite well.

STP is hallucinogenic in doses exceeding 3 mg. The average street sample contains 10 mg, making this one of the most potent illicit drugs.

STP is approximately 100 times more powerful than mescaline, but only one-thirtieth as strong as LSD (13). Emergency room treatment with phenothiazines has resulted in death secondary to cardiovascular collapse because of the summative cholinergic properties of the phenothiazines and STP. Consequently, management of adverse STP reactions should be by talking down and/or by the administration of benzodiazepines such as Valium (14, 15).

Myristicin

Myristicin is the volatile oil extract of nutmeg, a little-known hallucinogen available at most grocery stores. Hallucinogenic effects begin approximately an hour after ingestion and persist for 36–48 hours. Characteristically, this agent produces marked lability in mood, with initial jocularity followed by lethargy. Many subjects report extreme thirst and dehydration of the mouth and throat. The hallucinogenic effects are similar to those reported with LSD: exquisitely unreal and colorful visions, often accompanied by detailed musical illusions. Time distortion (slowing) is characteristic, as are vivid sexual images and increased sensuality. Many subjects report a dramatic increase in their appetite for sweets.

At the height of the drug experience, slowing of the heart rate, flushing of the face, reddening of the eyes, muscle and joint aches, and difficulty initiating urination and defecation may occur. Many individuals report a sense of stimulation following the ingestion of nutmeg rather than a direct hallucinogenic effect. Following the hallucinatory period, most subjects fall into a deep sleep, from which they awaken mentally clear.

Tryptamine Related Hallucinogens

All of these agents are indole compounds. They include LSD-25 (d-lysergic acid diethylamide), psilocybin (4-phosphoryloxy-N,N-dimeth-oxytryptamine), psilocin (dephosphorylated derivative of psilocybin), DMT (N, N-dimethyltryptamine), DET (N,N-diethyltryptamine), DPT (N,N-dipropyltryptamine), ALPHA-MT (dl-alpha-methyltryptamine), harmine, tetrahydroharmine, and ibogaine.

Many of the indole compounds occur naturally as plant products. The Haitian snuff, cohoba, contains bufotenine, DMT, and other indoles. The magic mushrooms of central and southern Mexico contain psilocybin; fly agaric contains bufotenine, muscarine, and piltzatropine. The African shrub iboga contains ibogaine, while the shrubs ritually used by the Indians of Ecuador, Colombia, Peru, and Brazil contain harmine and tetra-hydroharmine. Morning glory seeds contain several ergot alkaloids, including LSD and isolysergic acid amide (1).

These drugs are of particular interest because of their potency as hallucinogens and their chemical relationship to the central neurotransmitter, serotonin (5-hydroxytryptamine). The fact that LSD and harmine are powerful serotonin antagonists suggested that interference with serotonin metabolism might contribute to naturally occurring psychoses.

Let us turn our attention to two drugs of this class, psilocybin and LSD.

Psilocybin

Although used for centuries, psilocybin was not chemically identified until 1958, when its structure was defined by Hoffman, the Swiss scientist also known for the discovery of LSD. The drug was first brought to the world's scientific attention by the American banker R. G. Wasson, who in 1953 collected samples of the mushrooms used by some Mexican Indians in religious ceremonies. These mushrooms, *Psilocybe mexicana,* contain both psilocybin and its hallucinogenically active dephosphorylated metabolite, psilocin (16).

Psilocybin produces hallucinations in dosages of 10–50 mg. Thus, it is considerably more potent than mescaline but less potent than LSD. Unlike mescaline, it does not produce nausea or vomiting following ingestion. Physical changes are minimal: pupillary dilation and a slight elevation of blood pressure and pulse rate.

Approximately one-half hour following ingestion, subjects begin to feel extremely restless and anxious; within one hour, they begin to hallucinate, seeing bright colors and visual patterns playing over their retinas when their eyes are closed. The structural outlines of objects in the environment become blurred or sharpened and hearing becomes more acute. The subject begins to depersonalize and to experience a sense of unreality associated with a dreamlike state. Many subjects report sound distortions, particularly alterations of the tone and pitch of the human voice.

Hallucinations increase in intensity for two to three hours following ingestion, at which time they peak. At peak, visual changes, especially with the eyes closed, are pronounced. Objects seem to pulsate and develop wavelike qualities. The perception of distant objects is markedly impaired, as is the subject's ability to see objects in three dimensions. Time slows significantly. The subject may experience cyclical or ruminative thinking or develop a sensation of euphoria and mind expansion. The cosmic and euphoriant effects abate over the next three to four hours.

By 12 hours postingestion, the subject has returned to a normal state.

At the end of the experience, most subjects feel fatigued and contemplative. Many complain of headache (17).

LSD

On April 18, 1943, a chemist working in his laboratory in Switzerland began to feel ill and had to go home: "At home, I went to bed and got into a not unpleasant state of drunkenness, which was characterized by an extremely stimulating fantasy. When I closed my eyes, I experienced fantastic images of an extraordinary plasticity. They were associated with an intense kaleidoscopic play of colors. After about two hours, this condition disappeared" (18). Realizing that he might have experienced these symptoms because of something he was working with at the laboratory, Dr. Hoffman purposely ingested a minute amount of LSD the following day. He became nauseated, felt numb, and began to experience dramatic hallucinations with vivid colors and enhanced movement. This simple experiment ushered in one of the most profound sociological changes of the century, a change that has involved physicians, educators, the youth of all countries, scientists, lawyers, judges, churches, and a generation of anxious parents.

Chemical Properties and General Effects. LSD is a semisynthetic hallucinogen derived from the ergot fungus *Claviceps purpurea*. It is the most potent hallucinogen known to man and one of the most potent drugs ever developed. It is effective in microgram dosages, with as few as 30 mg producing profound hallucinogenic effects. LSD is odorless, tasteless, colorless, and water soluble, giving it potential as a chemical warfare agent. Effects occur 20–80 minutes after oral ingestion; autonomic effects are felt first, usually within 10–20 minutes (5). Pupils become dilated and react poorly to light. Reflexes are increased; feelings of numbness in the extremities, nausea, and a slight temperature elevation may occur. As is true with all hallucinogenic drugs, the mental reactions are determined largely by the dose, the subject's premorbid personality, and the setting in which the drug is administered, as well as the individual's reasons for taking the drug and whether or not any sudden changes in the environment occur during the drug experience. LSD hallucinations are similar to those produced by mescaline; however, the emotional response produced by LSD is more pronounced. While most subjects report an initial feeling of euphoria, perhaps 10 percent experience severe apprehension and sustained anxiety, which crescendoes to panic during the episode (18).

Other characteristic effects of LSD include an alteration of thought processes, with loosening of association and disruption of logical thought sequences. Although many subjects feel that they have an enhanced intellectual capacity during LSD trips, their performance on intelligence tests is significantly poorer than their nondrug performance (18). Subjects report increased fantasy production associated with disruption of ego and body boundaries, producing a state wherein self and fantasy objects blend. Depersonalization and derealization are common. Many subjects report a feeling of impending loss of control, as if they were astronauts "drifting away on a tether from a spaceship [i.e., the body]." "Going to the verge of insanity and then struggling to regain control of my mind," as one subject put it. "I get off on being able to get back in control of myself. When I have a bad trip is when I lose that control and float off into terrifying space."

The duration of the trip depends upon the dose and the subject's previous experience with the drug. Most trips last 4–12 hours. As the drug wears off, subjects experience "waves of normalcy (17). Unless excessive doses have been taken or the LSD has been consumed with some other drug, the subject's mental state returns to normal within 12–18 hours. The posttrip period is marked by fatigue and tension.

Although LSD was heralded as an agent to unlock the mind from its finite boundaries, serious and tragic side effects have resulted from its use: several homicides and innumerable cases of uncontrolled aggression; psychotic disorders; chronic states of intoxication; "schizophrenic reactions"; acute paranoid states; prolonged and intermittent psychoses in which visual hallucinations are common; and episodes of psychotic depression all have been reported. Multiple LSD related suicides have occurred, as have literally hundreds of cases of accidental death caused by misperception of space, time, or distance. Deaths also have resulted from delusions of omnipotence: intoxicated victims have leapt before railroad trains and ordered them to halt or jumped from buildings thinking they could fly (19). Finally, the drug has been reported to produce seizures in predisposed individuals and chromosome damage (20, 21). Let us briefly examine some of these effects.

Acute Panic Reactions. The "bad trip" is the most common adverse LSD reaction, occurring in as many as 1 in 10 LSD experiences (20, 22, 27). This short-term panic response, which subsides within 24 hours, frequently is precipitated by sudden changes in the environment or by a subjective sense of loss of control. The reaction is worsened by the absence of outside support or by interference with factors stabilizing one's reality orientation (e.g., stroboscopic lights) (22).

The majority of bad trips respond to environmental support and reassurance. In more severe cases, where users are agitated, violent, or injurious to self, sedatives (e.g., phenobarbital), minor tranquilizers (e.g., Librium or Valium), or major antipsychotics (e.g., chlorpromazine) may be required. In general, it is best to talk down the user rather than to administer drugs. If medication is required, a minor tranquilizer is preferable to a major antipsychotic since the latter may cause serious or even lethal complications if the user has ingested a drug other than LSD that possesses significant atropine effects (e.g., STP, strychnine, or PCP) (15, 16, 23, 27).

Acute Psychotic Reactions. These reactions have been estimated to occur in as many as 1 in 200 individuals using LSD. They represent a more serious complication than the bad trip as they are not necessarily self-limited. Characteristically, the subject experiences elements of a bad trip prior to becoming frankly psychotic, at which time he or she progresses to a state of hypervigilance, impaired emotional and behavioral control, and inability to make environmentally determined, discriminatory decisions. The subject begins to experience dissolution of bodily ego (derealization, depersonalization) and an impaired sense of autonomy. Later, he or she experiences marked lability of affect. The subject grossly misperceives reality, may develop delusional and/or paranoid symptoms, becomes intermittently aggressive or impulsive, and frequently is self-destructive. Severe chronic personality disorganization may also occur.

During the course of these psychotic reactions, the pain threshold is apparently elevated. Several reports of self-mutilation and suicide are available. Reactions are treated by immediate hospitalization and the administration of phenothiazines or other antipsychotic agents. If LSD consumption is unknown at the time of admission, these individuals are usually diagnosed as suffering from an acute schizophrenic reaction, a dissociative state, or a toxic psychosis (24, 25, 29, 31).

Prolonged Psychotic Reactions. These reactions are estimated to occur in up to 1 in 500 individuals who repetitively use LSD. Some investigators argue that the hallucinogen releases a latent psychotic disorder, while others believe that biochemical changes produced by this drug result in a schizophreniform psychosis in individuals who are not otherwise predisposed. Many investigators think that the premorbid personality of subjects who develop prolonged psychotic reactions are unstable, paranoid, psychopathic, hysterical, or schizoid (26, 36). Others have failed to demonstrate such premorbid psychopathology (37). Unfortunately, a significant number of patients fail to respond to any currently available psychiatric treatment (26, 33, 34, 36, 39, 45).

Flashbacks. Although the majority of individuals who use the term "flashback" do so when referring to the reexperiencing of visual hallucinations, other subjective states may also be reexperienced. Other "echo phenomena" include anxiety, agitation, disorientation, depersonalization, derealization, paranoid feelings, and nonvisual hallucinations.

Flashbacks may occur days, weeks, or months after the last LSD ingestion and are associated with the ingestion of other drugs (marijuana, alcohol, or amphetamine) or with episodes of sleep deprivation. Some flashbacks are reported as pleasant, but usually dysphoria is associated with them. The majority of LSD users who seek treatment for control of flashbacks are concerned about visual hallucinations and derealization, which occur without warning and thus place the patient in danger (e.g., while driving an automobile) (35, 37, 38).

Long-term Personality Disruption. The literature, though controversial, suggests that chronic use of LSD in ample quantity can produce profound personality change. Certain qualifiers, however, are necessary before reviewing these changes. The majority of case reports involve individuals who used LSD two or three times a week for several months or years. Moreover, most were multidrug abusers, which makes it difficult to attribute their personality changes exclusively to LSD.

On projective psychological testing, the chronic LSD user demonstrates a greater incidence of thought intrusion (disordered, nonconnected thoughts), more primitive drive material (i.e., violence, sex), and a higher Rorschach penetration score (stimuli seen as more unstructured) than non–LSD using matched controls. They also demonstrate higher emotional responsivity and more conceptual errors than do controls. Some investigators believe that such thought disturbances are determined more by the duration of drug abuse than by the variety of drugs ingested or the total amount of LSD consumed (32, 39–41).

Episodic loss of control with resultant physical aggression has been reported in chronic LSD users and has resulted in several homicides (42). Acute suicide attempts in chronic LSD users are also well documented (24, 25, 43, 44, 46). Some authors argue that the danger of suicide is considerably greater in individuals who have taken LSD in doses above 750 mg and in first-time users (47). The estimated incidence of suicide following the ingestion of LSD in carefully controlled medical settings is .4 per 1,000 patients; psychotic reactions occurred in .8 per 1,000 controlled subjects given the drug (46).

Typical Physical and Psychological Effects. The period of LSD intoxication is 8–24 hours (28). Following ingestion of the typical street dose (100–700 mg), the subject's pupils dilate, the pulse rate increases, and motor restlessness, hyperreflexia, and a fine tremor of the upper extremities result. Blood pressure becomes labile and elevated; the subject may experience headache, nausea, or vertigo. When observed, subjects appear hyperactive, restless, and excited; the restlessness, however, is not part of a purposeful activity.

If the dose of LSD is high, passive-depressed behavior predominates. Thought processes are slowed. Perseveration or total environmental nonresponsivity may occur. The subject appears perplexed or puzzled, looking much like the patient with a quiet organic mental disorder. Volitional thought processes are disrupted. The subject's train of thought is controlled by irrelevant external events or rapidly shifting internal associations; that is, the patient responds to rather than directs his or her thought processes and imagery.

These rapid mental changes may produce a hypomanic state with flight of ideas or, if high doses of the drug have been consumed, absolute incoherence. The patient may become paranoid or agitated and experience fleeting ideas of reference. Behaviorally, the LSD subject may go from a quiet, contemplative state to one of marked agitation, expressing great fearfulness and suspiciousness of others; characteristically, these states alternate rapidly. Some patients progress to a frankly grandiose state simulating mania.

Perception during the LSD experience is hyperacute. Subjects report flashing lights, colorful illusions, or complex visual hallucinations. Approximately a quarter of subjects experience auditory as well as visual hallucinations. The presence of the almost charcteristic visual hallucinations differentiates the LSD user from the schizophrenic patient, who rarely experiences such hallucinations. LSD hallucinations are further distinguished from those that occur during psychotic episodes by being "ego alien" and often by appearing as two- rather than three-dimensional images. That is, the subject finds the hallucinations fascinating but does not see them as an integral part of the self, as is the case with the schizophrenic. Subjects are intermittently able to distinguish the unreality of the hallucinations, as is illustrated by the following statement from an intoxicated patient:

> These are wonderful. There are bright colors everywhere. I can feel them vibrating in me. They keep changing and making me feel funny. Get away from there [nothing in the room is changing]; that's not real. I thought there was someone there, but I guess it's just them. They're beautiful. It feels like water is around. It's blue! No! Now it's greenish. What a beautiful plant! No, it's just colors. I never saw anything like it before. Now there are millions of them and the lights are flashing. The music is beautiful. Stay away. Don't get too close. Push it back from me. I've got to get out of here before they get too high. Now I'm okay again. I'm back in control. I know where I am.

As one can see from this example, subjects perceive the hallucinations as real but rapidly gain composure. This characteristic awareness-unawareness of the quality of the hallucinations distinguishes LSD psychosis from schizophrenia.

During the LSD experience, many subjects are unable to screen out irrelevant stimuli; for example, an individual may become acutely aware of various articles of clothing on the body or of the sound of a clock ticking in the room. In general, subjects' level of awareness becomes so low that they tend to respond indiscriminately to stimuli, making it impossible for them to maintain a focus of attention. Consequently, they become victims of outside stimulation.

Inability to focus attention, passivity, distractibility, and suggestibility all contribute to the marked emotional lability that occurs during the LSD trip. Episodes of distorted body image progress to derealization and depersonalization. Affect changes quickly, with the subject moving rapidly from euphoria to sadness, calmness to agitation. A depressed mood often persists following the period of acute intoxication.

In summary, a diagnosis of LSD intoxication is suggested by pupillary dilation, increased blood pressure, tachycardia, visual hallucinations of an ego alien quality, and inability to maintain perceptual focus. Moreover, the subject will show marked distractibility and lability of affect. Although these symptoms occur rarely in functional psychoses, colorful, geometric hallucinations do not; consequently, their presence is most helpful in diagnosing hallucinogen abuse.

Other Classes of Hallucinogens

PCP

No description of hallucinogens would be complete without a discussion of phencyclidine (sernyl). PCP, angel dust, or hog was developed during the 1950s as an anesthetic agent; it was found to be unacceptable for human use because of severe psychiatric side effects, which include agitation, psychosis, and delirium. However, the drug was marketed as an animal anesthetic.

PCP is chemically related to ketamine hydrochloride (Ketalar), which is employed as a human neuroleptic analgesic agent. It is easily manufactured in home laboratories and is often substituted on the street for other drugs, particularly mescaline and THC. When PCP is produced in home laboratories, the by-product 1-piperidinocyclohexane-carbonitrile is often present. This contaminant may produce violent abdominal cramps, bloody vomiting, bloody diarrhea, and coma (47–49).

PCP can be smoked, sprinkled, inhaled, swallowed, or injected. To date, no evidence of tolerance or physiologic withdrawal has been found. In whatever form administered, the drug produces an increase in systolic blood pressure, a quickening of the pulse, sweating, and increased deep tendon reflexes. Other symptoms may include nausea and vomiting, paresthesia, analgesia, and chills. PCP has a strong cholinergic component, which produces flushing, drooling, sweating, and pupillary constriction. Cerebellar disruption occurs frequently from moderate to high doses and produces sensations of dizziness accompanied by dysarthria, nystagmus, and ataxia. In the middle and upper dose ranges, subjects report sensory flooding, or hyperacusis, a feeling of being overwhelmed by external stimuli, which are impossible to sort out. As the degree of sensory overload increases, subjects become agitated, lose ability to test reality, experience dissolution of ego boundaries, and suffer severe intellectual and emotional disorganization. High doses may cause death by inducing seizures, cardiac or respiratory arrest, or acute hypertensive crisis with subsequent rupture of cerebral blood vessels (47, 50). The EEG changes characteristically produced by the drug include a Delta–Theta pattern with low voltage fast activity. The drug is thought to act on the nonspecific thalamocortical projections (51).

Cohen identified the major acute psychological effects of PCP as follows: disinhibition, toxic psychotic reactions, schizophreniform psychosis presenting with either stuporous or excited catatonic features, paranoia, anxiety, panic states, depression, or sensory blockade (47). Long-term PCP use may produce a severe, chronic, organic brain dysfunction or behavioral toxicity such as impaired impulse control—emotional outbursts, easily aroused assaultiveness, or uncontrolled belligerence. Some PCP users also develop an extreme condition of social withdrawal, remaining distant from all people and activities.

The magnitude of increase in phencyclidine abuse became clear when PCP emerged as the number one drug of abuse in the city of Detroit during 1975 (50). Phencyclidine represents a greater threat than any previously available hallucinogen because of its greater tendency to produce a severe, refractory psychotic state; liberate interpersonal violence and aggressivity; cause long-term central nervous system and cognitive impairment; and be surreptitiously substituted for other drugs (52–69).

Social, Cultural, and Environmental Aspects of Hallucinogen Abuse

The term "drug abuse" carries many connotations regarding what is socially acceptable and unacceptable behavior. For example, in our society, the use of caffeine is condoned and no one would call the executive drinking a second cup of morning coffee a drug abuser. On the other hand, if he or she took a second morning Demerol capsule, people would question that individual's mental stability unless the drug had been prescribed by a physician. The terminally ill cancer patient who becomes addicted to narcotics for the control of pain is not regarded as a socially deviant individual, but an adolescent consuming identical quantities of the same drug would be seen as socially impaired. In general, our society tolerates drugs that calm or stimulate but looks askance at agents that produce physiological dependence or alter sensory perceptions to the point of unreality. Consequently, we approve the social drinker but disapprove the drunk. We understand the use of caffeine but abhor the use of amphetamine. In the latter instance, society's fears stem from the drugs' ability to produce unpredictable responses. The innate fear that our society has of its unpredictable members is expressed by avoidance or confinement of such individuals, be they criminal, mentally subnormal, or psychiatrically impaired. This fear of erratic behavior, blown out of proportion, underlies many of the labels society places on individuals who use certain substances to excess.

Stereotyping is commonly applied to all individuals who use or abuse drugs. Yet, different drugs have different pharmacological and social qualities and tend to be used in different ways by different types of individuals. Making generalizations about the opiate user, the PCP user, and the intravenous amphetamine user is fruitless. A recent study of psychiatric patients admitted to a research unit found that drug use often followed, rather than preceded, the development of psychiatric symptoms (69). Many patients, in emotional turmoil produced by psychiatric disturbance, attempted to control their symptoms by self-medicating with various drugs; other patients began using drugs as a direct response to peer pressure; a third group did so as a result of characterological disorder. Some patients who reported drug use because it seemed fashionable had, in fact, never used drugs (70).

Many individuals in our country routinely abuse drugs that are defined as safe by the federal government; these substances are available over-the-counter. Most studies would not include this sizable population in discussions of drug—and particularly hallucinogen—users. Yet, many of these agents do have hallucinogenic properties and are taken for other than their intended purpose. For example, Sominex contains scopolamine and is capable of producing derealization, depersonalization, visual hallucinations, confusional states, and memory loss.

Before returning to the more traditional psychiatric explanations for hallucinogen abuse, let us look at some of the cultural and social factors that may also be responsible for the consumption of these drugs. America is a drug consuming society. Advertising for drugs is everywhere—newspapers, television, billboards, and sides of buses. Pharmacies are stocked with thousands of preparations for the treatment of every ailment and ill. Cigarette consumption is promoted by a billion dollar yearly advertising budget. Alcohol advertising likewise has become a major industry. Children grow up in an environment where their peers and parents readily consume drugs to relieve distress and promote a feeling of well-being. It is, therefore, a simple step for an adolescent to cross the line of discretion and begin using substances that produce "better living through chemistry."

One of the most frequently overlooked aspects of hallucinogen abuse is that the vast majority of users are casual, rather than chronic, and most do not experience the severe psychiatric or physical reactions described earlier. One in five Americans is presently, or has been, a casual user of marijuana. It is highly unlikely that many of these people have developed the much dreaded "amotivational syndrome," which occurs in some heavy marijuana users. One of two Americans has consumed alcohol, yet the vast majority of these individuals are not alcoholics. If agents can be safely and consistently used with a predictable response, they will be. One of the elements that separates the emotionally impaired hallucinogen abuser from the individual who smokes cigarettes or drinks liquor is that the hallucinogen user is never sure what he or she is buying. Of course, this was also the case for the vast majority of people who purchased alcohol during Prohibition; to be sure, people went blind from methyl alcohol, but most tolerated "the abuse" with no sequelae.

One element that produces fear of these drugs is their use by the young. Throughout history, laws have been passed to protect the young, along with people whose judgment is considered less than adequate, from undertaking actions that could harm them. The availability of hallucinogens to adolescents and preadolescents has created fear and outrage on the part of parents and those charged with the development of youth in our society—schools, churches, courts, and law enforcement agencies. Adolescents, who in Western society are seen as coming into inevitable conflict with their parents, chose in the sixties and seventies at least to threaten the use of drugs during this confrontation. The availability of hallucinogens to a youth oriented culture, which sought personal enhancement through greater self-awareness and "consciousness raising," produced a challenge from our youth to their elders: "If you can expand your consciousness through women's groups, athletics, Transcendental Meditation, yoga, psychotherapy, creative dramatics, etc., why may we not expand our consciousness through the social use of drugs? If you can relax by taking alcohol and Librium, why may we not relax by using pot? It's less harmful than the agents you use, you know."

The hallucinogens had potent social appeal. They were presented to youth as mind expanding, consciousness altering drugs. Successful use placed a premium on the user's intellectual and cognitive ability. Consequently, hallucinogens were regarded as drugs of the middle and upper class. They were more intellectually attractive than so-called ghetto drugs, such as heroin and barbiturates. In addition, they were viewed as drugs best taken in a group setting, which aspect satisfied the adolescent's need to belong and be accepted. In short, the youth of the 1960s and seventies brought into focus an ongoing societal conflict. They refused to accept the cultural norms and values of their parents in defining what substances or behaviors were harmful.

Epidemiologic surveys of youth supported the notion that hallucinogen use was epidemic. All classes of youth abused, and these drugs were everywhere—schools, playgrounds, parties, etc. Hallucinogens provided a means of rebellion, a ticket to belonging, a badge of courage, and a method of mind expansion. They raised questions about theology, ideology, social welfare, national policy, and the quality of human life, with which adults had to deal.

Not all individuals who used hallucinogens during this period did so because of interpersonal or societal crisis. Not all users were alienated from society or self because of the new affluence, social injustice, loss of creativity, or decline of Western ideals or aspirations. Some youths took drugs simply because they were available, their friends were doing it, and they had not seen anyone injured thereby. Some took drugs simply to experiment and having had the experience experimented no further. Such behavior can hardly be seen as different from that of adolescents who tried liquor during Prohibition. The major difference, however, is that hallucinogenic agents are several orders of magnitude more powerful and dangerous than alcohol.

Besides the casual users, some individuals did abuse hallucinogens. Scientists who studied this group identified numerous characteristics that differentiated them from the former category of user. Carey saw many college students who were socially ill at ease (71). He believed many of these students used hallucinogens in an attempt to belong, while others who were unable to express their dissatisfactions used drugs out of a sense of powerlessness or disillusionment. He thus described the chronic hallucinogen user as an individual severely disillusioned with and alienated from both society and his or her own peer group. Becker argued that hallucinogen use develops as a learning process and requires progression through definite steps, the first being the proper use of the agent; the second learning how best to perceive the elements of the high; and finally, learning how to control one's reaction so as to derive the "most fun" (72). Under this model, the drugs themselves have a "sociogenic" or "cultogenic" effect.

Goode and others saw the group process established by drug use as a potent social determinant for establishing a pattern of behavior in excess, since the drug defines one's ability to participate within a specific social group (73). Many of these drugs are used not merely in a group but within an *intimate* group of *significant* others. Freedman succinctly defined the sociological benefits as folows: "For this group, magical transformation of reality, omniscient union rather than the painful confrontation of separateness, is the lore" (22). Many authorities have identified peer pressure and desire for group belonging as the factors that initially prompt adolescents to experiment with hallucinogens (22, 69, 72, 73).

Other sociological factors that may encourage adolescent drug abuse include an inadequate national leadership, inappropriate parenting from a lost generation of parents, excessive permissiveness on the part of both the family unit and society, generalized disorganization of the family unit, suggested by an ever increasing national divorce rate, economic uncertainties, inflation, the past war in Southeast Asia, and the new affluence, which has produced a hedonistic society centered around a "cult of experience" (22, 72).

Psychological Correlates of Hallucinogen Abuse

While the sociological explanations may have merit, psychological motivators for the ingestion of hallucinogenic substances are the key to abuse. Three general theoretical assumptions have been offered to explain the psychology of drug abuse. The first is the concept of psychological dependence. The second is the notion that predisposition to the use of a particular drug is rooted in the individual's personality structure. The final hypothesis is that some individuals suffering from a tension state begin to abuse drugs in an attempt to self-medicate; the relief thereby obtained reinforces further use and abuse.

Although the composite that follows does not apply to every individual who repetitively uses hallucinogens, it separates the nonuser and the casual user from the abuser. Individuals with a true psychological drive for abuse and who later develop dependence upon these agents tend to be somewhat narcissistic and motivated by a rather immature need to seek immediate gratification. They tend to be easily frustrated and to have an excessive need for interpersonal acceptance and approval, which is difficult to satisfy. In addition, they usually have several dysphoric areas in their lives and shallow interpersonal relationships. Consequently, the hallucinogens serve as truly hedonistic, pleasure producing agents by reducing tension, anxiety, depression, boredom, or the user's sense of alienation. Perhaps a young man who was seen in an emergency room summarized this best:

> I get off on acid and dust [PCP] because I can do things when I'm taking them that I couldn't do otherwise. I'm a real bear on dust and everybody knows not to screw with me when I get mad when I'm on it. I usually drop acid with my friends and if something goes wrong, I know they care enough about me to look after me. We spend a lot of time [his friends and he] planning binges where we can just trip for a week or two. We'll even get it worked out so that somebody can bring in the food and look after the pad while we're doing it. That way we know if somebody freaks out, we'll have a straight man to make sure everyone's okay.

This patient has identified many of the elements that seem to differentiate the chronic hallucinogen user from other substance abusers. Their risk taking tends to be considerably greater, with the elements of excitement producing more camaraderie and cohesion than is seen in other varieties of drug abuse. The drug has a clear social context and often permits behaviors that would otherwise be seen as unacceptable or inappropriate.

The psychological dynamics of each abuser must be carefully defined by a skilled therapist since they are unique for each individual seen in therapy. For example, some individuals use hallucinogens to facilitate group belonging, others to express hostility, others to rebel, and still others to test the limits of their own control. The following case history illustrates this point. A young man was seen in the emergency room. On two previous occasions he presented with the same complaint, self-induced lacerations while under the influence of LSD. When he finally entered psychotherapy, it became evident that he felt extremely guilty for having precipitated a divorce between his father and alcoholic mother by continually playing one parent off against the other. Following the divorce, his mother committed suicide. Six months after her death our patient began to abuse a number of drugs, became increasingly despondent, and reported feelings of extreme guilt ("I killed her"). On two occasions, while under the influence of LSD, he lacerated himself severely with a knife while being able to "feel the harm that he has caused." Guilt and depression, as in this case, are frequently reported as core dynamics in individuals who abuse hallucinogens (74–77).

Nicholi argued that many youngsters who abuse drugs are depressed not because of some object lost but because of the disparity between what they wish themselves to be—gifted intellectual achievers—and what they are—one of a multitude of struggling students in a competitive and threatening environment (78). Grinspoon suggested that psychedelic abuse often results from boredom and the maladaptive control of sexual and aggressive impulses (74). He noted that such abuse may represent "identification with, or modeling after, a generation that has legitimized the taking of drugs." In addition, Grinspoon observed that some young abusers are acting out the repressed wishes of their parents. Bowers and associates were impressed with the need of psychedelic abusers for increased interpersonal closeness and their desire to fuse with others (80). Glickman and Blumfield also suggested that a desire for interpersonal fusion is a prime determinant of abuse, as is the subject's desire to create an illusion of power and intimacy (81).

Treatment

The treatment plan for hallucinogen abusers is determined largely by the definition of the patient's immediate problems, coupled with the therapist's insights into the psychological dynamics of the user.

If one is dealing with an acutely psychotic individual, the most appropriate course of action is identification of the substance(s) abused, evaluation of the patient's medical condition, and either treatment with appropriate environmental constraints and sedatives or simply talking down. Medical precautions should be taken to protect the patient from the sequelae of ingestion, such as status epilepticus, cardiovascular collapse, or respiratory insufficiency.

Chronic psychotic reactions produced by hallucinogens are treated rather like their naturally occurring counterparts. The administration of phenothiazines following a 72-hour period of observation is often the most salutary treatment. The majority of such patients improve considerably when monitored in a stable hospital environment. Administration of phenothiazines or thioxanthines is helpful. Unfortunately, a significant number of these patients, perhaps 10 percent, never fully recover.

Psychological treatment of the nonpsychotic and nonorganically impaired hallucinogen user is a complex issue. The psychotherapist needs to establish rapport and to obtain a detailed history. Over a period of several sessions, the possible motivations and rewards from hallucinogen use and abuse need to be defined. The psychotherapist should pay particular attention to drive reduction, goal substitutions, and the social gains derived from the use of hallucinogens. In general, one needs to consider that chronic hallucinogen use is symptomatic of an underlying problem that requires identification. Inappropriate social responses, which become evident during the course of therapy, need to be pointed out to the patient and corrected. The majority of individuals who chronically use hallucinogens are isolated and distanced from society and must learn to substitute people for drugs. They frequently have difficulty with their families, their girlfriends or boyfriends, or their spouses.

In general, treatment should be directed toward promoting membership in supportive drug-free groups and providing different psychological support systems for the individual. Group therapy, coupled with individual psychotherapy, is often extremely helpful in improving the individual's self-worth and sense of social comfort. The adaptive patterns that are learned in group therapy are readily generalizable. In addition, we have found it particularly useful for the patient's individual therapist also to function as the group therapist, as many of the reaction patterns seen in the group become a focus for individual psychotherapy. The fact that they are shared both by the patient and his therapist greatly enhances the therapist's ability to define areas of social distortion to which the patient often responds with feelings of rejection, inadequacy or hostility. The behavioral patterns of the patient, which in themselves distance him from other members of his group, are often extremely valuable to explore in the context of individual as well as group therapy.

The chronic hallucinogen user who suffers from a significant characterological disorder is unlikely to benefit greatly from this treatment. For such patients, treatment must consist of controlling the patient's environment and defining the manipulative aspects of his or her behavior by interpersonal confrontation. The patient with a true sociopathic personality disorder is unlikely to benefit from treatment in an outpatient situation since such a person's characteristic course of action is either to control the interpersonal relationship or to flee from it if it causes dysphoria or anxiety. Consequently, a longer term (6–12 weeks) inpatient treatment contract is recommended. Voluntary admission to drug abuse programs and halfway houses also has been reported as beneficial for some patients with sociopathic tendencies (16, 70, 76, 80).

Conclusion

Hallucinogen use and abuse in the United States has declined since the mid-1960s, except for marijuana and PCP, use of which has increased. Individuals who regularly use these agents to excess exhibit increased risk taking behavior and increased need for social approval. Hallucinogens represent a potential time bomb in our society: a significant number of people suffer long-term, adverse side effects, including central nervous system damage and chronic psychotic reactions, as well as episodes of precipitous violence. The treatment of the hallucinogen abuser poses a complicated psychotherapeutic challenge to substitute interpersonal gratifications for those produced by drugs.

References

1. Hoffer, A., and Osmond, H., *The Hallucinogens,* Academic, New York, 1967.
2. Elkes, J., The dysleptics: note on a no man's land, *Comp. Psychiat. 4,* 193–198 (1963).
3. Stoll, W. A., LSD-25: a hallucinatory agent of the ergot group, *Swiss Arch. Neuro. 60,* 279–323 (1947).
4. Elkes, J., Elkes, C., and Mayer-Gross, W., Hallucinogenic drugs, *Lancet 268,* 719 (1955).
5. Rinkel, M., LSD: problems connected with its use, misuse, and abuse in the United States, in *Recent Advances in Biological Psychiatry,* J. Wortis, ed., Plenum Press, New York, 1966, pp. 103–113.
6. Lester, E., Taking a trip with Leary, *N.Y. Times,* Dec. 4, 1966.
7. Chayet, N. L., Law, medicine, and LSD, *N. Eng. J. Med. 277,* 253–254 (1967).
8. Hirschhorn, K., LSD and chromosomal damage, *Hosp. Prac. 4,* 98–101 (1969).
9. Cohen, S., Trends in substance abuse, *Drug Abuse and Alc. Newsletter, 7,* 1–4 (1978).
10. Huxley, A., *The Doors of Perception,* Harper Colophon, New York, 1963.
11. Szara, S., The hallucinogenic drugs: curse or blessing? *Amer. J. Psychiat. 123,* 1513–1518 (1967).
12. Eddy, N. B., Halbach, H., Isbell, H., and Seevers, M. H., Drug dependence: its significance and characteristics, *Bull. WHO 32,* 721–733 (1965).
13. Snyder, S. H., Faillace, L. A., and Hollister,L., 2,5-dimethoxy-4-methyl-amphetamine (STP): a new hallucinogenic drug, *Science 158,* 669–670 (1967).
14. Solursh, L. P., and Clement, W. R., Hallucinogenic drug abuse: manifestation and management, *Can. Med. Ass'n. 98,* 407–410 (1968).
15. Solursh, L. P., and Clement, W. R., Use of diazepam in hallucinogenic drug crises, *JAMA 205,* 644–645 (1968).
16. Balis, G., The use of psychotomimetic and related consciousness-altering drugs, in *American Handbook of Psychiatry,* 2d ed., vol. 3, A. Silvano and E. B. Brody, eds., Basic Books, New York, 1974, pp. 404–446.
17. Jacobsen, E., The clinical pharmacology of the hallucinogens, *Clin. Pharm. Ther. 4,* 480–503 (1963).

18. *Hallucinogenic Agents: A Concise Review,* Shering Corporation, Bloomfield, 1963.
19. Cohen, S., Psychotomimetic agents, *Ann. Rev. Pharm. 7,* 301–318 (1967).
20. Cohen, S., A classification of LSD complications, *Psychosomat. 7,* 182 (1966).
21. Cohen, M. M., Marinello, M. J., and Back, N., Chromosomal damage in human leukocytes induced by lysergic acid diethylamide, *Science 155,* 1417–1419 (1967).
22. Freedman, D. X., On the use and abuse of LSD, *Arch. Gen. Psychiat. 18,* 330–347 (1968).
23. Abod, L. G., and Biel, J. H., Anticholinergic psychotomimetic agents, *Inter'l. Rev. Neurobiol. 4,* 217–273 (1962).
24. Cohen, S., LSD side effects and complications. *J. Nerv. Ment. Dis. 130,* 30–40 (1960).
25. Cohen, S., and Ditman, K. S., Complications associated with lysergic acid diethylamide (LSD-25), *JAMA 181,* 161–162 (1962).
26. Cohen, S., and Ditman, K. S., Prolonged adverse reactions to lysergic acid ethylamide, *Arch. Gen. Psychiat. 8,* 475–480 (1963).
27. Underleider, J. T., Fisher, D. D., Fuller, M., and Caldwell, A., The "bad trip": the etiology of the adverse LSD reaction. *Am. J. Psychiat. 124,* 1483–1490 (1968).
28. Bakker, C. B., The clinical picture of hallucinogenic intoxication, *Hosp. Med.,* 102–114 (1969).
29. Underleider, J. T., Fisher, D. D., and Fuller, M. The dangers of LSD: analysis of seven months experience in a university hospital's psychiatric service, *JAMA 197,* 109–112 (1966).
30. Fink, M., Simon, J., Haqueo, W., and Turan, I., Prolonged adverse reactions to LSD in psychotic subjects, *Arch. Gen. Psychiat. 15,* 450–454 (1966).
31. Frosch, W. A., Robbins, E. S., and Stern, M., Untoward reactions to LSD requiring hospitalization. *N. Eng. J. Med., 273,* 1235–1239 (1965).
32. Ditman, K. S., and Whittlesey, J. R. B., Comparison of the LSD-25 experience and delirium tremens, *Arch. Gen. Psychiat. 1,* 47–57 (1959).
33. Rosenthal, S. H., Persistent hallucinosis following repeated administrations of hallucinogenic drugs, *Amer. J. Psychiat. 121,* 238–244 (1964).
34. Cooper, H. A., Hallucinogenic drugs, *Lancet 268,* 238–244 (1964).
35. Hoffer, A., D-lysergic acid diethylamide (LSD): a review of its present status, *Clin. Pharm. Ther. 6,* 191–195 (1965).
36. Glass, G. S., and Bowers, M. B., Jr., Chronic psychosis associated with long-term psychotomimetic drug abuse, *Arch. Gen. Psychiat. 23,* 97–103 (1970).
37. Woody, G. E., Visual disturbances experienced by hallucinogenic drug abusers while driving, *Amer. J. Psychiat. 127,* 683–686 (1970).
38. Horowitz, M. J., Flashback: recurrent intrusive images after the use of LSD, *Amer. J. Psychiat. 126,* 565–569 (1969).
39. Tucker, G. J., Quinlan, D., and Harrow, M., Chronic hallucinogenic drug use and thought disturbances, *Arch. Gen. Psychiat. 27,* 443–447 (1972).

40. Ditman, K. S., Tiez, W., Prine, B. S., Forgy, E., and Moss, T., Aspects of the LSD experience, *J. Nerv. Ment. Dis. 145,* 464–474 (1968).

41. McGlothlin, W. H., Arnold, D. O., and Freedman, D. X., Organicity measures following repeated LSD ingestion, *Arch. Gen. Psychiat. 21,* 704–709 (1969).

42. Kletfisg, A., and Racey, J., Homicide and LSD, *JAMA 223,* 429–430 (1973).

43. Savage, C., The resolution and subsequent remobilization of resistance by LSD in psychotherapy, *J. Nerv. Ment. Dis. 125,* 434–437 (1962).

44. Savage, C., The LSD psychosis as a transaction between the psychiatrist and patient, in *Lysergic Acid Diethylamide and Mescaline in Experimental Psychiatry,* L. Cholden, ed., Grune & Stratton, New York, 1955, pp. 35–43.

45. Eisner, B. G., and Cohen, S., Psychoses with lysergic acid diethylamide, *J. Nerv. Ment. Dis. 127,* 528–539 (1958).

46. Schwart, C. J., The complications of LSD: a review of the literature, *J. Nerv. Ment. Dis. 146,* 174–186 (1968).

47. Cohen, S., Angel dust, *JAMA 238,* 515–516 (1977).

48. Liden, C. B., Lovejoy, F. H., and Costello, C. E., Phencyclidine: Nine cases of poisoning, *JAMA 234,* 513–516 (1975).

49. Tong, T. G., Benofitz, N. L., Becker, C. E., Forni, P. J., and Boerner, V., Phencyclidine poisoning, *JAMA 234,* 512–513 (1975).

50. *Calif. Soc'y. for Treatment Alc. and Other Depend. Newsletter 3,* 1–3 (1976).

51. Hollister, L. E., PCP, *Inter'l. Drug Ther. Newsletter 14,* 17–20 (1979).

52. Burn, R. S., et al., Phencyclidine: an emerging drug problem, *Clin. Tox. 9,* 473–475 (1976).

53. Shulgin, A. T., and MacLean, D. E., Illicit synthesis of phencyclidine (PCP) and several of its analogs, *Clin. Tox. 9,* 553–560 (1976).

54. James, S. H., and Schnoll, S. H., Phencyclidine: tissue distribution in the rat, *Clin. Tox. 9,* 573–582 (1976).

55. Wog, L. K., and Biemann, K., Metabolites of phencyclidine, *Clin. Tox. 9,* 583–591 (1976).

56. Bolter, A., Heminger, A., Martin, G., and Fry, M., Outpatient clinical experience in a community drug abuse program with phencyclidine abusers, *Clin. Tox. 9,* 593–600 (1976).

57. Ludeberg, G. D., Gupta, R. C., and Montgomery, S. H., Phencyclidine: patterns seen in street drug analysis, *Clin. Tox. 9,* 503–511 (1976).

58. Balster, R. L., and Chait, L. D., Behavioral pharmacology of phencyclidine, *Clin. Tox. 9,* 513–528 (1976).

59. Burns, R. S., Lerner, S. E., Corrado, R., Stuart, H. J., and Schnoll, S. H., Phencyclidine: states of acute intoxication and fatalities, *West. J. Med. 123,* 345–349 (1975).

60. Malcolm, R., Keeler, M. H., and Miller, W. C., Phencyclidine toxicity: "animal tranquilizer" reactions, *J. Nerv. Syst. 37,* 590–592 (1976).

61. Doran, R. D., Phencyclidine ingestion: therapy review, *South. Med. J. 70,* 117–119 (1977).

62. Luisada, P. V., and Brown, B. L., Clinical management of the phencyclidine psychosis, *Clin. Tox. 9,* 539–545 (1976).

63. Burns, R. S., and Lerner, S. E., Perspectives: acute phencyclidine intoxication, *Clin. Tox. 9,* 477–501 (1976).

64. PCP revisited, *Clin. Tox. 9,* 339–348 (1976).

65. Reynolds, P. C., Clinical and forensic experiences with phencyclidine, *Clin. Tox. 9,* 547–552 (1976).

66. Fauman, B., Aldering, G., Fauman, M., and Rosen, P., Psychiatric sequelae of phencyclidine abuse, *Clin. Tox. 9,* 529–538 (1976).

67. Showalter, C. V., and Thornton, W. E., Clinical pharmacology of phencyclidine toxicity, *Amer. J. Psychiat. 134,* 1234–1238 (1977).

68. Lawes, T. G. G., Schizophrenia, "sernyl," and sensory deprivation, *Brit. J. Psychiat. 109,* 243–250 (1963).

69. Bakker, C. B., and Amini, F. B., Observations on the psychotomimetic effects of sernyl, *Comp. Psychiat. 2,* 269–280 (1961).

70. Hall, R. C. W., Stickney, S. K., Faillace, L. A., and Gardner, E. R., Relationship of psychiatric illness to drug abuse, *J. Psychedel. Drugs 11,* 337–342 (1979).

71. Larey, J. T., *The College Drug Scene,* Prentice-Hall, Englewood Cliffs, 1968.

72. Becker, H. S., Marijuana use and social control, *Soc. Prob. 3,* 35–44 (1955).

73. Goode, E., Multiple drug use among marijuana smokers, *Soc. Prob. 17,* 48–64 (1969).

74. Grinspoon, L., *Marihuana Reconsidered,* Harvard University Press, Cambridge, 1971.

75. Louria, D. B., *Overcoming Drugs,* McGraw-Hill, New York, 1971.

76. Halleck, S. L., Psychiatric treatment for the alienated college student, *Amer. J. Psychiat. 124,* 642–650 (1967).

77. Hekimian, L. J., and Gershon, S., Characeristics of drug abusers admitted to a psychiatric hospital, *JAMA 205,* 125–130 (1968).

78. Nicholi, A. M., Harvard dropouts: some psychiatric findings, *Amer. J. Psychiat. 124,* 651–658 (1967).

79. Underleider, J. T., and Fisher, D. D., The problems of LSD and emotional disorder, *Calif. Med. 106,* 49–55 (1967).

80. Bowers, M., Chapman, A., Schwartz, A., and Dann, O. T., Dynamics of psychedelic drug abuse: a clinical study, *Arch. Gen. Psychiat. 16,* 560–566 (1967).

81. Glickman, L., and Blumfield, M., Psychological determinants of LSD reactions, *J. Nerv. Ment. Dis. 145,* 79–83 (1967).

5

Alcoholism

Frank A. Seixas

Both behavior and excess are such common words they may imply many shades of meaning. Cannon discovered the autonomic nervous system and separated urgent life-saving emergency responses of the sympathetic system from those of rest, recuperation, and relaxation, which he termed parasympathetic (1). Yet the deer would flee on sympathetic arousal, while the lion would attack. If behavior is the complex of reactions to environmental stimuli, we must be careful in assigning causes. In the Lesch-Nyhan's syndrome it is a congenital metabolic defect which eventuates in the cannibalization of the affected infant's extremities (2). The new discipline of psychobiology explores biological determinants of our behaviors.

In addition to biological determinants, internal stimuli can originate in parental instruction and in tribal, legal, and social influences. External stimuli may similarly vary.

Defining excess is also a challenge. We may put the cut-off point in varying places, choosing between fluctuating cultural, legal, or ethical determinants or else finding biological determinants which seem immutable. The term excess remains pejorative and insists a limit has been broached.

The psychopharmacological properties of ethanol have been known from ancient times, and the drinking of naturally fermented beverages like mead perhaps antedated agriculture. The effect of alcohol was powerful enough to generate strict taboos. Moderate drinking and even occasional drunkenness were observed as qualitatively different from that of the habituated drunkard whose intemperance looked involuntary, suggesting classification with disease. Benjamin Rush, physician, teacher, and signer of the Declaration of Independence, called alcoholism a disease, and at about the same time in England Thomas Trotter identified it similarly (3, 4). Throughout the nineteenth century, the disease idea persisted although the concept that drinking was a sin gained favor. In recent times, the students of many disciplines have looked at drinking and reached varied conclusions. Anthropologists explore socially approved practices of drink-

120

ing in different cultures, social surveyors determine the usual drinking practices of population samples by questionnaire (5), and behaviorists look at stimuli and their responses and postulate contingencies which might interrupt these sequences. Some sociologists have opposed the idea that alcoholism is a disease on pragmatic grounds. They reason that if the alcoholic adopts "the sick role" he will not provide the necessary cooperation to give a good result. But one requirement of the sick role as originally described by Parsons is participating to one's best ability to get well (6). Anything else is malingering and criminal rather than sick.

Synthesizing these varying strains in the service of understanding is difficult. Horn, Wanberg, and Adam administered questionnaires to patients at a treatment center (7). The questions examined general health, drinking history, and psychological symptoms. Analysis of regression separated eight clusters, which were seen as types of alcoholism, including such groups as the organically impaired public inebriate, the hysterical neurotic, and the sociopath. Schuckit and Morissey criticized their approach:

> These studies suffer from criticisms of many-factor analytic investigations where specific hypotheses were not being tested but subgroups were allowed to fall where they may . . . [and] the authors have not had the opportunity to demonstrate on followup the prognostic or treatment importance of their purported subdivisions (8).

Schuckit also looked at questionnaires in population surveys that "the population with the highest proportion of drinkers does not coincide with the population showing the highest rates of alcoholism." Thus "one would be ill-advised to generalize from . . . population studies of drinking directly to alcoholism rates" (8). As Room similarly observed, "Epidemiological truth is not the same as clinical truth (9). While debate continues among scholars, clinicians apparently widely accept the NCA definition of alcoholism:

> A chronic relapsing disease ending in death characterized by tolerance for alcohol, the presence of an alcohol withdrawal syndrome on the cessation of diminution of alcohol intake and/or physical diseases consequent to alcohol ingestion (10).

Genetic Predisposition

The last decade has provided "consistent and increasing evidence that a strong hereditary predisposition to alcoholism exists which is unaffected by environment" (8, p. 20). This conclusion was based on twin studies (11), adoption studies (12), half-sibling studies, and family geneologies. Animal studies have also given strong support to the hereditary predisposition hypothesis. The type of genetic influence likely in such a widespread disease as alcoholism would be polygenetic, such as is postulated for hypertension, schizophrenia, or diabetes. Thus it is no surprise that attempts to find "genetic markers" have not succeeded since these characterize diseases caused by single genes of large effect.

In some hereditary diseases, such as glucose 6 phosphate deficiency, one needs the ingestion of an external agent (fava beans or the drug Atabrine) to produce the symptoms. Also, one cannot have alcoholism without alcohol. Availability of alcohol, determined by social customs, taboos, price, and other circumstances, influences the number of susceptibles who develop the disease in a given population, or which of its symptoms they display. McAndrew and Edgerton have implied that in different cultures varying aspects of drunkenness may be favored although, in a given person, all the pharmacological behavioral changes may be observed (13). Imitation or role modeling could be a factor, but apparently a smaller one, since such influences have been ruled out in the genetic research.

Age, sex, and ethnicity also effect the manifestations of the disease. Alcohol addiction has been rare in youths since child labor laws and compulsory schooling removed from the streets young people with time and money on their hands (14). Only in female adolescents have reported recent increases in youthful drinking been verified (15). The aged, a significant and overlooked population among the alcoholics, respond less to counseling and more to environmental manipulation than do younger adults (16). Blacks, Chicanos, and American natives have a high incidence of alcohol problems also associated with cultural–historical factors. Moreover, metabolic differences may distinguish Mongoloid races from Caucasoid peoples (17), but studies on the possibility of different rates of metabolism have yielded mixed results. Striking racial sensitivity in initial drinking intolerance (facial flushing, palpitation, nausea, and giddiness) similar to the effect of the alcohol–antabuse reaction are well known. Experimentally determined differences in enzyme patterns of the Japanese and English now are continuing to be studied at an accelerated pace. Biochemical as well as emotional and cultural differences continue to require our interest in solving the puzzles.

A Profile of Alcoholism

Although the factors reviewed above make differences in treatment approaches and perhaps certain preventive efforts, the core of alcoholism is the individual's potential to develop tolerance to the substance. In the early stages of the disease, large amounts are ingested to produce euphoric feelings. Later on, the same high doses, no longer altering sobriety, result in high blood levels of alcohol, which cause blackouts (periods of amnesia while the individual appears normal to others). That the lethal blood level does not appear to be altered in these circumstances indicates that the adaptation of the central nervous system to alcohol described by the word "tolerance" is not perfect. Tests of performance on divided attention tasks also indicate that tolerance is selective.

Over months or years, the time spent pursuing alcohol and the misjudgment produced by heavy drinking may begin to interfere with business decisions and marital contentment, inevitably reflected in varying degrees in the accumulation of debts, domestic friction, and job imperilment. Unsuccessful restitutive efforts, such as changing jobs or moving to a new community (geographical cure), will be made. For each problem, more alcohol becomes the only solution; Edwards calls this the narrowing of the repertoire of the alcoholic (18). These social symptoms can only retrospectively be assigned to the unmeasurable "loss of control" classically associated with alcoholism. It is the central nervous system adaptation or tolerance which allows sufficient alcohol to be consumed to produce social and personality deterioration and, at the same time, to produce the physical deterioration involved in the development of liver cirrhosis and other alcohol-related diseases. The way the alteration of brain function might fit into the course of alcoholism is demonstrated by Begleiter, who produced abnormal electroencephalograms in mice after they had developed tolerance to alcohol (19). After a period of abstinence had caused the EEG to return to normal, a single drink would again cause reversion to the abnormal pattern, which heretofore had been present only after prolonged exposure. Eventually, in humans, the scene is set for one of the physical disabilities of alcoholism: cirrhosis of the liver, pancreatitis, anemia, gastritis, osteoporosis, alcoholic cardiomyopathy, and other diseases of every organ system. Persuasive evidence has been presented that many of these disorders depend directly on the effect of alcohol on the body; others come with associated vitamin deficiencies. The quantities of alcohol consumed are such as to suggest the necessity for developing tolerance to account for the very excessiveness of the behavior, both in amount and in persistence over time (20).

The alcoholic often appears to be the last to notice the association between his troubles and his drinking. Some when faced with alcohol dependence alone, others with some physical complication, or still others with social difficulties will stop drinking, but, for most, strenuous effort is required to enlist them into treatment. Many devices to encourage treatment are used: first, the advice of a knowledgeable physician; then the knowledge of handling the alcoholic person gained by his (or her) spouse, who may join Al-Anon, the spouse's organization associated with Alcoholics Anonymous (AA); third, labor–management alcoholism programs which use the threat of job loss for declining efficiency to mandate alcoholism treatment; fourth, highway safety programs which tie in a program of information and counseling with a direction toward alcoholism treatment. A fifth way has been provided by the discovery of the fetal alcohol syndrome (21). If pregnant women who are alcoholics are shown the possible harmful effects on their babies should they continue drinking, they can then sometimes be enlisted in a group therapy activity with other women in the same condition. Whereas is has been shown that a few people have moderated their drinking when presented with the problem, a major treatment *goal* must be complete abstinence. Other goals include improvement in work life, interpersonal relationships, and health.

Disulfiram (Antabuse) can be used as a deterrent against the impulse to drink. Alcohol taken while Antabuse is present in the body produces a violent, unpleasant response. Antabuse is contraindicated during pregnancy.

The term conditioned reflex therapy refers more specifically to associating the taking of alcohol with a carefully timed dose of emetine hydrochloride to induce vomiting. This type of procedure is used in a limited way. Enthusiastic participation in the fellowship of AA provides a cornerstone of treatment procedures in the United States.

Psychiatric, Personality, and Behavioral Considerations

No real success has resulted from attempts to discover an alcoholic or prealcoholic personality. Jones followed up children who had attended a mental health clinic (22). Those who were becoming alcoholic in adulthood were compared, for alcoholic or prealcoholic symptoms, with those who did not. There is a certain degree of agreement between her conclusions and those of similar studies by McCord and McCord, Berry, and Vaillant, in which we see the future alcoholic as a more outgoing, gregarious person with a shorter attention span who may depend on others for a sense of self-esteem (23–25). Other characteristics of the alcoholic merge into factors associated with minimal brain dysfunction. Stewart and Morrison investigated individuals having minimal brain dysfunction and found a suggestive correlation between parents with alcoholism and children with minimal brain dysfunction who later became alcoholics (26).

Similarities and Differences in Behaviors in Excess

The repetitive, self-destructive behavior exhibited by gamblers, narcotic addicts, alcoholics, and the obese suggests that a particular kind of person is susceptible to such excesses and chance factors may determine which such pattern is followed. This view may have validity; certainly one cannot out-of-hand call it incorrect. Indeed, the large correlation between alcoholism and excessive cigarette smoking (although not vice versa) and the large incidence of alcoholism in methadone clinics (here we have stong data showing the heroin addict as an alcoholic drinker before his heroin addiction) are factors that must be considered.

A few straws in the wind, though, point toward differences in these different situations. Hill investigated the "familialness" of alcoholism and drug addiction. Using the Weinberg Proband method and a tetrachoric correlation, she found separate heritabilities for alcohol versus heroin (27). An evaluation of the efficiency of combined versus separate treatment programs for alcoholism and/or drug abuse concluded that alcoholism and drug addiction are distinct, and that treatment is not a simple matter of dealing with addiction proneness in general (28). The specific chemical and perhaps also psychological factors that lead to either heavy alcohol or heroin use deserve higher clinical priority.

What Kind of Person Is an Alcoholic?

Two groups of psychiatric diagnostic terms are found along with alcoholism. In the first group "deviance," "sociopathy," "psychopathy," "personality disorder," and "character disorder" are included. In the second group of diagnostic terms "compulsion" and "obsession" are included. Obsessive compulsive states are said to be defenses to ward off deeply repressed impulses, chiefly of aggression and sexuality, which are too strongly associated with guilt to come to the surface. The words surrounding sociopathy are said to involve an *absence* of guilt. Zucker attempts to arrange these on a spectrum in an "opportunity structure of deviance theory" linked to degrees of affectional interaction deficit in families (29).

However, the trend toward descriptive phenomenalism at present makes it unlikely that one overall theory can be invoked with general agreement to explain the variations of personality in the alcoholic. DSM-III clearly rejected the compulsive label for alcoholism, defining compulsive disorders as behaviors that

> are not experienced as the outcome of an individual's own volition but are accompanied by both a sense of subjective compulsion and a desire to resist (at least initially). He (the patient) understands that the compulsive rituals are unnecessary in any realistic sense. He will insist that he doesn't want to give in to them but can't help himself. . . . Activities such as eating, sexual behavior, gambling, or drinking may be engaged in excessively. However, these activities are inherently pleasurable and the individual who engages in them excessively only wants to resist them because of secondary deleterious consequences. Such behaviors are often referred to as compulsive, but they are not, because the behavior is not ego alien (30).

Having brought forth both an hereditary influence, and eliminated by definition an immutable and commanding obsession, we must ask to what extent the choice of a drink is voluntary in the alcoholic. Skinner and his school trace many behaviors to their genesis in response to inescapable contingencies but cannot reduce behavior to such an extent that at the end there is no actor, the individual who makes choices that are more or less affected by outside contingencies (31). Many recovered alcoholics see all but their first drink as involuntary in the sense that the forces acting on them to take the second and subsequent drinks rendered them powerless to stop. Behaviorists argue that this view is self-fulfilling and attempt to prove that it is incorrect by inducing (thus far with minimal success) social drinking in alcoholics. They are denying that all but the first drink are involuntary. Ludwig, however, observed that exteroceptive or interoceptive stimuli mimicking remembered withdrawal symptoms might induce the desire for the first drink as the remembered antidote (32). This would decrease the voluntary aspects of the resolve to abstain, even for the first drink.

Freud postulated that alcoholism is a specific oral neurosis compensating for repressed homosexuality (33), but this is no more accepted today than are other specificity theories, when they attempt to relate an individual conflict to a specific behavior.

The social invention of AA was originally a makeshift pastiche that happened to work and persisted because of the organizational genius of its founder. But the alcoholic patients themselves had pioneered the concept of a disease, which in a new way mixed components of physical and psychiatric illnesses. When society later perceived an alarming threat in drug abuse, adaptations of AA were attempted which produced surprising failures and tragedies. The attempt to generalize treatment among "excessive behaviors" has had variable success. Society may be unready for some measures.

Excessive behavior of any kind might be stopped by force (34). This happens in total institutions. Other methods to control behavior include electric shock, administered in connection with showing pictures of the activity to be discouraged, to brain surgery designed to control excessive aggression, to stimulants for minimal brain dysfunction, and to other psychotropic drugs—all have aroused opposition in the community. The other side of the coin from mechanical methods to induce negative contingencies that inhibit certain behavior is the provision of alternatives, a strategy AA has used and which has gone beyond AA in other adaptations. In addition to strong personal relationships and group solidarity, an important aspect of these approaches is a spiritual side. Some of the more evangelistic of these groups have introduced their term for personal support in the first days as "love-bombing." The stigmatized condition is turned around and used as an asset. The power of group support substitutes for the defense mechanism which has been turned into excessive behavior. Alcoholics Anonymous has performed a strongly successful utilization of these principles. Organizations which have developed with similar goals have not (as in the case of Synanon and of The People's Temple of Guyana) avoided the large potential for abuse in this kind of approach. AA has so far avoided the excesses of its imitators by keeping its spirituality a common-sense one, avoiding an institutionalized charismatic leader, and avoiding cash contributions. The theory that indiscriminate sexual expression will diminsh hostility and aggression is also avoided by AA.

AA and Its Success

The success of AA in developing motivation for the maintenance of continued abstinence is witnessed by the large survey samples conducted by the organization: "The typical alcoholic sober less than one year has a 43% chance of getting through the next year without a drink and remaining in the fellowship. The corresponding number for a member of one to five years is 81% and that for a member of five years is 90%"(35).

For many patients, AA by itself is sufficient. For others, however, diagnostic differention after sobriety is achieved is important. Some alcoholics *are* also sociopaths; others suffer from manic depressive disease and require lithium carbonate; and still others are schizophrenic and should be administered phenothiazines in addition to maintaining their sobriety.

A great number of impulsive alcoholics will respond to disulfiram, which, when taken daily, is without pronounced effects but causes a pronounced toxic reaction shortly after alcohol is added. The offer of disulfiram effectively assesses motivation for abstinence, and therapy with disulfiram has produced positive results. Baekeland and co-workers reviewed the alcoholism treatment literature in 1977 and found seven follow-up studies with satisfactory controls (36). All of these concluded that disulfiram was an effective treatment modality. Costello, Brevier, and Baillargeon surveyed therapy outcome studies and found that disulfiram was used in nearly half the best studies and used aggressively and without ambivalence (37). It was used by only about one-third of the intermediate and good programs and almost never in the poorer programs.

Counseling or psychotherapy has been a constant ingredient in alcoholism programs, since hearing others with similar problems helps individuals recognize their own symptoms. Many varieties of group therapy are used, including psychodrama, transactional analysis, psychosynthesis, gestalt, and reality therapies (38). Both open and closed groups have proponents. More recently, family groups, couples groups, and female consciousness-raising groups have been used. Est reports success in treating alcoholism. Perhaps it will wind up, as Orford and Edwards have claimed, that at least in some hands of evaluation and advice in one visit may do as well as prolonged therapy (39).

There is no question, however, that the newly dry alcoholic has much to work over in his approach to life and interpersonal relationships and that help in resolution of these problems should be useful. Aversive conditioning, used for many years with alcoholics, continues to have its proponents (40). Happily, use of succinyl choline to induce apnea as an aversive stimulus has been abandoned as unnecessarily terrifying and dangerous. Electric shock conditioning is in rare use at present. The induction of nausea and vomiting that occur when alcohol is ingested after administration of emetine hydrochloride has been used successfully at Shadel sanatoria in Washington and other states. In recent times, AA programs have been added to this treatment. The termination of the manufacture of emetine may discourage this type of approach in the future.

Experimental psychologists have gone a step further in their search for new experimental models for alcoholism (41). Taking the stand that alcoholism is not a disease but a learning phenomenon, they have attempted to teach alcoholics to drink in moderation. In part, they instruct the individual to evaluate his or her blood alcohol level (alcohol discrimination training). Further, the person is taught how to refuse a drink, how to sip, to pace drinks, and to stop after one or two. In some such clinics, the drinking practice session is observed through a one-way screen, and inappropriate behavior (i.e., gulping drinks) is punished with an electric shock.

Although many have attempted this method of therapy and some clients have achieved moderate drinking for periods of time, thus far most treatment centers as well as clients have reached a consensus that the goal should be abstinence. Ewing attempted to control drinking by various means in volunteer active alcoholics (42). At 56 weeks, all had either opted for abstinence or had returned to uncontrolled drinking. And colleagues who used a paradigm of fixed interval drinking decisions in which patients were offered drinks in a hospital on an hourly basis found that those who refused all drinks not only remained sober after hospitalization but also showed more improvement in other aspects of their lives (43). The figures presented by Armor, Polich, and Stambul (44) in their study of alcoholism and treatment found but did not discuss the fact that the controlled drinking outcome was the least stable of all outcomes (45).

Finally, I shall mention detoxification, the initial treatment step. Many medications are cross-tolerant with alcohol and can help suppress temporarily the signs of alcohol withdrawal. Benzodioxepenes are the most popular these days because of their low toxicity. An alcoholic patient must be evaluated to determine his need for hospitalization, for temporary medication, and for other adjunctive treatment. Anyone hospitalized and given cross-tolerant medication should be drug-free well before discharge (at least 48 hours). In mild cases, sobering-up stations can be used, provided swift and guaranteed hospital backup is available for the patient. A guided withdrawal can be the first step toward a productive rehabilitative stay (46).

Labor–management programs (those set up jointly by the union and the management), programs for the drinking driver, and programs for pregnant women who are drinking utilize a threat to aspects of the person's life with which the alcoholic does not ordinarily associate drinking effects and have an increased chance of enlisting his or her aid in overcoming denial and starting treatment. Such programs use a kind of aversive conditioning since fear (of job loss, auto crashes, or birth defect) is an averse stimulus. This is behavior control and psychological conditioning, but these techniques may have a place, especially if they save a life, a family, or a job (47).

Conclusions

Alcoholism *in itself* is not a psychopathic disease. Any psychiatric diagnosis can coexist with alcoholism. Alcoholism is dependence on a psychoactive compound: ethanol. There is a strong hereditary predisposition. A good reason for characterizing alcoholism as a disease is that the same pharmacological quality responsible for many of its behavioral symptoms, the development of tolerance, also underlies the multiple organ damage that ensues over the long term.

Treatment for many excessive behaviors aims toward moderation. However, this approach has not proven effective in the rehabilitation of alcoholism. In the treatment of this disease, abstinence from alcohol is not only the goal but the rule for life.

References

1. Cannon, W. B., *The Wisdom of the Body,* Norton, New York, 1932.
2. Gordon, B. L., *Current Medical Information and Terminology,* 4th ed., American Medical Association, Chicago, 1971.
3. Rush, B., *Medical Inquiries & Observations on the Diseases of the Mind,* facs. ed., Hafner, New York, 1962.
4. Trotter, T., Medical, philosophical, and chemical aspects of drunkenness, thesis, University of Edinburgh, 1788.
5. Cahalan, D., Cisin, I., Crossley, H., *American Drinking Practices,* Rutgers Center of Alcohol Studies, New Brunswick, 1969.
6. Parsons, T., *The Social Structure,* Free Press, New York, 1964.
7. Horn, J. L., Wanberg, K. W., and Adams, G., Diagnosis of alcoholism: factors of drinking, background, and current conditions in alcoholics, *Q. J. Stud. Alc.,* *35,* 147–175 (1974).

8. Schuckit, M., and Morrissey, A., Alcoholism in women: some clinical and social perspectives, in *Alcohol Problems in Women and Children*, M. Schuckit and M. Rosenblatt, eds., Grune & Stratton, New York, 1976, pp. 5-31.

9. Room, R., personal communication, 1977.

10. Seixas, F. A., Blume, S., Lieber, C. S., and Simpson, R. K., Definition of alcoholism, *Ann. Int. Med., 85* (1976).

11. Seixas, F. A., Omenn, G. S., Burk, E. D., and Eggleston, S., Nature and nurture in alcoholism, *Ann. N. Y. Acad. Sci. 19*, 6 (1972).

12. Goodwin, D., *Is Alcoholism Hereditary?* Oxford University Press, New York, 1976.

13. McAndrew, C., and Edgerton, R. B., *Drunken Comportment: A Social Explanation*, Aldine, Chicago, 1969.

14. Keller, M., unpublished communication, 1978.

15. Youcha, G. A., *Alcohol: A Dangerous Pleasure*, Hawthorn, New York, 1978.

16. Seixas, F. A., Alcoholism in the elderly, *Alc.: Clin. and Exp. Res., 2*, 15-42 (1978).

17. Seixas, F. A., Racial differences in alcohol metabolism: facts and their interpretations, *Alc.: Clin. and Exp. Res., 2*, 59-92 (1978).

18. Edwards, G., and Gross, M. M., Alcohol dependence: provisional description of a clinical syndrome, *Brit. Med. J., 1*, 1058-1061 (1976).

19. Begleiter, H. H., Porjesz, B., and Youdin, R., Protracted brain hyperexcitability after withdrawal from alcohol in rats, *Alc.: Clin. and Exp. Res., 2*, 192 (1978) (abstract).

20. Seixas, F. A., Williams, K., and Eggleston, S., Medical consequences of alcoholism, *Ann. N.Y. Acad. Sci., 2*, 252 (1975).

21. Seixas, F. A., The fetal alcohol syndrome in the year of the child, *Toxicomanies, 12*, 319-329 (1979).

22. Jones, M. C., Personality antecedents and correlates of drinking patterns in women, *J. Consult. Clin. Psych., 36*, 61-69 (1971).

23. McCord, W., and McCord, J., *Origins of Alcoholism*, Stanford University Press, Stanford, 1960.

24. Berry, R., Antecedents of schizophrenia, impulsive character, and alcoholism in males, *Diss. Abstr. 28*, B2134 (1967).

25. Vaillant, G., *Adaptations to Life*, Harvard University Press, Cambridge, 1978.

26. Morrison, J., and Stewart, M., A family study of the hyperactive child syndrome, *Biol. Psychiat., 3*, 189-195 (1971).

27. Hill, S. Y., Independent familial transmission of alcoholism and drug abuse, *Alc.: Clin. and Exp. Res., 1*, 335-342 (1977).

28. Baker, S. L., Lorei, T., McKnight, H. A., Jr., and Duvall, J. L., The veterans administration's comparison study: alcoholism and drug abuse combined and conventional treatment settings, *Alc.: Clin. and Exp. Res., 1*, 285-291 (1977).

29. Zucker, R. A., Parental influences on the drinking patterns of their children, in *Alcohol Problems in Women and Children*, M. Schuckit and M. Rosenblatt, eds., Grune & Stratton, New York, 1976.

30. American Psychiatric Association Task Force on Nomenclature and Statistics, *Diagnostic and Statistical Manual of Mental Disorders,* 3d ed., American Psychiatric Association, Washington, D. C., 1980.

31. Skinner, B. F., *Beyond Freedom and Dignity,* Knopf, New York, 1971.

32. Ludwig, A. M., On and off the wagon: reasons for drinking and abstaining by alcoholics, *Q. J. Stud. Alc., 23,* 91–96 (1972).

33. Freud, S. *Collected Papers.* Hogarth Press, London, 1925, *4,* 203–216.

34. Rothman, D. J., Behavior modification in total institutions, *Hastings Center Rep., 5,* 17–24 (1975).

35. Norris, J. L., Analysis of the 1977 survey of the membership of A. A., paper presented to the 32d international congress on alcoholism and drug dependence, Warsaw, 1978.

36. Baekeland, F., Lundwall, L., and Kissin, B., Methods for the treatment of chronic alcoholism: a critical appraisal in *Research Advances in Alcohol and Drug Problems,* R. J. Gibbins, Y. Israel, H. Kalant, R. E. Popham, W. Schmidt, and R. G. Smart, eds., Wiley, New York, 1975, *2,* pp. 247–327.

37. Costello, R. M., Brevier, P., and Baillargeon, J. G., Alcoholism treatment programming: historical trends and modern approaches, *Alc.: Clin. and Exp. Res., 1,* 311–318 (1977).

38. Seixas, F. A., The person with alcoholism, *Ann. N.Y. Acad. Sci., 233,* 5–12 (1974).

39. Orford, J., and Edwards, G., *Alcoholism,* Oxford University Press, New York, 1977.

40. Franks, C. M., Behavior modification and the treatment of alcoholics, in *Alcoholism: Behavioral Research and Therapeutic Approaches,* R. Fox, ed., Springer, New York, 1967, pp. 196–201.

41. Pattison, E. M., Sobell, M. B., and Sobell, L. C., *Emerging Concepts of Alcohol Dependence,* Springer, New York, 1977.

42. Ewing, J. A., Some recent attempts to inculcate controlled drinking in patients resistant to Alcoholics Anonymous, *Ann. N.Y. Acad. Sci., 233,* 147–154 (1974).

43. Gottheil, E., Alterman, A. I., and Thornton, C. C., Variations in patterns of drinking of alcoholics in a drinking-decisions program, in *Currents in Alcoholism,* vol. 4, F. A. Seixas, ed., Grune & Stratton, New York, 1978, pp. 153–178.

44. Armor, D. J., Polich, J. M., Stambul, H. G., *Alcoholism and Treatment,* Wiley, New York, 1978.

45. Seixas, F. A., editorial, *Alc.: Clin. and Exp. Res., 1,* 281–283 (1977).

46. Seixas, F. A., ed., *Treatment of the Alcohol Withdrawal Syndrome,* National Council on Alcoholism, New York, 1971.

47. Seixas, F. A., Moving people into treatment for alcoholism, Proceedings of international symposium on prevention and research on alcoholism, Bloemendaal, 1980, 105–110.

6

Marijuana

Reese T. Jones

Defining Excessive Marijuana Use

Any definition of the level of marijuana use that should be considered excessive behavior will be disputed. Such is the case with many drugs used in nonmedical situations. Some claim use of marijuana at even low doses is potentially harmful (1, 2). Others as passionately argue that marijuana is a remarkable psychoactive drug: its effects even at high and frequent doses do not appear to be harmful to the user (3, 4). Proponents claim that legal controls are more harmful than the drug (5, 6). The nature of the value judgments made in this area is indicated by the recurring statements from senior scientists that the risks of chronic marijuana smoking are no greater than those associated with tobacco use (3, 4). If such optimistic (or pessimistic) judgments turn out to be true, the $25.9 billion cost and the 300,000 premature deaths annually attributed to tobacco smoking may give some idea of the potential price of excessive marijuana smoking (7).

Attempts have been made operationally to define excessive marijuana use. In the most recent edition of the American Psychiatric Association *Diagnostic and Statistical Manual* (DSM-III), used by psychiatrists in the United States, cannabis abuse was defined thus:

1. A pattern of use where intoxication is maintained throughout the day with use nearly every day for at least one month.
2. Continued patterns of use despite episodes of cannabis related delusional disorders.
3. Impairment of social or occupational functioning, including loss of interest in activities previously engaged in, loss of friends, repeated absence from work, loss of job.
4. Legal difficulties associated with cannabis use other than related to laws concerned with possession (8).

A related aspect of cannabis use, termed "cannabis dependence" in DSM-III, includes difficulty reducing or stopping use, repeated unsuccessful ef-

132

forts to control use, periods of temporary abstinence or restriction of use, intoxication throughout the day, use of cannabis nearly every day for at least a month, two or more episodes of cannabis related delusional disorders, and impairment in general functioning. A further element in the diagnosis of dependence is tolerance, or the need to use increasing doses of cannabis to achieve desired effects.

The DSM-III criteria for cannabis abuse and dependence represent the consensus of professionals who have had experience with cannabis users. As with other psychoactive drugs, satisfactory statistical data predicting consequences from a given pattern of use are lacking. The diagnostic criteria in DSM-III are based more on clinical experience and judgment than on hard numerical data as to consequences.

A recent and important attempt to arrive at objective criteria for marijuana abuse was a study of 97 chronic users evaluated over a five-year period (9). Marijuana abuse was operationally defined by behavioral criteria analogous to those used in diagnosing alcoholism. The majority of chronic marijuana users (91 percent) did not appear to have serious complications, either behavioral or physiologic, from their cannabis use. However, 9 percent of the group had persistent behavioral problems apparently produced by marijuana use: abusers were frequently involved in fights while intoxicated, more frequently received traffic tickets while intoxicated, and had more episodes of mental disturbance during intoxication. The abusing subgroup began using marijuana more frequently at an earlier age, used greater amounts than the majority of users, and tended to drink more alcohol than did the group defined as nonabusers. The abusers reported more health problems, more panic reactions or delirious episodes, and greater use of marijuana during morning hours. Although half of the abuser subjects thought their overall health had deteriorated because of marijuana use, none had specific medical complaints. The authors were appropriately cautious in drawing conclusions because of the relatively small sample. However, they pointed out that by employing objective criteria one could separate out a group of marijuana users with behavioral problems similar to those occurring in alcoholism. Worthy of note, the majority of the chronic users in the study took the drug without incident.

Why a Simple Definition of Excessive Behavior Is Unlikely

Because of the lack of good, controlled studies on long-term consequences, it is inappropriate to attempt a rigid definition of excessive marijuana use in a North American culture. The definitions in DSM-III and in the Weller–Hallikas study are only tentative (8, 9). Whatever the definition, it will have to be revised as experience accumulates, as has been the case with tobacco, alcohol, opiates, and many other drugs, both therapeutic and illicit.

In order properly to define excessive marijuana use, one needs to understand the health implications at various dose levels, over different periods of time, and with different frequencies of use. Clinical reports and observations from throughout the world suggest that frequent use of high potency cannabis can be associated with impaired pulmonary function and lung damage, abnormalities in reproductive and endocrine function, and impaired behavior, mental state, and brain function. Some of these effects have appeared in animal experiments, where dose and other variables can be controlled. However, animal data only indicate that similar phenomena are *possible* in human cannabis users, not that they will *necessarily* occur in a predictable way at a particular dose.

The level of use needed to produce health problems, the frequency with which they will occur, and the percentage of users who are at risk are disputed issues in regard to alcohol and tobacco use despite sophisticated and large-scale epidemiologic studies. Similar studies need to be carried out on large groups of marijuana users, with measurements made before, during, and after many years of regular use. Even after these data are available, uncertainty regarding individual risk undoubtedly will continue (10). However, marijuana related health and behavioral problems are likely to have the same pattern of low incidence in the general populaton of cannabis users as is the case with alcohol and tobacco related problems.

The research literature on marijuana has grown enormously over the past decade. Over 5,000 articles in the world literature discuss marijuana, with about 1,200 dealing with health effects. Still, much is unknown. Most articles only indicate what is possible, not what necessarily or predictably happens at any given level of marijuana use. Experimental data come largely from studies of highly selected young, healthy, adult males. Almost no human research has been done with females, adolescents, or people who are in some respect abnormal, say, suffering from diseases of the heart, lung, brain, or liver. With most drugs, however, such special populations are at greatest risk for adverse health consequences.

Sometimes it appears that greater proof of harm is demanded for marijuana than for other commonly used drugs. Conclusive *experimental proof* of many commonly accepted drug effects is unusual. For example, there is no completely accepted experimental proof in humans that alcohol causes cirrhosis or that tobacco causes lung cancer, though the associations seem clear to most observers looking at clinical and statistical data. Such important but relatively infrequent consequences of drug use like lung cancer in cigarette smokers and cirrhosis in alcoholics would not be apparent in small-scale studies such as have been done with cannabis users in Jamaica, Costa Rica, and other countries (3, 4). Thus, the absence of obvious adverse health consequences can be only marginally reassuring.

Patterns of Marijuana Use:
Is There Evidence of Abuse?

Much of what we know regarding incidence of marijuana use in the United States comes from questionnaire surveys of users asking about patterns of drug consumption. Marijuana appears to be an adolescent's and young adult's drug. Frequency of marijuana use reaches a peak in the 18–21-year age group. People in their late teens and early twenties are more likely to use marijuana than either younger or older persons (11). Most marijuana users begin between the ages of 14 and 18. The proportion of 12 or 13 year olds who have tried marijuana remains small (about 8 percent in 1977). A similarly small fraction of Americans over 35 years of age report having used marijuana at some time (about 7 percent in 1977). In contrast, the majority of people in the 18–25 age range report having used marijuana on some occasion (about 60 percent in 1977). Recent high school graduates have had more experience with marijuana than any other group in American history (11, 12).

Six out of every 10 high school seniors have tried marijuana. Over a third of the group that has tried marijuana reported using it in the month before the 1979 survey (12). Ten percent of the seniors who use marijuana reported using it on a daily or near daily basis. A majority of daily users reported smoking between one and six marijuana cigarettes per day, with a daily average of three and a half cigarettes. Assuming at least two hours of measurable intoxication following a marijuana cigarette—measurable by changes in both mental and physiologic functioning—the students are, on average, intoxicated by marijuana for six to eight hours a day. Some daily users (13 percent) reported smoking more than seven marijuana cigarettes per day. Most prudent individuals (relying more on common sense than on scientific data) might conclude that such behavior is excessive in high school students. However, there are no scientific data that cannot be challenged on one basis or another that would suggest such patterns of use are necessarily harmful.

Over the past few years daily or near daily marijuana use apparently has been leveling off. The reasons are unclear. Increased awareness of potential hazards may be a factor. Perhaps, too, at such levels of use most high school students cannot increase intake and still remain in the sampled population. The 1979 survey found a greater proportion of high school seniors who disapproved of regular marijuana use than did preceding surveys.

Other than for high school students, there are not good statistics regarding the number of marijuana cigarettes smoked per day or the contexts in which marijuana is used. The possible consequences of marijuana intoxication are different when driving or studying or sitting quietly before a television or stereo. To draw any conclusion about effects that might signal behavior in excess requires such data. They are not available. Unqualified claims like 43 million Americans have tried marijuana and 16 million are currently using can be very misleading when trying to interpret the presence or absence of certain consequences. It seems, however, that serious adverse effects are not associated with simply trying marijuana.

The Drug Cannabis: What Is an Excessive Dose?

To define excessive marijuana use, we must understand the chemistry of the drug. With marijuana this is another complex and uncertain area. Marijuana is one form of cannabis. The leaves and other small parts of the cannabis plant usually are dried, chopped up, and smoked in a pipe or cigarette. Hashish is the dried resinous exudate contained mostly on the flowering tops of the plant; it tends to contain more of the psychoactive resin than does the leaf.

For centuries cannabis has been cultivated throughout the world because of its fiber, oil, and resin. Like all other plants, cannabis is a complicated mixture of chemicals. Over 400 have been identified. About 50 or 60 are known as "cannabinoids" and are found only in this plant. One cannabinoid, delta-9-tetrahydrocannabinol (THC), accounts for most of the psychoactive and physiological effects of smoked marijuana.

One problem in specifying the effects of a given dose of marijuana or hashish is the tremendous range of THC content. Marijuana has from zero to 5 or 6 percent THC. Hashish may contain 12–15 percent, though some samples contain less than does marijuana. Crude extract of hashish, hashish oil, often available on the illicit market, may have up to 60 percent THC. Thus, the smoker of a marijuana cigarette may obtain a few milligrams of THC or 50–60 mg. Therefore, with cannabis determining dosage other than in numbers of cigarettes each day, week, or some other unit of time is difficult, and number of cigarettes is an inadequate criterion for precise research: low potency marijuana might entail a different set of experiences and consequences from that of high potency cannabis.

As users become dependent on a drug and seek higher doses, the marketplace may show increased demand for more potent material. However, systematic information on the quality of marijuana sold illicitly is not available. Scattered assays suggest the potency of marijuana being sold has increased markedly over the past several years. Dose and potency are relevant in defining excessive behavior (8).

Over the 1970s the THC content of the average illicit sample increased twentyfold (to about 2 percent). During this period greater numbers of users smoked greater numbers of cigarettes with no evidence of a decrease in the average size or weight of a marijuana cigarette (about a gram). Much marijuana on the illicit market, often of Colombian or Far

Eastern origin, now averages over 4 percent THC. Samples of hashish oil average 28 percent THC. If the increase in potency of marijuana seemed to be paralleled by decreased consumption (in terms of either frequency or total amount smoked), there would be less cause for concern. However, a pattern of increased drug potency suggests that a subgroup of marijuana users is ingesting increasing doses. This would be consistent with a population of marijuana users who might be considered dependent under various definitions (8, 9).

The complexity of the chemical analytic problem not only limits studies of the fate of THC and its metabolites in the body but also makes for uncertainty as to the relationship between marijuana use and various adverse consequences. THC is rapidly changed, mostly in the liver, to at least 20 metabolites (13). The measurement of THC concentrations in body fluids is complicated; measurement of metabolites is even more complex. Thus, there is not good information as to the amount of THC or other cannabinoids in accident victims, dead people, or unconscious people arriving in an emergency room.

Even if measurements were precise, the relationship between blood levels of THC and effects is more complicated than with alcohol. Blood levels of alcohol give a good indication of brain levels; however, blood levels of THC predict very little about brain or other organ levels (14). THC is rapidly removed from the blood and then more slowly metabolized; THC metabolites remain in the body in measurable amounts for 50–60 hours after a single dose. The relatively simple relationships between blood levels and effects, as is seen with alcohol, are not likely with THC.

Nahas and Paton speculated about the health consequences of the retained THC metabolites (15). Long retention of a drug in the body does not necessarily mean toxicity. However, if a substance is biologically active, even at a very low level, then long presence in the body increases the risk of cumulative toxicity even in users who take a dose only every few days. We have some understanding of the many effects of THC itself; these are described in sections that follow. Very little or no information is available on the in vivo effects of THC metabolites (15). After smoking a cigarette, the THC disappears rapidly with about half of the dose ingested disappearing in a matter of minutes. The metabolites remain for days.

The amount of THC absorbed—and thus its effects—depends on route of administraton. Absorption and transport to the brain via smoking take less than 30 seconds. Effects appear as rapidly. If the same THC dose is administered orally, most of it is eventually absorbed but in erratic fashion, taking as long as two or three hours for peak effects and lasting up to four to six hours after a single dose. Estimates vary, but the peak effects of THC are about three or four times greater by smoking than by oral ingestion (2). In the United States most marijuana is smoked; therefore, experience with cannabis in countries where it has been used for centuries but in high oral doses may not be relevant to the current American scene.

Behavioral and Mental Effects

The smoking of low to moderate doses of marijuana (about 20 mg THC or less) generally produces a subjective sense of well-being, often described in an imprecise way as euphoria, with relaxation, drowsiness, mild perceptual changes, an altered sense of time and distance, impaired memory of recent experiences, and impaired physical coordination, particularly in complex perceptual motor tasks. This mild level of intoxication lasts up to two or three hours after a single cigarette. For most smokers, an occasional period of mild intoxication is probably no more behaviorally or psychologically hazardous than would be the effects of a few bottles of beer or a few glasses of wine unless the intoxicated person attempted to drive an automobile, fly an airplane, engage in complicated intellectual or perceptual motor tasks, etc.

Here arises the problem of deciding when a given behavior, e.g., using cannabis, is harmful to the individual or to people around him or her. Such a decision necessarily is relative. The magnitude of the behavioral toxicity of a marijuana cigarette—the changes in reaction time, thinking, and perception—is determined by dose, setting, past experience, and demands of the situation, so that a rather predictable effect from a given dose might be considered either enjoyable or unpleasant, depending on the situation, the observer, and the user's and the observer's value systems.

In susceptible individuals significant behavioral toxicity can follow the ingestion of sometimes surprisingly small amounts of cannabis. Adverse mental reactions range from mild anxiety states to frank panic and paranoid delusions. The extreme is an acute toxic psychosis similar to that produced by a variety of psychoactive drugs (16, 17). Detachment from reality, delusions, illusions, occasionally hallucinations, and a variety of bizarre behaviors are possible (18). Such reactions rarely come to the attention of medical practitioners, but surveys of drug users suggest that mild versions of these reactions happen at least once in more than half of regular users (9). Adverse reactions occur more frequently in individuals suffering from stress or a psychiatric disorder such as schizophrenia. Their occurrence in seemingly normal users is more likely after more than the usual or expected THC dose is ingested. Most acute toxic reactions require no specific treatment and clear completely in hours or a day or so.

The relationship between such reactions and schizophrenia becomes clearer as more case reports are published (19). Patients with schizophrenia, or perhaps even patients who have a genotype for schizophrenia, seem more prone to develop acute schizophreniclike psychoses after consuming modest amounts of cannabis. The clinical signs and symptoms resemble those of schizophrenia, and the usual treatments for schizophrenia appear effective. Thus, it should not be surprising that there is uncertainty as to whether older case reports are discussing schizophrenia, cannabis induced psychosis, or some interaction between drug and disease

(17). Since schizophrenia is not that rare, the vulnerability of schizophrenics to adverse cannabis reactions has obvious health implications.

The descriptions of longer lasting cannabis induced psychoses appear largely in the Eastern and Middle Eastern medical literature and thus are drawn from cultures where cannabis is used both much more frequently and at higher dosages than in the United States (16, 17, 20). These psychoses can last one to six weeks or longer. Compared to schizophrenics, patients suffering from a cannabis psychosis show more bizarre behavior, more violence and panic, and a relative absence of schizophreniclike thought disorder. Patients relapse when they begin cannabis use again.

As is often the case with clinical reports, most studies describing cannabis psychoses rarely present data that would withstand rigorous scientific scrutiny. On the other hand, the reports suggesting no links between cannabis use and psychosis have the same methodological problems as studies claiming an association, making it very difficult to draw firm, unequivocal conclusions (5, 17). The studies of chronic marijuana users in Jamaica, Greece, and Costa Rica, often cited as not documenting such psychoses, looked at rather small and select samples so that the relatively rare occurrence of a lasting psychosis could have been missed (2).

Amotivation

An issue of more controversy is what has been termed the "amotivation syndrome." A pattern of apathy, lack of concern for the future, and loss of motivation persisting beyond the period of obvious intoxication has been described in some frequent marijuana users. The symptoms usually disappear over a period of weeks or months when regular use is discontinued but recur if drug use is started again. Some observers have expressed concern about a greater likelihood of such reactions in young marijuana users because of special sensitivity in that group. Others observe that the symptoms of amotivation are common in non–drug using adolescents or predate drug use. Many concerned people think that use of any psychoactive drug by adolescents is unwise and advance vague notions to support their position. Unfortunately, firm data on amotivation do not exist.

It appears that people most heavily dependent on alcohol or tobacco tend to have started drug use at an earlier age than other users. Thus, concern about the ultimate adverse effects of regular marijuana use on adolescents might have some basis if the experience with alcohol and tobacco can be generalized.

Impaired Learning and Memory

Experimental evidence from many animal studies suggests that long-term exposure to cannabis in doses equivalent to those consumed by habitual human users produces long-lasting impairment in learning and brain function and perhaps even cellular changes that persist for months after periods of chronic intoxication (21-23). Such findings are consistent with clinical observations in humans: immediate memory and intellectual performance associated with thinking, reading comprehension, and verbal and arithmetic problem solving are impaired during cannabis intoxication (1, 2, 24). Some long-term users also have reported lasting impairment (25).

Is Brain Damage Likely?

A study done in England reporting enlarged brain ventricles, consistent with the presence of cerebral atrophy, in a group of 10 young marijuana users stands alone as indicating anatomical brain changes in human marijuana users (26). Subsequent studies done in Missouri and Boston examined equally small groups of marijuana users and nonusers for evidence of brain atrophy (27, 28). Using computerized transaxial tomography, a relatively new brain scanning technique for visualizing brain anatomy, these more recent studies found no evidence for such changes in the marijuana smokers. The results from all three studies perhaps have received more attention in the popular press than they deserve.

The reports of normal brain size are reassuring in that they demonstrate that it is possible regularly to consume fairly large amounts of marijuana without obvious evidence of cerebral atrophy, as measured by CAT scans. However, the results underline one of the recurring problems in interpreting and reporting many marijuana effects. The English study used a measurement technique (pneumoencephalography) different from tomography. More important, this study used a population of marijuana users who were neurologically impaired or had neurological symptoms. In the studies finding no evidence of brain damage, subjects were preselected so as to represent healthy, normal marijuana users with no neurological complaints. It is possible that a population of abnormal, neurologically impaired marijuana users might show evidence of brain abnormality and a group of healthy and normal marijuana users would not show brain abnormalities. For example, it is possible to demonstrate organic brain toxicity from chronic alcohol use or not demonstrate it, depending on what sample of alcohol users is selected.

The sampling, or selection, process used by researchers is a general problem that confounds interpretation of many studies of chronic cannabis users. For example, the population of research subjects who finally appear in a laboratory may represent a subgroup relatively resistant to psychoactive drugs such as marijuana. None of the studies just mentioned either confirmed or totally ruled out the possibility that subtle changes in brain function may follow marijuana smoking. With many psychoactive drugs, severe impairment of brain function at a neurochemical level is not apparent from gross examination, microscopic examination, or any physical testing of brain tissue. Certainly, any dispassionate observer of marijuana intoxication would have to consider the signs and symptoms as evidence of impaired brain function lasting at least a few hours. Whether one considers this state as evidence of brain dysfunction or brain damage (albeit temporary) may be a matter of semantics only.

Physiological Consequences

Pulmonary Issues

Researchers widely agree that the smoking of marijuana, as with the inhalation of almost any substance, if done long enough and frequently enough will produce undesirable changes in lung function (29, 30). Marijuana smoke, although different from tobacco smoke in the sense of containing no nicotine, does contain a similar complex aerosol of tiny particles in a vapor phase that form what is commonly called tar. By weight, cannabis contains more tar than most tobacco. As with tobacco, marijuana tar includes literally thousands of substances, including the same variety of hydrocarbons that are suspected in tobacco tar to be associated with cancer causation. Simple equations specifying how many cannabis cigarettes equal how many tobacco cigarettes in regard to tar are misleading, no matter what the figures, since patterns of smoking cannabis and tobacco are so different and THC and the other cannabinoids have such different effects on the body from those of nicotine and its metabolites. The most conservative conclusion would be that with enough exposure as to both dose and duration one might expect very similar consequences from marijuana and tobacco smoking.

Certainly, long-term, frequent smoking of cannabis is associated with the same array of chronic respiratory symptoms as is tobacco smoking (31). These include sore throat, runny nose, and cough. In one study, bronchial biopsies taken from young heavy smokers of hashish and tobacco showed precancerous cellular changes of the sort that are not usually seen in smokers of tobacco only under the age of 40 (31). One confounding factor in any such research is that heavy cannabis users tend to be heavy tobacco smokers, too.

Cardiovascular Effects

Although the cardiovascular effects of marijuana smoking are among its most prominent and predictable (increased heart rate, decreased standing blood pressure, and increased supine blood pressure), these changes so far seem to be of little consequence in normal volunteer subjects. However, cardiovascular effects pose a problem in predicting chronic from acute effects. After long-term administration of cannabis, the patient shows a decrease in heart rate and a persistent mild lowering of blood pressure because of nervous system and cardiovascular adaptive changes. While these adjustments in themselves do not appear to have biological or functional significance, years of exposure may produce major consequences.

Lessons learned from chronic tobacco use are worth considering. Only after many years of use by millions of people was the increased potential for cardiovascular disease associated with tobacco smoking recognized. Even now the exact mechanisms for tobacco induced changes represent a topic of scientific debate. Cannabis smoking is similar to the smoking of tobacco in many respects, but THC has more marked effects on the cardiovascular system than does nicotine. As with nicotine, however, the long-term THC effects may be different from the easier to study and, in healthy individuals, relatively minor acute effects on the cardiovascular system. The chronic effects could turn out to be beneficial or harmful.

The health significance of tobacco-related pulmonary and cardiovascular effects was in dispute for years. They even now remain a topic of dispute by some scientists. One might anticipate a long period of observation of a sizable group of chronic cannabis smokers to establish the health implications of the pulmonary and cardiovascular changes. In the United States most cannabis users do not have the high level of drug exposure as is the case with tobacco, thus perhaps making for a longer period of incubation before the pathology becomes clinically apparent. The increased levels of marijuana smoking by very young people might provide the necessary 20 to 30 years of exposure needed to make an informed guess.

Endocrine and Reproductive System Effects

Animal studies and in vitro studies suggest that THC and other cannabinoids can interfere with sex hormones and reproduction in a variety of ways (2, 15). Although occasional use of marijuana does not appear to affect sexual function and may even enhance certain aspects of sexuality because of the time altering and disinhibiting aspects of intoxication, frequent users report decreased sexual drive and activity. In animals, chronic cannabis administration decreases blood levels of testosterone, produces cellular changes in the testes, and slows down, or makes for abnormal, sperm production. THC seems to act directly on the testes as well as indirectly by affecting hormone release in the hypothalamus. In female animals, THC suppresses ovulation by interfering with pituitary hormone release.

The reports of endocrine effects in humans are inconclusive. Some investigators have found small decreases in testosterone level in some male users (32). Since virtually no cannabis research has been done with women, there are no laboratory data; however, tentative evidence suggests decreased regularity of ovulation in female users of marijuana. In this area data from other countries are nonexistent: in cultures that have heavy cannabis use, females rarely take the drug.

In a few studies the chromosomes in the blood cells of cannabis users have shown abnormalities. However, this is a common finding in young people drawn from similar populations and thus may reflect general lifestyle rather than drug use. In any case, chromosome damage in blood cells has *never* been shown to indicate genetic damage or been associated with abnormal offspring.

With marijuana as with other psychoactive drugs, the definition of excessive behavior may be determined partially by the sex of the user. Any drug taking during pregnancy may eventually be considered excessive. The data from animal studies would suggest this is the most prudent position to maintain with cannabis use. Cannabis effects include an increased number of early fetal deaths, decreased birth weight, and increased perinatal mortality in the offspring of animals exposed to cannabis smoke during pregnancy. Of course, these findings may just as well implicate non–THC related factors—for example, carbon monoxide—though a similar pattern was found in animals given oral THC.

Immune System Effects

Much has been made of THC and marijuana effects on the systems controlling immune reactions in humans (15). Theoretically, the biological consequences of such effects could include increased susceptibility to infection and increased risk of cancer. The biological importance of these in vitro effects is unclear, but there is little doubt that the effects do occur and the findings cannot be dismissed as irrelevant. No one has yet noted increased frequency of cancer in countries where marijuana use is more established than in the United States; however, until recently the average lifespan in these countries was such that if there were an increased incidence of cancer with a long lag period, this trend might well have been missed in cannabis users. As with many reported cannabis effects, long-term epidemiologic studies are necessary.

Tolerance and Dependence

Tolerance and dependence are phenomena often associated with drug abuse (8). Tolerance, that is, a diminished response to a repeated dose, is clearly found with some effects of cannabis (33). For example, increasing doses must be given to obtain the same intensity of subjective effects and the same increase in heart rate that are observed initially with smaller doses; however, the conjunctival blood vessel dilation does not show a tolerance effect. The magnitude of the tolerance and the rapidity with which it develops depend on the amount and frequency of the repeated dose, as with any other drug (34). The more frequent and the higher the dose, the more rapidly tolerance develops. Even research subjects smoking as little as one marijuana cigarette per day in a laboratory demonstrate some tolerance on certain behavioral and physiologic measures. Most of the tolerance seems to be lost rapidly, but the rate of loss may vary with the sensitivity of the measure.

In recent years there has been much discussion of "reverse tolerance," or increased sensitivity to the psychological effects of marijuana. This term is probably a misnomer in the sense of evoking the phenomenon of tolerance. The most simple explanation for reverse tolerance is that with low doses of weak cannabis many of the psychological effects are so subtle that it takes experience to recognize them; thus, consumers of this type of marijuana seem to become increasingly sensitive to small effects. Such a phenomenon has not been documented in any experimental studies and seems less apparent now that high potency marijuana is widely available in the illicit marketplace.

Physical Dependence

With many drugs the appearance of withdrawal signs and symptoms following discontinuation of regular drug use is often associated with the existence of tolerance. Some have speculated that both tolerance and withdrawal symptoms reflect common underlying mechanisms of the body's adaptation to a drug's presence (34). It would be unusual for a relatively short acting drug that produces the marked tolerance associated with marijuana not to be linked to a withdrawal syndrome after drug administration stops. In both clinical and laboratory situations where the marijuana or THC dose and dose schedule were such that a sustained level of THC was maintained in the body, a set of signs and symptoms predictably appeared when drug use stopped (35). Within a few hours after the last dose of cannabis or THC, patients showed irritability, restlessness, decreased appetite, sleep disturbance, sweating, tremor, nausea, and occasional vomiting and diarrhea. These symptoms were reversed by small doses of marijuana and by other sedatives, including alcohol. The duration and magnitude of the withdrawal symptoms depended on the dose of THC and the duration of intoxication prior to the stopping of drug use. In experimental subjects who had smoked as few as five marijuana cigarettes per

day over a 64-day period, there was measurable restlessness, sleep disturbance, appetite change, and mild nausea when the smoking was discontinued (36). Most of the symptoms disappeared in a day or two, though
sleep disturbance as manifested by bad dreams and restless sleep persisted
for a few weeks in some cases.

Tolerance, Dependence, and Drug Seeking

An important question regarding dependence and tolerance is their effect
on drug-seeking behavior. That is, do the mild, transient withdrawal symptoms or the tolerance that develops make for more marijuana use? The
relationship among withdrawal symptoms, tolerance, and drug-seeking
behavior is not a simple one (37). Both clinical and laboratory studies indicate that physical dependence and increased drug-seeking behavior do
not necessarily go together. With marijuana, as with most psychoactive
drugs, drug-seeking behavior is shaped by a multitude of social, economic,
psychological, and other factors. For example, the role of the relatively
mild withdrawal symptoms from tobacco in determining tobacco seeking
behavior is uncertain, but most ex-smokers would agree that these symptoms do play a role. Similarly, if we understood why the relatively mild
withdrawal symptoms associated with the low potency doses of illicit
heroin generally used now in the United States are linked to vigorous
heroin seeking behavior, then we could better judge the importance of
tolerance to and dependence on cannabis in altering future cannabis use.
The information to answer such questions does not yet exist (37).

There is good evidence that frequent use of marijuana is sometimes
associated with psychological and physiological dependence, which seems
to include drug-seeking behavior. However, in the United States the
numbers of users who have reached this stage is not well determined and
probably will be a small percentage of users, as is the case with any
psychoactive drug. As we have learned from experience with alcohol,
however, a small percentage of dependent users (5–10 percent) can amount
to a tremendous social problem when one is dealing with a large total
population of users.

Treatment Considerations

It is premature to dwell on issues of treatment for marijuana users since the
characteristics of chronic use are poorly understood. Preventive education
as to consequences, mechanisms, and pharmacology of the drug is probably helpful. For many users, an understanding of the drug and its side ef-

fects may lead to more sensible use, such as avoidance of driving or similar activities while intoxicated.

For those who experience "bad trips," the metabolism of the cannabinoids is such that the signs and symptoms should disappear in a matter of hours. Treatment consisting of support and reassurance, avoidance of possible injury inducing situations, and, in general, a quiet environment should be adequate. For individuals suffering the more puzzling, long-lasting psychological changes, it appears that if the mental state resembles a schizophrenic psychosis, the cautious application of treatments appropriate for that condition, including hospitalization, environmental manipulations, and administration of antipsychotic drugs, is indicated. However, as with other drug induced adverse effects, overtreatment can be as much a danger as no treatment: the pharmacology of the cannabinoids is such that one might expect complicated and possibly unusual interactions in the presence of somatic treatments.

Legislative Controls

Legislation to change controls over marijuana possession and distribution are much debated. Many claim that liberalizing existing regulations would encourage use of this drug. Others reply that increased use has not been well documented in states like California, Oregon, or Alaska, which have eased laws on possession. The issues posed by changes in regulatory schemes are too complicated to pursue in a short chapter and have been discussed in detail elsewhere (6, 10, 38).

We presently do not have sufficient information to justify making the drug legally available. There are virtually no data on this potent agent in terms of its effects on women and individuals with various diseases, for example. Nor have proponents of legalization dealt adequately with the problems and costs of controlling use in adolescent populations or of combating continued illicit production and distribution of high potency marijuana. Indications are that relatively inconsequential or trivial marijuana effects in healthy and normal people might be of quite different significance for those with a disease; for example, heart disease or schizophrenia. Such considerations become important when attempting to predict the consequences of widespread relatively uncontrolled use of a drug like cannabis in a social situation where even the minimal controls and follow-up possible with prescription drugs become impossible. Generally, as the availability of a drug increases and absolute numbers of users increase, the potential for harmful effects increases as well. The financial and social costs of controlling availability must be evaluated against the benefits and risks of the drug. Despite the flurry of research activity in recent years, these costs, benefits, and risks have not been adequately calculated for cannabis (38).

It may well be that with cannabis we must proceed regardless of incomplete data, relying on value judgments to guide legislative action. This is a precarious undertaking at best.

Issues concerned with setting social policy and writing laws and regulations attempting to control not only cannabis use but other drugs similarly used have been discussed thoughtfully but have been relatively ignored by those engaged in the marijuana debate (10, 17). Any regulatory scheme will have to struggle with value judgments regarding the relative costs and benefits associated with cannabis use (38).

Conclusion

In closing this chapter, it would be nice to state that a given dose or frequency of use of marijuana is clearly excessive behavior with a predictable cost. This, of course, is not the case. It would be nice to report that cannabis use is so damaging that an all-out war on marijuana should be waged. Or it would be nice to report that the drug is harmless. However, the only fair conclusion is that the harm or harmlessness of cannabis use depends on many complicated things. The list of drugs that scientists first considered benign but later condemned is almost endless: cocaine, heroin, barbiturates, meperidine, minor tranquilizers, major tranquilizers, Thalidomide, amphetamines, LSD, tobacco, alcohol. A definitive statement on what constitutes excessive behavior vis-à-vis marijuana use is not likely. Partial definitions are likely to have to be continually redefined.

Research supported in part by Program Project Grant No. DA01696, Research Scientist Award No. DA00053 and Contract No. HSM-42-73-181 from the National Institute on Drug Abuse.

References

1. Jones, H. B., and Jones, H. C., *Sensual Drugs,* Cambridge University Press, New York, 1977.
2. Nahas, G. G., *Keep Off the Grass,* Pergamon, New York, 1979.
3. Stefanis, C., Dornbush, R., and Fink, M., *Hashish: Studies of Long-term Use,* Raven, New York, 1977.
4. Rubin, B., and Comitas, L., *Ganja in Jamaica: A Medical Anthropological Study of Chronic Marijuana Use,* Mouton, The Hague, 1975.
5. Grinspoon, L., *Marihuana Reconsidered,* 2d ed., Harvard University Press, Cambridge, 1977.
6. Kaplan, J., *Marihuana: The New Prohibition,* World, Cleveland, 1971.

7. Luce, B. R., and Schweitzer, S. O., The economic cost of smoking-induced illness, in *Research on Smoking Behavior* (NIDA Research Monograph No. 17), M. E. Jarvik, J. W. Cullen, E. R. Gritz, T. M. Vogt, and L. J. West, eds., GPO, Washington, D.C., 1977, pp. 221-227.

8. American Psychiatric Association Task Force on Nomenclature and Statistics, *Diagnostic and Statistical Manual of Mental Disorders,* 3d ed., American Psychiatric Association, Washington, D. C., 1980.

9. Weller, R. A., and Halikas, J. A., Objective criteria for the diagnosis of marijuana abuse, *J. Nerv. Ment. Dis. 168,* 98-103 (1980).

10. Edwards, G., Cannabis and the criteria for legalization of a currently prohibited recreational drug: groundwork for a debate, *Acta Psychiat. Scand. 251* (supp.), 1-62 (1974).

11. Abelson, H. I., Fishburne, P. M., and Cisin, I., *National Survey on Drug Abuse, 1977: A Nationwide Study of Youth, Adults, and Older People,* National Institute on Drug Abuse, Rockville, 1977.

12. Johnston, L. E., Bachman, J. G., and O'Malley, P. M., *1979 Highlights: Drugs and the Nation's High School Students,* National Institute on Drug Abuse, Rockville, 1980.

13. Agurell, S., Lindgren, J. E., and Ohlsson, A., Introduction to quantification of cannabinoids and their metabolites in biological fluids, in *Marihuana: Biological Effects, Analysis, Metabolism, Cellular Responses, Reproduction, and Brain,* G. G. Nahas and W. D. M. Paton, eds., Pergamon, New York, 1979, pp. 3-13.

14. Hunt, C. A., and Jones, R. T., Tolerance and disposition of tetrahydrocannabinol in man, *J. Pharm. Exp. Ther. 215,* 35-44 (1980).

15. Nahas, G. G., and Paton, W. D. M., *Marihuana: Biological Effects, Analysis, Metabolism, Cellular Responses, Reproduction, and Brain,* Pergamon, New York, 1979.

16. Halikas, J. A., Marijuana use and psychiatric illness, in *Marijuana: Effects on Human Behavior,* L. L. Miller, ed., Academic, New York, 1974, pp. 265-302.

17. Edwards, G., Cannabis and the psychiatric position, in *Cannabis and Health,* J. D. P. Graham, ed., Academic, New York, 1976, pp. 321-340.

18. Jones, R. T., Drug models of schizophrenia: cannabis, in *Psychopathology and Psychopharmacology,* J. O. Cole, A. M. Freedman, and A. J. Friedhoff, eds., Johns Hopkins Press, Baltimore, 1973, pp. 71-86.

19. Treffert, D. A., Marihuana use in schizophrenia: a clear hazard, *Amer. J. Psych. 135,* 1213-1215 (1978).

20. Thacore, V. R., and Shukla, S. R. P., Cannabis psychoses and paranoid schizophrenia, *Arch. Gen. Psych. 33,* 383-386 (1976).

21. Fehr, K. O., Kalant, H., and Knox, G. B., Residual effects of high dose cannabis treatment on learning, muricidal behavior, and neurophysiological correlates in rats, in *Marihuana: Biological Effects, Analysis, Metabolism, Cellular Responses, Reproduction, and Brain,* G. G. Nahas and W. D. M. Paton, eds., Pergamon, New York, 1979, pp. 681-691.

22. Fehr, K. O., Kalant, H., and LeBlanc, A. E., Residual learning deficits after heavy exposure to cannabis or alcohol in rats, *Science 193,* 1249-1251 (1976).

23. Heath, R. G., Fitzjarrell, A. T., Garey, R. E., and Myers, W. A., Chronic marijuana smoking: its effect on function and structure of the primate brain, in *Marihuana: Biological Effects, Analysis, Metabolism, Cellular Responses, Reproduction, and Brain,* G. G. Nahas and W. D. M. Paton, eds., Pergamon, New York, 1979, pp. 713-730.

24. Miller, L. L., *Marijuana: Effects on Human Behavior,* Academic, New York, 1974.

25. Soueif, M. I., Some determinants of psychological deficits associated with chronic cannabis consumption, *Bull. Narc. 28,* 25-42 (1976).

26. Campbell, A. M. G., Evans, M., Thompson, J. L. G., and Williams, M. R., Cerebral atrophy in young cannabis smokers, *Lancet 2,* 1219-1224 (1971).

27. Co, B. T., Goodwin, D. W., Gato, M., Mikhael, M., and Hill, S. Y., Absence of cerebral atrophy in chronic cannabis users, *JAMA 237,* 1229-1230 (1977).

28. Keuhnle, J., Mendelson, J. H., Davis, D. R., and New, P. F. J., Computed tomographic examination of heavy marihuana smokers, *JAMA 237,* 1231-1232 (1977).

29. Rosenkrantz, H., and Fleischman, R. W., Effects of cannabis on lung, in *Marihuana: Biological Effects, Analysis, Metabolism, Cellular Responses, Reproduction, and Brain,* G. G. Nahas and W. D. M. Paton, eds., Pergamon, New York, 1979, pp. 279-295.

30. Tashkin, D. P., Shapiro, B. J., Lee, Y. E., and Harper, C. E., Subacute effects of heavy marihuana smoking on pulmonary function in healthy men, *N. Eng. J. Med. 294,* 125-129 (1976).

31. Tennant, F. S., Jr., Histopathologic and clinical abnormalities of the respiratory system in chronic hashish smokers. *Substance and Alc. Actions/Misuse,* 1, 93-100 (1980).

32. Kolodny, R. C., Masters, W. H., Kolodner, R. M., and Toro, G., Depression of plasma testosterone levels after chronic intensive marijuana use, *N. Eng. J. Med. 290,* 872-874 (1974).

33. Fried, P. A., Behavioral and electroencephalographic correlates of chronic use of marijuana: a review, *Beh. Biol. 21,* 163-196 (1977).

34. Kalant, H., LeBlanc, A. E., and Gibbins, R. J., Tolerance to, and dependence on, some non-opiate psychotropic drugs, *Pharm. Rev. 23,* 135-191 (1971).

35. Jones, R. T., Benowitz, N., and Bachman, J., Clinical studies of cannabis tolerance and dependence, *Ann. N.Y. Acad. Sci. 282,* 221-239 (1976).

36. Nowlan, R., and Cohen, S., Tolerance to marijuana: heart rate and subjective "high," *Clin. Pharm. Ther. 22,* 550-556 (1977).

37. Cappell, H., and LeBlanc, A. E., Tolerance to, and physical dependence on, ethanol: why do we study them? *Drug and Alc. Depend. 4,* 15-31 (1979).

38. Kalant, H., and Kalant, O. J., *Drugs, Society, and Personal Choice,* General Publishing, Toronto, 1971.

7

Tobacco

Jacquelyn Rogers

Cigarette smoking and related tobacco use has been declared the "single greatest cause of unnecessary [preventable] illness and premature death in our society" by every surgeon general since Luther Terry issued his courageous report in 1964 in which he posited a relationship between smoking and cancer (6). Nevertheless, sales of cigarettes are increasing, children are starting younger (11 years old), and smokers are using age-old rationalizations.

Why do people continue to smoke in spite of obvious health hazards and recent social ostracism? I suggest that smokers continue to smoke because they do not know how to quit; once someone is hooked by a year or two of regular smoking (usually by age 16), casual attempts to quit cause such physical discomfort that the person puts off quitting until a major event occurs such as the smoking related death of a family member or friend.

Repeated unsuccessful efforts to quit cause discouragement and the smoker begins to rationalize this habit. Indeed, the nature of the behavior is more complex than most smokers can deal with; confronted by well-meaning friends, relatives, and doctors, the smoker becomes defensive, resisting most offers of help.

Smoking has been misunderstood and underrated as a condition like other addictions or compulsive behaviors; yet smoking is unique in its complexity. Massive and scholarly efforts to provide smokers with effective means of both cessation and long-term abstinence have been unsuccessful largely because most therapies have been too narrow. For instance, pharmacologists suggested lobeline sulfate as a substitute for nicotine, expecting eradication or reduction of craving following elimination of nicotine from the bloodstream. But what of smokers who abstained for several weeks or months—or years—and relapsed? Surely the nicotine had long vanished from the body. The psychologists proffered plastic pacifiers in the belief that smoking is an oral fixation. Religionists implored smokers to seek divine aid. The medical community relied upon reason: describe in vivid detail the physical destruction caused by smoking and surely rational people will quit. Behaviorists designed aversive conditioning models that too often increased smoking behavior because of heightened stress and discomfort. Psychotherapists delved into the past; hypnotherapists offered post-hypnotic suggestion; and so on. Each approach has aimed at cessation, an immediate result. But long-term success, not mere cessation, is the more important goal.

After trying most of the available therapies, I hypothesized that my heavy smoking habit consisted of a broad spectrum of physical, psychological, emotional, oral, and social components. I was obviously both physically addicted and psychologically dependent. In addition, I had developed many attendant rituals and implicitly held a reverent respect for the almost mystical capabilities of my cigarettes: lighting a cigarette could dispel worries and woes, fatigue, and downheartedness. I analyzed the habit piece by piece, identifying over 138 different elements. Then, over a period of six weeks, I systematically disconnected each element, simultaneously weaving positive reinforcement and strengthening motivation to change my behavior. My ultimate objective was to discard an old, outgrown "habit" without pain, remorse, or a sense of deprivation; I hoped to feel good about quitting. The technique produced a surprising sense of freedom. I enjoyed not smoking, feeling no self-righteousness or bitterness.

In addition, my sense of self-mastery acted as a catalyst for personal growth in other areas. These are the elements that insure lasting success. Resuming smoking is highly unlikely when it would mean giving up something of value (a free, clean feeling) for something the ex-smoker has come to view as a rather dirty and costly nuisance.

I successfully duplicated my results in a field trial: 23 of 25 participants in a 12-week program "cut off" at the sixth week; 2 dropped out following cutoff but the balance stayed abstinent for the remaining six weeks of the seminar, during which a variety of physical withdrawal symptoms were acknowledged and controlled. During the smoking phase, participants exhibited skepticism and a certain restrained hostility; in the postsmoking phase, a positive attitude emerged. Follow-up by mail every three months for the first year indicated a high abstinence rate. Now, 10 years after I founded Smokenders, essentially the same positive attitudes are evident in questionnaires received from graduates of these programs throughout the United States and Europe. This chapter looks at the complex problem of cessation and long-term abstinence.

Constituents of Tobacco and Smoke

The active principle of tobacco is nicotine, a very poisonous alkaloid, $C_{10}H_{14}N_2$. Various researchers have suggested that nicotine is the primary reinforcing agent in smoking addiction. In 1942, Lennox Johnson declared that "smoking tobacco is essentially a means of administering nicotine, just as smoking opium is a means of administering morphine." In 1971, M. A. Hamilton Russell wrote, "If it were not for the nicotine in tobacco smoke people would be little more inclined to smoke cigarettes than they are to blow bubbles or light sparklers."

Nicotine is generally considered to be the main cause of cardiovascular and circulatory problems in smokers since it dramatically constricts the blood vessels. Nicotine enters the bloodstream by absorption through the oral mucosa, as well as by inhalation, so noninhaling smokers of cigarettes, pipes, and cigars, along with tobacco chewers and snuff sniffers, are affected by nicotine.

Tar is the particulate matter left when moisture and nicotine are removed from smoke. Smokers recognize tar as the sticky, brownish substance that collects on the bottom of heavily used ashtrays. Tar, obtained from pipes and cigars as well as cigarettes, is widely considered to be the carcinogenic element in smoke and the cause of respiratory problems.

The carbon monoxide in tobacco smoke is potentially dangerous to the cardiovascular system. Recent evidence supports the theory that carbon monoxide causes exceptionally high levels of carboxyhemoglobin, which decreases the oxygen available to the cells. Many investigators argue that carbon monoxide may increase cardiovascular morbidity and mortality.

The Pull of Tobacco

While every smoker who has tried to quit and failed considers smoking an addiction, the scientific community is divided in its opinion. Until recently, smoking was labeled "habituative" and suggestions to the contrary were ridiculed. More recently, researchers have attempted to classify nicotine as an addictive drug. Indeed, the criteria of addiction are met: tolerance and measurable physiological changes upon withdrawal. Some researchers suggest that additional substances in cigarettes are addictive, such as other chemicals in the tobacco or the paper.

Perhaps the designation "addiction" has been withheld—apart from the scientific community's semantic preference—because of the term's connotations: cigarettes, pipes, and cigars might become socially unacceptable (to the industry's chagrin) if they were used by addicts; moreover, smokers would be embarrassed by the label.

I strongly support the designation "addiction": youngsters would be less likely to give way to initial curiosity and subsequently get hooked; the stigma of the label would render smoking in public an unacceptable social behavior (smokers are becoming uncomfortable and apologetic as a result of antismoking attitudes) and the knowledge that smoking is a pharmacological problem would reassure prospective quitters that they have not been guilty of lack of willpower in unsuccessful efforts to give up smoking.

Psychological Dependency

The nonphysiologic aspect of smoking behavior is dependency: the smoker mentally relies upon the cigarette, pipe, or cigar to maintain various emotional states—ability to cope, calmness, pleasure, relief from anxiety, etc. The physically addictive nature of smoking undoubtedly increases the intensity of the psychological dependence.

Smoking is viewed consciously or unconsciously as a reward by smokers. Unless they are helped to develop a stronger self-respect, which reduces the need for external recognition—either from others or from their cigarettes—they will continue to seek satisfaction from external sources. A truly successful cessation modality must aid the smoker in dissociating conditioned responses and ritualistic practices, as well as provide insight into how he or she uses cigarettes to enhance self-image.

Behavioral Habituation

A habit is a frequently repeated activity that becomes relatively automatic. When, as in cigarette smoking, a number of habits are combined, a "habit pattern" develops. External events, such as a telephone ringing, the drinking of coffee or cola, or turning on the television, act as reinforcers. Internal events can also act as reinforcers: anxiety, stress, feelings of inadequacy, lack of self-satisfaction, etc. Pavlov's conditioned reflex theory is clearly demonstrated by smokers.

Craving

Craving has been commonly described by smokers as "an empty, unsatisfied sense of restlessness which is very compelling and which despite great effort of will is very difficult to distract." This condition is often confused with "climbing the walls," which is a result of the physiological deprivation of nicotine, as indicated by dramatic changes in pulse, respiration, blood pressure, and skin temperature. While climbing the walls usually occurs at the onset of cessation and may last several days, until the bulk of the nicotine is out of the system, craving is experienced for considerably longer (in some instances, over five years). I suggest that craving is the principal cause of recidivism and that craving continues when the smoker has not completely disconnected the numerous psychological, emotional, and social triggers that activate the craving mechanism. From personal experience and from case histories of thousands of participants in Smokenders, I am convinced that craving can be eradicated permanently and suggest that this be the objective of all therapists and clinicians. Craving has several components that must be addressed: conditioned reflexes to numerous visual, aural, olfactory, taste, and physical sensations; need for oral satisfaction produced by repeated attention to the mouth in smoking; and relief from malaise (the body responds to nicotine, a poison, with adrenalin, which elevates blood sugar level and produces an immediate but temporary burst of energy).

Considerations in Smoking Cessation Programs

Evaluation of Efficacy

The efficacy of cessation efforts depends in the short run on the skill of therapists; in the long run, on participants. A first step in evaluating any antismoking program would be to look at the following areas.

1. *Attrition.* How many attended the first session and how many of these completed the treatment? A good therapy must be palatable and honest and quickly give the smoker a sense that the effort is worthwhile. Current educational and consumer marketing techniques are helpful in discouraging dropout.

2. *Compliance.* How faithful are participants? Mere attendance does not insure compliance.

3. *Success Rate.* Kanzler and colleagues evaluated the effectiveness of a Smokenders program at a state psychiatric hospital (2, 3). Of the 67 percent who completed the program (this figure, lower than the Smokenders' national average, was depressed because participants had to give blood samples), 67 percent of men and 57 percent of women were abstinent nearly a year after the program ended.

Total abstinence rather than reduction is the only acceptable measure of success since nicotine is addictive and tolerance is a major element of addiction. It is rare, indeed, to find smokers who have either reduced their consumption over the years or maintained a reduction for any length of time. Therapists do not agree about the length of time a smoker must remain abstinent before being considered cured. Opinions range from six months to five years. Dispute is understandable since many smokers abstinent for several years relapse; conversely, countless smokers have quit and never resumed smoking.

A Profile of Recidivism

The majority of smokers have suffered recidivism, whether or not they sought outside assistance in quitting. We classify smokers who have tried unsuccessfully to quit numerous times before seeking outside help as "active" quitters. "Passive" quitters think frequently about quitting but never forego their cigarettes because they have no confidence in their ability to withstand the physical repercussions (climbing the walls) or to function effectively without tobacco. This group cannot imagine themselves not smoking; the habit is as attached as a body part. Some smokers even have a love relationship with smoking. They view quitting as willful separation from a beloved and unless they are properly prepared for quitting, pseudomourning occurs (in these cases some psychologists find a grieving therapy useful).

The availability and social acceptability of smoking make this behavior pattern particularly resistant to change. Analysis of retrospective and prospective data collected routinely from participants in Smokenders during the past 10 years (over 100,000 subjects), has identified other major causes of recidivism. The following list includes items reported by all smokers for all their quitting attempts (inside and outside Smokenders).

1. *Alcohol.* For several months after withdrawal, alcohol has a considerably enhanced sedative effect on former smokers. When ex-smokers consume their usual quantity of alcohol but are unprepared for the stronger reaction, they can easily lose sight of the nonsmoking objective and reach for a nearby cigarette.

2. *Self-pity.* When the smokers perceive quitting as a form of self-denial or deprivation, they feel sorry for themselves. Soon the suffering becomes intolerable. So, as in the past, they use smoking as a source of solace (some smokers chose to substitute food as a source of comfort). If, on the other hand, quitting is perceived as a form of self-mastery and smokers have been programmed to consider the experience as a positive and pleasant achievement, the likelihood of resuming smoking is greatly reduced.

3. *Restlessness.* This condition may be associated with craving or with a new, unfamiliar increase in available time. Smokers report a "slowing down of pressures" and "more time" upon cessation. Although the act of lighting up and smoking is brief, the *rituals* of smoking consume vast amounts of time. For instance, smokers typically must finish their coffee and cigarette simultaneously. If the smoker on a coffee break finishes the coffee first, he or she drinks another cup while the cigarette is still burning and vice versa. Unless smokers can cope through training or other means with the restlessness consequent upon abandoning smoking rituals, continued abstinence is jeopardized.

4. *Availability.* A package of cigarettes especially one's old brand, is among the strongest of all the conditioned stimuli. This cue is almost impossible to ignore.

5. *Complacency.* Too often smokers succumb to the belief that they have conquered the habit and can control it. Virtually all smokers who attempt only to cut down quickly return to their normal level. In fact, many smokers report increased smoking after a bout of reduction or abstinence.

6. *Weight Gain.* When a smoker is unprepared for cessation and quits abruptly, the tendency is to substitute food for cigarettes. Consideration must be given to the need for oral gratification that exists *as a result of smoking,* whether or not this need has roots in early childhood. A smoker touches the lips and creates a sensaton in the mouth perhaps 200 times a day (20 cigarettes at 10 drags each), 700,000 times a year; for a 20-year smoker this means 14 million times. To compensate for the lack of oral stimulation following cessation, smokers turn to food and gain weight. There is also some indication that metabolic changes occur in certain individuals upon cessation, so that weight gain takes place without increased food intake. This field deserves considerable study. Women especially are loathe to view the additional weight as a suitable trade-off. The weight increase causes mild depression, which leads to self-pity, which overcomes the resolve to abstain!

Some smokers gain weight as an excuse to resume smoking: "I'd rather die of lung disease than have a heart attack from obesity." However, many smokers deal with weight gain in a positive manner: "If I can quit smoking, I can do anything. When I've got smoking licked, I'll deal with the weight gain." This is the ideal attitude. Finally, a small percentage of ex-smokers report weight loss as a result of cessation. Investigation reveals an increase in physical activity upon quitting, in many cases made possible by improved stamina and breathing ability. However, many ex-smokers who gain weight report increased physical activity as well.

7. *Completion of the Pleasurable Cycle.* Although smokers believe they are more likely to reach for a cigarette under pressure, we see very little recidivism from stress compared to resumption under enjoyable circumstances.

8. *Spite.* Smokers who quit for the sake of spouse or children may find reasons to be disappointed in some aspect of loved ones' behavior and resume smoking, saying, "Look what I did for you. I quit smoking. And you don't appreciate it. Look at what you've done to me. You've disappointed me, hurt me. So I'll start smoking again. You don't care."

9. *Stress* (anger, worry, shock, helplessness). The ex-smoker has a wealth of rationalizations on hand: "My husband was rushed to the hospital" or "I dented the fender" or "I thought I was going to be fired."

10. *Boredom.* This is one of the major causes of recidivism among widows and retirees. Involvement in people oriented activities is an effective antidote.

11. *Taste.* Because "taste" has been heavily promoted as a major reason for choosing a brand, most smokers assume each cigarette tastes good. Therefore, unless they have been trained to examine "taste" before they quit, the false memory of taste can cause relapse.

12. *False sense of control* following a short period of abstinence: "I

can limit my consumption to just a couple of cigarettes a day now that I have it under control!''

13. *Switch to Pipe or Cigars.* (Because this option is not commonly available to women, studies of recidivism in which it appears that more women than men resume cigarette smoking may be distorted since the question is frequently stated as "Have you ever smoked cigarettes? If yes, have you ever quit? If yes, have you ever resumed smoking?" The implication is in regard to cigarettes so many men, who have switched to cigars or pipe, respond "No.")

14. *Belief in a "safe" cigarette.* Resumption of smoking due to heavy promotion of low tar-nicotine cigarettes which reduce smoker's resolve to remain abstinent.

15. *Physical withdrawal problems.* (See "Erudite Insights" for discussion of specific withdrawal symptoms.)

Psychological Withdrawal Conditions

In seeking to establish a basis of "relapse predictability," we examined responses from recidivists and developed some interesting criteria.

Several groups of smokers have predictably high recidivism rates. When spouses or parent and child both successfully quit smoking during the Smokenders program, one might relapse and respond to the standard questionnaire sent to all graduates thus: "I really went to the program because my husband [or wife, or son, etc.] wanted to go and urged me to do it, too." Such respondents frequently add, "Although I wasn't interested in quitting then, having been off for a short while was rather nice and I will rejoin and do it right." Clearly, motivation cannot be forced.

The second major group of recidivists are people suffering physical conditions whether caused by smoking or not, who are told by a physician or dentist to "stop smoking or else!" These smokers are difficult to motivate, too, inasmuch as they feel the damage has already been done. "It's too late," they say. Furthermore, quitting is not their choice.

Another group that has a lower chance of remaining abstinent are women who attempt to stop smoking during menopause. Not only because her physical condition is likely to be unstable and unusual, but also because this period often coincides with the "empty nest" syndrome, the smoker relies heavily upon her familiar and reliable cigarettes. Conversely, some menopausal women view quitting as a fresh start and are exceptionally successful in spite of physical and emotional stresses.

1. *Titration.* Smokers adjust smoking behavior to maintain a comfortable level of nicotine in the bloodstream. Titration can be achieved by deeper inhalation, more rapid smoking, smoking more of each cigarette, cigar, or pipeful, or simply smoking a greater number of cigarettes, cigars, or pipes. Because of tolerance to nicotine, smokers increase their dosage

automatically, rather than consciously. Thus, the smoker who switches to a low tar and nicotine brand rather than remain abstinent will inevitably increase the number of cigarettes smoked.

A random sampling of Smokender participants in 1975 (prior to the surge of advertising in 1976 for low tar and nicotine brands) indicated 32.2 cigarettes smoked daily on average. In 1976, those participants who smoked brands low in nicotine (Carlton, More, Merit, Now, True, Vantage) had a daily average of 37.6 cigarettes. Smokers reported an increase in money spent on smoking because of changing to low tar and nicotine brands. Most said they felt "unsatisfied" with the new, so-called less hazardous brands unless they "tried harder" to satisfy themselves; eventually they either increased their consumption or switched back to the old brand.

2. *Less Hazardous Sources of Tobacco.* Large-scale smoking cessation efforts undertaken by government and voluntary health agencies following the 1964 report of the surgeon general, were costly and generally disappointing. By 1971, research was aimed at producing a "less harmful" form of tobacco. So-called safe cigarettes, however, are unsatisfactory for several reasons. First, the memory of taste, a factor heavily promoted by the tobacco industry, encourages smokers to return to old brands. Second, smokers consume an additional two packs per week on average. Third, the smoker is now subjected to increased intake of the products of combustion, in particular, carbon monoxide. Perhaps more harmful is the illusion that low tar and nicotine brands are an acceptable alternative to quitting: "The government obviously doesn't really believe that cigarettes are hazardous—otherwise, it would ban them entirely. But see, they've come up with safe cigarettes." This view was supported by statements to the press in 1978 by a prominent deputy of the National Cancer Institute, who implied that smoking under 10 low tar and nicotine cigarettes a day is "tolerable" (1). Finally, the greatest harm caused by low tar and nicotine brands is that children who try cigarettes are not repulsed by them: it is now easy to start—no coughing, choking, gagging, and dizziness as in first attempts in the past. The "less hazardous" label and the minimization of unpleasant physiological side effects may account for the increasingly early starting age.

A unique group of recidivists are people who enter treatment without previously having tried to stop smoking. When quitting is made easy, they are surprised. A high percentage of those who report resumption of smoking after treatment maintain, "Now I know I can quit when I want to, so I decided to resume smoking until I'm ready to quit." Unfortunately, cessation may not be so easy the second time and, indeed, it might be too late.

Smoking is rarely initiated in adulthood. The Center for the Study of Smoking Behavior reported in 1975 that of 250 Smokenders participants, constituting a broad geographic sampling and ranging in age from 20 to 70, 71 percent started smoking at age 18 or under; 95 percent began at age 22 or under. The majority of respondants were between the ages of 30 and 60. Projections of present trends toward lower starting ages are alarming: 75 percent of smokers who began smoking regularly in the late seventies were 15 or under!

Therapy

In 1969 Schwartz updated his earlier evaluation of 100 smoking cessation methods, concluding that "although health departments and voluntary health agencies have taken the lead in changing smoking attitudes, convincing smokers to stop, and bringing them to the point of seeing cigarettes as a personal threat, they have failed to establish a viable program of cessation clinics. Local cancer and heart chapters have held quit clinics but these have been only small efforts on a limited basis (7). As a result, in 1971 the World Conference on Smoking and Health recommended that health and government agencies concern themselves with prevention through education—in schools and through the media—rather than expend additional time, effort, or dollars on cessation clinics (8). Furthermore, public agencies were urged to encourage commercial withdrawal clinics and to evaluate them.

Schwartz reported that high dropout rates from many cessation programs frequently reflected low acceptance of the approach and he proposed criteria for smoking cessation methods:

1. Is the method acceptable to smokers wishing to stop?
2. Is it effective in helping them quit?
3. Is the method sensitive to individual needs, privacy, dignity, and financial means (7)?

An additional caveat has been added by clinicians since Schwartz's report:

4. Does the treatment entail high risk conditions that may adversely affect elderly or ill smokers?

The following survey of current treatment modalities is based on my experience as well as on research into the subject of smoking cessation.

Medical Intervention

The smoker's physician frequently provides counseling and encouragement after finding evidence of smoking related symptoms of disease. Unfortunately, most physicians and dentists shy away from helping patients quit—or even suggesting they quit—because they have met with frustration and disappointment in their past efforts to aid patients. It should be recognized that doctors have no special knowledge to help their patients stop smoking; in fact, they are laymen in this area. However, physicians and dentists are major influences in most people's lives—and their interest in patients' smoking history can persuade a considerable number to consider quitting. I recommend that doctors in all branches of health care routinely advise their patients to think about quitting. Smokenders offers specific ways to deal with patients in the pamphlet "Office Management of the Smoking Patient":

1. When taking patient's history, be certain to ask, "Do you smoke?" and if the answer is "Yes," ask, "How much? How long have you smoked?"
2. When using the stethoscope, pause for a moment and say, "Hmmm, how much did you say you smoke?" And the patient will likely answer, "Why, Doc, is there something wrong?" And you answer (if there is no evidence of smoking related disease), "No, I can't say there is. But professionally, this is as far I can go in regard to your smoking. In good conscience I must tell you that you must seriously *consider* quitting." Note that we urge the doctor to refrain from *insisting* they "quit smoking or else . . . " since that has proven counter productive in too many cases, because the anxiety produced by such ultimata is a condition which causes many smokers to reach for a smoke.
3. When the smoker then says, "OK, Doc, but HOW can I quit? I've tried many times, and it's not easy. Can you give me a pill or recommend something?" the doctor should have available names of books, clinicians, and treatment centers and say, "Here are some good possibilities. I suggest you look into any of them. Then, it's entirely up to you." This should be stated with confidence in the therapies and with firmness. Not equivocation. The smoker is quick to pick up the doctor's uncertainty about the therapy or his doubt about his patient's ability to quit. Both are self-defeating.

Psychotherapy and Psychoanalysis

Private or group counseling generally consists of one or two visits per week utilizing a variety of techniques—from classic Freudian psychoanalysis to psychodrama. It is difficult to appraise results since many smokers who choose psychotherapy or psychoanalysis generally present themselves with broader complaints regarding problems of adjustment rather than simply a smoking problem. In addition, most therapists do not maintain follow-up records, nor are they comfortable disclosing professional information of this nature.

Hypnosis

Treatment most often is completed in one session; follow-up support is occasionally provided by individual practitioners. Practitioners range from MDs to PhDs to entertainers; no licensing is required.

There is a wide assortment of hypnosis treatments increasingly available to smokers. Generally, this method proceeds by establishing a positive mental attitude toward hypnosis on the part of the smoker; hypnosis is then induced and suggestions are provided, most often directed toward self-preservation but also toward ego enhancement. The Third World Conference on Smoking and Health noted the lack of satisfactory studies that included adequate control data (9).

Group hypnosis programs are gaining in popularity; some are commercial. It is generally very difficult to obtain long-term results from hypnosis practitioners since they do not establish a long-term relationship with clients. I suspect that hypnosis is effective as a first step toward quitting for the "hard-core" smoker (a compulsive smoker who is both physically addicted and psychologically dependent); it may be somewhat more beneficial for the "social" smoker (one who is mildly habituated—as is a social drinker, for instance.) Moreover, weight gain seems to be an important reason for recidivism, since substitution of food for cigarettes (or pipe or cigar) is common. My opinion: various aspects of hypnosis may be used profitably in this area.

Acupuncture

New evidence indicates that acupuncture may produce good results if the clinician is professionally trained; if the smoker is only physically addicted (but not psychologically dependent); and if the patient is not using medications or drugs that might block pain receptors since acupuncture may activate brain chemicals (endorphins) that are capable of reducing or eliminating pain. Therefore, if a social smoker responds to acupuncture, he or she will be less likely to suffer the physiological pain of withdrawal during the period of nicotine detoxification. Generally, nicotine is largely out of the system in three or four days, so acupuncture aids the smoker by diminishing the risk of reaching for a cigarette during the first few days of cessation in response to relief from climbing the walls. However, most smokers succumb to cigarettes *after* the withdrawal period because of psychological dependence.

Pharmacotherapy

As mentioned previously, lobeline sulfate (Nicoban) and other nicotine substitutes have limited success since they deal solely with the physiological aspect of the problem. Results with tranquilizers and other stress reduction drugs have been poor. I believe that smokers must be motivated to a high level of resolve in order to succeed in quitting and that tranquilizers and depressants soften the resolve. The theory underlying smoking pharmacotherapy is that anxiety creates the need to smoke; therefore, reducing or removing the anxiety will eliminate the desire to smoke. This false assumption is based on the belief that smoking is a simple habit. In tests, placebo had better results than drugs. In light of new findings regarding the physiological implications of "the Placebo effect" the author's theory that smokers are hamstrung by their very strong belief that they are unable to free themselves from their smoking habit, and that if they are given specific instructions which give the smoker immediate sense of control of the habit and thereby a sense of hopefulness and soon, confidence in their ability to break free, the therapy has a chance for success.

Aversive Therapies

Based on the theory that negative reinforcement is a learning technique, aversion methodologies range from rapid forced smoking until nausea is induced; to a steady stream of warm, stale smoke blown into the face of the client; to full-color films of the surgical removal of a cancerous lung or of an emphysemiac in the last stages of self-induced suffocation; to display of a freshly excised cancerous lung; to noxious electrical shock. In another form of aversive therapy, covert sensitization, the therapist trains the subject to visualize that the cigarette contains one or several of the following: vomit, maggots, fecal matter, etc. Self-reports on these techniques provide a wide range of short- and long-term results; moreover, the attrition rate is high.

Positive Reinforcement Therapies

The best results—lowest attrition rate, short-term cessation, and long-term abstinence—have been produced by organizations, such as Smokenders, that offer the smoker positive reinforcements. The chapter has reviewed the principles and philosophy of this approach.

Conclusion

Smoking is a complex behavior. Quitting is therefore equally complex. The majority of smokers require sophisticated treatment approaches that address the physical, mental, emotional, and social aspects of the disorder. Preventive efforts are perhaps more critical than cessation programs. The stigma of addiction should be used to discourage children from starting and to promote the view of smoking as *socially unacceptable*.

Finally, a word on behalf of smokers. It is unfair to treat smokers like second-class citizens and to express dismay or disdain at their seeming unwillingness to heed health warnings and stop smoking. It is also counterproductive to harass smokers about their smoking or to imply that they lack willpower. Smokers are ordinary people who took up cigarettes when they were too young to understand the consequences; now they are unable to disengage themselves from the behavior without considerable direction, encouragement, and support. If the intention of the community is to reduce the incidence of disease and premature death, it can best serve smokers by creating an environment in which smoking is not a ready and accepted option.

References

1. Gori, G. B., and Lynch, C. J., Toward less hazardous cigarettes: current advances, *JAMA 240,* 1255–1259 (1978).
2. Kanzler, M., Jaffe, J. H., and Zeidenberg, P., Long- and short-term effectiveness of a large-scale proprietary smoking cessation program: a four-year followup of Smokenders participants, *J. Clin. Psych. 32,* 661–669 (1976).
3. Kanzler, M., Zeidenberg, P., and Jaffe, J. H., Response of medical personnel to an on-site smoking cessation program, *J. Clin. Psych. 32,* 670–674 (1976).
4. Zeidenberg, P., Jaffe, J. H., Kanzler, M., Levitt, M. D., Langone, J. J., and VanVunakis, H., Nicotine: cotinine levels in blood during cessation of smoking, *Comprehen. Psychiat. 18,* 93–101 (1977).
5. National Interagency Council on Smoking and Health, *Guidelines for Research on the Effectiveness of Smoking Cessation Programs: A Committee Report,* American Dental Association, Chicago, 1974.
6. U. S. Public Health Service, *Smoking and Health,* GPO, Washington, D.C., 1964.
7. Schwartz, J. L., A critical review and evaluation of smoking control methods, *Pub. Health Rep. 84,* 483–506 (1969).
8. *Proceedings of the Second World Conference on Smoking and Health,* Pitman, London, 1972.
9. *Proceedings of the Third World Conference on Smoking and Health,* GPO, Washington, D.C., 1977.
10. The magazine's smoking habit, *Columbia Journalism Rev. 17,* (1978).

8

Caffeine

John F. Greden

Definitions

Caffeine is a trimethylated xanthine derivative (1-,3-,7-trimethylxanthine), generally classified as a central nervous system stimulant (1–4). This alkaloid is found naturally in coffee seeds (beans), tea leaves, cocoa beans, cola nuts, and ilex plants (maté) and is common in large numbers of commercial products, including tea, coffee, cocoa, chocolate, and soft drinks (5). Many medicinal agents such as analgesics, stimulants, and diet preparations also contain caffeine (6–7) (Table 8–1). Alcohol, tobacco, and caffeine are the three most widely consumed psychoactive agents in the world. Annual caffeine consumption exceeds several billion kilograms (2, 5, 8). Although intermittently considered a substance of abuse throughout history (8), caffeine is now the prototype of a domesticated drug that most members of society volitionally consume in vast quantities.

Caffeinism is a clinical syndrome produced by the ingestion and consequent pharmacological actions of high doses of caffeine, whether from coffee, tea, cola drinks, over-the-counter pharmaceutical substances, or prescription medications (6, 9). Although common, the syndrome is frequently unrecognized (9). Major manifestations include mood changes, anxiety, sleep disruption, various somatic complaints, and occasional accentuation of other medical and psychological problems (6–12).

Caffeine withdrawal is an unpleasant physiological state produced by rapid decrease or discontinuation of daily caffeine intake, with resultant reductions in caffeine plasma levels (13–15). Found only among tolerant, chronic consumers who suddenly diminish their ingestion, this syndrome is characterized by irritability, lethargy, headache, alteration of sleep pattern, mood disturbance, and occasional physiological arousal. Caffeine withdrawal is inconsistent in onset; many chronic consumers deny experiencing any symptoms even if intake is precipitously stopped.

TABLE 8–1
Common Sources of Caffeine

SOURCE	APPROXIMATE DOSE
Beverages	
Brewed coffee	80–140 mg per cup
Instant tea	50–100 mg per cup
Tea (leaf)	30–75 mg per cup
Tea (bagged)	42–100 mg per cup
Decaffeinated coffee	2–4 mg per cup
Cola drinks	25–55 mg per cup
Cocoa	5–50 mg per cup
Many Over-the-counter Cold Preparations	30 mg per tablet
Many Over-the-counter Stimulants	100–200 mg per tablet
Small Chocolate Bar	25 mg per bar
Analgesics	
Anacin	32.5 mg per tablet
A.P.C.	32 mg per tablet
B C tablet	16 mg per tablet
Bromo-Seltzer	32.5 mg per tablet
Cafergot	100 mg per tablet
Capron	32 mg per tablet
Comeback	100 mg per tablet
Cope	32 mg per tablet
Darvon compound	32 mg per tablet
Dolor	30 mg per tablet
Easy-Mens	32 mg per tablet
Empirin compound	32 mg per tablet
Excedrin	64.8 mg per tablet
Fiorinal	40 mg per tablet
Goody's headache powder	32.5 mg per tablet
Medache	32 mg per tablet
Maranox	15 mg per tablet
Midol	32 mg per tablet
Migral	50 mg per tablet
Nilain	32 mg per tablet
P A C	32 mg per tablet
Pre-Mens	66 mg per tablet
Stanback tablets	16 mg per tablet
Stanback powder	32 mg per tablet
Trigesic	30 mg per tablet
Vanquish	33 mg per tablet

Description of the Disorder

Caffeinism is a multifaceted clinical syndrome (9, 16). Onset is frequently subtle and vague, symptoms are diverse, and the course usually fluctuates. Because of these confusing features, symptom subtypes associated with caffeinism must be discussed separately to achieve clarity. Anxiety is the most prevalent manifestation, so this symptom will be described first, followed by depression, sleep disorders, somatic complaints, delirium, delusional thinking, psychomotor abnormalities, and miscellaneous clinical aspects of caffeinism. Finally, I review withdrawal features and associated abuse of other chemicals.

Anxiety

Anxiety symptoms of caffeinism are dose related extensions of the drug's expected pharmacological stimulation (6). As consumption increases, many patients report being nervous, jittery, rattled, high-strung, irritable, tense, in turmoil, driven, or constantly on the go. Others complain predominantly about somatic symptoms such as trembling hands, quivering voice, twitching eyelids, jumpy feet, physical restlessness, hyperexcitability, jumpiness, muscle twitchings, flickering lights in front of the eyes, or increased perceptual sensitivity to touch. Approximately 10–20 percent of all caffeine consumers develop significant anxiety features at some time or another (8, 9, 16, 19–25). Most subjects who develop such symptoms consume at least 500–600 mg caffeine per day (9). Furthermore, the more drug consumed, the more severe the anxiety constellation tends to be.

The anxiety constellation associated with caffeinism closely resembles a classical textbook description of anxiety disorder. In actuality, it is a direct consequence of caffeinism, but mistaken diagnoses are probably common. Peculiarly, some patients with caffeinism complain most about psychological symptoms while others seem more preoccupied by somatic disturbances. In almost all cases, however, careful clinical questioning reveals that both psychic and somatic anxiety manifestations are present. Most patients are simply more aware of disruptions in one arena.

As early as 1811, an "anti-nervous" tea was offered for sale (17, 18), so recognition of the anxiety producing effects of caffeine is not new. In recent decades, lay descriptions of "coffee nerves" have been widely disseminated in mass media advertisements. Afflicted individuals are depicted as attractive, successful, and well functioning—but mildly anxious because of their coffee consumption. Such descriptions, rather than successfully alerting people to possible clinical risks, may produce and support an erroneous belief that the anxiety features of caffeinism are consistently mild. Although epidemiological investigations confirmed that the majority of caffeine consumers have negligible anxiety manifestations (9), some users are profoundly affected. Indeed, symptoms may be so severe that familial, social, and job difficulties ensue: home remedies may be used in an attempt to treat symptoms; over-the-counter medicines are often tried; and even professional treatment may be sought. Clearly, caffeinism is not always innocuous (8, 9. 16).

To determine whether caffeine consumption is quantifiably associated with anxiety, investigators have evaluated different caffeine using subgroups with the State-Trait Anxiety Index (STAI), a self-rating anxiety scale (9, 26, 27). In these studies, as caffeine intake increased, anxiety ratings climbed (9, 26). Specifically, trait anxiety items (which evaluate how one *generally* feels) and state anxiety items (which determine how one feels *right now*) were compared among high consumers (750 mg/day or more), moderate users (250–749 mg/day), or low users (0–249 mg/day) (9). High and moderate consumers consistently reported higher scores. A higher percentage described feeling tired, upset, nervous, tense, like crying, and that "difficulties were piling up." In comparison to low users, fewer felt happy, pleasant, calm, rested, content, or joyful. These findings, although not proof of causality, epidemiologically associated caffeinism with anxiety features.

How often does caffeine's socially sought stimulation become clinically disabling anxiety? This answer has not been completely determined. Gilbert estimated that 10 percent of North Americans may have caffeinism (19). Most users seem unaware of this possibility, however. Goldstein and Kaizer surveyed housewives to determine the effect of morning coffee and found that 47 percent felt "perked up," 43 percent felt "more alert," and almost one-third felt they could work more efficiently (24). Clearly, in an achievement oriented society, in which energy is prized and apathy criticized, such effects would be eagerly sought by many. Since studies have shown that risk of caffeinism greatly increases with daily dosage above 500 mg, and a number of these housewives exceeded this level, pharmacological principles would dictate that some respondents probably had undiagnosed caffeinism. If so, the beneficial feelings identified by a proportion of the women may simply have been the result of the daily treatment of an emerging caffeine withdrawal syndrome, a clinical possibility that subsequently will be discussed in greater detail.

High caffeine consumers often experience desirable stimulation and undesirable anxiety at the same time (28). They may seek and appreciate the subjective sense of clearer thoughts but simultaneously develop jitteriness. Individual tolerances to the drug differ. Some users react adversely to doses as small as 50 mg, while others insist they have no adverse symptoms despite intakes of 2,000–3,000 mg/day. Because of these aspects, longitudinal studies are required to determine how often the drug's desired properties meld into undesirable—and clinically important—tensions.

Many psychophysiological symptoms accompany caffeine's classical anxiety profile. These may enhance the experience of being anxious. To illustrate, caffeine commonly induces cardiac palpitations and arrhythmias (6, 14). If the etiology of such symptoms is not understood by the consumer, the worst may be imagined: hardening of the arteries, severe heart disease, an impending coronary, doom. The subjective response to such fears may further accentuate caffeine induced features. As described subsequently, this spiral of increasing anxiety symptoms—whether from naturally occurring stress or caffeinism—is mediated by central nervous system adrenergic mechanisms.

Epidemiologists are currently unable to conclude whether the anxiety reported by high users always follows caffeinism or occasionally predates it (9, 22). Some patients insist caffeine relaxes them, although clinical experience suggests this effect is not common. Some patients with years of hyperactivity, restlessness, and anxiety claim symptom relief with caffeine intake. Since stimulants in general, including caffeine to a mild degree, have been reported successful in treating hyperactivity, such claims are not farfetched and may have a sound neuropharmacological basis. In most cases, however, anxiety among subjects with caffeinism clinically seems to follow excessive intake rather than precede it.

Considering that 20–30 percent of Americans consume enough of this popular drug (500 mg or more per day) to make caffeinism a likelihood (9), and that anxiety features are probably the most prevalent manifestation, highest consumers should predictably report greater use of antianxiety agents. Studies have confirmed this possibility (9). In our survey of 205 subjects, 35 percent of those who ingested *less* than 750 mg/day reported some recent use of minor tranquilizers such as Librium, Valium, or Miltown. In contrast, 65 percent of those whose caffeine intake exceeded 750 mg/day had recently used antianxiety agents.

In summary, caffeinism is epidemiologically and clinically associated with diffuse anxiety symptoms. Anxiety rating scores are significantly higher among heaviest users. Simultaneous use of antianxiety agents is proportionately greater. Although cause and effect relationships are still vague, anxiety is clearly a major component of caffeinism.

Depression

Estimates suggest that more than 10 percent of individuals develop clinically significant depressions in their lifetime (29). Unfortunately, subcategories of depressive illness have been poorly defined. Clinicians often have difficulty determining possible associations between depression and other clinical conditions such as hypothyroidism, diabetes mellitus, alcoholism, or caffeinism. Depressive symptoms are remarkably similar regardless of their cause.

Recent data indicate that clinical relationships do exist between caffeinism and depression. Whether caffeine might cause, partially relieve, or confusingly modify depressive symptoms has not yet been determined (9, 30), but some support can be found for all of these possibilities.

On a theoretical basis, caffeine is a central nervous system (CNS) stimulant that alters those neurotransmitters associated with depression (31–43). Thus, the drug could be used by some already depressed people as self-medication to alleviate depressive symptoms. Since chronic use of other CNS stimulants (e.g., amphetamine or cocaine) is known sometimes to induce depressive features, however, chronic caffeine use could also cause depression. It is intriguing that in 1909 British doctors expressed concern that tea produced a "strange and extreme degree of depression" (17). More recent survey research indicated that individuals with high caffeine consumption reported *more* depressive symptoms. Among hospitalized patients who consumed more than 750 mg caffeine per day, for example, 50 percent scored higher than 23 on the Beck Depression Scale (a self-rating depression scale), a score that suggests severe depression. In contrast, 34 percent of moderate consumers and only 17 percent of low consumers scored higher than 23. Similar trends were found in nonpsychiatric and psychiatric patients.

It is revealing to compare these Beck scale scores with those compiled by Dorus and Senoy in assessing depression among opioid addicts (45). Twenty-nine percent of the multiple substance abusers, 23 percent of the short-term addicts and 15 percent of the long-term addicts reported Beck scores exceeding 23. Thus, even if causality has not been proven for caffeine, this drug has been associated with increased depressive symptomatology to an even greater degree than opiates.

Hospitalized nonpsychiatric patients who were high consumers reported more sadness, pessimism, dissatisfaction, self-dislike, self-accusation, and indecisiveness (9). More also described occasional crying and irritability. As with anxiety, this profile is sometimes diagnostically mistaken for a primary depressive episode. However, whereas highest caffeine consumers also reported greater use of antianxiety agents, we found no correlation between reported caffeine intake and treatment with antidepressants, suggesting that the depressive features may be unrecognized by treating physicians or mistakenly treated as anxiety manifestations.

Evidence that at least some high consumers use caffeine therapeutically is sketchy (16). First, approximately one-third of highest consumers reported that caffeine made them feel less depressed. This percentage was significantly greater than that among moderate or low consumers (9). However, we must consider the possibility that rather than treating depression, heavy users are simply recognizing and alleviating the dysphoria associated with recurrent caffeine withdrawal. Second, Neil and his colleagues observed that patients with depressive anergia and hypersomnia often self-medicated with large doses of caffeine and thus produced "mixed" depressive states, with simultaneous psychomotor deceleration and agitation (30). Indeed, the mean caffeine consumption among their mixed depressions exceeded 1,200 mg/day. A final observation suggesting that caffeine may be socially perceived as an antidepressant (even though there is no controlled evidence to support this claim) was contributed by Goldstein and his associates (23). They documented that caffeine unequivocally affected mood, as measured by a self-rating inventory: subjects who were most sensitive to the mood elevating effects were also most sensitive to the wakefulness caused by the drug, which suggested individual differences in pharmacokinetics or in sensitivity to the investigators.

In summary, some preliminary findings indicate that depressive symptoms may be a feature of caffeinism. Extensive studies, however, are clearly needed to delineate any precise relationships that might exist.

Sleep Disturbance

Perhaps the most prominent effect identified with caffeine is its antisleep action. Indeed, the earliest legends associated with coffee and tea emphasize the drug's antisoporific property (17, 18). Tea is claimed to have been discovered when a Chinese Buddhist tired and fell asleep during a nine-year meditation. He was so ashamed of his behavior upon awakening that he cut off his eyelids, which landed on the ground and sprouted into tea plants, used for ever after to combat sleep. A similar Arabian legend for coffee involves a goatherd (18). As early as 1660, tea was publicly promoted as a substance that "removeth lassitude, vanquisheth heavy dreams . . . overcometh superfluous sleep, and prevents sleepiness in general, so that without trouble whole nights may be passed in study" (46). Without doubt, caffeine's interference with sleep is responsible for much of the drug's popularity.

Pronounced sleep disruption from caffeine occurs predominantly among nontolerant users (9). Subjectively, caffeine before bedtime delayed sleep onset and caused more frequent nighttime awakenings. Objectively, the drug lengthened episodes of intervening wakefulness (47). The drug may also inhibit the deeper stages of sleep, but it does not alter REM sleep to the same extent as amphetamine (48, 49). Goldstein similarly concluded that nontolerant consumers were unequivocally kept awake longer by bedtime coffee (22). Commenting on the interaction between drug and psychological set, he also observed that many steady users denied that caffeine disturbed their sleep even when objective evaluations confirmed this effect. Futhermore, when a known caffeine sample was given to medical student volunteers and then blindly in a crossover design with lactose after the first night, subjects minimized the wakefulness produced by caffeine, so that caffeine's antisoporific effect *appeared* to be hardly greater than that of lactose. This minimizing of sleep disturbing effects among long-term users emphasizes the importance of developing objective measures for research studies (such as complete sleep EEGs) and the need for clinicians to treat subjective reports with slight skepticism.

Even accounting for some reverse-placebo bias, questionnaires have consistently documented huge reported differences in sleep activity across caffeine using subgroups (9). Highest consumers acknowledged fewest disruptions, suggesting tolerance or innate differences in response to the drug. To illustrate, 53 percent of low consumers (0–249 mg/day) in our studies said caffeine before bedtime prevented sleep; this decreased to 43 percent of moderate consumers (250–749 mg/day) and only 22 percent of high consumers (750 mg/day and above). Low users clearly seem more sensitive to nighttime caffeine.

Recent studies of sleep architecture have associated various phenomena such as reduced REM latency and increased REM density with endogenous depressions (50, 51). Since the preliminary data described above suggest that excessive caffeine use may also be associated with depression, the relationship between caffeine induced sleep disturbance and simultaneous depressive symptoms may be a fruitful area for study.

Caffeine's documented effect upon sleep is completely compatible with ancillary observations that highest caffeine users reported significantly greater use of sedative-hypnotic medications (9). Whereas only 1 percent of low users consumed sedative-hypnotics nightly, 8 percent of highest users had this pattern. A hospital study further revealed an interaction between caffeine and sleeping medications by pointing out that when caffeine was taken together with pentobarbital at bedtime, the soporific effect was approximately the same as that of a placebo (52). These antagonistic pharmacological effects predict that caffeine consuming patients would either escalate their requests for higher doses of sleeping pills or increase consumption of over-the-counter sleeping products.

In summary, caffeinism is clearly associated with sleep disruption. The recent development of sleep EEGs may provide more detailed information about the onset, cause, and significance of such disturbances and possible associations with other manifestations of caffeinism such as depression.

Somatic Manifestations

Caffeine has causally been implicated in such common medical conditions as hypertension, peptic ulcer, and headaches (53–56). Only recently, however has a profile of physical complaints been associated with caffeinism (28). When users were surveyed to determine which somatic symptoms they associated with caffeine use, almost two-thirds were aware of a caffeine diuresis. Approximately one in five associated caffeine use with occasional diarrhea, tachycardia, tremulousness, or abdominal pain. Only a few individuals felt that caffeine was likely to induce such symptoms as ringing in the ears, tingling of hands and feet, spots in front of the eyes, shortness of breath, or excessive perspiration. In contrast to "pure" anxiety symptoms, depressive complaints, or sleep disorders, perceived somatic complaints did not show a direct dose response relationship. Indeed, more low and high than moderate users reported somatic manifestations with caffeine use.

The somatic symptoms of caffeinism clinically tend to develop in late morning or midday, presumably because this is the time of peak plasma levels. Changes in consumption patterns could alter this timing, of course, since onset of physical features tends to occur one to two hours after a large consumption of the drug, regardless of time of day. As with sleep disruptions, tolerance may influence the severity of somatic symptoms, which may explain why low consumers more commonly associate somatic problems with caffeine use; low users have not developed tolerance.

Many of the physiological responses that follow high caffeine use are conventionally identified with anxiety. These include cardiac palpitations and arrhythmias (especially premature ventricular contractions), rapid heart beat, tremulousness, light-headedness, and diuresis. As noted earlier, recognition of such symptoms might launch, perpetuate, or exacerbate the subjective experience of being anxious, indicating why use of minor tranquilizers is greatest among heaviest caffeine users.

Delirium

Kraepelin, a wizard in his descriptions of psychopathology, suggested in 1892 that caffeine might precipitate a mild delirium (64). An actual case of caffeine induced delirium was not recorded until 1936, however (12). In that year, a 24-year-old female was reported periodically to consume large numbers of caffeine citrate tablets to "pep" her up. Although labeled manic by her treating physician, she actually presented with confusion and disorientation, symptoms more compatible with a delirious state. A similar delirium with disorientation, marked perceptual disturbances, and cognitive disruption was noted to follow high doses of caffeine in a dog sled racer who used commercially available caffeine products for energy and alertness (65). Since caffeine may alter perceptions, the possibility of a delirium from high doses must be considered.

Delusional Thinking

Caffeine has not been proven to induce delusions. Nevertheless, empirical evidence strongly suggests that the drug has the potential to cause or at least to accentuate psychotic thinking. Winstead, in his assessment of caffeine consumption among 135 psychiatric patients in a military hospital, observed that more high users were diagnosed as having psychosis (26). Mikkelsen suggested that schizophrenia flare-ups might occur following caffeine consumption (7). Specifically, he reported a catatonic patient who went on "a coffee jag," then presumably developed persecutory delusions that his mother was trying to kill him. A second patient reported feeling strange and increased paranoid thinking when she consumed coffee. Caffeine use has also been associated in hospitalized patients with increased psychopathology as measured by the Brief Psychiatric Rating Scale (BPRS). Vonnegut, in *The Eden Express,* a personal vignette, supported this possible association in a lay description of caffeine's effects upon psychotic thinking: "Coffee is nearly always bad for schizophrenics. Grass, hash, and especially the hallucinogens and speed can be real trouble. Good old alcohol, interestingly enough, can be helpful in a pinch" (66). Despite such warnings, coffee and tea have been advocated (perhaps unwisely) in treatment programs for psychiatric patients, generally because caffeine seems to combat the sleepiness commonly associated with most psychopharmacological agents (67, 68).

Psychomotor Abnormalities

With complete seriousness, a 1774 contribution to the *London Public Advertiser* observed that the Boston Tea Party may have had some surprising consequences: "Four or five hundred chests of tea have so contaminated the water in Boston harbour, that the fish may have contracted a disorder not unlike the nervous complaints of the body" (19). Numerous clinicians likewise have noted the common association of tremulousness with caffeine. Less well known are some rarer motor system abnormalities. In 1925, Powers described rhythmic tremors of the eyelid, hand, and tongue, accompanied by twitching of the facial muscles (11). All symptoms disappeared after caffeine intake was discontinued. Lutz recently claimed that the "restless legs syndrome" is caused by caffeine use (69). Predominantly occurring when resting, this syndrome consists of unpleasant, bilateral, creeping sensations in the lower legs. The original description of this condition, published in 1685 by the esteemed neurologist Willis, can scarcely be improved upon: "Wherefore to some, when being aBed they betake themselves to sleep, presently in the arms and Leggs, Leapings and Contractions of the Tendons, and so great a Restlessness and Tossings of their Members ensue, that the diseased are no more able to sleep, than if they were in a place of the greatest Torture" (70). Like patients with psychomotor akathesia secondary to neuroleptic administration, subjects with the restless legs syndrome feel the need to get up and move their legs but experience no relief thereby. Lutz maintained that elimination of caffeine intake relieved this perplexing syndrome. Replication of this claim is required.

Miscellaneous Clinical Manifestations

Although the number of case reports is small, excessive caffeine has been claimed to cause persistent lowgrade fever, impaired fetal development, cystic breast disease, and fluid retention (71–77). Though only a few published reports discuss these conditions, caffeine's possible role in coronary heart disease has been widely debated in the professional literature (8, 78). Findings are equivocal. Basic science investigators have been far more definitive and document that the drug has distinct toxic effects upon the cardiovascular and renal systems when used chronically (54, 55).

Genesis of the Disorder

Caffeine use has been heatedly debated on many occasions throughout history. Some have considered it a "loathsome poison," others have called caffeine containing drinks the "nectar of the gods." Historical societal responses to the drug have closely paralleled recent marijuana controversies. Critics have attacked caffeine use on moral, legal, and medical grounds. Despite these three-pronged attacks—so characteristic of societal responses to chemical substances—caffeine is very popular. This remarkable acceptance must be considered when discussing the origins of caffeinism.

From infancy, potential consumers are surrounded by caffeine users, attractive commercials, and business establishments that center their names (coffee chops) and activities around the ingestion of caffeine products. Society is not only permissive about beginning caffeine use; with few exceptions, it seems to encourage this practice. Peer example, modeling of adults, familial patterns, and cultural and ethnic patterns all contribute.

Consumption usually begins during adolescence. In the early stages, caffeine use is characteristically infrequent and often not considered especially pleasant. This is not surprising since caffeine containing substances are often described as tasteless or bitter (5). Many novices state that they had to learn to like coffee or tea. A few users promptly cease all ingestion after early sampling, usually because they developed unpleasant anxiety or somatic symptoms or strongly disliked the taste. For most early users, however, once launched, the habit flows; reinforcers are clearly strong because intake tends not only to continue but usually increases in frequency and quantity as well.

When asked why they consume, users invariably mention such qualities as taste, warmth, or aroma; association with other pleasant activities like eating and smoking; or a break from routine (coffee break). Subjectively, however, the drug's stimulation seems to be a far more potent reinforcer than any of these factors. The sense of well-being, the assistance in waking up in the morning, the lift during episodes of fatigue, the claimed increase in efficiency, the perceived clarity of thought—all are valued commodities. Students learn to study with the drug. Tired employees gird themselves for a day's work with it. Although perhaps more a social drug than other substances that are volitionally used, caffeine seems to be identified with work and productivity. In that sense, it is truly a domesticated drug.

Why does caffeine consumption often become excessive? Why do some consumers steadily increase their intake, even to the point of caffeinism? Definite answers to these questions are unknown. Certainly, classical Pavlovian conditioning contributes to the pattern (79). It is reasonable to hypothesize, however, that the drug neuropharmacologically stimulates reward systems of the brain (80). Whether in the hypothalamus, the median forebrain bundle, or unknown parts of the limbic system, caffeine may modulate CNS neurotransmitters and thus activate the brain's pleasure centers. Caffeine concentration in various preparations has been shown to be a factor in total coffee intake, suggesting that high users need to reach a critical level to achieve desired stimulation. Known parallels among caffeine, amphetamine, and cocaine, all of which produce many similar effects, make plausible the theory that the drug becomes habituating predominantly by reinforcing CNS pleasure centers.

Whatever the source of reinforcement, the caffeine habit is persistent and difficult to modify. Kings have failed in their attempt to alter it (17, 18). Doctors have commented upon how difficult it is to get patients to stop (81). As early as the sixteenth century, an observer noted that despite banishment

> the [coffee] habit had become so strong, and the use of it so generally agreeable, that the people continued, notwithstanding all prohibitions, to drink it in their own houses. The officers of the police, seeing they could not suppress the use of it allowed of the selling it, on paying a tax; and the drink-

ing it provided it was not done openly; so that it was drunk in particular
places, with the doors shut, or in the back room of some of the shopkeepers
houses (82).

Clearly, whatever they may be, reinforcements for caffeine consumption
are relatively potent.

Caffeinism tends to develop after years or even decades of use. Individuals with clear-cut caffeinism generally have consumed for more than
10 years. This pattern is predictable from known pharmacokinetics since
acute ingestion of large doses would produce such unpleasant consequences
that the user would quickly stop. Pharmacological tolerance, which increases slowly, must precede most cases of caffeinism.

Most chronic users report periodically stopping and restarting intake.
Such a pattern is intriguingly consistent with patterns of intravenous
stimulant self-administration among animals (regular cycles of drug intake
are interspersed with periods of voluntary abstinence).

The onset of caffeinism is inconsistent and rarely specific. Symptoms
come and go, probably because the tolerated plasma level is continually being readjusted. If tolerance is exceeded, palpitations, anxiety, headache, or
other symptoms may occur. The next day, dose may be readjusted (usually
not a conscious decision) and the symptoms fade. Another day, more drug
may be consumed late in the day and sleep may be disrupted. The following
day, the user compensates by decreasing intake and the insomnia disappears. Or, if he or she persists on a regular basis, tolerance to sleep interference develops and the problem seems to disappear. In this fashion,
the syndrome slowly and insidiously blossoms and fades, often without the
person's noticing a connection between clinical symptoms and caffeine intake. Clinicians frequently are told, "I've always been a coffee [or tea]
drinker, but I only recently started feeling this way," even when precise
clinical questioning documents years of symptomatology.

Most subjects with clear-cut caffeinism consume a total dose above
700 mg, usually approaching or surpassing 1,000 mg. Infrequently, chronic
consumers describe daily intake that seems frighteningly large, sometimes
near 5,000 mg/day (83). Among individuals whose intake is greater than
1,000 mg, clinicians can have a great deal of confidence that some
manifestations of caffeinism will be present even in patients who insist that
their caffeine consumption causes them no difficulties.

Sources of the drug differ across nations. In the United States, the
majority of caffeine is ingested via coffee (41). In some countries, tea,
cocoa leaf (84), or other sources may be more important. Probably many
of the other ingredients in caffeine containing vehicles produce their own
characteristic physiological effects. This phenomenon may explain reports
that tea and coffee affect people differently and claims that even decaffeinated products produce toxic manifestations among some users.

Biological and Biomedical Correlates

Caffeine is toxicologically a relatively safe drug (85), most notably because it is usually marketed in dilute form. Fatal caffeine doses for adults probably exceed 5–10 g (8); to consume this amount by coffee drinking, one would have to drink 50–100 cups in a short period!

Caffeine appears in tissues within minutes after oral ingestion (5, 86). Peak plasma levels occur after about 30–45 minutes. Studies of half-life suggest that about 15 percent of the drug is metabolized each hour. Plasma assays of caffeine levels are now possible but are available only in medical centers that have established the procedure (and usually solely for research purposes).

Caffeine's known pharmacological actions are widespread, influencing most physiological systems (2, 3). The recognized pharmacological actions clearly explain most of the clinical manifestations of caffeinism. As illustrated in Table 8–2, if initial dosage levels are exceeded, desired CNS effects such as alertness and diminished reaction time insidiously develop into restlessness, irritability, and tremulousness. Similar dosage relationships exist for effects within other physiological systems.

Various neurobiological substrates that might underlie psychopathologies such as anxiety, depression, and psychosis have recently been vigorously investigated. A number of CNS neurotransmitters have been implicated as important in mediating the manifestations. The evidence implicating norepinephine, dopamine, serotonin, and acetylcholine is especially strong (87). If anxiety, depression, and psychosis have been linked to certain CNS neurotransmitter abnormalities, a logical question is how caffeine might affect these various CNS transmitters.

Recent neuropharmacological investigations suggest that the drug produces a myriad of CNS effects. First, caffeine significantly increases CNS norepinephrine synthesis and turnover (33–35). It may also sensitize adrenergic postsynaptic receptor sites (37, 41). These effects possibly account for the anxiety symptoms associated with caffeinism, but this connection remains to be proven. These effects may also be responsible for some of the habituating (addictive) aspects of chronic users since increases in adrenergic activity might mediate reinforcement of hypothalamic and limbic system pleasure centers. Second, caffeine has been documented to raise serotonin concentrations in rat brainstems possibly by increasing synthesis or preventing release (88). Whether this effect also occurs in humans, or whether it relates to mood changes observed in some patients with caffeinism, is something about which we can still only speculate, but this surely is an important finding since serotonergic function has been linked to depression. Third, caffeine sensitizes central catecholamine postsynaptic receptor sites, particularly those for dopamine (41–43). The drug also produces biphasic changes in dopamine function, with a transient increase

TABLE 8–2
Pharmacology of Caffeine: Dose Relationship between
Expected Actions and Clinical Consequences

ANTICIPATED PHARMACOLOGICAL ACTIONS AT LOW DOSES	DOSE-RELATED MANIFESTATIONS OF CAFFEINISM
Central Nervous System	
Clearer thoughts	Insomnia
Diminished drowsiness	Restlessness, nervousness
Improved intellectual effort	Irritability, agitation
Diminished reaction time	Muscle twitching and fasciculations
Increased motor activity	Tremulousness, reflex hyperexcitability
Increased respiratory rate and depth	Headache
Decreased heart rate, constriction of	Sensory disturbances (hyperesthesia,
systemic vasculature	ringing in ears, flashes of light,
Increased reflex excitability	dry mouth, ocular dyskinesias)
	Tachypnea
	Lethargy, fatigue, yawning (biphasic
	reaction to large doses)
	Depression
	Secondary to withdrawal:
	Headache
	Inability to work effectively
	Lethargy
Cardiovascular System	
Increased rate and force of contraction	Palpitations, extrasystoles, tachycardia
Dilation of coronary arteries	Arrhythmias
Dilation of pulmonary and	Flushing
general systemic vessels	Marked hypotension and circulatory
	failure (very large doses)
Renal System	
Increased production of urine	Diuresis
Gastrointestinal System	
Increased volume and acidity	Nausea, vomiting, diarrhea
of gastric secretions	Epigastric "awareness" and pain
	Possible peptic ulcer
	Hematemesis
Basal Metabolic System (BMR)	
10–25% increase in BMR from .5 g	Fever, edema, dehydration

preceding a decrease (36, 43). Since dopamine has been strongly linked to schizophrenia and other psychoses, these effects of caffeine may explain why the drug seems to produce or exacerbate psychotic thinking among susceptible individuals.

Caffeine, like all methylxanthines (89), competitively inhibits an enzyme called cyclic nucleotide phosphodiesterase. Caffeine may change the concentrations of intracellular cyclic 3',5'-adenosine monophosphate (cyclic AMP), the important—but vaguely understood—"intracellular messenger" (90). Since alterations of cyclic AMP are produced by psychopharmacological agents (91), we can speculate that these effects might have causal or therapeutic implications. Finally, caffeine modifies CNS calcium release mechanisms (2), counteracts the stimulatory effects of adenosine (which may have long-term toxic effects) (39, 40), and alters acetylcholine activity (42).

Since the CNS effects of caffeine are so diffuse, it is reasonable to speculate that chronic consumption of high doses may sufficiently alter neurotransmitter balances to produce clinical consequences. Such phenomena are well described for other CNS stimulants, undoubtedly acting through similar neurobiological mechanisms.

Prior to concluding any discussion of biological or biomedical correlates of caffeinism, it would be prudent to consider whether some individuals might have genetic predispositions to caffeinism. Some investigators have suggested that coffee drinking and cigarette smoking showed a significant heritability when the amount consumed was considered (90). Others have hinted that there may be inherited variations in sleep disturbance after drinking coffee (93). Thus far, however, no genetic substrate that causes or contributes to caffeinism has been indentified.

Psychological and Behavioral Correlates

No precise personality profile of caffeinism has been established. Primavera and colleagues showed that caffeine users did *not* differ from nonusers on the Edwards Personal Preference Schedule (93). When self-descriptions were compared, caffeine nonusers tended to rate themselves more secure than users, but this was an isolated difference. The authors concluded that caffeine use (in contrast to tobacco use) was not related to the measures of personality they employed in their study. Furlong, in his assessment of coffee consumption among patients, did observe that the only significant correlation to the amount of coffee consumed was the presence of a "personality disorder" (81). Interactions were suggested by the fact that persons with personality disorder who simultaneously consumed 10 or more cups of coffee per day more often reported behavior disorders in childhood, school learning problems, impulsivity, and histories

of scholastic failure. He and others have suggested that many adult high
caffeine consumers may be patients with minimal brain dysfunction who
have learned to self-medicate with this drug (94). Cause and effect have not
yet been comfortably established, however. Gilliland noted that when individuals identified as either extroverts or introverts on the Eysenck Personality Inventory were given low doses of caffeine, the performances of
both groups were facilitated (95, 96).

In trying to understand why personality profiles of individuals with
caffeinism may be hard to identify, we must consider widespread use of
this substance. More than 60 percent of all persons 10 years of age and over
report recent coffee consumption, more than 80 percent of all adults
recently drank coffee, and more than 50 percent consumed tea within the
past month (97, 98). Thus, the phenomenon of caffeine consumption
almost certainly exists among *all* personality subtypes. If personality differences are ever to be found, emphasis will have to be placed upon *quantitative* differences.

Sociocultural and Environmental Correlates

Symptoms of caffeinism are undoubtedly influenced by life factors. Cobb,
for example, epidemiologically evaluated unemployed auto workers and
noted that those who drank coffee *after* experiencing the stress of job loss
had greater increases in norepinephrine output than they did drinking coffee at nonstressful times and greater increases than did controls (99). These
data suggest that sociocultural influences, caffeine use, and biological
substrates all seem to be integrated in a "final common pathway." Further
support for interaction between caffeine use and life events comes from
some of our unpublished work. We asked 205 hospitalized patients to indicate how they felt stress affected their caffeine intake. Only 13 percent of
low users noted their intake increased with stress, but 30 percent of
moderate users and 38 percent of heavy users reported this association. It
may be that high caffeine consumers are more driven to drink caffeine containing products at stressful times and that, paradoxically, consumption
under such circumstances synergistically produces more pathophysiological
symptoms than usual. Stated differently, consumption of large amounts
without clinical consequences might be possible when environmental
stresses are low, but similar intake under pressure might produce a spiral of
stress.

Demographically, highest caffeine users tend to be older, most commonly in their thirties or forties (89). Males and females appear equally
susceptible. Since some religions prohibit caffeine use, among a small seg-
ment of the population religion is certainly a factor in determining risk for
caffeinism. In large random populations, however, religious heritage or up-

bringing does not statistically predict the risk for caffeinism, while religious *activity* (regardless of religion) does differentiate, with more active individuals likely to consume less caffeine (9). Although educational differences among subgroups in our surveys were not significant, there was a slight tendency for highest consumers to be less well educated.

Caffeine Withdrawal

Pharmacological tolerance to caffeine has been disputed (8), but data support its existence (57). If a nonuser were to ingest 1,000 mg caffeine in a single day, the effects would be dramatic. Yet, perhaps as many as 10 percent of North Americans ingest this dose or more daily. Although most, when questioned carefully, have some manifestations of caffeinism, they lack the dramatic symptoms associated with large acute ingestions, a clear indication of clinical tolerance.

Once a pattern of chronic heavy intake is established, if consumption should suddenly drop, regardless of the reason, a caffeine withdrawal syndrome is likely to develop (13). Within 18–24 hours, consistent physiological manifestations appear among perhaps one-half of heavy users. Major complaints include irritability, lethargy, apathy, difficulty concentrating, inability to work effectively, nervousness, restlessness, and even mild nausea. Many withdrawing subjects become moderately somnolent; excessive yawning is not uncommon. Usually withdrawal symptoms are relatively mild and tolerable, but they occasionally impair functioning until the withdrawal phase has cleared.

The caffeine withdrawal headache may be the most important public health aspect of the withdrawal syndrome. First, it appears to be one of the more common and consistent features. Second, it is clinically the most perplexing to suffering patients. Third, it may lead to unnecessary analgesic use. Dreisbach and Pfeiffer initially described this headache and demonstrated that it can be experimentally induced (15). It starts with a feeling of fullness in the head, then phases into a diffuse, throbbing, painful, "typical" headache. Exercise accentuates the pain. If untreated, the headache persists for three to six hours. Goldstein noted a high incidence of caffeine withdrawal headaches among housewives who failed to consume their morning coffee (24). Similarly, Greden and Victor observed that 20 percent of 205 hospitalized patients reported having recognized previous caffeine withdrawal headaches, with the mean intake among headache subjects being significantly larger than among nonheadache subjects (618 mg/day versus 398 mg/day) (13). Caffeine withdrawal headaches subjectively occur most commonly on weekends, perhaps because work related caffeine consumption changes. Afflicted individuals do not report any significant differences in their history of receiving psychiatric treatment.

An intriguing public health aspect of the caffeine withdrawal syndrome is that the condition is most effectively relieved by further ingestion of caffeine. Thus, afflicted subjects are operationally reinforced to continue high ingestion (and thus avoid withdrawal headaches) and possibly to treat themselves with analgesics that contain caffeine should a headache develop (Table 8-1). A multitude of over-the-counter and prescription medications contain caffeine, so this pattern of treating "tension headaches" (which may often be caffeine withdrawal headaches) with more caffeine is probably quite common. Unfortunately, while consumption of two headache tablets several times a day may relieve the pain, these analgesics also contribute substantially to caffeine intake and thus aggravate the problem. The "treatment" predictably works, and the cycle just as predictably continues.

Associated Substance Abuse

High caffeine users consume more sedative-hypnotics and minor tranquilizers than do moderate and lower users (9). In addition, their drug use extends beyond these prescription drugs: they also utilize greater amounts of tobacco and alcohol (58).

In our surveys of hospitalized patients, we noted that 82 percent of high caffeine users were smokers, compared to approximately 60 percent of low and moderate users. Furthermore, 17 percent of highest users smoked more than two packs of cigarettes per day compared to only 9 and 5 percent of moderate and low users, respectively. Use of hard liquor, wine, and beer was also substantially greater among heaviest caffeine consumers. In fact, more than 8 percent of those who consumed above 750 mg caffeine per day also drank a case of beer per week (*plus* some liquor and wine). Consistent with these reported intakes, highest consumers compiled higher scores on the Michigan Alcohol Screening Test (MAST), an instrument designed to identify individuals with possible alcoholism (59).

Underlying reasons for this simultaneous volitional intake of other drugs are not clear. Gilbert documented that alcohol consumption among rats increased during periods in which caffeine was added to their marginally adequate diet and decreased once the drug was withdrawn, so perhaps some metabolic factor is operational (60). Erroneous claimed interactions between caffeine and withdrawal are, of course, legendary. As early as 1819, Benjamin Rush, the father of American psychiatry, claimed that a "love for tea in early life" prevented one from developing "the love of spiritous liquors" (61). In 1894 Walsh advised that "those who desire to rescue a drunkard from his bane will find no better substitute for strong, fresh-made coffee"(62). Objective studies have consistently refuted these pervasive myths, however (60, 63). Yet, it is intriguing that numerous ex-alcoholics are prodigious caffeine consumers, an observation subjectively made by many treatment personnel in alcohol rehabilitation units or Alcoholics Anonymous members.

Despite their greater use of commercially available drugs and alcohol, highest caffeine users reported no differences from low and moderate users in ingestion of lithium carbonate, antidepressants, other stimulants, or neuroleptic medications (9). Data unfortunately are unavailable about whether high caffeine users also overeat.

Treatment

Prior to treatment of caffeinism, accurate diagnosis is essential. Unfortunately, most people report some caffeine consumption. The clinician's task is to determine when such intake may be correlated to clinical problems. First, an accurate assessment of dosage—from *all* common sources—is necessary. Brief questionnaires might be utilized to compile these figures (9). Second, a high index of suspicion is required. If daily intake is high, 500 mg or more, a clinical association should be investigated. If dosage is not high, but a temporal association is found between intake and symptoms, caffeinism is highly likely. In other words, if symptoms regularly follow caffeine consumption, even if quantities consumed do not seem inordinately large, such a pattern may identify causality.

Patients should be educated about the likely etiology of their symptoms (including reading assignments if skepticism is rampant). A caffeine withdrawal and challenge should then be set up, ideally with the patient blind to the design. Specifically, patients should be told to refrain from all caffeine and given a list of caffeine containing substances. They should be encouraged to discard (not just sequester) all caffeine containing analgesics. Substitutes for oral stimulation might help, such as gum chewing or mint sucking. Tobacco smoking should *not* be suggested as an alternative, nor should other psychoactive stimulants be prescribed. Water should be recommended for quenching thirst. Patients should be informed that a number of transient withdrawal features may develop.

After one week of abstinence, symptoms of caffeinism—and also of withdrawal—should have abated among most users. At that point, for convincing demonstration of causality, a caffeine challenge can be implemented. Preferably, this is done by using placebo capsules for several days and then identical appearing caffeine capsules. The patient should be blind to the timing of the crossover. Predictably, symptoms will promptly resume when caffeine capsules are consumed. The code can then be broken and the patient informed. This procedure should be convincing, but clinical experience shows a great deal of denial and skepticism, which may well be unconscious mechanisms to avoid a dreaded abstinence from the drug. If use of matching placebo and caffeine pills is not possible, administration of caffeine containing substances such as coffee or tea can be alternated with abstinence or at least with ingestion of decaffeinated products. Other family members may be helpful in implementing a blind switch from decaffeinated to caffeinated products, although, as hinted earlier, decaffeinated products may also induce some symptoms.

For long-term prevention, in addition to eliminating known caffeine containing beverages, patients should be instructed to use only non–caffeine containing analgesics such as aspirin or acetominophen unless other medications are prescribed by the treating physician. Periodic reassessments of intake should be conducted since intermittent relapse with steadily increasing dosages is to be expected.

Although no published reports discuss this phenomenon, various adrenergic blockers, such as propanolol, may alleviate some symptoms of caffeinism.

Finally, anyone treating patients with caffeinism should consider the likelihood that a number of other substances are probably being simultaneously abused. Indeed, in some cases, the deleterious effects of these other agents may be more significant than those produced by caffeine. A comprehensive treatment approach is thus required.

Conclusion

Caffeinism is one of the most common volitional disorders in the world. Although more prevalent, this condition is happily not as disruptive as most other excessive behaviors. Yet the syndrome is still poorly understood and areas for future investigation are abundant.

Caffeinism closely resembles most other addictive drug disorders. Caffeine has, however, been rather thoroughly domesticated, and many users employ the drug in moderation and with relative safety. This means that future studies trying to understand why some users ingest excessive amounts ought also to consider why many users do not. Perhaps the lessons that are learned can be applied to other volitional disorders.

References

1. Peters, J. M., Factors affecting caffeine toxicity: a review of the literature, *J. Clin. Pharm. 7,* 131–141 (1967).
2. Ritchie, J. M., Central nervous system stimulants II: the xanthines, in *The Pharmacological Basis of Therapeutics,* 4th ed., L. S. Goodman and A. Gilman, eds., Macmillan, New York, 1970, pp. 358–370.
3. Truitt, E. B., Jr., The xanthines, in *Drill's Pharmacology in Medicine,* 4th ed., J. R., DiPalma, ed., McGraw-Hill, New York, 1971, pp. 533–556.

4. Weiss, B., and Laties, V. G., Enhancement of human performance by caffeine and the amphetamines, *Pharm. Rev. 14,* 1-36 (1962).

5. Levinson, H. C., and Bick, E. C., Psychopharmacology of caffeine in *Psychopharmacology in the Practice of Medicine,* M. D. Jarvik, ed., Appleton-Century-Crofts, New York, 1977, pp. 451-463.

6. Greden, J. F., Anxiety or caffeinism: a diagnostic dilemma, *Amer. J. Psychiat. 131,* 1089-1092 (1974).

7. Mikkelsen, E. J., Caffeine and schizophrenia, *J. Clin. Psychiat. 1,* 732-736 (1978).

8. Gilbert, R. M., Caffeine as a drug of abuse, in *Research Advances in Alcohol and Drug Problems,* R. J. Gibbons, Y. Israel, H. K. Alent, R. E. Pophan, W. Schmidt, and R. G. Smart, eds., vol. 3, Wiley, New York, 1970, pp. 127-168.

9. Greden, J. F., Anxiety and depression associated with caffeinism among psychiatric inpatients, *Amer. J. Psychiat. 135,* 963-966 (1978).

10. Orendorff, O., Letter to the editor, *JAMA 62,* 1828 (1914).

11. Powers, H., The syndrome of coffee, *Med. J. and Record 121,* 745-749 (1925).

12. McManamy, M. C., and Schube, P. G., Caffeine intoxication: report of a case the symptoms of which amounted to a psychosis, *N. Eng. J. Med. 215,* 616-620 (1936).

13. Greden, J. F., Victor, B., Fontaine, P., and Lubetsky, M., Caffeine-withdrawal headache, *Psychosomatics* 21: 411-418 (1980).

14. Greden, J. F., Victor, B., Fontaine, P., and Lubetsky, M., Caffeine-withdrawal headache: a neglected syndrome, paper presented to the 132d annual meeting of the American Psychiatric Association, Chicago, 1979.

15. Dreisbach, R. H., and Pfeiffer, C., Caffeine-withdrawal headache, *J. Lab. and Clin. Med. 28,* 1212-1218 (1943).

16. Greden, J. F., Coffee, tea, and you, *The Sciences 19,* 6-11 (1979).

17. Siegerist, H. E., Literary controversy over tea in 18th century England, *Bull. Hist. Med. 13,* 185-189 (1943).

18. Greden, J. F., The tea controversy in colonial America, *JAMA 236,* 63-66 (1976).

19. Gilbert, R. M., Letter to the editor: toxicity, *JAMA 263,* 1452 (1976).

20. Gilbert, R. M., Caffeine beverages and their effects, *Addictions 21,* 68-80 (1974).

21. Goldstein, A., Wakefulness caused by caffeine, *Exp. Path. and Pharm. 248,* 269-278 (1964).

22. Goldstein, A., Warren, R., and Kaizer, S., Psychotropic effects of caffeine in man I: individual differences and sensitivity to caffeine-induced wakefulness, *J. Pharm. Exp. Ther. 49,* 156-159 (1965).

23. Goldstein, A., and Kaizer, S., Psychotropic effects of caffeine in man II: alertness, psychomotor coordination, and mood, *J. Pharm. Exp. Ther. 150,* 146-151 (1965).

24. Goldstein, A., and Kaizer, S., Psychotropic effects of caffeine in man III: a questionnaire survey of coffee drinkers and its effects in a group of housewives, *Clin. Pharm. Ther. 10,* 477-488 (1969).

25. Goldstein, A., Kaizer, S., and Whitby, O., Psychotropic effects of caffeine in man IV: quantitative and qualitative differences associated with habituation to caffeine, *Clin. Pharm. Ther. 10,* 489–497 (1969).

26. Winstead, D. K., Coffee consumption among psychiatric inpatients, *Amer. J. Psychiat. 133,* 1447–1450 (1976).

27. Speilberger, C. O., Gorusch, R. L., and Lushene, R. E., *State-Trait Anxiety Inventory Manual,* Consulting Psychologists Press, Palo Alto, 1970.

28. Victor, B. S., and Greden, J. F., Somatic manifestations of caffeinism, *J. of Clin. Psychiatry,* in press.

29. Weissman, M. M., and Myers, J. K., Affective disorders in a U. S. urban community, *Arch. Gen. Psychiat. 35,* 1304–1311 (1978).

30. Neil, J. F., Himmelhoch, J. M., Mallinger, A. G., Mallinger, J., and Hanin, I., Caffeinism complicating hypersomnic depressive episodes, *Comp. Psychiat. 19,* 377–387 (1978).

31. Beer, B., Chasin, M., Clody, D. E., Vogel, J. R., and Horowitz, Z. P., Cyclic adenosine monophosphate phosphodiesterase in brain: effect on anxiety, *Science 176,* 428–430 (1972).

32. Bellet, S., Roman, L., DeCastro, O., Kim, K. D., and Kershbaum, A., Effect of coffee ingestion on catecholamine release, *Metabolism 18,* 288–291 (1969).

33. Berkowitz, B. A., and Spector, S., Effect of caffeine and theophylline on peripheral catecholamines, *Eur. J. Pharm. 16,* 193–196 (1971).

34. Berkowitz, B. A., Spector, S., and Pool, W., The interaction of caffeine, theophylline, and theobromine with monoamine oxidase inhibitors, *Eur. J. Pharm. 16,* 315–321 (1971).

35. Berkowitz, B. A., Tarver, J. H., and Spector, S., Release of norepinephrine in the central nervous system by theophylline and caffeine, *Eur. J. Pharm. 10,* 64–71 (1970).

36. Corrodi, H., Fuxe, K., and Jonsson, G., Effects of caffeine on central monoamine neurons, *J. Pharm. Pharmacol. 24,* 155–158 (1972).

37. Fuxe, K., and Ungerstedt, U., Action of caffeine and theophylline on supersensitive dopamine receptors: considerable enhancement of receptor response to treatment with dopa and dopamine receptor agonists, *Med. Biol. 52,* 48–54 (1974).

38. Levi, L., Effect of coffee on the function of the sympatho-adrenomedullary system in man, *Acta Med. Scand. 181,* 431–438 (1967).

39. Phillis, J. W., Kostopoulos, G. K., and Limacher, J. J., Depression of corticospinal cells by various purines and pyrimidines, *Can. J. Physiol. and Pharm. 52,* 1226–1229 (1974).

40. Phillis, J. W., Kostopoulos, G. K., and Limacher, J. J., A potent depressant action of adenosine derivatives on cerebral cortical neurons, *Eur. J. Pharm. 30,* 125–129 (1975).

41. Waldeck, B., Effect of caffeine on locomotor activity and central catecholamine mechanisms: a study with special reference to drug interaction, *Acta Pharm. and Tox. 36* (supp.), 1–23 (1975).

42. Waldeck, B., Modification of a caffeine-induced locomotor stimulation by a cholinergic mechanism, *J. Neural Trans. 35,* 195–205 (1974).

43. Waldeck, B., Some effects of caffeine and aminophylline on the turnover of catecholamines in the brain, *J. Pharm. Pharmacol. 23,* 824–830 (1971).

44. Snyder, S. H., Catecholamines in the brain as mediators of amphetamine psychosis, *Arch. Gen. Psychiat. 27,* 169–179 (1972).

45. Dorus, W., and Senoy, E. C., Depression, demographic dimensions, and drug abuse, paper presented to the 132d annual meeting of the American Psychiatric Association, Chicago, 1979.

46. Repplier, A., *To Think of Tea!* Houghton Mifflin, Boston, 1932.

47. Brezinova, V, Oswold, I., and Loudon, J., Two types of insomnia: too much waking or not enough sleep, *Brit. J. Psychiat. 126,* 439–445 (1975).

48. Brezinova, V., Effect of caffeine on sleep: EEG study in late middle age people, *Brit. J. Clin. Pharm. 1,* 203–208 (1974).

49. Soletu, B., Allen, M., and Itil, T. M., The effect of Coca-Cola, caffeine antidepressants, and chlorpromazine on objective sleep parameters, *Pharmacokopsychiat. 254,* 307–321 (1974).

50. Gillin, J. D., Duncan, W., Pettigrew, K. D., Frankel, B. L., and Snyder, F., Successful separation of depressed, normal, and insomniac subjects by EEG sleep diagnosis, *Arch. Gen. Psychiat. 36,* 85–90 (1979).

51. Kupfer, D. J., Foster, F. G., Reich, L., Thompson, K. S., and Weiss, B., EEG-sleep changes as predictors in depression, *Amer. J. Psychiat. 133,* 622–626 (1976).

52. Forrest, W. H., Bellville, J. W., and Brown, B. W., The interaction of caffeine with pentobarbital as a nighttime hypnotic, *Anesthesiology 36,* 37–41 (1972).

53. MacCormack, F. A., The effects of coffee drinking on the cardiovascular system: experimental and epidemiological research, *Prev. Med. 6,* 104–119 (1977).

54. Robertson, D., Frolich, J. C., Cain, R. K., Watson, J. T., Hollifield, J. W., Shand, D. G., and Oates, J. A., Effects of caffeine on plasma renin activity, catecholamines, and blood pressure, *N. Eng. J. Med. 208,* 181–186 (1978).

55. Henry, J. P., and Oused, J. C., Psychosocial factors in essential hypertension: recent epidemiological and animal experimental evidence, *Amer. J. Epidem. 90,* 171–200 (1969).

56. Roth, J. A., Ivy, A. C., and Atkinson, A. J., Caffeine and "peptic" ulcer: relation of caffeine and caffeine-containing beverages to the diagnosis and management of "peptic" ulcer, *JAMA 126,* 814–820 (1944).

57. Colton, T., Gosselin, R. E., and Smith, R. P., The tolerance of coffee drinkers to caffeine, *Clin. Pharm. Ther. 9,* 31–39 (1968).

58. Friedman, G. D., Siegelaub, A. P., and Seltzer, C. C., Cigarettes, alcohol, coffee, and peptic ulcer, *N. Eng. J. Med. 290,* 469–473 (1974).

59. Selzer, M. L. The Michigan Alcoholic Screening Test (MAST): the quest for a new diagnostic instrument, *Amer. J. Psychiat. 127,* 1653–1657 (1971).

60. Gilbert, R. M., Dietary caffeine and alcohol consumption by rats, *J. Stud. Alc. 37,* 11–18 (1976).

61. Rush, B. J. *An Inquiry Into the Effects of Ardent Spirits Upon the Human Body and Mind With an Account of the Means of Preventing, and of the Remedies for Curing Them,* 8th ed., Exeter, Philadelphia, 1819.

62. Walsh, J. M., *Coffee: Its History, Classification, and Description,* Winston, Philadelphia, 1894.

63. Newman, H. W., and Newman, E. J., Failure of dexedrine and caffeine as practical antagonists of the depressant effect of ethyl alcohol in man, *Q. J. Stud. Alc. 17,* 406–410 (1956).

64. Kraepelin, E., *Ueber die Beeinflussing einfocher psychischer; Vorgange durch einige,* Arznermittel, Pohle, Jena, 1892.

65. Stillner, V., Popkin, M. K., and Pierce, C. M., Caffeine-induced delirium during prolonged competitive stress, *Amer. J. Psychiat. 135,* 855–856 (1978).

66. Vonnegut, M., *The Eden Express,* Praeger, New York, 1975.

67. Ayd, F. J., Once-a-day neuroleptic and tricyclic antidepressant therapy, *Inter'l. Drug Ther. Newsletter 7,* 33–40 (1972).

68. Masnik, R., Bucci, L., Isenberg, D., and Normand, D., "Coffee and . . . " a way to treat the untreatable, *Amer. J. Psychiat. 128,* 164–167 (1971).

69. Lutz, E. G., Restless legs, anxiety, and caffeinism, *J. Clin. Psychiat. 16,* 693–698 (1978).

70. Willis, T., *The London Practice of Physick,* 1st ed., Bassett and Cooke, eds., London, 1685.

71. Reimann, H. A., Caffeinism: a cause of long-continued, low-grade fever, *JAMA 202,* 1105–1106 (1967).

72. Weathersbee, P. S., Olsen, L. K., and Lodge, J. R., Caffeine and pregnancy: a retrospective survey, *Postgrad. Med. 62,* 64–69 (1977).

73. Weathersbee, P. S. Caffeine: its effect on pregnancy, *Postgrad. Med. 63,* 48–49 (1978).

74. Consumer group urges warning on use of caffeine in pregnancy, *N.Y. Times,* Nov. 18, 1979.

75. Minton, J. P., Foecking, M. S., Webster, J. T., and Matthews, R. H., Caffeine, cyclic nucleotides, and breast disease, *Surgery 86,* 105–109 (1979).

76. Benign breast disease tied to coffee, tea, cocoa, cola, *Med. World News 20,* 11–12 (1979).

77. Ross, B. D., Caffeine and fluid retention, *JAMA 218,* 596 (1971).

78. Timson, J., How harmful is your daily caffeine? *New Scientist 78,* 736–737 (1978).

79. Wikler, A., Dynamics of drug dependence: implications of a conditioning theory for research and treatment, *Arch. Gen. Psychiat. 28,* 611–616 (1973).

80. Olds, J., *Drives and Reinforcements: Behavioral Studies of Hypothalamic Functions,* Raven, New York, 1977.

81. Furlong, F. W., Possible psychiatric significance of excessive coffee consumption, *Can. Psychiat. Ass'n. J. 20,* 577–583 (1975).

82. Ellis, J., *An Historical Account of Coffee,* Edward and Charles Dilly, London, 1774.

83. Molde, D. A., Diagnosing caffeinism, *Amer. J. Psychiat. 132,* 202 (1975).

84. Negrete, J. C., Coca leaf chewing: a public health assessment, *Brit. J. Addict.* *73,* 283–291 (1978).

85. Boyd, E. M., Dolman, M., Knight, L. M., and Sheppard, E. P., The chronic oral toxicity of caffeine, *Can. J. Physiol. and Pharm. 43,* 995–1007 (1965).

86. Axelrod, J., and Reichenthal, J., The fate of caffeine in man and a method for its estimation in biological material, *J. Pharm. Exp. Ther. 107,* 519–523 (1953).

87. vanPrag, H. M., *Depression and Schizophrenia: A Contribution on Their Chemical Pathologies,* Spectrum, New York, 1977.

88. Berkowitz, B. A., and Spector, S., The effect of caffeine and theophylline on the disposition of brain serotonin in the rat, *Eur. J. Pharm. 16,* 322–325 (1971).

89. Bulcher, R. W., and Sutherland, E. W., Adenosine 3',5'-phosphate in biological materials, *J. Biol. Chem. 237,* 1244–1250 (1962).

90. Kafka, M. S., and vanKammen, D. P., Reduced cyclic AMP production in schizophrenia, paper presented to the 131st annual meeting of the American Psychiatric Association, Atlanta, 1978.

91. Perry, A., The effect of heredity on attitudes toward alcohol, cigarettes, and coffee, *J. Appl. Psych. 58,* 275–277 (1973).

92. Abe, K., Reactions to coffee and alcohol in monozygotic twins, *J. Psychosom. Res. 12,* 199–203 (1968).

93. Primavera, L. H., Simon, W., and Camiza, J., An investigation of personality and caffeine use, *Brit. J. Addict. 70,* 213–215 (1975).

94. Schnackenberg, R. D., Caffeine as a substitute for schedule II stimulants in hyperkinetic children, *Amer. J. Psychiat. 130,* 796–798 (1973).

95. Eysenck, H. J., and Eysenck, S. B. G., *Eysenck Personality Inventory,* Educational and Industrial Testing Service, San Diego, 1964.

96. Gilliland, K., The interactive effect of introversion-extroversion with caffeine: induced arousal on verbal performance, Ph.D. dissertation, Northwestern University, 1976.

97. Abelson, H. I., and Fishburne, P. M., *Nonmedical Use of Psychoactive Substances: 1975–76 Nationwide Study among Youth and Adults,* Response Analysis Corporation, Princeton, 1976.

98. *Coffee Drinking in the United States, Winter 1974,* Pan-American Coffee Bureau, New York, 1974.

99. Cobb, S. Physiologic changes in men whose jobs were abolished, *J. Psychosom. Res. 18,* 245–258 (1974)

PART
TWO

9

Overeating and Obesity

Gordon G. Ball
Joel A. Grinker

Definitions

Obesity, defined as an excessive accumulation of body fat, is usually thought to be a direct consequence of overeating, or excessive food consumption. However, while overeating ("hyperphagia") alone can produce obesity, studies of genetically obese rodents have illustrated the importance of metabolic factors in this condition. Even when the food intake of genetically obese rats or mice was restricted to the level of lean controls, the obese remained fatter (1, 2). For purposes of the present discussion, we will concentrate on observable behaviors, such as excessive food consumption, hypoactivity, and affective disorders, that can differentiate the obese from the nonobese.

We have to eat to survive. How much we must eat depends upon an individual's activity level and metabolic rate. For instance, a sedentary man weighing 200 pounds could easily be depositing extra fat on a daily intake of 2,000 kcal, while an active individual of similar size would find it impossible to maintain his weight on a comparable regimen. Consequently, two similar eating patterns may have to be distinguished in accordance with lifestyle. Small deviations in daily caloric intake over a period of time also can lead to significant accumulations of fat. For instance, if a woman or man were to eat standard meals but consistently took in 150 kcal (two slices of bread) over daily requirements, she or he would gain 15 pounds of fat in a year's time; in five years, 75 pounds.

Editor's Note: Obesity as a result of excessive and/or compulsive overeating is the single most prevalent volitional disorder discussed in this book. In addition, of the various excessive behaviors eating is the only one that we cannot do without and therefore control must be exercised. The enormous complexity of overeating activity as viewed from psychological, sociological, physiological, and therapeutic perspectives required extensive and thorough attention. Therefore, we have included two complementary chapters on this subject: one clinical, the other comprehensive. These authors have provided the reader with an excellent description of all facets of the obesity problem.

Only by monitoring body composition over time can one determine whether or not hyperphagia has been occurring. The question then arises as to whether this type of eating should be classified an excessive behavior in the way the term is used in this book. The eating is excessive in the sense that attempts to reduce food intake (by dieting, behavior modification, or drugs) have produced uniformly poor results.

Weight alone is not a good indicator of obesity. Excess weight can also be a consequence of large amounts of muscle, so a distinction has to be made between obesity and overweight. To establish who is obese it is necessary to measure or estimate the amount of body fat and compare it to some standard of acceptable fatness in a specified population. Sex, age, and physical activity must be considered. As a working guideline, it is reasonable to call males obese if they have body fat in excess of 20 percent of total body weight; females, if body fat is in excess of 28 percent.

One aspect of hyperphagia occurs relatively infrequently but is clearly excessive. In binge eating, or "bulimia," an individual takes in an excessive amount of food in a relatively short period of time, varying from a few hours to a few days (3). Eating binges are usually planned and occur mainly late in the evening. The food consumed tends to be sweet, high in calories, and easily swallowed, allowing for rapid eating. Food is usually gobbled rather than chewed. The eating is usually done in secret or at least as inconspicuously as possible. Once eating has begun, the individual feels a loss of control and an inability to stop. The behavior may terminate because of excessive abdominal pain, sleep, or interruptions by others. Many people who indulge in bulimia learn to vomit in order to decrease the physical discomfort. The binge is sometimes terminated by the vomiting, but many binge eaters use this device as a means to continue the binge.

Although bulimia always results in intake far beyond immediate bodily needs, it does not necessarily lead to obesity as the outbursts may be infrequent. This eating pattern is exhibited by the obese, by people of normal weight, and by anorectics. Binge eaters report that their eating generally is not a consequence of hunger but a response to emotional disturbance.

Prevalence and Contributing Factors

It is difficult to find well-controlled studies providing accurate data on the prevalence of obesity. Most studies have used relative weight, which does not differentiate the obese from the overweight. Skinfold thickness at a variety of sites is generally regarded as a useful indicator of obesity. In the United States, the most quoted statistics come from life insurance companies, national health surveys, and studies looking for etiological factors in cardiovascular disease and diabetes. Insurance companies have analyzed the relationship between body weight and mortality rate among insured in-

group was biased in terms of people who could afford treatment. Most of the patients, 17–46 years old, were mildly obese. Bulimia was more common in anorectic and mildly obese individuals; least common, in the severely obese. However, in most cases the amount of bulimia correlated positively with the degree of dietary restriction the individuals had imposed upon themselves in the past. In no case was the behavior damaging to health, and in only a few cases did it produce rapid increases in weight.

Palatability and Meal Patterns

Our eating behavior is constantly affected by external circumstances. As children, we are implored to eat, threatened for being finicky, or reinforced for cleaning our plates. Later in life, we are bombarded by advertising attempting to trap us into ingesting more food. These external forces emphasize yet other variables that affect the amount a person eats. Two of the more important variables are the palatability and availability of food. The effects of variations in palatability have been extensively examined in animals (15, 16). Laboratory rats tend to maintain a relatively healthy weight on regular laboratory chow. When their food is made more bulky by the addition of bland, indigestible substances like cellulose, they adjust intake appropriately by increasing the volume of food eaten in order to maintain constant caloric intake. But if animals are fed a highly palatable diet containing sweet or greasy substances, they can become grossly obese (17). In these animals, eating for calories can be overriden by eating for taste. Restoring the regular laboratory diet results in undereating and weight reduction. On the other hand, adulterating the food with a bitter substance like quinine will reduce intake and produce a leaner animal. Taste factors and variety also play a significant role in determining food consumption during a meal: rats will eat more when offered a variety of palatable foods in succession than when offered only one such food (18). In people this phenomenon has been called the "French Restaurant Syndrome."

Schacter and Rodin suggested that obese humans are actually more responsive to sensory or taste factors and less responsive to internal physiological cues of hunger and satiety than normal weight humans (19). However, recent studies have indicated that the eating behavior of both obese and normal weight individuals can be influenced by external cues such as the appearance of food or the portion size (20, 21). Other studies have found that obese individuals are not hyperresponsive to sweetness (22).

Researchers have examined the meal patterns of the obese, hoping to find abnormalities directly related to the development or maintenance of his condition. Surprisingly, these studies have found many similarities in the eating behavior of obese and normal weight individuals; however, obesity is most often associated with larger and less frequent meals (23, 24). Stunkard and Kaplan reviewed 13 studies involving direct observation of the eating behavior of obese and normal weight individuals (25). The studies used different measures of eating, making them difficult to compare. However, the obese individual tended to choose more food and to eat more rapidly than the nonobese individual. In one laboratory study the rate of eating was manipulated and related to subsequent hunger: subjects who were instructed to eat rapidly showed more salivation (used as an index of hunger) several hours later than did subjects who consumed the same amount of food at a slower rate (26). Another observational study found that overweight children aged two to six gulped their food and chewed less, demonstrating a faster rate of food consumption than normal weight children (27). It remains unclear whether these behaviors are merely correlated with the appearance of obesity or can actually produce excessive intake.

Psychological Aspects

Although clinical observations suggest that emotions play a role in chronic hyperphagia and bulimia, no specific personality constellations have emerged. Two studies have indicated that anxiety and depression may be correlated with obesity. One study, using the MMPI, reported that the obese tended to exhibit a moderate degree of anxiety and a mild to moderate degree of depression (28). Another study found obese adolescent girls to be considerably anxious, with some degree of immaturity and depression (29). On the other hand, other studies have pointed to the emotional stability of the obese. Studies comparing the obese with psychosomatically ill individuals found the obese to be stronger, more dominating, and more independent (30). At least two other studies were also impressed with the relative infrequency with which obese patients needed psychiatric help (31, 32) Nevertheless, the obese suffer from stigmatization (33). They are less liked and less sought out and have fewer educational and job opportunities (34). These obstacles may play a decisive role in producing psychological problems in this group.

Bruch, with her immense clinical experience, classified obese individuals into two categories (35). One type of obesity is purely developmental, with minimal emotional problems; the other is a reactive type wherein the ingestion of excess food is part of an emotional response to environmental factors. She argued that the latter pattern reflects inappropriate responses to the feeding situation during the growth and development of the child.

In assessing over 100 clients, Gordon Ball found this subdivision useful. A small percentage constituted a class of individuals who had gained weight steadily over a number of years; emotional problems concerning weight were minimal. The group tended to be sedentary and to show little concern for weight control. In general, they appeared to be well adjusted and relatively successful. Their eating habits were both regular and appropriate for their bodily demands. Their motivation to lose weight was often generated by fear of cardiovascular complications; as the fear decreased with weight loss, these people tended to drop out of treatment.

Obese patients who reported eating in response to emotional factors could be subdivided into two groups. One group consisted of relatively active, middle-class suburban housewives. Most had a history of successive weight loss and gain. They exhibited mild depression, extreme boredom, and resentment of their lifestyles. Most were bulimic on occasion: the bulimia appeared to be related to the degree of food deprivation during dieting attempts. The second group of individuals showing reactive eating tended to be only mildly obese but also had a history of cyclical weight gain and loss. The clinical sample consisted mainly of relatively successful, professional, single women. In treatment they expressed boredom, loneliness, and fear of failure in personal relationships. Weight control was seen as necessary and was related to their emotional stability. Bulimia was highly prevalent in this group and increased in probability with strict dieting and low weight. Fears of specific foods, of specific situations surrounding food, and of loss of control also were extremely common in this group. In general, the stronger the fear, the better control over weight. In some cases individuals developed anorexia nervosa.

Several of these clinical observations have been examined in laboratory studies. A series of experiments attempted to relate anxiety and lack of control to increased food intake in the obese. Greater food consumption by obese subjects in anxiety provoking situations reportedly helped to reduce the anxiety (36). Another sequence of studies categorized obese and normal weight individuals as restrained or unrestrained eaters on the basis of dieting or controlling food intake (37).

Activity Level

The more active the individual, the more calories are required to maintain weight. Consequently, active people can consume more food before becoming obese. As Table 9-3 shows, obesity and sedentary work are highly correlated (6).

Obesity is incompatible with activity: whether obesity leads to inactivity or vice versa is not known. Possibly both factors are operating. In one study, thin infants were more active and ate more food than fat infants, who moved less and ate less (38). In adolescence, similar findings

TABLE 9-3
Obesity and Sedentary Occupation by Country

% OBESE	COUNTRY	% SEDEN-TARY	COUNTRY
0–20	Japan Finland Greece	0–20	Japan Finland Greece Italy
20–40	Italy Yugoslavia Netherlands	20–40	Yugoslavia Netherlands
Over 60	United States	Over 60	United States

have been obtained (39). Obese girls were found to have a lower caloric intake than lean girls but showed significantly lower levels of activity, emphasizing again that hyperphagia is a relative term. The same phenomenon has been observed in adolescent boys (40).

An informative study on the interaction between eating and activity was performed in India, where food intake was compared with caloric requirements of men in different occupations (41). For active individuals caloric intake accurately matched caloric demands. As long as individuals were at least moderately active, little obesity occurred. However, there was a breakdown in the correlation between eating behavior and caloric needs in men who were less than moderately active. Rather than reduce food intake to compensate for lack of activity, these sedentary individuals increased their daily intake well above that found among the moderately active men. As one would expect, a large proportion of these individuals were obese.

In the interaction between food intake and exercise, it appears that if individuals are required by their lifestyles to be relatively active, caloric intake is regulated by caloric demands. Little obesity is seen in such individuals. However, if people are not forced to be active, one group tends to become sedentary and obese, with a breakdown in the energy balance; the other group stays spontaneously active, maintaining the energy balance to prevent excessive fat accumulation. The increased fatness often observed with increasing age is probably a result of decreased physical activity.

Physiological Factors

It is hypothesized that the body has a system that signals the failure to meet caloric needs. Since the hyperphagic consumes more food than is calorically required, such an individual probably is not responding to the signals or else the signals are not functioning properly. Search for such signals has gone on for years. Many biological and biochemical factors appear to be at work in the control of food intake and the stabilization of body weight, including neural factors (the adrenergic neural system), gastrointestinal factors (gut hormones), humoral factors (blood glucose), and hormonal factors (thyroid hormones). Only a few of the more established internal control theories can be mentioned here.

Most of the research in this area involves animals. Two types of animals have been useful to study: animals whose obesity is related to known genetic factors and animals made obese either by the administration of specific chemicals or by the production of electrolytic lesions, both of which methods destroy fibers in an area in the lower part of the brain known as the ventromedial nucleus of the hypothalamus. The larger the destruction, the more ravenous the eating. Tripling of body weight is quite common. In the early stages following the brain damage, the animals exhibit behavior very similar to bulimia. They eat inordinate quantities of food, appear unable to stop, and show agitation if prevented from eating. Once the new weight has been established, meal patterns are only slightly different from the normal pattern. If the animals are deprived so that they lose weight, at the first opportunity they will start eating excessively until their new weight is again reached.

One theory of internal control suggests that heat production, reflected in changes in body temperature, regulates food intake. The preoptic area of the anterior hypothalamus appears to be involved. Slightly raising the temperature of this area by artificial means produces drastic increases in food intake. Artificially cooling the area reduces food consumption. When the area is destroyed, body temperature control is unimpaired, but animals eat too much in the heat and too little in the cold (42). The modern version of this theory suggests that the thermogenic regulation of obese animals is faulty. In particular, the obese animal shows an altered response to diet induced thermogenesis (43).

Researchers have looked for biological mechanisms that monitor fat storage. The lipostatic theory postulates that the fat cell itself may give off the appropriate signal in some form of biochemical message. This view is based on investigation into the formation of adipose tissue in developing animals and the cell morphology of obese and lean animals (44). The evidence suggests that the number of fat cells is determined by genes as well as by environmental experiences. When an individual loses weight, nutrients in the fat cells are consumed and the cells become smaller. The fat cell itself does not disappear. When an adult gains weight, this is the result initially of storing extra nutrients in the fat cells. However, it appears possible in both adult animals and humans also to increase the number of fat cells (44, 45). The lipostatic protagonists have carefully examined the intricate biochemistry of fat cells for possible chemical messages that could be released from these cells in different states of distension. So far, no clear-cut evidence has appeared to show that animals or people eat in response to biochemical signals from fat cells.

Hormones are prime candidates for controlling eating behavior. One hormone definitely involved in regulation is insulin (46). Injections of insulin result in increased food intake and body weight. This increased eating can result from peripheral hypoglycemia or from direct action of insulin on the central nervous system. When eating begins, there is an initial rapid rise in insulin; this release is correlated with food palatability and meal size (47).

Another candidate for the control of eating behavior is the gastrointestinal tract. Mechanical theories related to stomach distension and emptying have been proposed by researchers studying ways to curb eating. Strong contractions in the empty stomach are to some extent correlated with sensations of hunger (48). More recently, attention has focused on the release of hormones from the intestine during feeding. One such hormone, cholecystokinin, appears to be involved in the onset of satiation (49). High levels of cholecystokinin have also been found in the brain in a number of animal species (50). Current research is attempting to relate cholecystokinin and other brain-gut peptides, as well as the endorphins (the naturally occurring, opiatelike, brain substances), to the control of eating and body weight.

Treatment

The time-honored way of attempting to control chronic hyperphagia and bulimia is some type of restricted caloric intake. Chronic hyperphagia can be brought under control temporarily by this method. Clinical observations on bulimia suggest that restricted caloric intake may actually increase the frequency of binge eating.

All diets work relatively well as long as people adhere to them. The rate and the amount of weight loss depend primarily upon the degree of caloric restriction. Variations in rate associated with high protein or high carbohydrate diets apparently reflect different rates of sodium or water excretion. Restrictions below 800 kcal per day are not advisable since little extra fat is catabolized by this extreme deprivation and a reduction in basal metabolic rate may occur (51). In sum, caloric restriction rather than the type of diet appears to be the most important factor in weight loss. Unfortunately, dieting tends to be temporary, with most people eventually returning to old eating habits and regaining the lost weight.

Failure to maintain weight loss following a diet led to a search for alternate ways of taking and keeping weight off. New approaches emphasize modifying people's eating habits. Under this behavior modification format, patients keep detailed records of time and place of eating, amount of food consumed, rate of eating, and social interactions during eating. Analysis of these detailed records yields structured eating strategies. To achieve lifetime change, the patient must progress through four major stages of control of eating: learning appropriate decisionmaking processes, developing new eating skills, acquiring strategies for handling the posttreatment period, and finding ways of coping with new challenges in the extended posttreatment phase (52). Behavior modification techniques that emphasize these skills facilitate long-term maintenance of weight loss (52).

Self-help groups for controlling excessive eating have become quite popular in this country and abroad. Weight Watchers is the best known. Many of its methods have been adapted from behavior modification programs. Results published by the organization indicate that people who continue to go to Weight Watchers tend to lose weight steadily and gradually. The few results available on people who drop out of the Weight Watchers program show that they tend to regain lost weight. Overeaters Anonymous is another self-help group having a modicum of success, although there are no published records on its results. Anecdotal evidence suggests that those who stay with the organization and continue to seek out support from its members tend to keep their eating behavior relatively under control. The premise on which the organization functions is that overeating is an addictive disease similar to alcoholism; the program is loosely modeled on the abstinence techniques of Alcoholics Anonymous. Gordon Ball's clinical experience is that Overeaters Anonymous tends to attract the binge eater. The organization's emphasis on the problem as an addiction, along with its social support network, appears to be useful for such an excessive behavior. A third popular organization is TOPS (Take Off Pounds Sensibly), which has chapters around the country. Many of these chapters have incorporated behavior modification techniques into their programs with increasing success.

Many advocate the use of exercise as a means of changing the balance between caloric input and output. However, exercise alone as a method of reducing is inefficient simply because the increased output required to use up a significant amount of fat necessitates more activity than people can easily incorporate into their lifestyles (53). However, several reports have indicated that continued exercise can be helpful for some patients, especially if accompanied by reduction in food intake. Moreover, mild exercise appears to depress appetite rather than increase it. One drawback to exercise is that many obese patients have to overcome large psychological barriers in order to participate—their size makes it difficult and embarrassing for them to engage in such activities.

The major attempts to control obesity have come from drug companies. They have concentrated on finding drugs to reduce appetite and thus discourage excessive intake. They also have investigated ways of preventing food, once eaten, from being absorbed. So far, no ideal agent in either category has been found. An ideal drug should be free of long- and short-term toxicity, should be well tolerated, and should have no deleterious metabolic effects.

In the past the most popular drugs for controlling eating were the amphetamines, which increase activity and decrease appetite, with an accompanying reduction in food intake and weight. In no way do these drugs increase metabolic efficiency. Today, amphetamines are counterindicated because of the high degree of tolerance and the occurrence of psychotic episodes following withdrawal. Two other compounds now being used are mazindol and fenfluramine, but problems of habituation and addiction remain. The Food and Drug Administration analyzed data on these agents and found that weight loss per week tended to be only slightly greater than on placebo (54).

Rather than attempting to modify the eating behavior, other researchers have looked for a compound which would leave the eating behavior intact, but would decrease the absorption of food from the intestine. They have concentrated on compounds which decrease fat absorption, such as Neomycin and cholecystymamine. This approach to weight control mimics in many ways the effects produced by the intestinal bypass operations to be discussed later. However, no agents without many unpleasant side effects are currently available.

Thyroid hormones offer another avenue of investigation since they appear to enhance weight loss in obese people by increasing oxygen consumption, with increased utilization of endogenous fuel. However, this treatment leads to increased protein catabolism and increased nitrogen excretion and has a deleterious effect on cardiac muscle.

Recent research suggests that some bulimic outbursts may be related to neurological dysfunction. Rau and Green, examining 59 compulsive eaters, found a disproportionately high number with EEG irregularities (55). The possibility of a neurological dimension in bulimia was further supported by the fact that an anticonvulsant medication, diphenylhydantoin, significantly reduced the incidence of binges. In general, however, there is presently no safe, effective, and permanent way of curbing hyperphagia or enhancing metabolic efficiency by the use of drugs.

The most drastic method for controlling overeating is a surgical procedure, the gastrointestinal bypass operation, which has been performed since the 1950s. The procedure involves sectioning and reattaching the small intestine so that food bypasses most of that portion of the gastrointestinal tract involved in the normal breakdown of food (56). Over 1,000 patients have had this operation, with heavier patients losing more rapidly than lighter ones (57). The benefits from this operation are longer lasting weight loss, lowered cholesterol and triglyceride levels, reduced blood pressure, improved pulmonary function, increased self-esteem, and enhanced body image.

The interesting fact about the bypass procedure is that is was conceived as a means of reducing the absorption of food in the overeater rather than of controlling excessive eating. As it turns out, hyperphagia disappears after the operation. Caloric intake drops to about 20 percent of preoperative intake for the first 6 months and then gradually increases to half the preoperative level 12–18 months postsurgery. The present view is that the altered eating habits in these patients may be more important than malabsorption in producing weight loss. Nevertheless, all patients who lose weight also develop diarrhea; less than a quarter of patients report diarrhea at the end of one postoperative year. Malnutrition is a major problem in the early months, and patients need special care in terms of levels of fat soluble vitamins, electrolyte maintenance, and protein absorption. Between the sixth and the eighteenth month postoperative, however, there are gradual adaptations in intestinal absorption and eating patterns. Major postoperative problems include liver disease and calcium loss. Overall mortality from the operation is about 3 percent.

Conclusion

Overeating is commonly regarded as the major cause of obesity, with the reduction in food intake as the solution. This chapter emphasizes that the picture is considerably more complicated. Eating becomes excessive only in relation to a person's metabolic processes and energy expenditure. The interaction among these three variables determines the final percentage of adipose tissue. Sociological and psychological factors play important roles in determining obesity, but it is not clear how much they affect activity levels and eating behavior.

The standard treatment plan for obesity has concentrated on controlling eating as a means of controlling weight. The lack of success of this method indicates that treating the excessive eating behavior alone is not sufficient. In order to control obesity, eating behavior as well as activity level and metabolic processes need to be considered.

References

1. Cox, J. E., and Powley, T. L., Development of obesity in diabetic mice paired with lean siblings, *J. Comp. Physiol. Psych. 91,* 347–358 (1977).
2. Cleary, M. P., Vasselli, J. R., and Greenwood, M. R. C., Development of obesity in Zucker obese (fafa) rat in the absence of hyperphagia, *Amer. J. Physiol. 238,* E284–E292 (1980).

3. American Psychiatric Association Task Force on Nomenclature and Statistics, *Diagnostic and Statistical Manual of Mental Disorders,* 3d ed., American Psychiatric Association, Washington, D. C., 1980.

4. *Ten State Nutrition Survey, 1968–1970,* Department of Health, Education, and Welfare, Washington, D. C., 1972.

5. Goldblatt, P. E., Moore, M. E., and Stunkard, A. J., Social factors in obesity, *JAMA 192,* 1039–1044 (1965).

6. Keys, A., Coronary heart disease in seven countries, American Heart Association, Monograph 29, 1–211 (1970).

7. Muller, F., Paul, I., and Brasch, C., The incidence in the German Democratic Republic, *Z. Gesamte Inn. Med. 25,* 1001–1009 (1970).

8. Johnson, T. O., Prevalence of overweight and obesity among adult subjects of an urban African population sample, *Brit. J. Prev. Soc. Med. 24,* 105–109 (1970).

9. Stone, C., Gompel, B., Abramson, J. H., and Scotch, N., Weight, height, and skinfold thickness of Zulu adults in Durban, *S. Afr. Med. J. 34,* 505–509 (1960).

10. Jansen, A. A., Skinfold measurements from early childhood to adulthood in Papuans from western New Guinea, *Ann. N.Y. Acad. Sci. 110,* 515–531 (1963).

11. Shields, J., *Monozygotic Twins Brought Up Apart and Brought Up Together,* Oxford University Press, New York, 1962.

12. Robinson, S. C., and Brucer, M., Hypertension, body build, and obesity, *Amer. J. Med. Sci. 199,* 819 (1940).

13. Charney, E., Goodman, H. C., McBride, M., Lyon, B., and Pratt, R., Childhood antecedents of adult obesity: do chubby infants become obese adults? *N. Eng. J. Med. 295,* 6–9 (1976).

14. Poskitt, E. M. E., and Cole, T. J., Do fat babies stay fat? *Brit. Med. J. 1,* 7–9 (1977).

15. Carlisle, H. J., and Stellar, E., Caloric regulation and food preference in normal, hyperphagic, and aphagic rats, *J. Comp. Physiol. Psych. 69,* 107–114 (1969).

16. Strominger, J. L., and Brobeck, J. R., Mechanism of regulation of food intake, *Yale J. Biol. Med. 25,* 383–390 (1953).

17. Sclafani, A., and Springer, D., Dietary obesity in adult rats: similarities to hypothalamic and human obesity syndrome, *Physiol. Beh. 17,* 461–471 (1976).

18. Le Magnen, J., Hunger and food palatability in the control of feeding behavior, in *Food Intake and Chemical Senses,* Y. Katsuki, M. Sato, S. F. Takagi, and Y. Oomura, eds., Japan Scientific Societies Press, Tokyo, 1977, pp. 263–280.

19. Schachter, S., and Rodin, J., *Obese Humans and Rats,* Wiley, New York, 1974.

20. Grinker, J. A., Obesity and taste: sensory and cognitive factors in food intake, in *Obesity in Perspective,* vol. 2, G. A. Bray, ed., GPO, Washington, D. C., 1973, pp. 73–80.

21. Pliner, P. L., Effect of liquid and solid preloads on eating behavior of obese and normal persons, *Physiol. Beh. 11,* 285–290 (1973).

22. Grinker, J., Obesity and sweet taste, *Amer. J. Clin. Nutr. 31,* 1078–1087 (1978).

23. Stunkard, A. J., Grace, W. J., and Wolff, H. G., The night-eating syndrome: a pattern of food intake among certain obese patients, *Amer. J. Med. 19,* 78–86 (1955).

24. Fabry, P., and Tepperman, J., Meal frequency: a possible factor in human pathology, *Amer. J. Clin. Nutr. 23,* 1059–1068 (1970).

25. Stunkard, A. J., and Kaplan, D., Eating in public places: a review of reports of the direct observation of eating behavior, *Inter'l. J. Obes. 1,* 89 (1977).

26. Wooley, O. W., Wooley, S. C., and Turner, K., The effects of rate of consumption on appetite in the obese and non-obese, in *Recent Advances in Obesity Research,* vol. 1, A. Howard, ed., Newman, London, 1975, p. 212 (abstract).

27. Marston, A. R., London, P., and Cooper, L. M., A note on the eating behavior of children varying in weight, *J. Child Psych. Psychiat. 17,* 221–224 (1976).

28. Atkinson, R. M., and Ringuette, E. L., A survey of biographical and psychological features in extraordinary fatness, *Psychosom. Med. 29,* 121–133 (1967).

29. Werkman, S. L., and Greenberg, E. S., Personality and interest patterns of obese adolescent girls, *Psychosom. Med. 29,* 72–80 (1967).

30. Silverstone, J. T., Psychosocial aspects of obesity, *Proc. Roy. Soc'y. Med. 61,* 371 (1978), pp. 13–17.

31. Weinberg, N., Mendelson, M., and Stunkard, A. J., A failure to find distinctive psychological features in a group of obese men, *Amer. J. Psychiat. 117,* 1035–1037 (1960).

32. Friedman, J., Weight problems and psychological factors, *J. Consult. Psych. 23,* 524–527 (1959).

33. Allon, N., The stigma of overweight in everyday life, in *Obesity in Perspective,* vol. 2, A. Bray, ed., GPO, Washington, D. C., 1973, pp. 83–102.

34. Canning, H., and Mayer, J., Obesity: its influence on college acceptance, *N. Eng. J. Med. 275,* 1172–1174 (1966).

35. Bruch, H., *Eating Disorders,* Basic Books, New York, 1973.

36. Slochower, J., and Kaplan, S. P., Anxiety, perceived control, and eating in obese and normal weight individuals, *Appetite 1,* 75–84 (1980).

37. Herman, C. P., and Polivy, J., Anxiety, restraint, and eating behavior, *J. Abnorm. Psych. 84,* 666–672 (1975).

38. Mack, R. W., and Kleinhenz, M. E., Growth, caloric intake, and activity levels in early infancy: a preliminary report, *Hum. Biol. 46,* 345–354 (1974).

39. Johnson, M. L., Burke, B. S., and Mayer, J., Relative importance of inactivity and overeating on the energy balance of obese high school girls, *Amer. J. Clin. Nutr. 4,* 37–43 (1956).

40. Stefanik, P. A., Heald, F. F., and Mayer, J., Caloric intake in relation to energy output of obese and non-obese adolescent boys, *Amer. J. Clin. Nutr. 7,* 55–62 (1959).

41. Mayer, J., Roy, P., and Mitra, K. P., Relation between caloric intake, body weight, and physical work: studies in an industrial male population in west Bengal, *Amer. J. Clin. Nutr. 4,* 169–175 (1956).

42. Hamilton, C. L., and Brobeck, J. R., Food intake and temperature regulation in rats with rostral hypothalamic lesions, *Amer. J. Physiol. 207,* 291–297 (1964).

43. Bray, G. A., *Obesity in America,* Department of Health, Education, and Welfare, Washington, D.C., 1979.

44. Hirsch, J., and Batchelor, B. R., Adipose tissue cellularity in human obesity, in *Clinics in Endocrinology and Metabolism,* vol. 5, no. 2, M. Albrink, ed., Saunders, Philadelphia, 1976, pp. 299–311.

45. Faust, I. M., Johnson, P. R., Stern, J. S., and Hirsch, J., Diet-induced adipocyte number increase in adult rats: a new model of obesity, *Amer. J. Physiol. 235,* E279–E286 (1978).

46. Woods, S. C., Decke, E., and Vasselli, J. R., Metabolic hormones and regulation of body weight, *Psych. Rev. 81,* 26–43 (1974).

47. Louis-Sylvestre, J., and LeMagnen, J., Palatability and preabsorptive insulin release, *Neurosci. Biobeh. Rev. 4,* 43–46 (1980).

48. Stunkard, A. J., and Fox, S., The relationship of gastric motility and hunger: a summary of the evidence, *Psychosom. Med. 33,* 123–134 (1971).

49. Smith, G. P., and Gibbs, J., Cholecystokinin and satiety: theoretic and therapeutic implications, in *Hunger: Basic Mechanisms and Clinical Implications,* D. Novin, W. Wyrwicka, and G. Bray, eds., Raven, New York, 1976.

50. Schneider, B. S., Monahan, J. W., and Hirsch, J., Brain cholecystokinin and nutritional status in rats and mice, *J. Clin. Invest. 64,* 1348–1356 (1979).

51. Blondheim, S. H., Kaufman, N. A., and Stein, M., Comparison of fasting and 800–1000 calorie diet in obesity, *Lancet 1,* 250–252 (1965).

52. Stuart, R. B., Weight loss and beyond: are they taking it off and keeping it off? in *Behavioral Medicine: Changing Health Lifestyles,* P. O. Davidson and S. M. Davidson, eds., Brunner/Mazel, New York, 1980, pp. 151–194.

53. Kenrick, M. M., Ball, M. F., and Canary, J. J., Exercise and weight reduction in obesity, *Arch. Physiol. Med. Rehab. 53,* 323–327 (1972).

54. Scoville, B. A., Review of amphetamine-like drugs by the Food and Drug Administration, in *Obesity in Perspective,* vol. 2, G. A. Bray, ed., GPO, Washington, D. C., 1973, pp. 441–443.

55. Rau, J. H., and Green, R. S., Compulsive eating: a neuropsychological approach to certain eating disorders, *Comprehen. Psychiat. 16,* 223–231 (1975).

56. Payne, J. H., and DeWind, L. T., Surgical treatment of obesity, *Amer. J. Surg. 118,* 141–147 (1969).

57. Bray, G. A., *The Obese Patient,* Saunders, Philadelphia, 1976.

10

Obesity: The Psychology of a Multifaceted Volitional Disorder

Sandra Haber

Overview

Despite research efforts over many years and enormous sums of money devoted to cures, both the cause and the control of obesity remain obscure. To date, 40 percent of the U. S. population is considered obese (1), and there is evidence that this figure has increased in recent years. And although there are thousands of programs devoted to helping people lose weight, "there is no known way to sustain weight loss in the substantially obese" (2). Bray noted that "in long term follow-up studies, it is apparent that every program has some success, but that for most, less than 10 to 20 percent of the individuals who enter a treatment program other than surgery will solve their problems" (3).

This disease has spawned a weight loss industry that promotes thousands of new diets and countless books and gadgets each year. Simonson noted that there are 28,096 weight reducing methods and gadgets, of which no more than 6 percent are safe and effective (4). Blackburn has estimated that the dieting industry accounts for $10 billion a year (5). The desperation of the obese individual has led to vastly popular fad diets—the ice cream diet, grapefruit diet, drinking man's diet, rice diet, etc. None of these has met with long-term success.

Obesity has serious medical and psychological consequences. Medically, this condition has been related to diabetes, respiratory insufficiency, cardiovascular disease, gallstones, liver damage, increased risks from surgery, hernia, carcinoma of the colon, and varicose veins (6). Vickery and Fries observed that overeating costs the average individual one year of life, with each additional pound over and above the 10-pound range for ideal weight costing a person one month of life (7). Psychologically, the costs of obesity are equally high. Obesity is a disorder with a dual set of psychological consequences, one being society's reaction to the excess weight, the other being the psychic burden of guilt and shame associated with being fat (1).

Psychosocial Costs of Obesity

"We live in a culture that pays extensive lip service to the notion that fat is morally and sexually repulsive (1). This society abhors the overweight individual and is intolerant of his or her problem. The social and psychological repercussions of this attitude cannot be minimized. Studies have indicated that the obese are discriminated against in both job and educational settings (1); certainly, interpersonal discrimination is obvious. Unlike disorders such as alcoholism, compulsive gambling, or general psychoneurosis, obesity is necessarily public. According to Bruch, being fat is a "public display of transgression, a demonstration of self-indulgence and lack of control and willpower" (8). In our culture, we stereotype the obese as jovial, irresponsible, and uncaring about their appearance (6). The process of ascribing a particular constellation of personality traits frequently leads to a set of negative assumptions about obese people, who in fact may have nothing in common but their fat.

Intrapsychic Costs of Obesity

"One's reputation, whether false or true, cannot be hammered, hammered, hammered, into one's head without doing something to one's character" (9). The obese are a visible minority and suffer from social and psychological limitations, the most devastating of which is self-hatred. The attitudes of many fat people closely resemble the minority group attitudes described by Allport in his analysis of racial prejudice: "A child who finds himself rejected and attacked on all sides is not likely to develop dignity and poise as his outstanding traits. On the contrary, he develops defenses" (9). Obese individuals frequently experience despair, self-hatred, and disapproval in response to their inability to stop eating (2). Orbach noted that "being fat isolates and invalidates women. Almost inevitably, the explanations offered for fatness point a finger at the failure to control weight, appetite and impulses" (10). Intolerance of themselves and intolerance from others contrast with the typically bland façade of the obese, for under this façade lie pain and devaluation (11).

These feelings persist even in patients who lose weight. Clearly this disturbance in body image has a major impact on self-esteem and dramatically influences one's interactions with the world. In spite of the serious medical and psychological consequences, however, the patient, the public, and the practitioner have been intolerant toward the obese. This attitude is of major importance in understanding the limitations of research on obesity. It is difficult to explain why these shared feelings exist, but perhaps they can be understood if one looks at the nature of the disorder. In obesity, unlike alcoholism, total abstinence vis-à-vis food is not possible.

And unlike the drug abuser, the obese patient shares with the public and the practitioner an important behavior—eating—as well as a frequent desire and tendency to engage in overeating. However, whereas normal weight individuals inhibit this tendency, the obese person cannot. This commonality of experience, then, leads all parties to attribute obesity to lack of caring or lack of self-control; as such, obesity is considered a volitional disorder. It is difficult to empathize with a patient whose illness seems so willful.

Patterns of Overeating

Extra weight is gained by eating in excess of the body's need for calories, but not all overeating occurs in the same way. Obese patients follow their own style of overeating, which pattern forms the core of their obesity problem. To overlook the particular method by which these calories are ingested would be to miss one of the most important aspects of obesity. To date, three types of overeater have been identified: the sociocultural overeater, the nighttime eater, and the binge eater.

Sociocultural Overeating

Some types of obesity seem to result simply from overeating high calorie food in a food oriented social environment. This pattern is environmentally or situationally triggered. However widespread these cues may be, overeating and excess weight are condoned only in certain groups or subcultures. For example, Stunkard found that 24 percent of his sample of foreign-born women were obese versus 5 percent of women without foreign-born grandparents (11).

Apparently, the more Americanized an individual is, the less likely he or she is to be overweight; yet the American ideal of slenderness is a circumscribed norm. Overweight is valued in a number of cultures. Indeed, foreign countries, in particular those with precarious food supplies, tend to value women who are of rounder proportions, as did many ancient cultures, which were similarly concerned with food scarcity and fertility.

Nighttime Overeating

A second pattern of overeating has been termed "nighttime eating." Originally identified by Stunkard, patients with this pattern are generally "good" all day long, meaning that they have little desire for food or have no appetite at all (11). In the evening, they have long eating episodes that terminate only when they fall asleep. Three characteristics are needed for the diagnosis of nighttime eating: lack of appetite in the morning, overeating in the evening, and combined agitation and insomnia. Stunkard concluded from these features that this pattern is a response to life stress and is therefore resistant to change. Bruch confirmed these findings, although she observed that the syndrome occurred in few of her patients (8).

Available clinical material suggests that the nighttime eating syndrome occurs infrequently in the pure form described by Stunkard. In my experience, the more common pattern consists of heavy nighttime eating coupled with morning anorexia and moderately controlled diurnal eating behavior.

Binge Eating

Food binges are the ingestion of enormous quantities of food at a very fast pace. Binges are neither social events nor occasions of celebration. Bingers report eating standing by the kitchen sink or walking down the street. The binge is a totally uncontrolled, seizurelike experience, with bingers usually feeling dissociated from their behavior. Binging is frequently followed by self-induced vomiting and, at the very least, by feelings of self-condemnation and hatred. Stunkard noted "the sudden-out-of-the blue way it came on, its orgiastic quality, the feeling of loss of control, and the compulsion to eat until the stomach was full, even painful (11).

Etiology of Obesity

What causes these often dramatic patterns of overeating? Answers to this question are by no means clear, and theoretical attempts at explaining them are unsatisfying.

Medical Approach

For some patients, physiology clearly figures in the etiology of obesity. Mayer classified the origins of different types of medical obesities as genetic, hypothalamic, other CNS caused, and endocrinological (12). Some skeptics argue that genetic factors extend no further than a familial preference for sweets and inactivity (13). Proponents of a genetic explanation note that hereditary obesity can easily be demonstrated in most animals.

However, even ardent geneticists usually concede that in humans the relationship between genetics and environmental variables makes purely hereditary obesity uncommon. Although evidence from twin studies does point to a genetic component, it is more likely that genetic factors set up a predisposition to obesity that will result in the condition given the proper environmental variables (inactivity and food abundance). When obesity occurs in early childhood, the condition is termed "hyperplastic," indicating that the individual has an increased number of fat cells. In later life, these cells can be shrunk by dieting but are not lost. On the other hand, "hypertrophic" obesity involves an increase in fat cell size and seems to have a better prognosis. However, these divisions are neither simple nor clear-cut, and many individuals exhibit characteristics of both syndromes.

Behavioral Approach

The behavioral approach began with the work of Stunkard, who correlated gastric motility with identification of hunger. He found that normal weight subjects reported subjective feelings of hunger true to their physiological state, while obese subjects showed significantly less accuracy in relating the physiological event to psychological experience. These findings led Schachter to study where, when, and why obese feeding patterns differ from those of normal weight subjects (14). Schachter wondered whether the obese eat when they are not hungry and, if so, why. He found that obese subjects did eat when they were not hungry. Schachter assessed the second question by manipulating different variables while hunger was held constant. For instance, subjects worked on a task while clocks ran slow or fast. When given crackers, obese subjects ate twice as many when they thought the hour was later (past dinner time) as when they thought it earlier (before dinner time). The actual time was the same in both conditions. Obese subjects seemed to respond to environmental variables (leading Schachter to propose an externality theory of overeating), whereas normal weight subjects responded to the internal stimulus of hunger as the trigger for eating.

Additional tests of Schachter's hypothesis were made in a series of field studies by Goldman and colleagues (15). Here, obese Jewish subjects were more likely than nonobese subjects to fast on the religious holiday of Yom Kippur. These obese subjects found fasting less unpleasant than the nonobese when both groups spent the time in synagogue, that is, away form food cues. These findings confirmed Schachter's externality theory and challenged the stereotype that fat people lack self-control. In a followup study, overweight intercontinental fliers had eating patterns that were significantly less affected by discrepancies in time than did their normal weight counterparts, again indicating that obese subjects responded more to environmental than to internal hunger cues.

What must be noted is that each researcher tends to define obesity by his or her own criteria. Limitations to Schachter's theory are caused at least in part by definitional problems. Other legitimate criticism also has been aimed at the externality theory. While still valid, the theory has less usefulness than previously assumed.

Milich, for example, criticized Schachter's work primarily on the ground of limited generalizability (16). Most of Schachter's work used college-age students, thereby combining juvenile and adult onset obesity, so valid conclusions could not be drawn. Milich also cautioned that obesity is a cultural phenomenon and value: findings will not generalize to lower socioeconomic groups underrepresented in the usual college sample. Finally, each of the studies was correlational in design, so it is difficult to determine which factors were responsible for which results.

Although external responsiveness seems a rather limited principle to explain such a complex phenomenon as overeating, discarding this theory may be premature. Perhaps a more parsimonious view would be to let Schachter's dimensions explain some types of obesity, granted that obesity is a multidetermined, complex disorder.

Psychodynamic Approach

Food and thoughts of food are used by many individuals to cope with their problems. Some people overeat out of joy and happiness in social occasions, others overeat out of sadness and depression when they are alone. Food is more than calories; it is laden with meaning, reflecting maternal care, religious symbolism, or significant events. For some people, food becomes the sole coping mechanism and in these cases it proves to be a destructive force.

Bruch, in her landmark research, has provided insight into the complex and painful conflicts in the development of obesity (8). Food, from the first moments of life, is associated with another person, the mother, and with this figure comes the stimulation of the senses: touch, smell, sound, sight, and taste. Food is a physical comfort; being fed is a psychological comfort. From these associations feeding comes to mean much more than the satisfaction of physiological hunger; the presence of an eating disorder, more than mere overeating. In some people eating may be a way of controlling anger that threatens this interpersonal security, for when anger and autonomy jeopardize the mother-child relationship, the child learns that it is not safe to feel angry and "swallows the anger" in the form of excess food. Bruch noted that the first characteristic of developmental obesity is the inability to discriminate feeling states: hunger, anger, loneliness, and love are confused and dealt with by overeating. The second characteristic of developmental obesity is a lack of control over one's own life (8).

Psychoanalysts have carried this view further, hypothesizing that when conflicts occur over food, the child often needs to suppress feelings of anger toward the mother, leading to personality traits designated as an "anal cluster." This anger at the mother and the lack of control over one's own life can be illustrated through case histories.

Case studies show that the psychodynamic view has considerable face validity. Unfortunately, there has been little experimental assessment of this process using traditional scientific paradigms. This lack leads to an artificial division among psychologists: on one side are investigators, like Schachter, who use experimental analysis to test hypotheses, producing empirical findings that are limited by the narrowness of the constructs; on the other are clinicians, like Bruch, who formulate theories on obesity by studying case histories, yielding a paradigm that has face validity and intuitive appeal but lacks the methodological rigor commensurate with scientific validation.

Current Trends

Many researchers now recognize the limitations of both views and agree that obesity is a multifaceted disorder of varying causes and differing degrees of psychopathology. More complex paradigms are being developed, and some attempts to link obesity with other addictive disorders are under way (17). One model aims at a differential diagnosis of obesities by taking into account both the time of onset and the degree to which excess weight is integrated into the personality (18). The first variable is analogous to Bruch's identification of developmental and reactive obesity types. Some patients exhibit chronic (developmental) obesity, a lifelong problem with relatively few fluctuations in weight; others manifest an acute (reactive) obesity pattern in which current weight is significantly different from the idiographic weight level of the individual. The second variable, the degree to which obesity is integrated into the personality, combines the clinical observations of Bruch and Stunkard and the experimental findings of Schachter. The dangers of weight loss, noted by Bruch and Stunkard, can be understood in that for some patients, the obese state is all they have known. Some patients have known the obese state all their lives; obesity is part of them and although they may desire weight loss, large body size is harmoniously integrated into the sense of self. In these cases, the symptom appears "ego syntonic" with the personality. For other patients, however, the opposite dynamic occurs: the obesity is perceived as foreign. They exhibit hatred of and disgust at their condition. In these cases the symptom is "ego alien." For still others, excess weight is a problem with little affective value connected to it ("ego environmental").

The six obesity types derived from this model provide us with a way of integrating the major theoretical positions into one framework. For example, "homeostatic obesity" describes the developmental obesity cases of Bruch; the patient has been obese throughout life but the excess weight is an integral part of the identity (8). "Integrated obesity" pertains to those chronically obese individuals in whom the condition resulted from socioenvironmental factors, often excessive food related activity in childhood. Schachter's externally oriented subjects would be placed here (14). This patient dislikes the obese condition. There is a marked desire for cure but the strong affective dimension present in both the ego syntonic condition (attachment to and need for body size) and the ego alien condition (intolerance of and disgust toward body size) is absent. "Dysfunctional obesity" refers to patients who have lifelong eating problems and manifest hatred of their disorder and eating problems. These patients vacillate between total control of their food intake and chaotic lack of control. Patients in this category are analogous to Stunkard's binge eaters (11).

For some patients, the experience of increased body weight occurs later in life. Bruch assigned an overall classification of reactive obesity to these patients. However, a more accurate label would be acute onset obesity with subdivisions in this category. For example, the fourth type, "systemic obesity," includes patients who develop their condition as a coping response to a difficult lifestyle. This family dynamic view has been supported by the work of Granat (20). Unlike the systemic conditions, "circumstantial obesity" is brought about by a specific change in the environment. As with the integrated obese patient, the circumstantially obese are responding strongly to external cues. However, these cues have not been present since childhood but are relatively recent. Frequently, an increase in business and social obligations precipitates this condition. In these cases, the obesity is neither ego syntonic nor ego alien; the patient has a clear perspective on the magnitude of the problem, the causes of the illness, and what effects treatment will realistically produce. The last type, "acute onset obesity," describes the patient who is using food to cope with a traumatic loss.

As a descriptive model, this paradigm provides a framework for incorporating the major theories of obesity. Researchers are beginning to note the presence of multiple types of obese patients and some have gone so far as to speak of this condition in the plural, "obesities" (12, 21, 22).

Treatment

Surgical Intervention

Having a dramatic effect, the surgical remedies for obesity are of outstanding interest to all professionals treating the morbidly obese. This procedure involves a surgical bypass of part of the absorbing intestine, thereby limiting the availability of nutrients to the body. Psychologically this procedure eliminates the individual's responsibility over food intake monitoring as the surgery, at least in principle, allows the patient to overeat while losing weight. Quaade and colleagues made one of the most comprehensive assessments of surgical procedures for obesity (23). They followed up surgical results over a three-year period. Weight loss in these patients was dramatic. However, postoperative complications were extensive, including electrolyte imbalance and liver damage. Side effects appeared significantly more often in this group of patients than in obese controls. Surprisingly, though, other physical problems were more common in the control group. These included pain in the hip, back, knees, and feet, as well as intolerance to heat and excessive perspiration. The control group remained more subject to teasing and depression, whereas the surgical group reported better spirits, less loneliness, and less insecurity. Finally, surgery seems to have normalized patients' responses to everyday life; for example, they were more inclined to partake in sports and to have normal sexual activity than was the control group.

Behavior Modification

Behavior therapy or behavior modification is the treatment approach derived from the learned behavior view of obesity. Behavior modification does not produce dramatic results, but it is a relatively inexpensive therapy that can be used with large numbers of patients; it has a low attrition rate; and it produces uniformly positive results, be they modest. This treatment is attractive because it is a focused and limited therapy lacking the mysterious aura of more traditional therapies. In addition, behavior modification fosters a sense of personal control through the self-management strategy it teaches.

Psychodynamic Treatment

As behavior modification is clear and methodologically simple, psychoanalytically oriented therapy is difficult to summarize. According to this approach, if overeating and obesity are signs of psychological conflict, one can identify and treat a cohesive set of psychological characteristics separating obese individuals from normal weight counterparts. Unfortunately, most studies have failed to find a common obese personality. For example, Crisp found that the correlation between obesity and psychiatric status was too small to be clinically meaningful (24).

Is psychodynamic treatment then inappropriate? The answer is affirmative only if one agrees that the effectiveness of treatment rests on the presence of common personality traits. An alternative explanation is that the absence of an "obese personality" is indicative of the multiple causes of obesity.

Various reports document the emotional results of weight loss. The most dramatic occur with patients who have chosen the bypass operation. Following weight loss, most patients experience positive gains, particularly in the areas of body image, assertiveness, and sexuality. A minority are unable to cope with their reduced body size. Neill and co-workers, in a careful study of 14 patients and their spouses, noted that the postoperative period was marked by emotional lability (25). There were serious changes in most of the marital relationships. Stresses seemed to stem from personality changes in the patient—increased assertiveness, greater expression of autonomy, etc. One explanation consistent with the psychodynamic view is that obesity is a manifestation of personal conflict and surgery leads to weight loss not controlled by the patient, forcing the individual into confrontation with self and others.

If we review the nonsurgical studies on weight loss, particularly the clinical data of Stunkard and Bruch, we see depression and psychological conflict manifested in patients attempting to lose weight, with psychotherapy being the only treatment available at the present time to cope with these emotional reactions. However, there is little conclusive evidence on the efficacy of psychotherapy as a treatment modality.

Possibly, the psychodynamic view used in conjunction with behavior modification could yield an effective treatment. Perhaps initial weight loss is purely a matter of external cue control, while later loss involves intrapsychic problems. Crisp postulated a critical level of weight loss and hypothesized that 25 percent above normal weight is a threshold below which denial of personal problems is no longer possible (24).

As with understanding the etiology of obesity, a key to treatment might be the combination of various modalities. Medical, psychoanalytic, and behavior modification therapies, as well as nutrition counseling and exercise programs, could be fruitfully integrated.

Conclusion

There are far fewer attempts to understand the causes of obesity than there are attempts to cure it: "We now use methadone to cure heroin addiction, Valium to cure alcoholism, amphetamines to cure carbohydrate and sugar addiction. I would suggest to you that the medical model, which plays a kind of addictive musical chairs, is a total failure because it actually escalates the problems in severity (17).

Obesity will be a growing problem in this culture for social conditions contribute to its generation (5). We live in a world of instant gratification and are called the narcissistic generation—me, myself, and I—manifested in everything from our divorce rate to our modes of activity—disco and jogging. The pressure for quick results increases the appeal of fast therapies—behavior modification, medication, etc. Used appropriately, these techniques have advanced knowledge and provided help to large numbers of patients. The problem, as noted by Wachtel (26), is that modern psychology often has been limited by monolithic research and training skills and a distorted emphasis on quantity instead of quality. For advances in the understanding and treatment of obesity, we need practitioners and researchers who have immersed themselves in the data currently available (26).

References

1. Beller, A. S., *Fat and Thin: A Natural History of Obesity,* McGraw-Hill, New York, 1977.
2. Sash, S. E., Why is the treatment of obesity a failure in modern society? *Inter'l. J. Obes. 1,* 247–248 (1977).
3. Bray, G., Testimony presented in *Diet Related to Killer Disease,* vol. 2, GPO, Washington, D. C., 1977, pp. 96–107.
4. Simonson, M., Obesity as a health factor, *Fem. Patient* 85–87 (1978).
5. Blackburn, G. L., Pathophysiology and metabolism, in *Obesity,* G. L. Blackburn, ed., Center for Nutritional Research, Boston, 1977, pp. 1–22.
6. Craddock, D., *Obesity and Its Management,* Churchill-Livingstone, Edinburgh, 1978.
7. Vickery, D. M., and Fries, J. F., *Take Care of Yourself: A Consumer's Guide to Medical Care,* Addison-Wesley, Reading, 1976.
8. Bruch, H., *Eating Disorders: Obesity, Anorexia Nervosa, and the Person Within,* Basic Books, New York, 1973.
9. Allport, G. W., *The Nature of Prejudice,* Doubleday, New York, 1958.
10. Orbach, S., *Fat Is a Feminist Issue,* Berkley, New York, 1978.
11. Stunkard, A. J., *The Pain of Obesity,* Bull, Palo Alto, 1976.
12. Mayer, J., Obesity, in *Modern Nutrition in Health and Disease,* 6th ed., R. S. Goodhart and M. E. Shils, eds., Lea and Febiger, Philadelphia, 1980, pp. 721–740.
13. Briggs, G. M., and Galloway, D. H., *Bogert's Nutrition and Physical Fitness,* Saunders, Philadelphia, 1979.
14. Schachter, S., Obesity and eating, in *Social Psychology Research,* A. Snadowsky, ed., Free Press, New York, 1972, pp. 16–33.
15. Goldman, R., Jaffa, J., and Schachter, S., Dormitory food and the eating behavior of obese and normal persons, in *Beyond the Laboratory: Field*

Research in Social Psychology, L. Bickman and T. Henchy, McGraw-Hill, New York, 1972, pp. 280–285.

16. Milich, R. S., A critical analysis of Schachter's externality theory of obesity, *J. Psych. 84,* 586–588 (1975).

17. Cummings, N. A., Turning bread into stone: our modern anti-miracle, *Amer. Psych. 34,* 1119–1129 (1979).

19. Haber, S., Differential diagnosis and the treatment of obesity, paper presented to the Divison of Psychotherapy of the American Psycho. Assoc., San Diego, American Psychological Association, 1980.

20. Granat, J. P., Obesity: a family problem, *Obes. Bariatric Med. 8,* 178–180 (1979).

21. Bray, G. A., To treat or not to treat—that is the question? in *Recent Advances in Obesity Research,* vol. 2, G. A. Bray, ed., Newman, Washington, D. C., 1977, pp. 248–265.

22. Van Itallie, T. B., testimony presented in *Diet Related to Killer Disease,* GPO, Washington, D. C., 1977.

23. Quaade, F., Intestinal bypass for severe obesity: a randomized trial, in *Recent Advances in Obesity Research,* vol. 2, G. A. Bray, ed., Newman, Washington, D. C., 1977.

24. Crisp, A. H., Some psychiatric aspects of obesity, in *Recent Advances in Obesity Research,* vol. 2, G. A. Bray, ed., Newman, Washington, D. C., 1978, pp. 336–344.

25. Neill, J. R., Marshall, J. R., and Yale, C. E., Marital changes after intestinal bypass surgery, *JAMA 240,* 447–450 (1978).

26. Wachtel, P. L., Investigation and its discontents: some constraints on progress in psychological research, *Amer. Psych. 35,* 399–408 (1980).

11

Anorexia Nervosa

Daniel C. Moore

Superficially, anorexia nervosa seems to be a strange subject for a book dealing with behaviors of excess since in most cases excess implies the intake of too much alcohol, tobacco, tranquilizers, narcotics, caffeine, food, vitamins, or television. By comparison, anorexia nervosa appears to involve aversion toward food and fear of the consequences of eating too much—obesity. In actuality, anorexia nervosa is a behavior in excess because, as Bruch pointed out, the core symptom is a *relentless pursuit of excessive thinness* (1). Anorexic patients do not dislike food and eating; on the contrary, they usually feel hunger, think constantly about food, enjoy preparing food for others, and frequently work at food related jobs such as waitressing. What they fear are the calories in food, which might compromise their all-consuming desire for thinness.

In its development, anorexia nervosa follows a pattern similar to that in all behaviors of excess. Initially, dieting is mild and intentional. The patient feels good because she has finally gained control over her eating and appears more attractive. Gradually but increasingly, she becomes involved with losing weight to the exclusion of other activities. Finally, the patient reaches the stage where starvation begins to take its toll in terms of debilitation, fatigue, susceptibility to disease, and family upset. At this point, some anorexics realize the harmfulness of their excessive dieting but feel powerless to stop. They analogize their self-starvation to alcoholism or drug abuse or to being controlled like a robot by some outside force (1).

Although they may compare their pursuit of slimness to other behaviors of excess, on a deeper level anorexics experience their excessive dieting as being in control and view any miniscule relaxation of their caloric restriction in order to gain weight as a terrible loss of control. As one patient said: "Once you get started [eating], you don't know how to quit" (2). Indeed, many anorexics experience a loss of control with excessive eating and elevated weight at some point in their lives. Some are overweight before adolescence and about half the patients show weight regulation problems or difficulty with eating or digestion during childhood (3, 4). Some patients who are overweight are so frustrated by lack of success in their attempts to diet that they resort to continual binging and vomiting as a way to accomplish weight loss. Others with better willpower have less frequent episodes of gorging on carbohydrates, usually followed by deep shame and remorse for their excesses. After treatment aimed at restoration of normal weight, about one-third of patients begin to eat excessively and are found to be obese on follow-up (5). The desperate efforts of anorexics to establish "control" over their weight by relentless pursuit of thinness are not without risk—in about 5–8 percent this excessive behavior results in death attributable to malnutrition (6, 7).

Symptoms and Progression of the Disease

By the time the patient with anorexia nervosa comes to clinical attention, a striking picture has emerged. In the classic phrase of Richard Morton, who first described anorexia nervosa in 1689, "I do not remember that I did ever in all my practice see one, that was conversant with the Living, so much wasted with the greatest degree of Consumption (like a Skeleton only clad with Skin)" (8). Yet despite their shocking gauntness, anorexics remain surprisingly resolute, with vigorous exercise schedules and an implacable refusal of food. Typically, the anorexia nervosa patient is an adolescent girl whose feeding difficulties began at age 15–19 years of age, but the variation is wide, with a range of 11–40 years in reported cases (6). Seventy percent fall ill before age 26. Anorexia nervosa is a rare disease in males, occurring only about once in 15 cases (9). When this condition does affect males, it is usually at a prepubertal age, while the great majority (89 percent) of females have passed through puberty and menstruated for at least two years before the onset of food refusal or amenorrhea (6).

The patient's stubborn weight loss is particularly difficult for parents to understand because in many cases the anorexic had been their best child (1). Usually these patients are described with a list of superlatives: most cooperative, intelligent, helpful, considerate, eventempered, self-directed, and obedient. Other children in the family might have been expected to cause trouble, but not this "perfect" daughter. Often the excessive dieting begins innocently enough, with a desire to lose a few pounds and become more attractive. Since some patients are a bit overweight and dieting is almost universal among adolescent girls, the idea is not viewed as unusual. Perhaps most confusing to parents is the tendency for the anorexic daughter to remain conscientious, studious, and compliant in every area of her life except one—her eating.

Possible precipitating events are mentioned in 66–100 percent of cases (2, 3, 6, 10). These include separations or losses such as going to college, death of a family member, or loss of a parent through divorce or remarriage (2, 3). Other frequent precipitants are physical illness, dissatisfaction with personal appearance ("too chubby'), or critical remarks about weight (2, 6). Some patients begin to diet after sexual teasing (e.g., a boy commenting on the girl's breast size) or the first heterosexual experience (3, 6). These events highlight a sense of poor self-esteem and self-doubt, which has been there all along but is now being stressed by the experiences of puberty and adolescence, with their new demands for autonomy and self-control (2). All adolescents must deal with these issues and troubled teenagers often look to drugs, alcohol, sexual activity, or delinquency for a solution. Anorexics have such a pervasive sense of ineffectiveness and powerlessness that they turn to the only thing over which they have any control—the growing curves of their own bodies—and begin to diet excessively (1, 2).

Initially, some parents try to ignore the dieting and wait for the child "to grow out of this fad." A few families deny the anorexia until a doctor or school nurse questions the emaciation in their daughter. The majority pass through several approaches as their daughter's weight continues to drop alarmingly. They reassure her that her weight is now normal and she can stop dieting. However, they soon discover that she has a distorted body image and still views herself as fat, especially about the hips, thighs, and abdomen. This distorted view is extremely self-specific. One anorexic will comment upon another's thinness but maintain vehemently that she herself is too fat and must lose more weight. Slade and Russell documented this distorted body image by using a visual size-estimation apparatus consisting of a horizontal bar with movable lights operated by a pulley (11). Each anorexic was asked to estimate the width across her face, chest, waist, and hips by indicating when the distance between the lights matched the width of each part of her body. Slade and Russell found that anorexics overestimated their body size by 25–50 percent, while normal women had a fairly accurate body perception and a tendency, if anything, toward underestimation (11). They also found that anorexics tended to overestimate the size of a normal female, but not as greatly as they overestimated their own figures. Finally, Slade and Russell showed that the body image distortions of patients with anorexia nervosa tended to decrease as patients put on weight, especially if this were done gradually.

Many parents attempt to lure their daughter off her diet with a favorite meal or dessert, only to find that their daughter barely samples the food. When questioned, she may praise the food as delicious but refuse it for having "too many calories." Most anorexics become self-taught nutritionists and usually have large libraries of calorie and diet books. They can estimate the calories in any plate of food in a matter of seconds and some spend time obsessively counting and recounting their calories to make sure that their estimates are not too high. Alternatively, an anorexic who puts herself on an 800 kcal diet may cut the amount to 400 kcal daily to reassure herself that errors in calculation will not put her over her limit. To this end, carbohydrates and fats are avoided as high in calories, while limited amounts of protein are allowed.

Despite the rigid diet, anorexics are by no means indifferent to food. Most are preoccupied with food or cooking. Often, food is cut into miniscule pieces and eaten over a period of hours in order to savor the taste fully. These behaviors may be explained partly by the effects of starvation. Prisoners from concentration camps and volunteers in a study of semistarvation both reported a striking increase in thoughts and daydreams of food and eating (12). When given their small portions, they obsessively divided their food into little bites to prolong the pleasurable experience of eating. However, the biological effects of starvation do not explain other anorexic preoccupations with food such as cooking a gourmet meal for the family on a daily basis but refusing to partake of it. Nor do they explain the behavior of the patient who forces excessive amounts of food on her family while resisting normal amounts herself.

When pushed to eat by their familes, anorexic patients usually protest that they are not hungry, that they do not need to eat, or that they are full after a few bites. In many cases, a denial of hunger is simply a bargaining point used with family or friends. Bruch found that anorexics who deny hunger early on will often admit later in therapy that they were hungry but did not want to admit it (1). Garfinkel documented differences between anorexia nervosa patients and normal women in their reactions to hunger and perception of satiety (13). He had 11 anorexics and 11 controls come for a noonday meal after 12 hours of fasting. Before eating, they filled out a questionnaire consisting of multiple items concerning emotional and bodily experiences of hunger. They then ingested a standard meal of soup, sandwich, dessert, and beverage and completed a questionnaire on satiety. Garfinkel found that both anorexics and controls experienced hunger as a feeling of gastric emptiness. There were no differences in mouth, throat, or cerebral sensations. The only significant differences were a strong preoccupation with food, a strong urge to eat, and a nervous, irritable, tense, or depressed mood associated with hunger in anorexics. By comparison, the satiety questionnaire indicated that controls tended to eat until they felt satisfied, accompanied in all cases by gastric fullness, while anorexics stopped because a "diet limit" was reached. The typical gastric experience for patients was bloating (seven), though some did experience gastric fullness (five). Only anorexics reported nervousness, irritability, or depression about having eaten. Overall, Garfinkel concluded that bodily perception of hunger was normal in anorexia nervosa patients but that there was a disturbance in the perception of satiety. Since there was no difference between acute and discharged patients or good and poor outcome patients, these abnormalities of perception could not be attributed to the effects of starvation alone.

Continued refusal to eat is such an upsetting symptom for parents to see that when pleading, coaxing, and cajoling fail, they often resort to threats of physical violence to get the anorexic daughter to eat. Even when these threats work, their success is often only temporary and the family finds that the patient has redoubled her efforts to lose weight. They may discover that the patient is pretending to eat normal amounts but disappears quickly to the bathroom to vomit. Some patients vomit only when they occasionally lose control over their hunger and eat more than they had intended, but other patients make a habit of overeating and vomiting, defending this pattern as a way of enjoying eating while still losing weight. The patient may consume donuts, ice cream, pizza, candy, or other high carbohydrate foods forbidden by her diet and then find a safe and secluded place to vomit. Once that is accomplished, she may feel hungry again and begin another round of eating and vomiting. In cases where this cycle is compulsive, the patient is unable to concentrate on anything else, runs out of money, and becomes physically exhausted. Some of these patients continue their cycles by stealing small amounts of food or money when their finances get low. Compulsive food bingers usually find vomiting easy to do, while the patients who find vomiting difficult or esthetically undesirable may resort to other means. Laxatives are available over-the-counter, and anorexics try to reduce the amount of calories that their intestines absorb by speeding the food through their system. Purging may also give them a feeling of having a slender stomach since the large intestine and colon stay empty and flat most of the time. Both vomiting and purging severely disturb the gastrointestinal tract, producing epigastric burning, stomach bloating, and intestinal cramps. When these symptoms become chronic, they further distort the patient's ability to perceive hunger and satiety. They also disrupt the body's electrolyte balance. When extensive, vomiting or purging can be life threatening. A few anorexics compulsively use diuretics to reduce their weight further. Diuretics act quickly and the weight loss is fast, but continued use of them can cause dehydration and severe electrolyte imbalance, which are particularly dangerous for an already debilitated patient.

Anorexics miss no chance to lose calories, and most resort to excessive exercise soon after their dieting begins. They may run or bicycle for long periods during the day or develop ritualistic patterns of running a certain number of miles, doing a certain number of situps, or swimming a certain number of laps. Often the exercise increases rather than decreases as they become more emaciated. Even when admitted to an inpatient unit and restricted in activity, anorexics find ways to use up calories such as pacing the floor or doing pushups or situps in their own rooms. In fact, hyperactivity is so important to many patients that the threat of restricted activity is one of the few inducements that can be used to get an anorexic to eat. In this way, they differ significantly from patients in studies of semistarvation, who become listless and avoid movement in order to conserve energy and calories (12).

Amenorrhea is one of the hallmarks of anorexia nervosa. However, there is considerable debate whether it has the same psychological or etiological importance as slimness and fear of eating. The facts are undisputed. Most anorexics go through menarche at a normal age of 12.7 years (SD ± 1.18 years) and menstruate regularly for several years before developing secondary amenorrhea (6). A small group, about 11 percent, who begin dieting at or before menarche never menstruate and are diagnosed as having primary amenorrhea (6). The average patient begins feeding difficulties at a mean age of 15.5 years (SD ± 3.14) and develops amenorrhea at a mean of 18.2 years (SD ± 6.43) (6). Specifically, the illness beings within two years of menarche in 32 percent, within five years in 87 percent, and within seven years in 92 percent (6).

Forced starvation during wartime and famine often lead to high rates of amenorrhea, and many investigators have assumed that the cause of amenorrhea in anorexia nervosa is malnutrition. This is undoubtedly the case in some patients. In her studies of normal adolescent girls, Frisch pointed out that menarche and menstruation are dependent on a critical composition of fat as a percentage of body weight (14). Her studies elegantly showed that puberty is dependent upon the attainment of this ratio rather than simply upon age factors. When anorexics regain their normal weight as a result of treatment and begin menstruating again, they do so at weights that coincide with Frisch's critical fat to body weight ratio. In this view, amenorrhea is a secondary symptom of the primary eating disturbance rather than a primary symptom of the disorder. Bruch concurs with this view (15). Though conceding that her patients do have disturbed sexual functioning, she does not see sexual conflicts or fear of pregnancy as being at the core of the patient's difficulties, except in some atypical cases. She points to cases of older, married patients with anorexia nervosa who have sought and received treatment of their amenorrhea in order to become pregnant and have a child, all the while maintaining their anorexic attitude toward eating. While these arguments are convincing, they do not explain all the observed facts. In Morgan and Russell's study of the relationship between onset of feeding difficulties and amenorrhea, weight loss came first in 45 percent, but amenorrhea preceded eating problems in 18 percent and coincided with feeding disorders in 34 percent of cases (6). Kay and Leigh found amenorrhea prior to repugnance for food in 25 percent of patients and coincident in 25 percent (3). Thus, in 50–55 percent of cases, amenorrhea precedes or coincides with the onset of dieting. These figures suggest that amenorrhea is not a secondary symptom in all cases and may be related to the etiology of anorexia nervosa. This question is discussed in more detail in the section on biological correlates of anorexia nervosa.

Typically, the patient with anorexia nervosa first comes to psychiatric attention after a year or two of dieting, surreptitious vomiting or purging, hyperactivity, and family disruption. By then, the patient has usually lost 20–40 percent or more of her ideal body weight. On the average, this amounts to a loss of 13.5 kg, though much more weight will have been lost in patients overweight prior to starting a diet (10). Usually by this time the patient looks like the starved skeleton of Morton's description but continues to deny her emaciation: "I do not need to eat. I am not too thin." Typically the patient does not see herself in need of help and is uncooperative. After months or years of dieting, the anorexic attitude has hardened into a character style that derives its only satisfaction from the independence obtained by refusal of all food or help. If the anorexic feels some unhappiness about her desperate condition and expresses a desire for help, she nevertheless will resolutely reject any suggestion of liberalizing her diet. When anorexia reaches this stage, hospitalization is usually required for medical as well as psychiatric reasons because of the physical changes in the severe, or late, stage of anorexia nervosa (2). In addition to the wasting of subcutaneous adipose and muscle tissue, which is so visible, hypotension and bradycardia occur, leading to frequent dizzy spells and continual fatigue, so that maintaining their original hyperactivity may be impossible for patients. Hypothermia causes decreased tolerance to cold, resulting in pale and cold extremities. They show loss of hair and the growth of lanugo type hair on the arms and legs. Other signs of advanced starvation include edema, constipation, polyuria, and insomnia. When anorexic patients die, the cause generally is an infection to which the body could not respond, even to the point of an elevated temperature or white cell count.

Diagnosis

During the eighteenth and nineteenth centuries, and even in the earlier part of the twentieth century, the most significant diagnostic task was to separate anorexia nervosa from the physical illnesses with which it might be confused. In particular, anorexia resembles the slow wasting of tuberculosis and even when correctly differentiated was initially referred to as a "nervous consumption." Likewise, cancer can cause loss of appetite and rapid weight loss similar to that in anorexia nervosa. Various endocrine disorders, especially hyperthyroidism and panhypopituitarism, can present similar symptoms: extreme hyperthyroidism results in an increase of nervous hyperactivity and weight loss, as well as menstrual symptoms, though usually the appetite is good; panhypopituitarism was at one time suggested as a model for anorexia nervosa because of the symptoms of amenorrhea, weight loss, cold intolerance, loss of hair, bradycardia, and hypotension. Even though this condition occurs postpartum and involves fatigue rather than hyperactivity, the symptoms explain why it might be confused with anorexia nervosa. Nowadays, sophisticated medical tests make it easy to distinguish anorexia nervosa from all of these diseases.

In modern psychiatry, attempts have been made to separate a loose clump of anorexic behaviors associated with weight loss into diagnostic subgroups. These efforts have aimed at creating subgroups that are more uniform in terms of etiology or prognosis, so that treatment can be applied more specifically. In her pioneering work, Bruch took the lead in dividing anorexic behavior into psychogenic malnutrition, atypical anorexia nervosa, and primary anorexia nervosa. She attached the term "psychogenic malnutrition" to a group of psychiatric conditions that may at one time or another present with weight loss (15). Examples include neurologic disorders such as multiple sclerosis with decreased appetite secondary to hypothalamic lesions or chronic schizophrenia with delusional ideas about poisoned food and voices telling the patient not to eat. Similarly, patients who do not eat because of depression, mental retardation, esophageal strictures, or political convictions would be excluded from the anorexia diagnosis. In each of these cases, the diagnosis of anorexia nervosa is inappropriate because refusal to eat represents a short episode in the course of a chronic disease and does not involve preoccupation with achieving thinness. Atypical anorexia nervosa is more difficult to differentiate from primary and, as Bruch has admitted, can sometimes be distinguished only after extensive contact (15). These patients may have just as severe weight loss and amenorrhea but they are usually not as hyperactive or concerned with thinness. They also begin their anorexic behavior at a later age, averaging 20.3 years instead of 15.9; nevertheless, the age difference is not significant enough to tell the two apart in any individual case. The chief point of differentiation for Bruch is the meaning of the refusal to eat. Atypical anorexia nervosa patients with neurotic or hysterical personality may refuse to eat for a variety of reasons, often with an unconscious sexual conflict as the basis. She has argued that the original theory of anorexia as a fear of oral impregnation fits such patients. Thinness is not of primary value, and patients use not eating as a way of coercing parents to allow further dependent behavior. Bruch noted that schizoid personalities have a near delusional fear of eating unrelated to fear of calories or weight gain; they reject food for reasons such as feelings of unworthiness, fear of contamination, etc. Finally, some adolescents with depressions etiologically related to repeated experiences of separation may show anorexic behavior and desire for slimness for some time but never crystallize an identity around thinness, hyperactivity, and perfectionism, so the anorexic phase is only transient.

In contrast, the central issue for the patient with primary anorexia nervosa is a struggle for a sense of identity, competence, and effectiveness, which comes to be represented by thinness (15). Bruch identified three areas of disordered psychological functioning that are pathognomic for genuine anorexia nervosa:

1. "A disturbance of delusional proportions in the body image and body concept." The desire for excessive slimness is primary and the true anorexic relentlessly seeks this state, identifies with it, and defends it.

2. "A disturbance in the accuracy of perception or cognitive interpretation of stimuli arising in the body." These patients either do not recognize or deny hunger or fatigue, with the result that they feel full when they are starving and remain hyperactive when exhausted.

3. "A paralyzing sense of ineffectiveness." This psychological characteristic explains why anorexics choose refusal to eat and pursuit of thinness. It is the only aspect in their lives over which they feel they have any control. When they submit to hunger and gorge, they see this behavior as a loss of control and are humiliated and ashamed. The genesis of this self-concept is discussed in the section on psychological correlates (15).

Bruch's criteria for primary anorexia nervosa are psychological, while other researchers, particularly the British, rely on descriptive criteria for diagnosis and do not try to infer psychological conflicts. For instance, the criteria of Beaumont and colleagues for anorexia nervosa include a pattern of behavior aimed at inducing weight loss; a persistent pursuit of thinness, an admitted aversion to regaining a normal weight, and a denial of the severity and extent of weight loss; emaciation to a body weight of at least below 80 percent of standard; amenorrhea of at least three months' duration; and absence of other physical or psychiatric illness (10). Beaumont and colleagues have admitted that some of Bruch's atypical anorexics might be included in this group. They divided patients who satisfied their criteria into those who achieved weight loss by dieting alone and those who also employed vomiting and purging. Significant differences appeared. The "dieters" were not obese prior to the onset of their weight loss, which was precipitated by a psychosocial stress. They had mainly obsessional personality traits and were highly competitive academically but socially withdrawn and lacking in dating or sexual experience. They usually presented for treatment at less than 70 percent of ideal body weight. On the other hand, the "vomiters and purgers" had been big eaters and obese prior to their anorexic symptoms, which were precipitated by teasing remarks about their weight. Over half had histrionic character traits and were socially extroverted. All had had regular boyfriends and 79 percent had experienced sexual intercourse (as compared to 18 percent of the dieters). They had fluctuating courses of gains and losses in weight and seldom fell below 70 percent of body weight. Interestingly enough, the dieters, though lacking in social skills, were found to have a shorter course of illness and better prognosis.

In preparing the third edition of the *Diagnostic and Statistical Manual of Mental Disorders* (DSM-III), the Task Force on Nomenclature and Statistics of the American Psychiatric Association created diagnostic formulations similar to those of Beaumont and other British authors (16). The classification of anorexia nervosa corresponds to Beaumont's dieters, while bulimia corresponds to the vomiters and purgers. Russell recently proposed the catchy name "bulimia nervosa" for this latter category of anorexics with a prominent pattern of gorging and vomiting (17).

Sociocultural Correlates

As in most other areas of psychiatry, no single cause of anorexia nervosa is known or verifiable. Instead, research reveals a large number of factors, each of which correlates with anorexia nervosa but is not sufficient by itself to explain the disease. For this reason, theories of psychiatric illness tend to be multicausal, taking into account all of the factors that influence behavior. These factors include the biological substrate of the child, the sociocultural milieu in which she or he grows up, and the psychological concepts and conflicts that arise. In the case of anorexia nervosa, all three correlates are quite important in both the genesis of the disorder and the approaches to treatment.

The sociocultural context of anorexia nervosa has several dimensions. The most obvious dimension is the increasing preoccupation of modern Americans with dieting, exercise, and slimness. From earliest times, representations of the female figure have tended to be fat, or at least hefty, thereby symbolizing physical beauty and fertility. In times when crop failures and famines were not uncommon, fatness also signified health, wealth, and general well-being, as well as protecting against unexpected shortages of food. A look at the rounded contours of the famous *Venus de Milo* or the sizable proportions of Renoir's *Bathers* serves to show that slimness has only recently become the ideal of beauty. Today, both advertising and the media extol youth and slimness as the key to success in love, sex, business, and friendship. Even the cigarettes for the "modern" woman are called Virginia Slims. This concern with ultrathinness has increased to the point that some of the great beauties of the 1940s and 1950s look heavy by today's standards. However, as Bruch pointed out, this recent veneration of the excessively slim figure is not found everywhere (15). In countries like India and Bangladesh, where famine is a very real possibility, a certain plumpness is considered most attractive for both women and men. Bruch noted that anorexia nervosa is unknown in other underdeveloped countries, where food is still scarce (15). Even in the United States, there is no anorexia nervosa reported in blacks or other underprivileged minority groups, though we might expect that cases will begin to appear with increasing affluence (15).

Anorexia nervosa, therefore, is primarily a disease of the economically secure, who have never faced the danger of poverty or food scarcity. Both American and British authors have remarked upon the disproportionate degree to which the upper classes are represented in studies of anorexia nervosa (1, 6, 21). In Morgan and Russell's experience, 44 percent of anorexic patients came from social class I, even though this highest class represents only 3.3 percent of the population. Similarly, class II accounted for 21 percent of patients as compared to 14.6 percent of the general population, whereas classes IV and V contributed 2.4 percent and zero, respectively, even though they comprise almost 24 percent of the population (6).

Some investigators report that anorexia nervosa has been increasing in the past few years, possibly as a result of the cultural concern with slimness. At the very least, this condition is being more frequently identified than in the past. Crisp and associates studied the prevalence of anorexia nervosa at seven independent schools and at two comprehensive schools (9). In the British school system, girls at independent schools tend to be from the middle and upper classes; as might be expected, these schools had much higher rates of anorexia nervosa. Indeed, only one case was discovered at the comprehensive schools, while there was an overall prevalence of 4.6 per 1,000 at the independent schools. Among girls 16 years and older, this prevalence rose to an astounding 10.5 per 1,000, or about 1 percent. In this study the criteria for anorexia nervosa were very strict, including a loss of 30 percent of body weight, as well as amenorrhea and bizarre eating habits. When milder criteria such as weight loss plus secondary amenorrhea of at least six months' duration were used, the rate increased to 4 percent of "normal" adolescent girls (19). The authors concluded by pointing out that rates were probably even higher in older age groups and in university women.

Other sociofamilial data besides social class have correlated significantly with anorexia nervosa: 42 percent of anorexics had poor childhood social adjustments, especially at school, or neurotic problems in childhood (21). Studies differ as to whether they had infant or childhood feeding difficulties (4, 6). However, all studies agree on the importance of disturbed family relations. Specifically, anorexia nervosa patients showed higher rates of abnormal parental marriages when compared to matched neurotic patients and healthy controls (4). In another study, 49 percent of anorexics had parents with poor marital relationships prior to onset of the daughter's disease (18). Even more important, 63 percent of patients had a disturbed relationship with their family before developing anorexia nervosa (18). This poor relationship with family is also the one measure that correlates significantly with poor outcome, whereas familial mental illness, social class, sibling rivalry, and anomalous family structure are not good predictors (6). The influence of a disturbed family structure on outcome has loomed large in Bruch's long experience with anorexics: "Whenever I have succumbed to pressure to accept a patient without involving the family . . . I have come to regret it" (1). In her case studies, she often found that the preanorexic child was intertwined with her parents in such a way that her own desires and feelings were denied. Instead, the child's role was to make the parents feel good about themselves by being extra good or useful or bright. In some cases, the child also had the task of preventing overt marital discord by supplying a parent with satisfaction otherwise missing in the marriage.

Minuchin and his group at the Philadelphia Child Guidance Clinic extensively studied the structure of families having children with psychosomatic diseases and anorexia nervosa (20, 21). They found that the family of an anorexic usually presented itself as untroubled except for the symptom of noneating in the child. When asked about medical or interpersonal difficulties, they minimized or denied them compared to the anorexic symptom. Minuchin uses a lunch session with the patient and family to identify disturbed family relationships and begin the process of revealing the noneating behavior as an attempt to ward off other intrafamilial issues. Once the marital discord, lack of parent-child boundaries, or lack of individual autonomy and privacy become the focus, anorexic behavior begins to decrease in intensity (21).

Despite the usefulness of the family structural model in treatment of anorexia nervosa, this conceptualization does not predict why certain children from particular families develop anorexia rather than, for instance, asthma or delinquent behavior. Social and family concepts provide a context for the symptom, but the choice of this particular symptom may be governed by constitutional (biological vulnerability) or psychological (personal meaning) correlates.

Biological Correlates

As already mentioned, anorexia nervosa was originally confused with physical diseases such as panhypopituitarism but was later conceptualized as being a purely psychological disease with the biological changes secondary to advanced malnutrition. This view is not surprising since anorexia nervosa at base is a disorder of self-starvation. However, there are differences between the anorexic and the victim of famine in symptoms such as onset of amenorrhea, awareness of hunger and satiety, and hyperactivity. Though some psychological explanations have been presented, they are not always adequate to explain these symptoms in their entirety, which suggests that the disease may have biological correlates. In considering this possibility, the reader should keep in mind diseases like asthma and depression as models of psychological-biological interaction. Asthma is a psychosomatic disease with a clear biological basis of bronchiolar hypersensitivity to allergens and pollutants, but the degree to which this condition causes impairment and hospitalization can be strongly affected by psychological factors, such as reactions to life stresses. Likewise, depression can be precipitated by a loss of another person or of one's self-esteem, but once this condition is established, a constellation of symptoms including biological factors such as deficits in sleep, appetite, and sexual functioning take over. At this stage, antidepressant drugs acting at a biological level can often lift the patient far enough out of depression to begin psychological work again. Prior to antidepressants and the neurochemical studies they stimulated, depression was seen as a primarily psychological illness.

Research in anorexia nervosa is nowhere near establishing that sort of biological relationship or effective drug treatment, but some provocative findings have been uncovered in the past 15 years as endocrine tests have become increasingly sophisticated. As already mentioned, though malnutrition is generally given as the reason for amenorrhea in anorexia nervosa, this theory does not explain the approximately 50–55 percent of patients who stop menstruating at or prior to beginning dieting and before significant weight loss has occurred (3, 6). Looking at amenorrhea as a measure of outcome, one finds that return to normal body weight is not always followed by return of menstruation. In one recent study, 48 of 102 patients had maintained normal weight when followed up four to eight years after hospitalization, but 11 (23 percent) still had amenorrhea and 8 (17 percent) had only sporadic periods (18). Russell studied human pituitary gonadotrophins (HPG)—follicle stimulating hormone (FSH) and luteinizing hormone (LH)—and estrogen levels in seven anorexic females when they were malnourished and then upon return to normal weight (22). While emaciated, the women had low estrogen and HPG levels. On refeeding, estrogen level increased in all patients, while HPG increased in two and remained low in five. One patient had normal HPG levels throughout the study. Only one of the patients had returned to normal menstruation 11 months after refeeding. Russell contrasted this investigation to a study of malnourished Mexican patients who had a prompt increase in HPG and resumed normal menstruation on return to normal weight. Russell further studied this issue by comparing seven anorexics who developed amenorrhea along with or preceding weight loss with seven patients with amenorrhea late in the illness (23). He found that on refeeding, the response of HPG was lower in the group with early amenorrhea. Of the whole group, only four had resumed menstruation by the end of the study. He concluded that weight loss or regain may affect the level of HPG, but rhythmic secretion of FSH and LH must be controlled by other factors. Studies with modern methods reveal that LH is more frequently decreased while only some patients have lowered FSH (24,25).

These studies raise the question as to whether there is a defect in the pituitary or the hypothalamus of anorexics. This question has been examined using synthetic preparations of the luteinizing hormone–releasing hormone (LH-RH) normally secreted by the hypothalamus to control release of LH from the pituitary. While some studies have suggested that there may be pituitary resistance to LH-RH at very low body weights, all studies found that in anorexia nervosa the pituitary responds to test doses of LH-RH with release of normal LH (26–28). Thus, whatever defect exists in the release of LH occurs above the pituitary.

Boyar's revent investigation of the 24-hour LH secretory pattern in anorexics showed that during the acute phase of the illness, with weight loss and amenorrhea, patients had a flat (or immature) LH secretory pattern, similar to that in prepubertal girls, instead of an adult pattern of episodic secretion of LH (29). Patients with other types of amenorrhea, such as gonadal dysgenesis (Turner syndrome), polycystic ovaries (Stein–Leventhal syndrome), menopause, or functional amenorrhea-galactosemia, do not show this immature pattern (30). Patients who recovered from anorexia nervosa, with voluntary maintenance of normal weight and return of menstruation, reverted to the normal adult pattern (29). A further study demonstrated that the mature circadian LH secretory pattern was not present in anorexic women who had been pressured to return to ideal weight but who otherwise remained symptomatic in terms of attitudes toward eating, weight, and their figures (31).

These studies indicate that the amenorrhea of anorexia nervosa is controlled on the level of the hypothalamus or above, in the midbrain or cerebral hemispheres. In the case of anorexia nervosa, it is doubtful that this control is simply a sensing of low weight since menstruation would then always resume when ideal weight returned, as in the case of the malnourished Mexican women discussed by Russell (22). So-called pschogenic amenorrhea provides a model for cessation of periods caused by stress rather than malnutrition. Gathering together a large number of studies, Drew showed increasing rates of amenorrhea associated with increasingly stressful situations (32). This ranged from 2 percent prevalence among WAVE inductees leaving home and entering the navy, to 60 percent in inmates of the concentration camp Theresienstadt, to 100 percent in prisoners before execution. Drew pointed out that the Theresienstadt women ceased menstruating immediately upon entering the concentration camp and realizing their danger, that is, before their nutritional status altered. Conversely, when liberated, they began menstruating again "immediately—long before we had gained weight" (32).

These studies suggest two possible models for amenorrhea and other symptoms of anorexia nervosa. One possibility is that a preexisting hypothalamic defect or vulnerability is activated by stressful events in puberty or adolescence. Once activated, this mechanism follows a course of its own, just as some depressions seem to do, producing continued amenorrhea despite weight gain. Case histories of patients with tumors in the hypothalamus show that changes in that region can duplicate all the behavioral symptoms of anorexia nervosa: amenorrhea, anorexia, aversion to any form of carbohydrate, weight loss, indifference to emaciation, and continued activity (33, 34). It is not surprising that this constellation of symptoms could occur secondary to a tumor or other change in the hypothalamus because it contains the higher control centers for all vegetative functions, including hunger, satiety, heart rate, temperature, water regulation, sleep cycle, sexual functioning, menstruation, and a host of endocrine hormones.

The second model involves control of a normal hypothalamus by higher cortical structures that alter hypothalamic function during times of stress. Teleologically, periods of stress ranging from normal separations up to starvation are not the right time to become pregnant, so ovulation ceases and menstruation stops. For the preanorexic patient, adolescence poses maximum stresses in the areas of changing body image, sexual maturity, and increased independence. Recent advances in neurophysiology and neuroendocrinology have revealed neurochemical pathways through which stress felt in the cerebral cortex or the limbic system (the so-called seat of the emotions) could be transduced into amenorrhea, anorexia, hypothermia, and hyperactivity. The hypothalamus is known to be innervated by multiple neurotransmitters, of which the best known and studied are norepinephrine, dopamine, serotonin, and acetylcholine. Each of these neurotransmitters has been implicated in the control of LH-RH secretion, either on a stimulatory or on an inhibitory basis and acting at different sites within the hypothalamus (35–37). Norepinephrine appears to stimulate release of LH-RH at both the preoptic and the arcuate–median eminence regions of the hypothalamus, and alpha-adrenergic receptor blocking drugs, which block norepinephrine, inhibit LH release (34). The cell bodies for these noradrenergic neurons lie in the locus ceruleus of the brain stem, which has recently been heavily implicated in mechanisms of anxiety (38). The locus ceruleus gives rise to an ascending pathway called the dorsal forebrain bundle, which courses through the lateral hypothalamus to terminate in the preoptic, anterior hypothalamic, and median eminence regions (35). Destruction of hypothalamic nuclei in the areas through which these noradrenergic neurons pass has been noted to have interesting effects on eating behavior. Lesions in the lateral hypothalamus cause aphagia, while similar destruction in the ventromedial hypothalamus causes overeating and obesity (39). Thus, initially eating was thought to be regulated by a balance between a lateral hypothalamic "feeding center" and a ventromedial hypothalamic "satiety center." Studies have indicated that norepinephrine from the dorsal forebrain bundle may act by inhibiting suppressor brain areas such as the satiety center and allow eating (40). Other researchers have suggested that adrenergic agents act on alpha-adrenergic receptors in the ventromedial hypothalamus, causing increased hunger, while adrenergic agents applied to the lateral hypothalamus suppress feeding by acting on beta-adrenergic receptors (41). The exact control of hunger and satiety in the hypothalamus is still in debate, but the existence of a norepinephrine system that can effect eating and menstruation is well established.

Dopamine may exert similar influence on menstruation through the tuberoinfundibular system, which terminates at LH-RH containing neurons in the median eminence, and on eating through the nigrostriatal system, which passes through the lateral hypothalamic feeding center (36, 39). Barry and Klawans pointed out that compounds that mimic or release dopamine (such as amphetamine, apomorphine, and L-dopa) can cause amenorrhea, anorexia, hyperactivity, and hypothermia (42). They admitted, however, that some drugs, like amphetamine, have effects on norepinephrine as well as dopamine and that amphetamine induced hyperactivity is related primarily to increased norepinephne activity.

Both the dopamine and the norepinephrine theory are too simple at present to explain all the complex systems of anorexia nervosa, but they do suggest how a central defect could produce such seemingly unrelated symptoms as anorexia, amenorrhea, hypothermia, and hyperactivity in response to stress. In fact, recent clinical studies and drug trials have provided some support for these theories.

In a follow-up of anorexia nervosa patients and their families, Cantwell and co-workers found significant amounts of psychopathology, especially affective disorder (43). Patients were found to have manifested depressive symptomatology premorbidly, postmorbidly, and in follow-up. Depressive disorder was also particularly common in the mothers of anorexic patients. Cantwell and associates hypothesized that anorexia nervosa might be a variant of affective disorder, with atypical symptoms presenting in adolescence. Following a similar line of reasoning, Halmi and colleagues measured 3-methoxy-4-hydroxyphenylglycol (MHPG) concentrations in acutely ill anorexics with secondary depressive symptoms and again after weight gain (44). MHPG is a urinary marker for brain norepinephrine metabolism that is decreased in some patients with primary depression. The Halmi study found that urinary MHPG was significantly lower in acutely ill anorexics than in normal control females. Although the MHPG level increased with treatment, it remained lower than in controls. Halmi and co-workers noted an apparent relationship between MHPG and degree of depression in a group of anorexics who did not carry a primary diagnosis of depression. Antidepressant drugs such as amitriptyline and imipramine are thought to increase norepinephrne and therefore MHPG in some depressed patients. Case reports indicate that when these drugs are tried in anorexia nervosa, some patients experience a decrease in preoccupation with eating, thinness, and binging and vomiting (45–47). Success has also been reported with L-dopa, which increases dopamine, and with phenoxybenzamine, an alpha-adrenergic blocking agent that selectively blocks certain norepinephrine receptors (48, 49). Unfortunately, none of these drugs works in all cases, indicating that the neurophysiological aspects of anorexia nervosa are either more heterogeneous or more complex than our present knowledge.

Psychological Correlates

The sociological and biological correlates of anorexia nervosa deal with symptoms observable from a relatively exterior vantage point. The psychological correlates are often revealed only much later, after patients have begun to recover. They tell more about the internal viewpoint of the anorexic and how excessive concern with slimness becomes a temporary, but dysfunctional, solution to the problems of adolescence and adulthood. As already described in family structural terms, the patient's role in the family often is to prevent family discord by being excessively considerate, sweet, and obedient—that is, a perfect child—to make the parents feel good about themselves. The child obviously is not consciously aware that she is passively responding rather than actively expressing wishes and desires. Adolescence has as its age-appropriate task the consolidation of an identity separate from the parents, with different wishes and goals. Having been so successful as obedient children, anorexic patients are shocked by the difficulty of this new decision-making task; they have no childhood framework on which to build. Most patients report consternation and fear at normal adolescent activities—dating boys, choosing a major, separating from parents, making personal decisions—before becoming preoccupied with dieting. For the first time in their lives, these "perfect" children experience themselves as imperfect and ineffective because they have had no experience in satisfying their own desires, only in satisfying those of their parents. In many cases, they set about frantically to become perfect at everything, trying to maintain top grades in all courses, excel at the piano, be athletic, and attract boys. Soon they find that it is impossible to be good at everything, and they must choose which activities are most important to them. This realization is both a blow to their self-esteem and a dilemma, for how will they choose?

Bruch suggested that dieting is often begun casually in an attempt to correct one of the many imperfections (1). When it turns out that they are good at dieting and receive praise, this bolsters their sense of effectiveness. They pursue dieting further for the sense of superiority and pride in accomplishment it gives them. Finally, they feel they can be different and perfect in one area—no one else can diet and lose weight as well as they can. At this point, excessive preoccupation with weight begins. Having linked self-esteem rigidly to thinness, the anorexic feels shame and self-loathing at any "indulgence" in food or gain in weight, even an ounce. Thinness thus becomes the brittle focus for a self-identity, a sense of independence and separateness. Nevertheless, the feeling of hunger and preoccupation with food persist, so these patients begin a process of redefining hunger. Formerly a deprivation, hunger now comes to symbolize their superiority and therefore turns into an oject for enjoyment. Anorexics talk about the empty feeling in their stomachs as showing them that they are thin and therefore not too fat. They procrastinate as they eat, waiting for the slightest feeling in the stomach that they can define as fullness (1).

Just as losing weight gives anorexics a sense of pride and effectiveness, the thought of gaining weight fills them with terror. Their new self-concept is built on a single, limited foundation—thinness. From this turned around viewpoint, it is not dieting that is excessive; rather, eating is excessive and out of control. To be really safe, they must lose still more, but each successive reduction in weight is not enough to protect against the dread of losing control and gaining weight. In fact, the lower the weight, the greater the physiologic need to eat and the greater the likelihood of losing control and eating. So the weight is further lowered to protect against that risk. In other words, the psychology of the anorexic is a vicious circle. At this stage, some patients begin to realize that self-respect will not come from thinness and feel desperately unhappy, but they are trapped by the fear of fatness just the same. They realize that they are not independent and their lives are not full, but thinness is still their only source of self-esteem. At this stage, the effects of starvation also begin to influence their thinking. The Minnesota study of semistarvation in normal volunteers showed that chronically malnourished people lose the ability to concentrate and thinking becomes confused, probably from biochemical changes in the brain secondary to the malnutrition (12). In addition, they become preoccupied entirely with thoughts, dreams, and discussions of food. For the anorexic, this means that just when her ability to reason out alternative routes to independence and self-respect is most impaired, thoughts of food loom larger and larger. In this state of chronic starvation, the only focus becomes the struggle between eating and not eating. As one patient stated, "It is as if you were slowly poisoned, something like being under the chronic influence of something like alcohol or dope. . . . You're in a constant daze—you don't feel as though you are really there. It came to the point that I doubted the people around me—I was unsure whether they truly existed (1).

The artificial conflict over eating and the confused thinking also serve to protect against the anxieties generated by the more important and disturbing issues of their lives: the isolation from others, the absence of true autonomy, the lack of a sense of effectiveness. Most authors agree that the longer the anorexic stance persists before treatment, the harder the patient is to treat (6, 15, 18). The longer this condition goes on, the more anorexic thinking becomes embedded in the personality as the cornerstone of a sense of self. All personality traits are more flexible and amenable to change in early adolescence than in the late teens and twenties, when the personality begins to consolidate around learned behaviors and experiences. If anorexic behavior goes on long enough, preoccupation with weight becomes the major psychological mechanism and mode of interpersonal contact. Bruch has seen women in their forties and fifties still vigorously defending their excessively slim figures as the major concern of their lives (1).

Treatment

The treatment of anorexia nervosa can be divided into two phases: acute, lifesaving inpatient treatment aimed at restoration of weight to safe levels and longer term outpatient care directed at the personal and family issues that led to the weight loss in the first place. Although there are no good figures, it seems that a large number of anorexic patients have mild enough weight loss or come to treatment early enough that they can be treated as outpatients. A smaller but much more visible and psychiatrically ill group lose weight to such a spectacular degree that the danger of electrolyte imbalance, cardiac arrhythmia, and intercurrent infection makes hospitalization mandatory.

The cornerstone of all inpatient treatments of anorexia nervosa is a stepwise increase in weight to within 10–15 percent of ideal body weight, at least partly and sometimes totally against the patient's wishes. However, there is wide disagreement about how this goal can best be accomplished. At one extreme, some wards use a strict behavioral approach based on the assumption that refusal to eat is a learned response that can be modified through a reward and punishment system (50, 51). Typically, a requirement for a certain amount of weight gain per day is set—for example, three pounds per week. If the patient fails to gain, she is placed on strict bed rest and denied social or physical activities. Some programs also recommend sedation with a tranquilizer such as chlorpromazine, though this procedure has become much less popular in recent years. Usually, restriction from physical activity is enough of a punishment for the hyperactive anorexic. Reward consists of freedom to exercise, interact socially, or leave the ward on a pass. Often patients are offered a high protein–high calorie nutrient drink as a more acceptable way to gain weight since they may find solid food difficult to take early in treatment. Reactions range from violent refusal to temper tantrums to passive acceptance, but almost all anorexics try the same subterfuges successful in preventing forced weight gain at home. They may vomit after meals unless watched or continue to purge with a supply of laxatives smuggled into the hospital on admission. They drink large amounts of water and void only after weigh-in. With good nursing communication, such tricks are easily detected and prevented. The ultimate negative reinforcement is tube feeding and few anorexics persist in their refusal to eat after one or two experiences with this method.

There is little dispute that the behavioral approach is the fastest method of weight gain, but some critics point to the high frequency of relapse after behavior modification patients are discharged (1, 52). More important, according to Bruch, such systems remove the last bulwark of self-control and source of self-confidence too rapidly. She pointed out that many anorexics feel coerced and helpless, lose all control, and resort to binging on unhealthy, "junk" foods, which practice may continue after discharge (1). Other anorexics become depressed and suicidal at their uncontrolled weight gain. Instead, Bruch has recommended a carefully planned, healthful diet, which will allow a patient to gain weight slowly enough to adapt to her new body image gradually; this slower approach protects the patient from the fear of gaining too fast, losing control, and becoming obese. Though not completely repudiating tube feeding as a last resort, Bruch observed that the newer technique of intravenous hyper-alimentation can provide essential weight gain without creating struggles over eating. Unfortunately, this technique carries with it the danger of sepsis and is not foolproof; one patient avoided weight gain by surreptitiously turning off the IV at night. British authorities such as Crisp and Russell provide a balance of these two extremes, taking a medical tack that the anorexic patient is ill and needs someone else to make dietary decisions for a period of time but tailoring the treatment program to individual needs (53, 54).

Once the patient has reached a sufficient weight, such that starvation effects no longer hamper her memory or cloud her thinking, outpatient treatment can begin. Usually there is an agreed upon weight below which the patient cannot go without readmission to the hospital, and this rule may be invoked several times before the patient settles at a low but safe weight. Outpatient treatment generally consists of individual psychotherapy, family therapy, or, ideally, a combination. The goal of restructuring the family to reduce the need for a symptomatic child was described in the section on sociocultural correlates. Minuchin and his group have recommended family therapy and a continuation of the behavior modification paradigm on an outpatient basis (51). The patient is required to gain at least two pounds per week or be confined to the house on weekends. Since a family member is required to stay with the grounded patient, this technique places stress on the rest of the family and forces them to work together to be sure the patient eats.

Individual psychotherapy has been investigated in greatest detail by Bruch (15). She found that classical psychoanalysis with an aim toward an understanding of psychodynamics, followed by interpretation by the therapist, is unproductive, even counterproductive. The anorexic is expert at figuring out what others, especially parents, want to hear and then parroting it back. Classic psychotherapy gives them a superficial understanding that cannot be put to use in their own lives. More important, since anorexics have no previous experience with sensing their own desires, interpretation by the therapist becomes a repetition of being told what their feelings are, increasing the sense of ineffectiveness and inadequacy. Bruch developed a psychotherapy based on a fact-finding, noninterpretative approach in which the therapist and patient collaborate (15). Together, they discover thoughts and impulses to which the patient has never previously paid attention. For the patient, the essential change is from passively experiencing life to actively participating in self-discovery. This approach gradually addresses the general lack of bodily awareness, which has led to hyperactivity, distorted body image, and denial of hunger. Over time, the anorexic begins to discover with genuine pleasure her *own* awareness of hunger or fatigue. By this slow, often tedious process, anorexic patients can build a sense of self-respect and effectiveness based on an awareness of their own thoughts and desires.

Outcome

Anorexia nervosa is noted for its intractability. Typical case histories often show multiple hospital admissions for dangerously low weight and long periods of outpatient treatment during which dieting and excessive preoccupation with weight remain prominent. Until recently, attempts to look at recovery rates have been clouded by differing diagnostic criteria, variable durations of follow-up, small numbers, and reliance on anecdotal information. Fortunately, two excellent studies have now been published with uniform diagnostic criteria, large numbers of patients, and a long (four to eight years) duration of follow-up (6, 18). Morgan and Russell rated overall recovery using an average outcome score based on outcome in five areas: nutritional status, menstrual function, mental state, sexual adjustment, and socioeconomic status (6). Using this scale, they rated patients at least four years after treatment and found a good outcome in 39 percent, intermediate in 27 percent, and poor in 29 percent. Five percent of patients had died (6). With the same scale, Hsu and colleagues rated 48 percent as having a good outcome, 30 percent as intermediate, and 20 percent as poor, with 2 percent dead (21). Despite the reasonably high percentage with good outcome, few patients were completely free of anorexic symptoms. More than half had had at least one readmission for anorexia nervosa during the four-year follow-up (6). Even after four years, Hsu and associates found only 28 percent not concerned about weight, while 44 percent still worried continually about weight (18). These statistics show that while the most serious symptoms of anorexia nervosa can be ameliorated in 66–78 percent of cases, it is a chronic disease that continues to trouble patients for years after the acute phase is over.

Although there is as yet no way to predict good outcome, certain factors predict a poor prognosis in anorexia nervosa. Some of these factors are rather expectable, such as long duration of illness, lower body weight at presentation, and unsuccessful previous treatment (6, 18). Other factors speak to psychological and family issues, with poor childhood social adjustment, school phobia, disturbed parental relationship, and disturbed parent-child relationship all suggesting a bad prognosis (18). Some predictors are intriguing but not easily explained: vomiting, older age at onset, marriage prior to illness, and lower social class all point to poor outcome (18).

Conclusion

Despite recent strides in understanding the biological, psychological, and sociocultural aspects of anorexia nervosa, it remains an enigmatic disease that is highly resistant to treatment. Like many other diseases of excess, anorexia nervosa presents dramatically to others but is denied by the patient. For this reason, it is essential that family and friends resist the impulse to ignore anorexic behavior and instead help the patient seek medical attention while the excessive dieting is still in the early and most treatable phase.

References

1. Bruch, H., *The Golden Cage,* Vintage Books, New York, 1978.
2. Casper, R. C., and Davis, J. M., On the course of anorexia nervosa, *Amer. J. Psychiat. 134,* 974–978 (1977).
3. Kay, D. W. K., and Leigh, D., The natural history, treatment, and prognosis of anorexia nervosa, based on a study of 38 patients, *J. Ment. Sci. 100,* 411–431 (1954).
4. Kay, D. W. K., Schapira, K., and Brandon, S., Early factors in anorexia nervosa compared with non-anorexic groups, *J. Psychosom. Res. 11,* 133–139 (1967).
5. Halmi, K., Brodland, G., and Loney, J., Prognosis in anorexia nervosa, *Ann. Inter'l. Med. 78,* 907–909 (1973).
6. Morgan, H. G., and Russell, G. F. M., Value of family background and clinical features as predictors of long-term outcome in anorexia nervosa: four-year followup study of 41 patients, *Psych. Med. 5,* 355–371 (1975).

7. Nemiah, J. C., Anorexia nervosa, *J. Digest. Dis. 3,* 249–274 (1958).

8. Morton, R., *Phthisiologia—Or a Treatise of Consumption,* 2d ed., Smith, London, 1720.

9. Crisp, A.H., Palmer, R. L., and Kalucy, R. S., How common is anorexia nervosa? a prevalence study, *Brit. J. Psychiat. 128,* 549–554 (1976).

10. Beumont, P. J. V., George, G. C. W., and Smart, D. E., "Dieters" and "vomiters" and "purgers" in anorexia nervosa, *Psych. Med. 6,* 617–622 (1976).

11. Slade, P. D., and Russell, G. F. M., Awareness of body dimensions in anorexia nervosa: cross-sectional and longitudinal studies, *Psych. Med. 3,* 188–199 (1973).

12. Schiele, B. C., and Brozek, J., "Experimental neurosis" resulting from semi-starvation in man, *Psychosom. Med. 10,* 31–50 (1948).

13. Garfinkel, P. E., Perception of hunger and satiety in anorexia nervosa, *Psych. Med. 4,* 309–315 (1974).

14. Frisch, R. E., Food intake, fatness, and reproductive ability, in *Anorexia Nervosa,* R. A. Vigersky, ed., Raven, New York, 1977, pp. 149–161.

15. Bruch, H., *Eating Disorders,* Basic Books, New York, 1973.

16. American Psychiatric Association, Task Force on Nomenclature and Statistics, *Diagnostic and Statistical Manual of Mental Disorders,* 3d ed., American Psychiatric Association, Washington, D. C., 1980.

17. Russell, G. F. M., "Bulimia nervosa": an ominous variant of anorexia nervosa, *Psych. Med. 9,* 429–448 (1979).

18. Hsu, L. K. G., Crisp, A. H., and Harding, B., Outcome of anorexia nervosa, *Lancet 1,* 62–65 (1979).

19. Fries, H., Secondary amenorrhoea, self-induced weight reduction, and anorexia nervosa, *Acta Psychiat. Scand. 248* (supp.), 1–66 (1974).

20. Rosman, B. L., Minuchin, S., and Liebman, R., Family lunch session: an introduction to family therapy in anorexia nervosa, *Amer. J. Orthopsychiat. 45,* 846–853 (1975).

21. Liebman, R., Minuchin, S., and Baker, L., An integrated treatment program for anorexia nervosa, *Amer. J. Psychiat. 131,* 432–436 (1974).

22. Russell, G. F. M., Loraine, J. A., Bell, E. T., and Harkness, R. A., Gonadotrophin and oestrogen excretion in patients with anorexia nervosa, *J. Psychosom. Res. 9,* 79–85 (1965).

23. Russell, G. F. M., Psychological and nutritional factors in disturbances of menstrual function and ovulation, *Postgrad. Med. J. 48,* 10–43 (1972).

24. Garfinkel, P. E., Brown, G. M., Stancer, H. C., and Moldofsky, H., Hypothalamic-pituitary function in anorexia nervosa, *Arch. Gen. Psychiat. 32,* 739–744 (1975).

25. Warren, M. P., Jewelewicz, R., Dyrenfurth, I., Ans, R., Khalaf, S., and VandeWiele, R. L., The significance of weight loss in the evaluation of pituitary response to LH-RH in women with secondary amenorrhea, *J. Clin. Endocrin. and Metab. 40,* 601–611 (1975).

26. Palmer, R. L., Crisp, A. H., Mackinnon, P. C. B., Franklin, M., Bonnar, J.,

and Wheeler, M., Pituitary sensitivity to 50 mg LH/FSH-RH in subjects with anorexia nervosa in acute and recovery stages, *Brit. Med. J. 1*, 179–182 (1975).

27. Mecklenberg, R. S., Loriaux, D. L., Thompson, R. H., Anderson, A. E., and Lipsett, M. B., Hypothalamic dysfunction in patients with anorexia nervosa, *Medicine 53*, 147–159 (1974).

28. Katz, J. L., Boyar, R. M., Roffwarg, H., Hallman, L., and Weiner, H., LH-RH responsiveness in anorexia nervosa: intactness despite prepubertal circadian LH pattern, *Psychosom. Med. 39*, 241–251 (1977).

29. Boyar, R. M., Katz, J. L., Finkelstein, J. W., Kapen, S., Weiner, H., Weitzman, E. D., and Hellman, L., Anorexia nervosa: immaturity of the 24-hour luteinizing hormone secretory pattern, *N. Eng. J. Med. 291*, 861–865 (1974).

30. Medical News: Hormonal abnormality found in patients with anorexia nervosa, *JAMA 232*, 9–11 (1975).

31. Katz, J. L., Boyar, R. M., Roffwarg, H., Hellman, L., and Weiner, H., Weight and circadian luteinizing hormone secretory pattern in anorexia nervosa, *Psychosom. Med. 40*, 549–567 (1978).

32. Drew, F. L., The epidemiology of secondary amenorrhea, *J. Chron. Dis. 14*, 396–407 (1961).

33. Lewin, K., Mattingly, D., and Millis, R. R., Anorexia nervosa associated with hypothalamic tumour, *Brit. Med. J. 2*, 629–630 (1972).

34. Heron, G. B., and Johnston, D. A., Hypothalamic tumor presenting as anorexia nervosa, *Amer. J. Psychiat. 133*, 580–582 (1976).

35. McCann, S. M., Luteinizing-hormone–releasing hormone, *Physiol. in Med. 296*, 797–802 (1977).

36. McCann, S. M., Krulich, L., Cooper, K. J., Kalra, P. S., Kalra, S. P., L'Libertum. C., Negro-Vilar, A., Orias, R., Rønnekleiv, O., and Fawcett, C. P., Hypothalamic control of gonadotrophin and prolactin secretion; implications for fertility control, *J. Reprod. Fert. 20* (suppl.), 43–59 (1973).

37. Hery, M., LaPlante, E., and Kordon, C., Participation of serotonin in the phasic release of LH: evidence from pharmacological experiments, *Endocrinology 99*, 496–503 (1976).

38. Redmond, D. E., Jr., New and old evidence for the involvement of a brain norepinephrine system in anxiety, *Life Sci. 25*, 2149–2162 (1979).

39. Grossman, S. P., Role of the hypothalamus in the regulation of food and water intake, *Psych. Rev. 82*, 200–224 (1975).

40. Mawson, A. R., Anorexia nervosa and the regulation of intake: a review, *Psych. Med. 4*, 289–308 (1974).

41. Liebowitz, S. F., Hypothalamic ß-adrenergic "satiety" system antagonizes an α-adrenergic "hunger" system in the rat, *Nature 226*, 963–964 (1970).

42. Barry, V., and Klawans, H. L., On the role of dopamine in the pathophysiology of anorexia nervosa, *J. Neur. Trans. 38*, 107–122 (1976).

43. Cantwell, D. P., Sturzenberger, S., Burroughs, J., Salkin, B., and Green, J. K., Anorexia nervosa: an affective disorder, *Arch. Gen. Psychiat. 34*, 1087–1093 (1977).

44. Halmi, K. A., Dekirmenjian, H., Davis, J. M., Casper, R., and Goldberg, S., Catecholamine metabolism in anorexia nervosa, *Arch. Gen. Psychiat. 35,* 458–460 (1978).

45. Needleman, H. L., and Waber, D., Amitriptyline therapy in patients with anorexia nervosa, *Lancet 580* (1976).

46. Moore, D. C., Amitriptyline therapy in anorexia nervosa, *Amer. J. Psychiat. 134,* 1303–1304 (1977).

47. White, J. H., and Schnaultz, N. L., Successful treatment of anorexia nervosa with imipramine, *Dis. Nerv. Syst. 38,* 567–568 (1977).

48. Johansson, A. J., and Knorr, N. J., Treatment of anorexia nervosa by Levodopa, *Lancet 591* (1974).

49. Redmond, D. E., Jr., Swann, A., and Heninger, G., Phenoxybenzamine in anorexia nervosa, *Lancet 307* (1976).

50. Agras, S., and Werne, J., Behavior modification in anorexia nervosa: research foundations, in *Anorexia Nervosa,* R. A. Vigersky, ed., Raven, New York, 1977, pp. 291–303.

51. Liebman, R., Minuchin, S., and Baker, L., An integrated treatment program for anorexia nervosa, *Amer. J. Psychiat. 131,* 532–546 (1974).

52. Pertschuk, M. J., Behavior therapy: extended follow-up, in *Anorexia Nervosa,* R. A. Vigersky, ed., Raven, New York, 1977, pp. 305–313.

53. Crisp, A. H., A treatment regime for anorexia nervosa, *Brit. J. Psychiat. 112,* 505–512 (1966).

54. Russell, G. F. M., General management of anorexia nervosa and difficulties in assessing the efficacy of treatment, in *Anorexia Nervosa,* R. A., Vigersky, ed., Raven, New York, 1977, pp. 277–289.

12

Nymphomania and Satyriasis

Jerome D. Goodman

Excessive sexual appetite is a subject that has been less seriously studied than most other behaviors in excess. Theology and ethics have universally condemned this disorder whereas sexual humor and erotic literature have served as conduits for wishful thinking. Jokes about nymphomania, we are told, "serve to reassure men who are unable to form deep commitments that somewhere, someday, they will find a willing and appreciative woman who will want pure physical sex without emotional involvement" (1).

We can speculate as to why nymphomania has been so little studied. It is well-known that the overall incidence of nymphomania and satyriasis is lower than the incidence of hyposexuality. In addition, potential researchers may have been threatened by acknowledgment of the problem's existence of they may have felt so compromised by moral positions that they were unable to remain objective. Moreover, the prevalence of excessive behavior is generally underestimated, since fewer people seek help for this condition. From the patient's viewpoint, it may be that embarrassment, pride, denial, or a combination of these keep many potential subjects from seeking therapy.

Definitions

A large number of terms refer to nymphomania, satyriasis, or the generic condition of excessive sexual behavior. Nymphomania has been called the Messalina complex (after the wife of the Roman emperor Claudius) or furor uterinus. Satyriasis is most closely linked to the term "Don Juan complex." Both nymphomania and satyriasis have been labeled sexual hyperversion, compulsive promiscuity, erotomania, and, more recently, cryptoperversion. Nymphomania, literally translated, is madness referable to the external female genitalia. In Greek mythology, a nymph is a semidivine female being, especially young and beautiful. The Greek term was modified in Latin to *nympha,* meaning bride; in the combined form *nympho* Greek and Latin roots are joined. Satyriasis derives from the mythological satyr, a woodland minor god or demon, half man and half beast (usually goat), of lustful propensities. Satyrs were closely associated with the god Dionysus, whose ecstatic worship involved wild dance and drunkenness. As Homer noted, this god was the most popular figure of the pantheon; yet Dionysus had ominous qualities having to do with the frenzy of his rites and his ability insidiously to take possession of the psyche of his followers.

Among the most famous historical or literary examples of excessive sexuality are Don Juan, a legendary Spanish nobleman who cunningly seduced women under the riskiest circumstances; Casanova, an Italian adventurer who lived in the eighteenth century; Thomas Walter, the Victorian who wrote *My Secret Life,* a frank confession of satyriasis; and Frank Harris, who chronicled his countless sexual escapades. By the middle of the twentieth century either the occurrence of satyriasis plummeted or Western society accepted the notion of men with large sexual appetites or the behavior was modified. In either case, the literature and fantasy projections turned from men toward women as architects of prodigious sexual feats. This new sexual liberation has led some observers to acknowledge the existence of an advantage for women in terms of both performance and desire. Others deny the intrinsic sexual superiority of women, clinging to sex role stereotyping or other myths.

In 1898, Beard noted the nervous exhaustion produced by sexual activity (4). In his textbook he considered nymphomania and satyriasis *physical* conditions whereas what he termed erotomania was described as "a mental state, in which the victim is exclusively occupied by the object of her [his] thoughts." Beard's discussion and recommended treatment would now be deemed moralistic and primitive. However, Beard thoughtfully described a clergyman who had insatiable longings for women. This patient encapsulated the differential diagnosis of biological and psychological hypersexuality in the following statement to his physician: "If this terrible longing is due to some disorder of my system, I want the physician's help; if it comes from a wicked heart, I'll fight it to the day of my death; you, perhaps, can help me to decide" (2).

Some researchers have explored the possible role of environmental factors in excessive sexual behavior. Allen listed a number of contributing elements in what he called sexual hyperversion: hot climate, slight fever, obstruction to the normal expression of sexuality, and certain attributes of the object of attraction: "It is well known that sexual desire increases with the approach of warmer weather in the spring and summer, and those who inhabit tropical and sub-tropical zones are more desirous" (3). Later research has verified a weak positive correlation between frequency of conception and warmer months of the year. To date, however, there is little information other than anecdotal reports on enhanced sexuality in warmer climes.

In any case, it is important for the clinician to differentiate between biological hypersexuality and excessive sexual behavior of psychological origin. Table 12-1 compares the etiology and correlates of the two conditions. Obviously, entirely different modes of therapy are indicated for these disorders.

Biomedical Correlates

Biological hypersexuality is commanding increasing attention in medical circles. This disorder is rarely associated with other behaviors in excess (Table 12-2). Additionally, as shown in Table 12-1, one of the chief differences between biological and psychological hypersexuality is the true sexual excitement found in the former. In the biological disorder, multiple orgasm is common and sexual excitement is the rule.

Perhaps the closest approximation to an interface between biological and psychological hypersexuality occurs in those psychiatric disorders listed in Table 12-2 as bipolar psychosis and schizophrenia. In both, the biological substrate requires emotional triggering in order to come to full pathological development. It is usual to find excessive sexual stimulation accompanied by flagrant social behavior on the wards of psychiatric

TABLE 12-1
A Comparison of Biological and Psychological Hypersexuality

BIOLOGICAL	PSYCHOLOGICAL
Usually regarded as ego alien and undesirable	May be troublesome yet not typically regarded as ego alien
Multiple orgasms common	Often unsatisfying sexually
Secondary sex characteristics often affected (e.g., virilization)	No discernible effect on secondary sex characteristics
Multiple partners less common	Many partners typical
History of developmental precocity or sudden onset in adult life	Possible history of precocity, but onset gradual
Usually not associated with other behaviors in excess	Often associated with kleptomania, gambling, or other behaviors in excess
Treatment is medical with supportive psychotherapy	Treatment is psychological (either behavior modification or insight oriented)

TABLE 12-2
Biological Disorders Associated with Hypersexuality

Neoplasms
      Primary and metastatic brain tumors
      Adrenal tumors[a]
      Ovarian tumors

Endocrinopathies
      Hyperthyroidism
      Adrenal hyperplasia (congenital or acquired)[a]

Infection
      Early tuberculosis[b]
      Leprosy[b]
      Tertiary syphilis (paresis)

Neurological Disorders
      Psychomotor epilepsy
      Irritative temporal lobe lesions
      Lesions of pyriform cortex and amygdala

Neuropsychiatric Disorders
      Bipolar psychosis (manic states)[a]
      Schizophrenia

Iatrogenic Disorders
      Anabolic steroids
      L-dopa
      Androgenic substances $<$ men / women[a]
      Progestins in pregnancy (later expression in offspring)[b]

[a] High correlation.
[b] Speculative correlation.

hospitals, where these patients are in acute crisis. Repetitive masturbation and exhibitionism, as well as open gestures toward personnel and visitors, are common.

A most circumscribed and reversible clinical example of biological hypersexuality was caused by ingestion of anabolic steroids. A young woman of particularly small stature wished to join the Women's Army Corps. She had to gain weight in order to meet the size requirement, but overeating did not result in weight gain. Finally, she consulted a physician who had utilized steriods for "beefing up" professional athletes. She obtained orally administered steroids from this physician to increase her muscle mass and gained the requisite 10 pounds within a few months (7).

This woman was virginal prior to entry into the service and had no

history of excessive sexual activity. In fact, her sexual attitudes were re-
served and fastidious. Within a few months, this woman experienced intense desires beyond her control. Repetitive sexual relations and incessant
masturbation were unsatisfactory in providing her with what she termed
"relief." She consulted me because she found herself frightened over the
many sexual liaisons, which brought the risk of military discipline. Physical
examination revealed an enlarged and hypersensitive clitoris.

The patient had affairs with numerous soldiers and was preoccupied
with flirtations. She masturbated while on duty and had received
reprimands for late hours and notorious behavior in the town near the
military base. She also had made certain to provide herself with an adequate source of the anabolic steroid medication, regarding it as essential
for her continuance in the armed services. The patient was concerned that
she would lose weight and no longer meet military fitness standards. She
did not recognize the connection between the steroid and her uncon-
trollable sexual desire.

Once hormone administration ended, the woman's sexual desires
receded. Moreover, the woman became less aggressive and demanding.
Ambition and aggression appear to be more prominent features of the
female whose hypersexuality is mediated by hormones rather than the
psychological, or compulsively driven, hypersexual female.

Double-blind studies of estrogens, androgens, placebos, and hormone
combinations administered in a random fashion to women for the management of menopause have found that libido was markedly increased during
those intervals when either androgen or a combination of androgen and
estrogen was given (4). Cautioning that dosages should be restricted to sub-
virilizing levels, clinicians noted that when other factors were controlled
(health, domestic situation, etc.), androgens in the female increased libido.
Likewise, sudden increases of androgenic substances caused by adrenal
tumors result in a pronounced strengthening of sexual desire in both
sexes (5).

A central nervous system disorder, the Kluver-Bucy syndrome includes hyperphagia, hypersexuality, and other features related to ablation
of the anterior portion of the temporal lobe. Cases of limbic system
dysfunction associated with hypersexuality and a fugue state have also been
reported. In one case, a 28-year-old female presented with a marked change
in sexual behavior from naivete, shyness, and fear of intercourse to promiscuity and increased libido (6). The authors noted that this patient enjoyed intercourse despite the absence of orgasm. She also experienced
fugue episodes of increasing duration, with one episode lasting 36 hours.

Summing up the varieties of biologically based hypersexuality, these
conditions often have sudden onset and can at times be medically reversed.
They are not well described in literary invention and are distinct from the
fantasized conception of promiscuous adventures (7). Hypersexuality of a

biological variety is usually both intense and alien to the basic personality structure. For this reason, such sexual behavior is often more covertly and less relentlessly pursued than is the case with psychological hypersexuality. This disorder represents a driven quest for satiation of heightened libido. There is often an aggressive component and a secondary emotional response of bewilderment, guilt, and depression.

Psychological and Behavioral Correlates

The psychoanalytic view of sexual behavior in excess emphasizes the impulsive nature of repetitive liaisons. Psychoanalysts routinely search for the essentially nonsexual or primitive sexual satisfactions that underlie the disorder. The pseudoerotic form of high frequency sexuality is described as incidental to the human encounter. For women, it is a means to fulfillment of infantile needs (caressing and holding). Excessive sexuality in women can be a plea that childhood longings may yet be fulfilled. For men, aggression is most frequently the basis for repetitive sexual activity. Aggression expressed by high frequency sex in men resembles a competitive sport. Basic to understanding this pseudo sexual activity is the tenet that excessive sexual desire will remain unrequited no matter how frequently fulfillment is attempted.

Referring to women, Fenichel attempted to explain the need for repeated liaisons: "An accurate anamnesis by itself often shows that nymphomanic women are by no means the most excitable sexually, and do not regularly have an orgasm. Even when they have an orgasm, it is not true in pleasure and gives them no satisfaction" (8). In psychodynamic theories sexually driven women are thought to harbor homosexual impulses, to behave in an active rather than a passive way, and to be constantly seeking a father surrogate. In this view, intense and unfulfilled sexual urges symbolize unconscious incestuous desires.

Bergler (9) defined nymphomania as *compulsive* promiscuity combined with lack of orgasm (9). He emphasized that despite a voracious appetite for indiscriminate sex and despite the multiplicity of affairs, such women do not find satisfaction. A succession of "*nearly* reached climaxes" makes these women depressed and deeply dissatisfied. For Bergler they represent exquisitely masochistic beings, specializing in being refused: "They love to shock people with their sexual freedom, only to disguise their slavery to the hidden psychic masochism."

Female psychoanalysts, notably Bonapart and Deutsch, have argued that compulsive sexual excess in women is related to pregenital considerations and is unconsciously experienced as maternal succoring behavior.

Other theories of compulsive sexual behavior in women describe the rebellious, defiant aspect of such activity as a substitute for direct hostility.

Similarly, hypersexual women are often kleptomaniacs. According to the
psychoanalytic theory, compulsive stealing is the collection of trophies or
prizes compensating for the prized genital that was denied at birth. Yet attempts to correlate excessive sexual behavior, particularly in women, with
psychopathic behavior have usually yielded negative results. Cleckley
found psychopaths lacking in

> "particularly strong sex cravings even in this uncomplicated and poverty
> striken sense. Indeed they have nearly all seemed definitely less moved to ob-
> tain genital pleasure than the ordinary run of people. The impression one gets
> is that the amativeness is little more than a simple itch and that even the itch is
> seldom, if ever, particularly intense. . . . the familiar record of sexual pro-
> miscuity found in both male and female psychopaths seems much more
> closely related to their almost total lack of self-imposed restraint than to any
> particularly strong passions or drives" (10).

The same negative correlation between excessive sexual activity and antisocial behavior pertains to frankly sexual offenses (11). Sex offenders require intense or bizarre stimulation to shore up a weak sexual appetite.

In psychoanalytic interpretations of male compulsive sexual behavior,
the term "Don Juan" is central. The Don Juan type is not at all interested
in his partner. His sexual activities are attempts to compensate for inferiority feelings by repeated proof of success. Most authors emphasize
that a Don Juan personality type is frequently a defense against unconscious homosexual impulses. Fenichel stated flatly that the Don Juan's
behavior is no doubt produced by oedipal conflict. According to Fenichel,
the Don Juan character seeks his mother in all women but cannot find her
(8). This particular form of oedipal conflict is aggravated by narcissistic
impulses and colored by sadistic impulses. There is strong pregenital fixation in the sexual encounter, which has unconscious narcissistic components; the love usually is mixed with hostility; and the ambivalent relationship includes incorporation of the object. Fenichel concluded that the
sadism contained within this personality is not always directed toward objects but is often directed against the ego so that the vigorous sexual activity
is truly masochistic, or self-punitive.

As Adlerian theory implies, the drive for power and prestige in men
can be coupled with excessive sexual encounters. Sexual gratification can
discharge anxiety and temporarily satisfy the man's need to be nurtured.
As Bird observed: "[In] prominent men [the] drive for power derives from a
pathological identification with powerful parents in order to counteract
feeling unloved. In this process, they put themselves in the position of
either or both parents and love themselves as they had hoped their parents
would love them. Their sexual desire is expressed consistently to satisfy
their craving for love, warmth, and nurturance" (12).

Commenting on Bird's article, Salzman noted that it is not surprising that "aggressive, driven individuals are frequently overly demanding in terms of frequency of sexual activity and number of sexual partners. The status-seeker who sees multiple outlets as the symbol of success will become involved in many affairs" (13). The link between the drive for power and the drive for sexual conquests is their mutual compulsive underpinnings. Compulsive behavior represents recurrence with routinization followed by attempts to overcome the repetitive drive with consequent guilt and annoyance. Similarity with other behaviors in excess is striking.

In a more contemporary reworking of some of these psychoanalytic views, Stoller described nymphomania and satyriasis as "cryptoperversions" (14). He emphasized the dehumanization of the sexual partner in these disorders. Wondering how the delight in perversions is engendered by the destruction and humiliation—in fact, deformation—of the perverse individual and the partner, Stoller asked: "If perversion is the result of threat and the resultant hatred, whence comes pleasure? Unmitigated trauma or frustration has no lust in it, nor does rage. Pleasure is released only when fantasy—that which makes perversion uniquely human—has worked. With fantasy, trauma is undone, and in a daydream—the manifest content, the conscious, constructed storyline of fantasy—it can be undone, over and over as necessary."

Stoller later developed a general theory of derivation of sexual excitement (15). He stated that in the absence of physiological factors, hostility, whether overt of covert, is responsible for generating and enhancing all sexual excitement. Conversely, the absence of hostility leads to sexual indifference and boredom. For Stoller, the central position of hostility in eroticism is necessary as an attempt to undo childhood traumas and frustrations that threatened the development of gender identity. Stoller noted that the same sort of dynamics, although assorted and recombined differently, are found in everyone—from those labeled perverse to those labeled normal. According to this view, repetitive sexual behavior correlates directly with degree of hostility and the strength of the infantile trauma.

Another point of view, less analytic, has been presented by Cauthery, who argued that everyone is potentially promiscuous; he called the potential for promiscuity a powerful socializing force (16). Cauthery observed that flirting, as well as the general interaction between sexes, has an almost exclusively beneficial social effect on the behavior of individuals. Potential for promiscuity, then, makes every member of the opposite sex a possible partner. He described individuals of both sexes who are frequently or even routinely prepared to behave sexually on grounds other than emotional involvement. Giving an example of "real sexual promiscuity," Cauthery noted that "it seems to the superficial observer as if 5 to 10% of the population so involved are sex mad. . . . in fact, on closer observation it is usually—if not invariably—discovered that the promiscuous have weak

libidinal drives. . . . their personal psychosexual histories tend to be im-
poverished, and they are usually depressive in the sense that they feel inferior, useless, unlovable and lacking in merit." According to Cauthery,
hypersexual women believe that no man would ever want them; so they
reduce males to sexual partners in order to escape the scrutiny that they
would otherwise receive. These women do not have typical romantic fantasies. They are described as unhappy people who require psychotherapy
aimed not at stopping the sexual behavior but at strengthening the ego.
Cauthery further described promiscuous men as fundamentally afraid of
women. Out of their fear come wishes to dominate and humiliate women;
should they fall in love, these men are often impotent. Such men clarify the
saint-whore dichotomy: sexual objects are depreciated, whereas women
who are the object of love are deemed unattainable.

Orford attempted to integrate hypersexuality into a larger field theory
of dependency (17). Orford widened the discussion of the nature of
dependence to include an example of what he labeled "excessive appetitive
behavior, namely sexual behavior which is compulsive or excessive." He
listed the typical features of any excessive appetitive behavior: preoccupation with the object of the desire and with the means of consuming and par-
taking; behavior felt to be inappropriate and in excess of what the
individual, other people, or both would consider normal; activity com-
menced in response to the experience of unpleasant affect; experience
described as conflicted that results in guilt; and attempts at self-control
with a variety of tactics. Orford's list places some forms of hypersexuality
within the general category of behavior in excess. Orford noted striking
similarities between debates over definitions of hypersexuality and such
disputes on alcoholism or gambling. Control is the central psychological
concept. As in other behaviors in excess, "very heavy, frequent, or immoderate indulgence is abnormal only in the statistical sense, but almost
always carries greater risk of the incurring of varying costs." He went on to
note: "As the heaviest users are likely to be those with the strongest ap-
petitie for the activity concerned, the incurring of costs creates conflict and
dissonance about behavior" (17). Were it not for the conflict and
dissonance engendered by the behavior, therapy would be of no avail.

Behaviorists argue that sexual excesses must be understood as self-
reinforcing behavior. Behaviorists are interested primarily in recording the
behavior itself and less interested in how it is embedded in the personality.
If hypersexuality is merely a self-reinforcing behavior with high frequency,
then decrease in frequency can be accomplished through avoidance conditioning or through shaping and/or fading. In addition, behaviorists
emphasize the possibility of teaching the subject methods of self-regulation—which implies that hypersexuality stems from a lack of self-
control.

Behaviorists use learning theory to understand the genesis of heightened sexual behavior. In examining the patient's history they look for those reinforcing conditions that did not permit a satisfactory experience in the absence of frequent repetition. In general, the behavior therapy literature emphasizes altering deviant sexual behavior, rather than nondeviant but excessive heterosexual behavior.

Men who have high frequency sexual experiences have been called sexual athletes. Possibly, such excessive behavior results from an addiction to the physical concomitants of high energy levels. Perhaps if not indicative of addiction, such behavior counters boredom or depression. Athletes have long known about the altered state of consciousness that occurs when exercise is continued beyond usual levels. Described as elating, exhilarating, or extremely pleasant, this altered state creates a floating sensation (i.e., the individual becomes detached from an awareness of what he or she is doing). The loss of self-consciousness and the heightened sense of physical involvement result in euphoria and a timeless feeling. Certainly the intense and sustained physical effort made by many so-called sexual athletes is in itself an antidepressant.

For women the muscular exertion is frequently less, but many do experience the euphoria associated with the physical demands of sexual activity. Occasionally, a woman will speak of fainting, losing consciousness in a paroxysmal fashion, upon reaching orgasm. Perhaps this effect is related to hyperventilation.

Excessive sexual behavior has been correlated with borderline personalities ranging from hysterical to schizoid and prepsychotic (18, 19). The more contemporary view of the borderline personality considers it fluid in terms of personality organization and intermediate between neurotic levels of integration and psychotic disintegration. Such personalities tend toward impulsive decisions and primitive judgment; sexuality is often promiscuous and perverse. These individuals combine frequent sexual activity with dependency on alcohol or drugs for the relief of tension and the gratification of impulse. The borderline personality needs immediate gratification and epitomizes the acting out of unconscious conflicts. The problems of such personalities are primitive and pregenital. They have magical expectations of caretaking and gratification from men or women that are rarely realized. As such, the tempo of their sexual excursions remains high. For them, sexuality is a search for nurturance, a quest for instant acceptance, that continues to be unsuccessful because the premise is basically untenable. Many women considered nymphomaniacs may be borderline personalities who retain remnants of earlier symbiotic interaction.

Borderline variety hypersexual patients are driven personalities who are generally aware of social conventions and the accepted boundaries of behavior. Their excess sexual activity is unconsciously defiant. Self-destructive behavior is part of an impulsive pattern in which unconscious material is acted upon with little delay. Such patients can wreck havoc upon their partners because their behavior is predicated on hostility.

Case Studies

Nymphomania

This young woman was first seen at age 17 via court order for a series of shoplifting incidents. Her family was intact, and she was the youngest of three girls. The family was bewildered by this first example of extralegal behavior and made no attempt to come to the aid of the patient. The mother stated that she did not know "this person" and lamented that her daughter had become notorious and rebellious. Her father, making plain his disgust, informed the patient that she would be on her own at age 18.

The patient described a relatively happy early childhood, during which she had played as "one of the boys," and often recalled the time spent in street games as "carefree days." These halcyon years ended with precocious development and menarche at age nine. Her classmates in grade school were "in awe" of her, and although she recalled being told about sexual matters early, she thought she was "bleeding to death" with her first menses. She was not examined for possible sexual precocity, and an endocrinological workup at age 15 found only a minor thyroid problem.

She had been masturbating "as long as [she could] remember." She recalled the sounds of parental sexual relations, noting that her bedroom was located next to theirs. Her first sexual relations—at age 10 with a girlfriend—were followed by other homosexual encounters during sleepover visits. At age 14 she attempted to hang herself with a blanket and was hospitalized briefly. She had repetitive dreams of being chased by monsters. Sexual intercourse began at age 15: "It was high time to get broken in." She bragged of numerous sexual encounters, cynical about the inadequacy of partners. She would often "wear out" male partners and alternated between male and female lovers. The patient particularly enjoyed performing multiple fellatio and other varieties of group sex. From 14 to 17 she masturbated frequently, often as much as eight times daily. Her favorite place for masturbating was the classroom and she wore clothing that let her manipulate herself unseen. She had cultivated an interest in sadomasochism, often asking partners to flagellate her if they were sexually exhausted prior to her satiation. She claimed to be incapable of forming any deep interpersonal "attachments." She frequently used pseudonyms, derived from television soap operas, and ran away to New York City for "thrills."

Court involvement began at age 15, when she was apprehended for shoplifting. At age 16 she had an abortion. The court referred the patient for psychiatric consultation at age 17 following another series of shoplifting incidents. When seen at age 17, she described her sexuality as "tension relieving" and was "proud of [her] appetite." She explained her stealing as another type of thrill, recognizing that there was no necessity for it yet not conceiving of shoplifting as basically wrong. The patient was bright and creative and did not evidence any psychotic thought. She managed to curb her shoplifting while on probation, and when she turned 18 she left therapy and home—for a supposed career in modeling.

Four years later she returned to therapy, this time voluntarily, because of recurrent depression. In the interim she had lived in Manhattan and worked as a cocktail waitress. The modeling career had been a failure; she occasionally posed for less well-known pornographic magazines. She returned to therapy because she found to her amazement that she had become frigid. Consultation with a sex therapy clinic in New York City had uncovered no physical basis for her lack of sexual response. The frigidity set in despite increasingly frantic efforts to find "good enough" partners. The woman described herself as "burnt out . . . my body is dead."

In the summer prior to her return for therapy she had slept, without satisfaction, with over 20 men and had participated in mixed group sex on three occasions. Masturbation was no longer successful, nor had there been any true sexual excitement except twice during dreams and once with a total stranger in an airplane restroom. Without orgasm, the patient began to feel guilt and shame about sexuality and realized that her appetite had become excessive. For the first time, she attempted to curb her need to find new sexual partners and became apathetic and depressed. She thought that her life could be restored to happiness if only she could be resexualized. The idea of other young people happy together and in love caused her great pain and brought on weeping.

Therapy centered on her difficulties in forming meaningful relationships. She agreed to abstain from *all* sexual activity until she could improve her self-image. She entered college, taking courses at night, and began working in the dining room of that institution. She met a foreign graduate student and dated "as though [she] were an inexperienced virgin." The risk inherent in her former multiple sexual adventures was transformed into the risk inherent in a close relationship. Unfortunately, her family resisted any attempts at reconciliation, and she finally resolved that she would have to re-create her own family ties.

After five months of abstinence, the woman slept with her new lover and experienced satisfaction. They were married shortly thereafter and she became pregnant within three months.

The case of this young woman illustrates that psychological excessive sexual behavior is a quest without satisfaction. At first, the patient's nymphomania was an attempt to master overwhelming feelings of sexual precocity. Her excessive behavior in early adolescence served to displace depression and emphasized her fluid gender identity. The excessive behavior continued in middle adolescence, now driven by counterphobic defiance and the desire for new and thrilling experiences. By young adulthood, the nymphomania had become compulsive, serving to counteract a depreciated self-image. Interestingly, the shoplifting served parallel functions. Finally, the patient experienced guilt and painful affect associated with her sexual behavior, which made it unpleasant. Only at that point was she ready for therapy.

Satyriasis

This 31-year-old male was referred for chief complaints of anxiety and depression. The precipitating antecedent for the anxiety was a scalp infection secondary to hair grafting to eliminate baldness. The patient's vanity and self-image had been seriously threatened when it appeared that the hair graft would be unsuccessful. After consulting a number of dermatologists, he became depressed.

As a young boy, this patient was generally pushed into competitive sports by an athletic father, who was a proclaimed self-made man. The father, a World War II hero and the coach of the town football team, owned a small construction company. The mother was distant and aloof, preferring painting and pottery to family involvement. The patient had one sister, a year older, who remained very close to him until high school, when their intimacy was challenged by her first boyfriend. The older sister and the patient had shared exploratory sexual games from early childhood, although without frank incestuous intercourse.

The patient recalled that in early adolescence he was of small to medium stature; his father prodded him to lift weights, starting a life history of physical training and competitive sports. By age 15 he had become husky. He wrestled and played linebacker in football and carried on a lively correspondence with various purveyors of so-called training and health food supplements. The patient's scholastic work was acceptable although he was suspended several times for fighting during school hours. He had a tendency to bully "soft" boys and fought with anyone who resisted his dictatorial direction.

In terms of psychiatric symptomatology, the patient had a need to exercise compulsively and was unduly interested in athletic records. He saw a psychologist once in high school after a suspension for fighting, but he had "gotten over" (i.e., successfully manipulated) that professional and there were no follow-up visits.

His first sexual experiences were unformed encounters with his sister. At day camp he discovered masturbation (age 11). An older boy taught

him, saying that he would not be "a man until [he saw] jit [semen]."
Masturbation became compulsive and frequent: often he masturbated so
vigorously that he abraded the skin of his penis, temporarily precluding
further masturbation. At age 13 ("my happiest day"), he ejaculated for the
first time. From that point, he intermittently kept a diary of sexual prowess.

His first experience with intercourse (age 14) was the result of a
"teaching lesson" administered by a 15-year-old girl. At 16, he tried to
"set the record" for frequency of intercourse, once achieving eight
orgasms in five separate couplings with two girls. Following that experience, he suffered prostatic pain, which served as a caution for "trying
to break that record." By age 21 he had slept with over 100 women.

The patient met his match on two occasions when partners proved to
be equal or superior to his aggressive desires. He found these women repug-
nant. One of these women invited another male (without the patient's
knowledge) for group sex. This interlude produced a certain amount of
panic and resulted in a flight from sexuality that lasted approximately three
months, the only period of abstinence the patient could remember in his
adult life.

His fantasies concerned bringing women close to orgasm and then
abandoning them. It was necessary for the patient to monitor his partner's
orgasms and he became enraged if she attempted either to suppress or to
simulate orgasm. Most particularly, he required the illusion of total control. He depreciated lasting relationships and regarded women as distinct
only in terms of sexual responsivity.

When the patient was 23, his father was killed in a construction accident. He responded to this loss without emotion, blocking his feelings, and
immersed himself in running the construction company. Shortly thereafter,
he became engaged to an airline stewardess. His fiance broke off the
engagement when she discovered his notebook on recent sexual adventures.
The patient did not form another serious relationship until therapy was
under way.

In the early stages of psychotherapy the patient spoke about his conquests and mistrust of women, gradually admitting that he was worried
about maintaining pace and facing competition from younger men. He still
worked out with weights and jogged compulsively. His first major insight
in therapy was the realization that he had dichotomized women into accessible (therefore depreciated) and inaccessible (therefore idealized)
categories. The compulsive infrastructure of his fitness regime was interpreted as the need to control angry feelings. The patient recognized that
setting records reflected his need to please father and was not appropriate
to human sexual interaction. He was able, via therapy, to channel most of
his ambition into construction projects and associated business ventures.
Accordingly, the frenetic pace and the compulsiveness of his sexual activity

eased and he was able to reduce his anxiety level about aging and decompensating as a sexual athlete. However, he still found it necessary to keep a catalogue and diary of sexual experiences. The hair grafting project was abandoned. He accepted his balding appearance, noting that it did not interfere with his ability to attract women.

Perhaps the most humanizing experience for the patient was the delayed emotional response to his father's death, which took the form first of anger and then of sorrow. The therapeutic experience enabled him to renew contact with his sister, and he found himself easing into the role of primary male in the extended family.

The patient had previously identified with the aggressor role of his father. He had also experienced homosexual panic and was uncomfortable about any men who were less competitive or creative than he. His satyriasis functioned primarily to reassure him about his masculinity and secondarily to depreciate women. After he was able to understand and to express anger over his mother's aloofness, the patient recognized that he was punishing women for his early emotional deprivation.

Therapy

Treatment depends on accurate diagnosis. If the excessive sexual behavior is biologically based, treatment can be quite specific. In general, excessive sexual behavior issuing from biological causes is fairly sudden in onset, foreign to the personality of the patient, and regarded as an embarassment and an encumbrance. This behavior is often accompanied by some accentuation of secondary sexual characteristics, usually virilization: an increase in body or facial hair, an increase of muscular mass and strength, acne, and male pattern hair loss. As in the case described earlier, if medications prescribed for another condition are implicated in the etiology, obviously they must be discontinued. If a cerebral or endocrinological tumor is suspected, referral to a surgeon is indicated.

To facilitate treatment of psychologically based hypersexuality, the therapist must form an alliance with the patient to facilitate control. The therapist must recognize that the treatment of excessive sexual behavior requires growth in the entire personality of the patient. These patients are often emotionally starved. They are therefore particularly vulnerable to separations and losses and are more than usually dependent on others for self-esteem. In other words, in the beginning they will look toward the therapist as the arbiter of their reality. As therapy progresses, they will become more capable of making their own decisions.

Fundamental to all forms of psychological therapy is the traid of support, persuasion, and education. The nonmoralistic attitude of the therapist and the reassurance that positive change can be achieved support the patient. At times, such support needs to reach family members as well. This nonjudgmental position indicates that the therapist will provide the emotional commitment necessary to sustain the patient through the treatment. The element of persuasion runs the spectrum from suggestion, in terms of interpretation, to more direct influence, as in hypnotherapy. Intrinsic here is the concept that the therapist will do *something* (but will do no harm) if in fact the excessive sexual behavior is unsatisfactory, the force behind persuasion holds forth the hope that the behavior can become much more pleasurable and satisfactory. As in other forms of excessive appetite, the patient needs to be reassured that progress will be gradual. The third principle of therapy, education, is most applicable to the treatment of excessive sexual behavior. Many patients do not recognize that they have the potential for satisfactory and fulfilling sexual relations. They are often ignorant of basic sexual physiology so education in this area provides self-reinforcing opportunities for direct learning. At times, education can take the form of group therapy in which a particular excessive appetitive behavior can be identified with the general problems of the appetitive syndrome. For patients whose excessive behavior is polymorphous—for example, those who are hypersexual and also involved in compulsive stealing or drug abuse—the benefits of group therapy are considerable.

Sex therapists suggest that repetitive and excessive sexual activity is mechanically unsatisfactory. A sex therapy program would therefore concentrate on humanizing these experiences by setting up experiences for pleasuring that capture the essence of eroticism without requiring orgasm. Such nondemand sexuality would theoretically relieve anxiety about performance while permitting relationships with partners to become more sensate. Similarly, behavior therapists would focus on modifying the behavior so that it did not interfere with daily living.

As with all psychological conditions of uncertain cause, one-third of patients improved with therapy, one-third show no change, and the remainder deteriorate. Understanding excessive sexual behavior within a larger field theory of dependence appears promising for developing psychotherapies that are more specific and therefore possibly more effective.

Conclusion

Nymphomania and satyriasis are poor terms for excessive sexual behavior. There is no room for making moral or value judgments about these suffering patients. The professional should first attempt to assess whether the patient represents biological or psychological hypersexuality. Characteristics of the disease, as treatment, differ with the etiology.

The literature is biased in several regards. First, reports often belie a moralistic or judgmental attitude on the part of researchers. Second, researchers tend to report more on women than on men. Third, hypersexual men are stereotyped as especially virile and accomplished and hence receive approval; hypersexual women are viewed as threatening to men, morally degraded, and therefore reprehensible.

Many hypersexual patients exhibit other excessive behaviors and consequently often fit into a larger behavioral complex emanating from a general dependency base. Psychotherapy must provide support, persuasion, and education. Group therapy is often efficacious. The therapist need remain mindful of the emotional deprivation in these patients and seek to remedy the barrenness of their lives.

References

1. Fry, W. F., Psychodynamics of sexual humor: nymphomania, *Med. Aspects Hum. Sex. 12,* 120 (1978).
2. Beard, G. N., *Sexual Neuroasthenia,* rep. ed., Arno, New York, 1972.
3. Allen, C., *A Textbook of Psychosexual Disorders,* Oxford University Press, New York, 1962.
4. Greenblatt, R. B., et al., Evaluation of an estrogen, androgen, estrogen-androgen combination and a placebo in the treatment of the menopause, *J. Endocrin. 10,* 1547 (1950).
5. Goodman, J. D., The behavior of hypersexual delinquent girls, *Amer. J. Psychiat. 133,* 662–668 (1976).
6. Mohan, K. J., et al., A case of limbic system dysfunction with hypersexuality and fugue state, *Dis. Nerv. Sys. 36,* 621–624 (1975).
7. Goodman, J. D., Biologic and psychogenic nymphomania, *Med. Aspects Hum. Sex. 11,* 93–94 (1977).
8. Fenichel, O., *Outline of Clinical Psychoanalysis,* Norton, New York, 1934.
9. Bergler, E., *Counterfeit Sex,* Grune & Stratton, New York, 1958.
10. Cleckley, H., *The Mask of Sanity,* 5th ed., Mosby, St. Louis, 1976.
11. Meiselman, K., *Incest,* Jossey-Bass, San Francisco, 1979.
12. Bird, H. W., Sex and power: a study of men of prominence, *Med. Aspects Hum. Sex. 13,* 8–23 (1979).
13. Salzman, L., Commentary on "sex and power," *Med. Aspects Hum. Sex. 13,* 23 (1979).
14. Stoller, R. J., *Perversion: The Erotic Form of Hatred,* Pantheon, New York, 1975.
15. Stoller, R. J., Sexual excitement, *Arch. Gen. Psychiat. 33,* 899–909 (1976).
16. Cauthery, P., Sexual problems of young adults, in *Psychosexual Problems,* . S. Crown, ed., Grune & Stratton, New York, 1976.

17. Orford, Jr., Hypersexuality: implications for a theory of dependence, *Brit. J. Addict. 73,* 299–310 (1978).

18. Hartocollis, P., *Borderline Personality Disorders,* International Universities Press, New York, 1977.

19. Shapiro, E. R., The psychodynamics and developmental psychology of the borderline patient: a review of the literature, *Amer. J. Psychiat. 135,* 1305–1315 (1978).

13

Excessive Work

Wayne E. Oates

In 1968 I coined the term "workaholic" while counseling persons addicted to alcohol (1). I was seeking a basis of empathy with their compulsive drinking and discovered that my own addiction was to work (2). Soon, television situation comedies and talk shows, radio programs, newspapers, national news magazines, etc., were using the term widely but lightly. The seriousness of the excessive work syndrome got lost in the laughter, the jests, and the resulting superficiality of thought and word.

Because excessive work is highly regarded in business, industry, colleges, and universities, and religious living, the potential of this behavior to cause human suffering in its own right has been largely missed. A few persons nevertheless have taken the matter seriously, investigating the nature, dynamics, and treatment of this condition (2, 3).

This chapter, written from a clinician's perspective, deals with harmful patterns of work behavior and the pathological conditions of the work situation. Though the creative use of leisure time is often dismissed by the public as either an exotic or a contrived concern, a growing body of data indicates that rest and recreation are important human needs. Accordingly, I touch on these issues throughout the chapter.

Parameters of the Disorder

Work is excessive when it threatens to destroy a person's health, family, or sense of perspective. Physical well-being may be jeopardized by cardiovascular breakdown, gastrointestinal failure, exhaustion, and/or clinical depression. Family problems may lead to marital liaisons on the part of either partner or sexual disorders of competence and/or frequency of intercourse. Finally, the workaholic may become suspicious, making unfounded accusations against work associates and/or spouse, and show poor judgment in health, safety, or business matters. These symptoms have been clinically identified; well-controlled interdisciplinary experimental studies are needed. Any one of the chief complaints described above can be documented by several cases seen in our clinic. While confirmatory research has not yet been initiated, techniques for more rigorous observations are being developed so that an interdisciplinary therapeutic team can test comparative populations with a reasonably clear cut research design.

The elusive syndrome of work addiction blends into other addictions. The wife of a U.S. senator became "morbidly depressed, fighting with her husband and his staff, angry that the time he was spending putting together a presidential campaign was forcing them apart, feeling cut out of his life, taking shots and popping pills to keep herself going" (4). Alcoholism may develop in a family member trying to cope with the fallout from excessive work. Adolescent protest in the form of breaking and entering, shoplifting, vandalism, etc., often exists against a family background of workaholism.

Clinically, too, psychotic decompensations of depressive and/or schizophrenic disorders occasionally are presaged by work obsession (as we shall see, biogenic and genetic factors were potentiated by the work addiction). Long before observable pathology, however, the work pattern itself can be seen as aberrant: prepsychotic socialization of the sense of worthlessness in the unipolar depressed person; hypomanic hyperactivity in the bipolar depressed person; grandiosity and sense of persecution in the schizophrenic person; or manipulative behavior in the overly ambitious sociopathic person. In brief, the pathology of work addiction is part and parcel of cardiologic, psychotic, and/or behavioral decompensation—"working like crazy" may be a very accurate description. Similarly, "work paralysis," to use Erikson's term, has a part in psychiatric disorders: the passive-aggressive person does *not* work as a means of expressing unresolved anger of which he or she is unaware; the neurotic fear of failure keeps a bright student from performing; grandiose fantasies keep the schizoid person "waiting for the big break" (5). Suspicious, paranoid ideation may cause a person so to distrust fellow workers and employers that his or her performance deteriorates to the point of dismissal. The depressed person's despair and loss of initiative may prompt him or her to quit a job on sudden impulse. Though co-workers commonly label these persons incompetent or lazy, their behavior is often a reaction to demands for work efficiency. Inasmuch as all clinical branches of medicine use work efficiency as a diagnostic indication of wellness or illness, recognition of the excessive work syndrome calls this criterion into question.

Meyer built a unique classification of behavioral disorders around the idea of work. He called health "ergasia," or mentally integrated activity. Meyer noted that "a false sense of competition which does not allow the human being as he is" endangers psychic health and he called attention to "insufficient hygiene of work." In 1933, Meyer wrote that there were "occupations in this country which no American parent would want his children to be engaged in and for which we need 'immigrants to do the dirty work.'" He added that "there is a need of reciprocity between the satisfaction in the worker's life (literally the duration of the organism) both as to dependability, and the respect offered on the part of the social medium in which the individual has to live" (6).

Clinical Models

The various diagnostic and therapeutic categories of psychiatry are helpful in the differential diagnosis and treatment of the work addict.

Social Inadequacy

Work addiction may often provide a sense of security to persons who are highly expert on the job yet socially inadequate at home, especially when they have preadolescent and adolescent sons and daughters. Sometimes one or both parents are unable to cope with their demanding children. They experience massive anxiety in setting and enforcing limits. The most common clinical case is the successful business or professional man who leaves childrearing entirely to his wife and immerses himself in work. He justifies abdication of parental responsibility by the heavy demands of his job. This creates a martyred feeling in his wife, who upbraids the husband so much that he becomes passively angry toward her. The passive-aggressiveness often expresses itself in partial or complete sexual impotence. This in turn further lowers the wife's sense of self-worth. Remarkably enough, such couples tend to be symptom-free if and when they take a vacation from both his job and her care of the children. Yet marital crisis is common when all the children have finally left the home, which points to underlying problems in the marriage.

A useful approach to this kind of work addiction is to involve the couple in parent effectiveness training, marriage enrichment workshops, etc. Specific interventions, for example, nights out together, long weekends together, and vacations, are also helpful. Intensive psychotherapy with the father is most beneficial if he can thereby identify the source(s) of his feelings of inadequacy and develop more assertiveness. Most assertiveness training courses are tailored for women, but men also suffer from a lack of assertiveness and need reeducating away from their passive-aggressiveness.

Hyperactive Response to Marital Collapse

Other cases of work addiction stem from marital alienation and collapse. The work behavior of persons in such a crisis often becomes bizarrely hyperactive. The person talks little about the marriage problem, but generally attributes the impending or recent divorce to work demands. Such patients are cognitively deeply involved with work and have only narcissistic relationships with their spouses. Typically, they are involved with a workaholic co-worker.

This kind of clinical situation is not an established pattern of work addiction. To the contrary, it is a symptomatic or transient personality disturbance. Once the marital dissolution is grieved through, the work pattern takes on a nonmorbid character. Therefore, a grief therapy approach of a supportive and rational nature is indicated. Life support groups in churches or Y's, single parent groups, and postdivorce therapy groups are the treatments of choice. Often a job change offers the person a whole new work and social arena in which to relate without the painful associations of the scene of the marital breakup. Thus, job change must be evaluated in counseling; at the very least, renegotiation of the present job is needed.

Emotional Deprivation

The chronic work addict tends to have a long history of both emotional and economic deprivation. The typical family history and psychosocial development pattern includes the following elements:

1. History of death of or abandonment by one or both parents in the earliest years of life.
2. History of rejection and sibling rivalry for the remaining parent's approval, praise, and affection.
3. History of significant upward mobility from the lower classes into the upper middle and lower upper clases; mobility achieved by education and/or long hours of work and acute business judgment; fear of poverty sustains excessive work pattern.
4. Present profile of self-made success (rejection of school and attraction to entrepreneurial self-employment such as car dealerships typical in workaholics from upper middle class).
5. Hard work used to "earn" respect, love, appreciation, and even salvation; anxious loneliness and guilt overwhelming if they are not working.
6. Very high intelligence test scores on items evaluating manual performance and concrete operations; task oriented, pragmatic, and active personalities.

Biogenic and Temperamental Correlates

Whatever can be said of the affective disorders, treated quite successfully today by clinical psychiatrists, can also be said of a large proportion of work addicts. The affective disorders are disorders of mood and energy output. For example, the person who exhibits marked mood swings suffers from a "bipolar depression," characterized by alternations of energy depletion and overmobilization. Work addiction seems to be a precarious socialization of these mood swings. In the manic phase, the workaholic becomes hyperactive and overproductive. As Rhoads observed:

> Some persons seem to lack an inner monitoring device for regulating the work-rest-recreation balance. Cursed with a compulsive need to work, they deny the existence of fatigue and push themselves beyond reason. They attempt to cope with diminished ability to concentrate, ease of distractibility, and drowsiness (early signs of fatigue) by forcing themselves to stay at the appointed task. In fact, they usually lengthen the workday to compensate for their lessened ability to produce efficiently (7).

He then presented a brief case history:

> A 34-year-old tax attorney was admitted to the medical services with a complaint of chest pain. Four months earlier, he had noted the onset of leg pains, followed a month later by constant substernal and left-sided chest pain, dizziness, shortness of breath, and tremor. He stopped working and consulted his family doctor. The symptoms continued for the next three weeks, accompanied by intestinal overactivity, a lump in the throat, and palpitations. He gave a history of similar episodes, one occurring eight years previously and the other during college. It was estimated that for at least three years he had worked 80 to 100 hours per week. He took no vacations and seldom took any weekends or days off. Three months prior to the onset of the symptoms noted, he had been aware of fatigue, lessened ability to concentrate, and sleep disturbances, for relief of which he took several drinks. Relevant family history included the sudden death of his father resulting from a heart attack when he was in his mid 40s (7).

Another dimension of the hyperactive phase of bipolar depression is pathological boredom, which explains, at least in part, other symptoms such as irritability, memory loss, and inability to concentrate. The flight of ideas does not allow interest to develop. Bieber noted that for work addicts "the easiest escape from free time boredom is immersing themselves in work and taking on assignments that preclude free time" (8).

The critical elements in the manic phase of bipolar depression seen in workaholics are acknowledged fatigue, faulty perceptions, impaired judgment, and confusion. In this state the person makes impossible promises that come back to haunt him or her, producing sleeplessness in the later depressed phase of the bipolar depression. The person begins to bemoan the amount of work necessary to fulfill the promises made in the earlier cycle of the mood swing.

Tricyclic antidepressants are effective short-term remedies for sleep deprivation. Some physicians will shift the person to a lithium regimen after the antidepressants have alleviated the depression. The whole episode of illness seems to be nature's way of regulating the organism so as to preserve life.

Friedman and Rosenman have identified a particular personality pattern—"Type A"—as the key cause of heart attacks. The Type A personality shows the following characteristics:

1. Incessantly struggles to achieve more and more in less time.
2. Readily bucks the system and opposes efforts of others to stop him or her.
3. Often exhibits a free-floating and well-rationalized hostility.
4. Does not manifest Type A behavior unless environmentally challenged.
5. Has a habitual sense of time urgency.
6. Perpetually sets deadlines for himself or herself "to an exclusion of life's loveliness" (9).
7. Evaluates his or her worth by *number* of achievements.
8. Indulges in polyphasic thinking (tries to think two or more things at once).

Friedman and Rosenman's argument deserves to be taken seriously. The coronary care units of general hospitals abound in Type A personalities. I have also observed that heart patients handle stress by a fight response rather than a flight response and rarely by apathy.

Type A behavior and work addiction are remarkably similar. One question that can be raised regarding Friedman and Rosenman's hypothesis centers on the organ *specificity* in their model: the heart is the wear and tear focus in the Type A organism. Other systems of the body must surely be involved: for example, the respiratory, gastrointestinal, and endocrine systems have all been implicated in the stress syndrome. Overweight and obesity are related to the fatigue, often warded off by food, and lack of exercise characteristic of many work addicts.

On-the-Job Factors

Work addicts enjoy both affectionate chiding and indulgence in our culture. Many job situations assume that workers will devote themselves primarily or even exclusively to their tasks. Several writers have defined such conditions as *slavery*. Paul La Fargue, son-in-law of Karl Marx, spoke of the chains of middle-class people to work and their "right to laziness." He hoped that machines would release man from the bondage of drudgery and boring work. Leo Tolstoy observed that such servitude reflects the desire to live like the privileged and wealthy classes (10). Today, social climbing is generally approved though it demands repudiation of one's origins and a singleminded quest for money.

If one views excessive work as a maladaptive response to the demands of a job, one makes the therapeutic mistake of assuming that the work addict is totally responsible for his or her addiction. To the contrary, the job may demand round-the-clock performance, with quitting the only means to effect a change. This situation in turn can be understood only within the context of larger social and economic arrangements.

In some cases, of course, employees make the organization for which they work the *sole* investment of their ego; they perceive themselves as indispensable to the company and their job as indispensable to their self-worth. Executives and administrators call this loyalty. John Calvin, the Protestant reformer, would have called it idolatry! Such idolatry and self-delusion provide the stuff of work addiction and very often employers are as trapped as those they employ.

The absence of ego strength, a requisite for making and implementing decisions, is common in patients who have been hospitalized for heart attack or agitated depression. Well-controlled research into this pattern is vital in elucidating the stress syndrome. To what extent do breaches of contract and inordinate work demands produce semi-indentured service and contribute to work addiction? Do overspecialization and lack of flexibility in job structures result in enslavement to dead-end jobs? To what extent does chronic neurotic depression prevent employees from renegotiating job responsibilities or moving to new positions? In short, how do company policies and working conditions interact with the work addict's psyche to produce chronic excessive working? A different situation exists with self-employed persons such as physicians, building contractors, lawyers, plumbers, or artisans and research would have to be modified accordingly. The contending forces of job and nonjob demands are contained within the work addict himself or herself.

Treatment

The Methodist Hospital in Indianapolis has had for several years a health hazard appraisal program for ministers, teachers, etc. The evaluation combines several day's respite from work stresses with a thorough medical and/or psychiatric appraisal. Patterns of sleeping, eating, smoking, alcohol use, self-medication, exercise, and sexual behavior are scrutinized. Both the cardiovascular and the gastrointestinal system are examined carefully. The specific risks to longevity by reason of overwork are discussed with the patient. *Both* marriage partners participate in this evaluation as a matter of course.

Similar preventive programs are available at other hospitals and many companies require their executives to participate. Airline pilots are mandated by law to undergo such appraisals.

I suggest that emergency attention to the work addict's sleep disorder be given top priority. A sleep disorder outpatient-inpatient clinic should be the first site for treating work addiction.

Stress management seminars can identify the most troublesome issues for work addicted persons. Selye (11), Levinson (12), and Grinker and Spiegel (13) have published remarkably relevant data for developing instructional formats and rational therapies for work addicts. Retreats in quiet settings are ideal locations for discussing and accomplishing stress management and reduction in work addicts.

A welcome sign of the times is the appearance of "positive" addictions to replace work addiction; for example, the widespread participation in running, walking, swimming, tennis, and racketball. The reader is cautioned, however, that excessive involvement in these activities may represent a new variation on an old theme. Food regimens that exclude caffeine, cholesterol, and other harmful substances have been associated with a marked reduction in cancer among special populations such as the Mormons and the Seventh-Day Adventists, and the incidence of death by heart disease has shown a general decline in this country. Meditation is another experiment in ritualized "effortlessness" that can become a positive addiction offsetting work addiction (14, 15).

At base, however, the *act of surrendering* one's feelings of omnipotence and the desire to avoid a premature death caused by superhuman effort triggers the need for "magnificent obsessions" that can lure the work driven person into enjoyment of being human and permitting himself or herself to rest. Such capitulation may succeed either a religious experience of surrender to a god of grace who delivers the person from the slavery of work or the shock of recognition (after a close brush with death) that time is a joy to savor. A severe heart attack, a partial loss of sight, hearing, or movement, or a disabling accident may inspire a total reappraisal and result in what is called a positive act of surrender that releases the powerful grip of an addictive work pattern.

The act of surrender means in part setting aside the urgent sense of time that plagues the work addict. As Friedman and Rosenman observed, the work addict has "a stereotyped sense of time." He or she "more and more substitutes 'faster' for 'better' or 'different' in his way of thinking and doing. . . . The Type A man . . . tries to accomplish more and more in less and less time" (9). The person who finally breaks the siege of time is in fact coming to terms with his or her own mortality. As Don Juan told Carlos Castaneda, "Death is our eternal companion." How we accept the presence of this companion determines our pace of doing. "The thing to do when you're impatient is to turn to your left and ask advice from your death. An immense amount of pettiness is dropped if your death makes a gesture to you, or if you catch a glimpse of it, or if you just have a feeling that your companion is there watching you" (14). This advice should be well taken not only by the work addict but by all of us as well.

References

1. Oates, W. E., On being a workaholic: a serious jest, *Pastoral Psych. 19*, 16–20 (1968).
2. Oates, W. E., *Confessions of a Workaholic: The Facts about Work Addiction,* Abingdon, New York, 1971.
3. Oates, W. E., *Workaholics, Make Laziness Work for You,* Doubleday, New York, 1978.
4. Nocera, J., Marvella (Bayh's) wonderland, *Louisville Courier Journal Magazine,* Sept. 23, 1979.
5. Erikson, E., *Identity and Youth in Crisis,* Norton, New York, 1965.
6. Meyer, A., Spontaneity, in *The Common Sense Psychiatry of Dr. Adolph Meyer,* A. Lief, ed., McGraw-Hill, New York, 1948, pp. 553–583.
7. Rhoads, J. M., Overwork, *JAMA 237,* 2615–2618 (1977).
8. *Louisville Courier Journal,* Aug. 11, 1978.
9. Friedman, M., and Rosenman, R. H., *Type A Behavior and Your Heart,* Fawcett Crest, Greenwich, 1974.
10. Tolstoy, L., *Slavery in Our Times,* Walker, New York, 1900.
11. Selye, H., *The Stress of Life,* McGraw-Hill, New York, 1976.
12. Levinson, D. J., *The Seasons of a Man's Life,* Knopf, New York, 1978.
13. Grinker, R. R., and Speigel, J., *Men under Stress,* rep. ed., Irvington, New York, 1978.
14. Castaneda, C., *Journey to Ixtlan,* Dell, New York, 1972.

14

Gambling

Ralph G. Victor

Life is a gamble. Every moment has its uncertainties and risks. How we cross a street, choose a mate, earn a livelihood, and spend leisure time—all require making decisions with an element of uncertainty. It is difficult to face existence realistically. Since confronting facts can be so painful, magical thinking and the denial of reality have been an essential part of man's attempt to lessen his anxieties. In appealing to a magical power man seeks an ally to bend fate in a favorable direction.

This chapter deals with aspects of gambling, not with magic or fortunetelling or man's relation to the supernatural; however, there is a connection. The individual who gambles to excess denies facts, replacing them with unrealistic beliefs about having fate on his or her side.

Liber de Ludo Aleae, a delightful little book written about 1520 by Gerolamo Cardano, is one of the earlier descriptions of the psychological aspects of gambling (1). Cardano was a physician and a mathematics teacher. A man of many faults who lived a stormy life, he was an inveterate gambler. Cardano apologized for writing about gambling: gambling might well be an evil, he stated, but since so very many people gamble this activity should be discussed by medical doctors as one of the incurable diseases.

Gambling was an established institution in the most diverse cultures throughout the ages. Cohen and Hansel noted that gambling was prevalent in the ancient civilizations of China, Japan, India, Persia, Egypt, Palestine, Greece, and Rome and among numerous native American peoples (2). Indeed, one form of gambling, divination, was widely used to decide major questions. Likewise, the outcome of every contest or trial of strength was considered a sacred sign from the gods. Bergler noted the preservation of superstitions and magical rituals in modern gambling situations (4). Players superstitiously alternate seats, walk around chairs, change decks of cards, wear or place good luck charms on the table, rub their cards or dice on various parts of the body, look at their cards in a prescribed order, wager high stakes on poor cards because of hunches and little on good hands because they feel unlucky, etc.

Americans eagerly share the worldwide and ageless passion for gambling: Mark Twain recounted several stories and anecdotes about gambling; as far back as 1863, horses raced at Saratoga Springs; boxing and wrestling matches are heavily bet on, and legalizing various forms of gambling is hotly debated in state legislatures. In a 1976 report, the National Gambling Commission estimated that about 1.1 million Americans (.77 percent) were addicted to gambling. The commission estimated another 3.3 million potential gamblers. In Nevada, where gambling is permitted, 2.6 percent of adult citizens or permanent residents are thought to be compulsive gamblers, which suggests that gambling is more prevalent where it is legal (Monte Carlo has recognized the destructive appeal of gambling: only tourists may gamble there legally; and local people are forbidden to enter the casinos).

Definitions

How is gambling defined today? According to Moran, gambling exhibits the following characteristics: there is a voluntary agreement between two or more persons to engage in this activity; one individual's gain is another's loss; and the results are dependent on the outcome of an uncertain situation; i.e., participation involves risk taking (3). Gambling activities can either be based entirely on chance, as with roulette, bingo, or slot machines, or require skill as well, as in various card games and in horse racing.

Bergler defined compulsive gambling as follows: it is a chronic and repetitive activity in the gambler's life; superseding all other interests; the gambler is pathologically optimistic about winning; he or she cannot stop when ahead but eventually risks more than he or she can afford; the gambler seeks and enjoys a thrill that cannot be logically explained; and the activity is compounded as much of pain as of pleasure (4). The third point is crucial: the gambler cannot stop when he or she is winning, which has been widely interpreted to mean that he or she really gambles to lose.

Though definitions vary, all investigators agree that the compulsive gambler has a paramount preoccupation with this activity, which is pursued in spite of a succession of bad experiences.

Terms such as "compulsive" or "pathological" suggest that gambling is an illness. This at once raises some basic questions, reminiscent of long-standing arguments about alcoholism. Is gambling a disease or a character weakness? The former suggests that gamblers cannot help themselves and are possessed by their sickness; the latter points to individual choice and either a need to harm others or an abdication of responsibility. Clearly, etiology is a crucial consideration in treatment. The 1980 *Diagnostic and Statistical Manual* of the American Psychiatric Association listed pathological gambling as an illness. As noted in the *Seattle Times,* this official action may "increase awareness and will stimulate research and treatment just as it did when alcoholism was recognized" as an illness in 1957 (5).

In discussing compulsion, Ogman observed that the potential conflict between the view of the gambler as a victim of drive and the view of the gambler as purposeful and calculating is a conflict that has always dominated man's thoughts about himself (6). Ogman argued, with some force, that we have made it too easy for the gambler. If gambling behavior is determined by forces outside the individual and does not in any way represent rational choice of ends, means, and values, then this condition can be considered as a chronic illness that is never completely cured. However, Oldman noted that the regular gambler does not inevitably end up in an economic mess (one could reply that the regular gambler is not necessarily the compulsive gambler). He suggested that the gambler prefers to be seen as a patient needing treatment rather than an individual with a deviant personality. Generally, Oldman's paper leaves open the possibility that many gamblers are more sociopathic than ill and that they are suffering from a character disorder stemming from self-centeredness and indifference to the needs of others.

I agree with Oldman that the polarization of views on gambling goes to the crux of psychotherapy generally. In a large group of psychological afflictions no changes can occur unless the patient is an active participant in the treatment process. Therapy (individual or group) may be based primarily on insight or on behavior modification, but in either case there is an appeal to volition and self-awareness. Existential psychiatry takes the most radical view in declaring that man has a choice; thus, the object of therapy is to mobilize this will to choose. Most addictions, including alcoholism and gambling, are neither pure illness nor pure badness, but a mixture of the two. Yet the mixture is always there, even if the proportions differ.

Psychological and Behavioral Dimensions

The casual gambler may enjoy the companionship of others and the ambience of the gambling place. This situation lessens loneliness but does not call for intimacy. Just as male alcoholics tend to be very uncertain of their masculinity (not necessarily their sexual potency or performance) and use liquor to help them overcome shyness or anxiety with women, compulsive gamblers tend to become animated when they are gambling and initially less anxious (7).

Boyd and Bolen studied a group of male gamblers, whom they described as passive-dependent and schizoid and in whom feelings of isolation and unrelatedness were primary (7). Their marital relationships usually were turbulent; the men were hostile to their wives, rebelled against them, and tended to treat them as mothers, not spouses. The men came from homes where there was a controlling, critical, and authoritarian parent, typically the mother. The presence of at least one noticeably domineering parent probably contributed to or caused the feeling of inferiority and uncertainty about masculine adequacy in this group.

While many factors converge to produce compulsive gambling, a sense of inadequacy and isolation, highly conflicting feelings about one or both parents, and then a recurrent depression secondary to losses are dominant. Gambling is an attempt to overcome these feelings: the excitement this activity generates is a defense against depression and winning gives a transient sense of adequacy and connectedness with others.

Bergler observed that the psychology of consciousness is inadequate to the task of unraveling the complex personality of the gambler (4). Only the psychology of the unconscious can expose the illogical and senseless certainty of winning deeply rooted in the gambler's psyche. Bergler related this faith to childhood megalomania, which encompasses grandiose and omnipotent beliefs. In the normal course of development young children think of themselves as all-powerful. Bergler, a psychoanalyst, suggested that the gambler remains a child and has never given up fantasies of omnipotence. Bergler noted, too, that rebellion, guilt, and self-punishment play a major role in gambling. According to Bergler, gambling is an aggressive, rebellious activity; in losing the gambler pays the penalty for his or her hostility. Though on many levels, Bergler's approach is very sensible, his theory accounts for only part of the phenomenon. As indicated in the following case history, however, the masochistic dimension in gambling is significant. The masochist enjoys punishment not for its own sake but because the suffering experienced compensates for highly aggressive, unacceptable impulses. Not to win is a form of atonement.

> C. G. sought help because his gambling kept him too busy to attend to his business. Likewise, his marriage was stressed; there was little overt fighting but no real intimacy. The patient was sexually potent yet emotionally indifferent.
>
> He spontaneously stated that he got much more excited about gambling than about sex, but he did not have physical manifestations of sexual excite-

ment when gambling. C. G. would gamble for higher and higher stakes until losses were so severe that he could not raise any more cash. He would then abstain until he had sufficient funds to resume gambling. C. G. stated that he felt joyful and tremendously excited driving to his place of gambling. Knowing on one level that he would probably lose, he nevertheless felt that "today things may be different." When he came home after gambling, he would tell his wife that he had been with a customer. C. G. generally felt very guilty, "dirty," and compelled to take a bath to cleanse himself upon his return.

This patient had a very powerful, authoritarian father (who also gambled, but to a much lesser degree). C. G.'s father overemphasized achievement and equated masculinity with financial success. The patient tried simultaneously to appease and to compete with his father. In many ways, C. G. hated and rejected this punitive, powerful man. Hating encompassed a desire to destroy—"to make a killing"—but to win this game would be intolerable since it would mean displeasing or destroying the father. Losing, then, meant to give in to his father and at the same time to keep aggressive impulses under control.

Several authors have identified depression as a possible cause of gambling (3). There is a real question, however, whether depression is a cause or a result of gambling, which might lead to further gambling. Among the cardinal symptoms of clinical depression is the patient's difficulty making decisions. Also typical is an exaggerated concern about spending money and about having enough money for the future. Gambling requires specific decisions unlikely to be forthcoming in a significant depression. However, severe depression resulting from excessive gambling is not uncommon, and there are many reports of suicides in individuals ruined by gambling. Zola observed a group of men who gambled heavily (12). He mentioned depression but emphasized that such depressions were remarkably short-lived—lasting only until a new opportunity arose for placing bets. C. G. reported experiencing profound depression almost every night after gambling. But this state would pass the next day, when he would be happily excited as he again went off to gamble.

The basic question of whether depression in gamblers is primary and leads to gambling or whether it results from gambling cannot be answered with certainty. Unfortunately, the clinical term "depression" covers a wide range of moods below a presumably normal level. Since compulsive gamblers so often feel happy only when they start gambling or anticipate the gambling activity, they seem chronically depressed. The reasons for this depression probably include a conscious reaction to the reality of the life situation, combined with a less well defined anxiety stemming from unfulfilled and unsatisfied longings and drives. Depression also is often associated with diminished sexual drive: sexual closeness in a loving relationship is rarely found among gamblers.

Freud's contribution to the problem of gambling is found in his study of Dostoevski, who apparently had a need to lose (8). In fact, he could return to creative writing only after he had rid himself of guilt feelings (4). Freud argued that gambling was a substitute for and derivative of masturbation. The parallels between these behaviors are many: the exciting activity of the hands, the irresistibility of the urge, the repeated resolutions to abstain, the intoxicating quality of the pleasure, and the enormous guilt feelings generated.

In addition to theories linking both masochism and masturbation to gambling, other psychoanalytic perspectives describe this behavior. Though some of these approaches have been helpful to analysts treating gamblers, in general they seem farfetched. Greenston analyzed five male patients (9). He observed regression to the pregenital phases of libido in all five. Greenston described the gambler as unconsciously striving to restore infantile omnipotence and the mother–infant unity. Lintner also identified incestuous longings and death wishes toward the father in gamblers (10). Deer noted that the gambler does not necessarily wish to lose (11). Through punishment, however, he wishes to relieve guilt, but his hopes and dreams are first and foremost to win the mother's body and "from the possession, the world's treasure house will pour its wealth upon him" (11). Geha discusses male gamblers only.

Treatment

There is no certain cure for the compulsive gambler. Nevertheless, various approaches have at times been successful.

Boyd and Bolen worked intensely with couples in which one spouse was a compulsive gambler (7). Participants agreed to remain in treatment for an entire year. Boyd and Bolen described the chaotic and symbiotic nature of the marital relationships, the complementary pathology present in the partners, and the vicious villain-victim style of interaction. They personally found the therapy time-consuming and emotionally draining because of perpetual crises, depressions, gambling episodes, and eruptions of marital discord. As therapists they had to be constantly available and make vigorous interventions; yet their treatment results were impressive. There were no dropouts in spite of low initial motivation in some of the patients. All gambling activities stopped before the year ended and marital relations had improved.

There are few other successful treatment efforts in the literature. One reason is that few gamblers have the time, funds, or inclination to undergo prolonged psychotherapy. Second, the very nature of intensive, prolonged psychotherapy prevents any one therapist from seeing many patients with the same illness. Thus, most case reports deal with only a single or a few individuals.

Gamblers Anonymous has had the most success with gamblers in England and the United States, although there are no reliable statistics for this organization. In general, the compulsive gambler will seek treatment only when forced to do so by external circumstances such as financial trouble—bankruptcy or debt accumulation—family pressure, or probationary status following conviction for a crime related to the need to acquire money.

GA involves both the gambler and his or her spouse in treatment. Group sessions and the overall treatment process help the individual develop a sense of adequacy by encouraging confession, which establishes that the gambler has achieved *something* in being more irresponsible or foolish than any other gambler. GA also encourages religious faith but avoids religious dogmatism; for some, this may give life a new direction and purpose. Finally, group membership and support lessen the gambler's sense of isolation. The real success of Gamblers Anonymous again raises the question of illness versus weakness of character. GA suggests that sociopathic features may cause gambling behavior since the compulsion is so successfully broken by a powerful appeal to morals, group pressure and support, and new activities—without any significant attempt to deal with psychodynamic factors.

Miller and Barker defined compulsive gambling as a "progressive illness which can never be cured but which can be arrested" (13). They described several cases in which gambling was cured or improved after only 12 hours of treatment. In their aversion therapy a one-armed bandit was connected to a electrical deconditioning apparatus. A careful attempt was made to simulate the typical gambling room atmosphere. With the cuff of the deconditioning apparatus applied to the left wrist, the patient slowly sipped a beer and inserted gambling discs into the machine. As he gambled with his right hand, electric shocks were repeatedly delivered to the left. The authors pointed out that the natural history of compulsive gambling may be punctuated by long periods of abstinence followed by relapse. They therefore recommended regular booster treatments. However, since less and less has been heard about aversion therapy during the last decade, it is presumed that this procedure has had very limited usefulness.

I successfully used paradoxical therapy with C. G., the patient discussed earlier (14). Unfortunately, at follow-up after several years he was divorced and gambling again.

Finally, antidepressants have been used with gamblers but without reported successes.

Conclusions

Gambling can best be looked at as an addiction, most usefully compared to alcoholism. Both types of addiction probably have a number of causes, yet commonly the afflicted person has a great sense of inadequacy and feels uncertain about his or her social and sexual role. Addictive activity temporarily gives the individual a feeling of competence or superiority. Inhibitions are decreased while acceptance and sociability are increased, often with people having similar inner conflicts.

Neurotic behavior generally leads to discomfort. A subject engages in such behavior, however, because without it he or she would be even more uncomfortable. The choice is between the lesser of two evils: gambling or facing loneliness and one's inadequacies.

The treatment of choice for gamblers is a therapy group that understands and accepts the affliction. The key to treatment is not insight but confrontation of the gambler's dishonesty, callousness to others, etc., from either a group or committed therapists.

With the removal of legal barriers to gambling, the problem is likely to increase. There is thus reason to be deeply concerned.

References

1. Cardano, G., *Liber de Ludo Aleae,* in *The Gambling Scholar,* O. Oystein, ed., Princeton University Press, Princeton, 1953.
2. Cohen, J., and Hansel, M., *Risk and Gambling,* Longmans, Green, London, 1956.
3. Moran, E., Pathological gambling, *Brit. J. Psychiat. 127,* 416–428 (1975).
4. Bergler, E., *Psychology of Gambling,* International Universities Press, New York, 1970.
5. Psychiatric association classifies compulsive gambling as illness, *Seattle Times,* Oct. 7, 1979.
6. Oldman, D., Compulsive gamblers, *Soc. Rev. 26,* 349–371 (1978).
7. Boyd, W. H., and Bolen, D. W., The compulsive gambler and spouse in group psychotherapy, *Inter'l. J. Group Psychother. 20,* 77–90 (1970).
8. Freud, S., *Dostoevsky and Parricide* (1928). *Collected Papers,* vol. 5, Basic Books, New York, 1959, pp. 222–242.
9. Greenson, R. R., On gambling, *Amer. Imago 4,* 61–77 (1947).
10. Lintner, R., *Explorations in Psychoanalysis,* Julian Press, New York, 1953.
11. Geha, R., Jr., Dostoevsky and the gambler: a contribution to the psychogenesis of gambling, part II, *Psychoanal. Rev. 57,* 289–302 (1970).

12. Zola, I. K., Observations on gambling in a lower class setting, in *Gambling,* R. D. Herman, ed., Harper, New York, 1967.

13. Miller, M. E., and Barker, J. D., Aversion therapy for compulsive gambling, *Nursing Mirror 18,* 21–25 (1968).

14. Victor, R. G., and Krug, C. M., "Paradoxical intention" in the treatment of compulsive gambling, *Amer. J. Psychother. 21,* 808–814 (1967).

15

Too Much Television

Arthur Asa Berger

The unabridged *Random House Dictionary of the English Language* gives six definitions of "excess." They all add up to the same thing. Excess involves "going beyond ordinary or proper limits," "immoderate indulgence," and "more than or above what is necessary, usual, or specified." In certain areas, "immoderate indulgence" has obvious physiological, psychological, and/or physical consequences. What about television viewing? How much is too much? The relationship that exists between television and human behavior is so complicated and problematic that any answers are necessarily tentative.

Despite some 2,500 English-language studies on television and human behavior it is difficult to establish a causal relationship between what we see and what we do. But there are reasons to *suspect* all kinds of things. This chapter looks primarily at this somewhat gray area. Nevertheless, ample scientific evidence links television watching to violent behavior, and we have grounds to believe that both program content and the medium itself may have negative consequences that we must consider carefully. For example, the report to the U.S. surgeon general concluded that "a modest relationship exists between the viewing of violence on television and aggressive tendencies," noting that the relationship between violence on television and aggressive behavior by viewers is "embedded in a complicated set of related variables (1). As Comstock and associates pointed out: "The evidence is that television may increase aggression by teaching viewers previously unfamiliar hostile acts, by generally encouraging in various ways the use of aggression, and by triggering aggressive behavior both imitative and different in kind from what has been viewed" (2).

A Note on the Structure of Addictions

Television addiction, as all addictions, can be analyzed from a structural point of view. Structuralism can be defined as a mode of thought which

282

studies phenomena in terms of their organizational makeup and the formal attributes and relationships underlying these phenomena. From this perspective, addictions are behavior codings which function within the larger collection of master codings dominant in a given culture. One way to describe "culture," then, is a system of codings. Addiction is a deviant coding or subcoding practiced, generally, by subcultures within the general culture, as the following indicate:

1. *Process Codes* refer to the methods by which the addict learns how to become a drug-user, how he or she is indoctrinated into the subgroup, and how he or she is taught how to use whatever paraphernalia is necessary.

2. *Consumption Codes* describe how the addict learns to become a discriminating consumer of drugs, the routines necessary to purchase them, and other related matters.

3. *Activity Codes* relate to the life-style the addict learns to enable him or her to function effectively—that is, maintain access to drugs. These activities frequently involve crime, prostitution, and so on. For people in this subculture, drug use becomes the central organizing activity of their lives—a role occupied, for example, by religion, work, childrearing, and hobbies in most other people's lives.

4. *Pleasure Codes* delineate the gratifications obtained. In the case of addictions we find such things as escapism, sensation, excitement, and group solidarity as the sought-after goals.

It is obvious that many of the codings characterized for hard drug addictions are analogues to television addiction, although the gratifications may not be as powerful nor the risk as evident. If we can view addictions, as well as other kinds of behaviors, as coded—that is, made up of various rules of procedure that interlock with one another—we may make some progress in finding out how to break these addictions. Evidently, the problem is individual and cultural, complicated further by the fact that culture influences the individual often without his conscious awareness. Other, less destructive codes have to be found which will enable people to escape their addictions more easily. To ask a heroin or television addict to go "cold turkey," on his own, without any help or substitute activity, is futile.

Viewing Patterns

Television developed in the 1920s and 1930s. The technical breakthrough was the invention of an electronic scanning device and picture tube in 1931. Commercial television began in July 1941, having been approved by the Federal Communications Commission. Life in America has never been the same. By the end of the first year there were some half dozen TV stations and about 10,000 sets in use; now there are hundreds of stations and 97

TABLE 15–1
Weekly Time Budget

ACTIVITY	TIME (HOURS)
Sleep	50
Work	40
TV viewing	21.5
Eating	8
Reading books	.06

percent of U.S. households have at least one TV set (one reason that television has spread so rapidly, especially of late is low price: a 12" black and
white portable sells for under $100 now). Americans currently spend a lot
of time watching TV. In 1978, according to the Roper Organization, the
median number of viewing hours per day was 3.08—that comes to 21.56
hours per week and 1,121.12 hours per year. This figure, up from the 2.17-
hour daily average in 1961, represents an enormous investment in time on
the part of the public (Table 15–1). The average American spends almost as
much time watching television in one week as he or she spends reading
books in one year!

The amount of television viewing varies with age, educational level,
race, sex, etc. That is, some elements of the American public tend to watch
a good deal more than three hours per day and others watch a good deal
less. For example, college educated people watch 2.31 hours per day; those
in "upper economic levels" watch 2.52 hours per day. A typical household
has its set on 6.82 hours per day, which represents almost all the leisure
time people spend at home.

Television, Psyche, and Society

The data on television suggest that the average amount of television viewing in America is excessive. As the Greeks taught, proportion and harmony
are proper in all things. When one activity dominates our lives something is
wrong.

We all have a limited number of hours at our disposal in any one day.
As a rule, there are various things we must do with these hours if we are to
be emotionally and physically healthy. We are social animals and need
companionship and interaction with others. We have a physical body to
look after and require exercise, food, etc. And we have many other needs:
spiritual, psychological, and sexual. All too often, television monopolizes
our time and unless we are highly disciplined, we are unable to attend to
many of the things we should be doing. For too many Americans, televi-

sion *is* the content of their lives aside from work and sleep. They schedule meals so as not to miss their favorite news program and spend holidays absorbed in televised sports events.

The fact that television is an entertainment medium makes it difficult for people to recognize its power and influence. We assume that entertainments are basically trivial, harmless ways of spending time, but this kind of thinking can lead us astray: television is not simply an entertainment. It is a socializing agent of awesome power that has profoundly affected all of us. As Gerbner testified:

> In only two decades of massive national experience television has transformed the political life of the nation, has changed the daily habits of our people, has molded the style of the generation, made overnight global phenomena of local happenings, redirected the flow of information and values from traditional channels into centralized networks reaching into every home. In other words, it has profoundly affected what we call the process of socialization, the process by which members of our species become human (3).

The situation is complicated by several factors. First, most of us underestimate the amount of television viewing we do. Second, the average amount of viewing is not seen by most people as unusual or problematic. Third, television is addictive; there are many self-confessed "television junkies" who are, in effect, prisoners of their sets.

Research has indicated that substantial numbers of people will watch anything on television and that once a given channel is selected early in the evening they will stick with that channel regardless of programming. Television has a hypnotic fascination. People spend hours almost mesmerized in front of the set. The "boob tube," as it is sometimes called, has become the all-pervasive background against which we play out our lives.

The saturation of the American market by television is important for a number of reasons. For one, television is a medium for selling goods and services. As a television station producer told me, "You've got to realize that television exists for one reason and only one reason: to carry commercials. The rest of the stuff that goes in between the commercials is important only insofar as it provides viewers for the commercials." Thus, television is instrumental in keeping the U.S. economy going. Commercials fuel the "consumer lust" that is so prevalent in American society. The widespread use of television also has important cultural consequences. Even low rated programs are seen by many millions of people, who are affected by the values implicit and explicit in the shows: the roles people play, the kinds of characters held up for emulation, the goals pursued, the style of life sought, etc. Some critics of television are worried that TV encourages "cultural homogenization."

In recent years there has been a technological revolution in electronics: videotape recorders (VTR), videodiscs, and numerous other wonders. Although costing more than television sets, these devices are not terribly expensive and economies of scale will probably bring down their prices considerably. In the relatively near future, most households probably will have VTR units and videodisc players of one sort or another. This equipment will certainly intensify our relationship with electronic media in general and television in particular: we will spend even more time viewing TV, though perhaps more selectively.

Were I to adopt medical jargon here, I would say that television viewing is something which almost always becomes addictive, with larger and larger "doses" or "video-fixes" becoming necessary for the addict. The disease is highly contagious and has reached endemic proportions; but since everyone is afflicted, and most seem to enjoy their affliction, hardly anyone pays much attention to the matter. Indeed, those who do not watch television, or who do not at least watch the "required" three-hours or so a day, are now defined as abnormal, weirdos, or elitists. And since a goodly amount of conversation between people seems to be about television programs, these critics or "light viewers" find themselves isolated from their fellow men and women to a considerable degree.

Was there life before television? Many young people, and some not-so-young cannot conceive of this.

The Debate on TV Viewing

It is difficult to talk about television, other mass media, or popular culture without sounding either naive or shrill. Defenders of television, the most important carrier of the popular arts, make the following arguments:

It is democratic. People have a right to watch what they like.

It is informative. People learn a great deal about the world from watching television.

It is moralistic. Generally, the virtuous triumph and socially approved behaviors are reinforced.

It raises people's consciouness and cultural level. Miniseries like Roots and Holocaust and ballets, operas, and other such programs play an important role; for many people TV provides exposure and access to cultural events they would not otherwise experience.

It unifies. By providing a common ground of experience, TV makes it easier for people to relate to one another.

It is functional. TV satisfies various needs people have and provides important gratifications.

Those who are negative about television look at many areas defenders do, but from a somewhat different perspective. At what point does cultural unification become cultural homogenization? When does moralizing become brainwashing? These are not easy questions to answer. Let me review some of the criticisms commonly leveled at television:

It is a narcotic and leads to addiction.

It promotes escapism.

It appeals to the lowest common denominator. This approach is taken to secure as large an audience as possible so networks can charge higher prices to run commercials.

It distorts life.

It is overly sentimental and violent and exploits sexuality.

It trivializes everything. Much programming is mindless, repetitive, and uncreative.

It bombards us with commercials. These commercials disrupt our sense of continuity and foster consumer lust as well as powerful feelings of relative deprivation in those who cannot afford to buy all the so-called good things of life.

It arouses anxieties in us. TV does not, however, offer us adequate relief to these anxieties and we are left in a disturbed state. TV overstimulates us while at the same time promoting passivity.

It encourages privatism and alienation.

These two lists indicate the general contours of the great debate about television.

The factor that weighs most heavily here is *volume*—the incredible amount of time devoted to this medium by viewers. Even if only some of the criticisms of television are correct, the amount of viewing time gives us good reason to be apprehensive. Although people do not always pay strict attention to the set when it is on and often more than one person at a time views television in a given household, people do not relate to one another in significant ways while watching TV. The following statistics suggest what a powerful force television is:

- By age 16, the average child has spent 4,000 *more* hours in front of a television set than in the classroom. This adds up to about 16,000 hours of television viewing.
- By this time he or she will have viewed more than 640,000 commercials, many of which advertise food products with high sugar content.
- The average American is exposed to approximately 150 commercials a day and 1,100 commercials per week. This adds up to more than nine hours per week.
- There are approximately 720 commercial television stations in

America and they broadcast some 4.7 million hours of programming (on an estimated 18-hour day).
In the average household the television set is normally on 47.41
hours per week (1).

To an alarming degree, then, television *is* our leisure time.

Marxist critics argue that the mass media are agents of social control
and manipulation directed by the dominant, or ruling, class in society.

> Applied to any aspect of culture, Marxist methods seek to explicate the
> manifest and latent or coded reflections of modes of material production,
> ideological values, class relations and structures of social power—racial or
> sexual as well a politico-economic—or the state of consciousness of people in
> a precise historical or socio-economic situation. . . . The Marxist method,
> recently in varying degrees of combination with structuralism and semiology,
> has provided an incisive analytic tool for studying the political signification of
> every facet of contemporary culture, including popular entertainment in TV
> and films, music, mass circulation books, newspaper and magazine features,
> comics, fashion, tourism, sports and games as well as such acculturating in-
> stitutions as education, religion, the family and child rearing, social and sex-
> ual relations between men and women—all the patterns of work, play and
> other customs of everyday life. . . . The most frequent theme in Marxist
> cultural criticism is the way the prevalent mode of production and ideology of
> the ruling class in any society dominates every phase of culture, and, at pre-
> sent, the way capitalist production and ideology dominate American culture,
> along with that of the rest of the world that American business and culture
> have colonized. This domination is perpetuated both through overt propagan-
> da in political rhetoric, news reporting, advertising and public relations, and
> through often unconscious absorption of capitalistic values by creators and
> consumers in all the above aspects of the culture of everyday life (4).

Since television is the dominant medium in American society, it is
supremely responsible for the manipulation of people and for the generation and maintenance of alienation. According to the Marxists, this alienation fuels the fires of consumerism and distracts people from identifying
and fulfilling their true interests.

From the Marxist perspective, the psychological problems that many
people have are rooted in the social and economic system. Thus, television
addiction and its correlates—alienation, passivity (political as well as
physical), anxiety, privatism, and a host of others—are spawned by social
and economic arrangement. The ways in which these "symptoms of
malaise" are generated are complicated; the economic system does not
simply "determine" culture—a position held by the so-called vulgar Marxists—but it does affect culture profoundly.

One need not be a Marxist to accept some of the insights of Marxist
critical thought. If they or the radical critics are correct, and I believe that
their argument is strong, our means of dealing with television addiction will

be different from what they would be were excessive TV watching defined as a purely personal problem. It is very difficult for Americans, who have a strong sense of individualism, to see any addiction as having social, cultural, and economic roots. Furthermore, one addict, no matter what the addiction, does not represent a social problem, and in general each addict tends to see his or her behavioral excess as unique. Yet each addiction is part of an elaborate system of cultural, social, and economic arrangements that foster or facilitate certain behavioral excesses—in the most obvious way by making addictive substances or activities available.

A Closer Look at TV Addiction

The language used in writing about television is full of drug jargon. Many people look upon television watching as a "mild addiction"; television "junkies" are "hooked" on television and experience "withdrawal symptoms" if they cannot watch TV. A television set in need of repair is returned to the customer in an average of three days. Evidently, being deprived of television for longer is considered a minor catastrophe. Let us now look closer at this addiction.

The Detroit Experiment

The *Detroit Free Press* wanted to see what would happen when people went without television for a month and offered to pay them $500 to participate in an experiment on TV deprivaton. The paper picked 25 names from the telephone book certain it would have more than enough people to insure a good socioeconomic mix; the *Free Press* eventually approached 120 households but was turned down by more than 90:

> A couple that gives up all television watching for a month is likely to suffer nervous withdrawal symptoms. They may also read more, listen to the radio more, and possibly spend more time together in bed. In Detroit, five such couples also are $500 richer for their withdrawal pains. The money came from the Detroit Free Press, a newspaper that wanted to investigate the effect of going cold turkey on television watching by paying five families $500 to let the repairmen come in and disconnect their sets for a month. [An experimenter] "was surprised that there really did seem to be an addiction to television with serious withdrawal symptoms. Some of these people literally went crazy. They didn't know how to cope" (5).

One couple was described as television junkies who averaged 70 hours of viewing per week. When deprived of television both husband and wife became markedly nervous, as indicated by increased smoking and complaints of headache. However, the couple also went out more, talked more, read more, played with their children more, and spent more time in bed, not necessarily sleeping.

Most of the other families acknowledged difficulties but managed to adapt. All were pleased to resume TV watching when the experiment ended, though one couple, the most affluent, cut down on their viewing time. The reported increase in sexual activity is noteworthy: is television leading us to become scopophiliacs, who derive sexual gratification from looking rather than loving? Is celluloid "wiggle and jiggle" and "tits and ass" somehow replacing our interest in the real thing?

Chance (alias Chauncey Gardiner)

Chance is the hero of Jerzy Kosinski's brilliant novel *Being There* (6). He is a symbolic figure whose life tells us a great deal about the role of television in society. Chance, so named because he was born by chance of a mother with a damaged mind (like his), lives on a big estate. He has no family name nor is there any record that he exists. He lives with an old man, a person of some mystery. All Chance does is work in the garden and watch television. He cannot read or write.

When the old man dies, Chance must leave the house. Shortly thereafter he is hit by a car. The driver, E. E. Rand, the wife of a wealthy industrialist, asks Chance his name. He answers, "Chance, the gardener," which she mistakenly hears as "Chauncey Gardiner." She takes him to her home, where he stays until his injury heals.

All that Chance knows about the world comes from television, but that seems to be enough to carry him along. In the course of a few days he meets the president of the United States, appears on television, and becomes such a sensation that the end of the tale finds Chance being considered for the vice-presidency, in part because he has no background and thus cannot be objectionable to anyone.

Kosinski implies that we are not that different from Chance. And Chance may be the norm in the future—a "vidiot" living on the thin surface of life, with no relationships, no history, no pleasures save those of the garden and the television set.

An Explanation of Excessive Viewing

Interest has recently focused on "uses and gratifications" research, which studies not the effects (real or alleged) of television (and other media) but the ways people use this medium and the gratification they derive

FIGURE 15-1.
Focal Points in Media Analysis

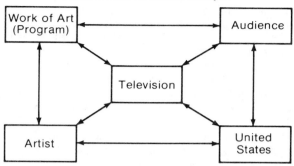

therefrom (7). Whereas audience research studies have tended to concentrate on reactions of audiences to programs without much concern for the way different aspects of programs generate meaning, uses and gratifications research takes into account the thematic content of programs, esthetic matters, powers and limitations of media, and the numerous needs we all have and the gratifications we seek (Figure 15-1).

Obviously, a medium as much a part of our lives as television must be supplying a number of gratifications to large groups of people. To be more precise, the programs carried by the medium (and, if McLuhan is correct, the medium itself) deal with our needs, fears, and desires and help satisfy them in various ways. Hyde identified some of the more important needs and desires (to be gratified not only by television, however):

The need for fictitious models of agents and actions.
The need to experience the beautiful.
The need or desire to experience the ugly.
The need for periodic spiritual cleansing.
The need to be purged of unpleasant emotions.
The need to see order imposed on the world.
The need to have shared experiences with others.
The need to share in the sufferings of others.
The need to be distracted from the realities of life.
The need to feel "informed."
The need for vicarious, and controlled, emotional experiences.
The need to explore taboo subjects with impunity.
The need to live vicariously in a world of significance, intensity, and larger-than-life-size people.
The need or desire to believe that spiritual or moral values are more important than is mere physical existence.
The need to believe that spiritual or moral values are more important than material goods.

The need to see authority figures exalted.

The need to see authority figures deflated.

The desire to see others make mistakes.

The need or desire to feel superior to a societal deviant.

The need to find outlets for the sex-drive in a guilt-free context.

The desire to believe in romantic love.

The desire to believe that meaningful existence is not cancelled out by death.

The need to identify with the Deity and the Divine Plan.

The desire to believe in the miraculous.

The desire to experience, in a guilt-free arena, the extreme emotions of love and hate.

The need to confront, in a controlled situation, the horrible and the terrible.

The desire to see evil punished and virtue rewarded.

The desire to imagine oneself a hero or heroine.

The desire to see villains in action.

The desire to believe in "the good old days."

The desire to be amused (8).

Evidently, television is a functional alternative to religion, public ceremonies, schools, and many other institutions important earlier in American society. But are the gratifications offered effective and to what degree does television take care of peoples' needs in positive and humane ways? Critics of television would argue that TV uses the public airwaves to exploit and manipulate people in the worst possible ways (for reasons dealt with earlier).

I suggest that excessive television watching occurs because we become caught in a vicious cycle in which television creates the very dependencies that we are trying to overcome through its use. Events during childhood disturb us and generate fear of becoming adults and being involved in grown-up conflicts. These fears are reinforced or exacerbated by television. Fairy tales and folk tales are very functional for children, helping them to deal with conflicts at *their* level. Television, on the other hand, exposes children to problems too difficult for them, which may be responsible for their often becoming psychologically stunted. This fear of growing up is costly: large numbers of young people find themselves unable to have sustained emotional relationships (9). This incapacity for emotional involvement leads, in turn, to promiscuous sex, fear of marriage, egocentric behavior, etc.—an unsatisfying lifestyle that needs escape mechanisms such as drugs and television. Since television is readily available and socially sanctioned, it becomes a major vehicle to obtain, even if only vicariously, gratifications. Watching television becomes our means to escape from imprisonment within ourselves. It provides vicarious experiences to fulfill the various needs we have. But television also activates the very fears and apprehensions that initially led to our television watching. In other words, TV provides relief from the anxieties it simultaneously arouses.

Treatment

How can something as trivial, banal, and silly as television be a danger to our health and well-being? As I argued earlier, television is a social and cultural force of awesome power whose importance extends far beyond its value as an entertainment medium. People often fail to recognize the significance of ubiquitous features of their environment—e.g., television—and certain myths prevent us from seeing television in its true light. For example, we assume that the federal government would not allow television if it were dangerous and that networks are responsible and would not broadcast anything they knew to be in any way harmful. In addition, we overestimate our ability to exercise restraint and self-control. "You can always turn off the set," we are told, but this is often more easily said than done especially when children are involved. Thus, although Action for Children's Television and some individuals in government, the universities, and the media are concerned about the dangers inherent in TV, the public largely takes television for granted, assuming it to be benign. Some steps could be taken to lessen the influence of television on our lives.

Children should not be allowed to watch more than one hour per day, or a total of seven hours per week, of television. This means, of course, that parents cannot use television as a babysitter, that they will have to spend more time with their children, and that children will have to discover other ways of amusing themselves, such as playing with friends, reading, and working on hobbies.

In order to enforce this rule, parents must have control over the set. If placing the television where the parents can control it is inconvenient, a plug lock can be purchased. Once children realize their limit, they will stop arguing and become quite selective about what they watch. Each child can be assigned a different hour and though there are scheduling conflicts, these can be resolved.

Adults should learn how to watch television selectively and not allow television to dominate their leisure time. This means we should not look upon television viewing as our typical evening activity. When we do watch, we should tune in only the programs we want to see and not fill in the gaps between these programs with shows we do not really care for. This, of course, requires willpower. Once we turn on the set, we find ourselves strangely reluctant to turn it off: what will we do with the gaps between programs?

Those who analyze institutions or activities in terms of their functions and dysfunctions have a useful concept: functional alternatives. An activity like television watching is clearly functional in certain ways. As such, it cannot be modified or controlled unless a satisfactory alternative exists. That is, unless we can find other means to meet the needs television satisfies, we will never be able to overcome our addiction. I suggest as the functional alternative to excessive television a lifestyle in which television is nor perceived as a necessary component. Modern-day existence has *programmed* us to excessive TV viewing. We must reorganize our leisure time priorities so that television watching becomes one of many options—and not necessarily at the top of the list. As one kind of activity in a diverse group, television becomes a preference rather than a need.

To complement and assist these efforts, the federal government could take a stronger position vis-à-vis the television industry. For example, the government could mandate that we not be overly exposed to violent or otherwise antisocial and potentially destructive programming. Of course, government censorship and/or control of television or other media is to be feared, but does free speech mean that young children should be enticed into eating junk food or that the viewing public be heavily exposed to violence and sexual exploitation? Oftentime to avoid these messages we must avoid television altogether: what about freedom *from* as well as freedom *to*?

Finally, the schools must turn their attention to media literacy as well as print literacy, with a particular focus on television since it is the dominant medium of our time. Children must be made aware of how television affects people—its psychological, social, political, and economic aspects. When media literacy courses become more common, children, adolescents, and even adults should accordingly be harder to manipulate (for example, research suggests that children can be taught to resist commercials).

Conclusion

We watch an immoderate amount of television, and each year the numbers go up. The quantity of commercials we are exposed to each day is by itself cause for grave concern. Every year, billions of dollars are spent to make us act in certain ways. That such manipulation may be extremely destructive often has been discussed.

Television is not simply an entertainment medium but is a social and cultural force of great power and subtlety that operates in ways many people may not understand. A large number of Americans have become dependent on television and are, in effect, addicted to it. However, since we do not as a rule define television viewing as an addiction, people do not define themselves as addicts. The terms used to discuss viewing behavior nevertheless suggest subliminal awareness of this status.

We must deal with television by limiting our exposure to it and by studying it. We must deprogram ourselves and restructure our lifestyles so that television does not occupy the central position it now enjoys. The government also has clear responsibilities in this area.

I am afraid of television. I am concerned about its psychological and social consequences. We must remember that television carries programs, but only immediately so. It also carries, through these programs, *culture,* and not necessarily the best, most positive, humane culture available to us. Since culture, as I understand it, can be defined as a collection of codings, of which we are frequently unaware, we may be in the process of being changed by this medium in dramatic ways that we do not recognize and whose ultimate effects we cannot anticipate.

References

1. Surgeon General's Scientific Advisory Committee on Television and Society, *Television and Growing Up: The Impact of Televised Violence.* Report to the Surgeon General, United States Public Health Service, Washington, D. C.: GPO 1972.
2. Comstock, G., Chaffee, S., Katzman, N., McCombs, M., and Roberts, D., *Television and Human Behavior,* Columbia University Press, New York, 1978.
3. Gerbner, G., Testimony before the National Commission on the Causes and Prevention of Violence, 1968.
4. Lazere, D., Mass culture, political consequences, and English studies, *College English 38,* 755–756 (1977).
5. Tube unplugged: five families describe painful ordeal, *San Francisco Sunday Examiner and Chronicle,* Jan. 8, 1978.
6. Kosinski, J., *Being There,* Bantam, New York, 1972.
7. Blumler, J., and Katz, E., eds., *The Uses of Mass Communications: Current Perspectives on Gratifications Research,* Sage, Beverly Hills, Cal., 1974, and Frank, R., Greenberg, M., eds., *The Public's Use of Television: Who Watches and Why,* Sage, Beverly Hills, Cal., 1980.
8. Hyde, S., Course materials for Broadcast Communication Arts 321: Analysis of the Public Arts, San Francisco State University, mimeograph 1973.
9. Hendin, H., *The Age of Sensation,* Norton, New York, 1975.

Selected Bibliography

Barnouw, E. *The Sponsor: Notes on a Modern Potentate.* New York: Oxford University Press, 1978.

Berger, A. A. *Pop Culture.* Dayton: Pflaum/Standard. 1973.

———*The TV-Guided American.* New York: Walker & Co. 1975.

———*Television as an Instrument of Terror: Essays on Media, Popular Culture and Everyday Life.* Rutgers, N. J.: Transaction Books. 1979.

Goldsen, R. K. *The Show and Tell Machine: How Television Works You Over*. New York: Delta Books, 1978.

McLuhan, M. *Understanding Media: The Extensions of Man*. New York: McGraw-Hill. 1965.

Real, M. R. *Mass-Mediated Culture*. Englewood Cliffs, N.J.: Prentice-Hall, Inc. 1977.

Schwartz, T. *The Responsive Chord*. Garden City, N.Y.: Anchor Books. 1974.

Williams, R. *Television: Technology and Cultural Form*. New York: Schocken Books. 1975.

16

Compulsive or Excess Sports

G. Hartley Hartung

Emile J. Farge

The topic of excess or compulsive sports may seem out of place among the other disorders discussed in this volume. Indeed, for the majority of persons, sports participation is an enhancement of life rather than a detriment. It is perhaps not widely recognized that excesses in sports or other physical activities even exist. To our knowledge, this is the first treatment of the topic in the professional literature; hence, many of the ideas presented have not been tested experimentally. This does not mean that the material lacks scientific merit but rather our attempt to use a multidisciplinary approach to the problem has no precedent.

Our assumption is a psychobiological one. Morgan reported that over 50 percent of all medical and surgical patients suffer from illnesses that are primarily emotional in nature and more than half of these conditions are depressive disorders (1). It hardly needs to be defended that low physical states lead to low psychological states and vice versa. Scholars in diverse fields have investigated this relationship at length and journals such as *Psychosomatic Research, Psychosomatic Medicine, Psychophysiology, and Psychopharmacology* are concerned primarily with biological and psychological connections.

Evidence accumulating over the past several years indicates that lifestyle has a great impact on mental health. Both long-term and acute physical activities have been linked to greater stability and less anxiety (2). Questions must arise, however, concerning the degree of physical stress or exercise and effects on mental health and illness, especially the point at which physical stress becomes excessive or compulsive.

Excess might be compared to negative addiction, in which the individual is willing "to give up principles, ideas, family, friends, or spouse; nothing in life is allowed to stand, against the . . . addiction. He lives by one set of values which is that whatever promotes his addiction is right, everything else is wrong" (3). Our notion of excess involves surpassing or going beyond sufficiency, necessity, or duty or exceeding what is usual, proper, or proportionate.

Our notion of compulsion includes behaviors marked by forced action or assent. Compulsion bespeaks an irresistible impulse to perform an irrational act, the performance of which tends to disturb a neurotic doer but not a psychotic.

By sport we mean any physical activity involving individual skill or physical prowess and further we distinguish primary and secondary sports. Primary sports are the more physical forms, involving use of bodily function quite beyond that in ordinary activities such as walking or driving. Hence, running, tennis, skiing, and contact sports (football, soccer, etc.) are primary sports while golf, horseshoes, and bowling are secondary sports.

Bearing these definitions in mind, we consider compulsive sports to be undue participation in physical activities that the majority of persons call sports or games. Undue participation can mean either overly long, intense, or frequent indulgence or the disregard of contraindications such as the presence of disease or discomfort. Compulsive sport can be motivated either neurotically (conscious) or psychotically (unconscious).

Overexertion has some obvious signs: tightness or pain in the chest, severe breathlessness, light-headedness, dizziness, loss of muscle control, and nausea. Cooper cautioned that when one experiences any of these symptoms one should stop exercising immediately because the workout is too vigorous (4). He counseled a subsequent reduction in the intensity or duration of the activity. Psychological manifestations of overexertion include poor eating or sleeping habits, lack of interest in family and other social contacts, or alienation from work.

By the mid-1980s distance running will be the most heavily pursued sport. To the occasional chagrin of comrades, colleagues, and family members, millions of persons who began by running or jogging short distances apparently have become highly dedicated to this avocation. Running has attracted a great deal of scholarly as well as popular interest. The physical stresses are studied frequently (5–7). The relationship of physiological and psychological traits in runners also has received considerable attention (8–10). Nevertheless, there is no shortage of controversy on running and exertion, specifically on possible cardiac advantages and disadvantages. Bassler and Opie are at odds in this area: Bassler contends that he could not document a single death from ischemic heart disease among marathon finishers of any age (11, 12); Opie, however, argues that even the best trained runner is not exempt from heart disease and death from overexertion (13, 14).

Genesis of the Disorder

The origins of the disorder of overexerting through running, or indeed through other forms of physical activity, are not well studied. In the context of compulsive sports, however, some conjectures are warranted. Table 16-1 shows how compulsive or excessive sportsmanship might progress from early success in the sporting endeavor, through increased investment in the sport and reinforcement by others (of the involvement), to confusion of means and ends, excessive participation, illness or injury, and finally reappraisal and either moderation or abandonment of the activity or continued excess.

Often the decision to take up a sport is based on vague dissatisfaction with a sedentary lifestyle. Stories of the reluctant novice shooting a 10-point buck and suddenly becoming a confirmed hunter are legion. Tennis players, oarsmen, and skiers also get hooked by early success. In the case of running or jogging such success can be attained very soon because these sports do not require combined skills such as hand-eye coordination (as does squash) or especial muscular strength (as does rowing or cross-country skiing); the initial success can be privately measured by the individual running a mile without stopping or jogging for half an hour.

TABLE 16-1

1	Inactivity ↓	Sedentary lifestyle
2	Initial success ↓	Self-satisfaction from participation
3	Increased investment ↓	More time and money committed; lifestyle changes to support participation
4	Reinforcement from others ↓	Approval from peers or authority figures of some aspects(s) of the practice
5	Confusion of means and ends ↓	Approval of *outcome* of the practice confused with need to pursue the sport
6	Excessive participation ↓	Means has become an end; the sport overshadows other activities
7	Illness or injury ↓	Acute or chronic problems associated with excess
8	Reappraisal ↓	Examination of time, money, interest devoted to the sport
9	Return to 1	Decison to end participation
	Return to 3	Decision to moderate practice
	Return to 6	Decision to proceed at excessive level
	Vacillation among 1, 3, and 6	Alternating abandonment, moderation, or indulgence

The third step toward excess involves a heavier investment in the sport in terms of time and money. When a new activity, perceived as beneficial, begins to affect one's family and social life, it is obviously important to the participant. In a humorous effort to describe the runner as perhaps enmeshed in the sick roll, Hessler posed a set of 10 questions (see Table 16-2) based on the Alcoholics Anonymous test for dependence (15).

The fourth step toward developing an obsessive attitude toward sports entails the reinforcements that the participant receives for achievements related to the sporting endeavor, for example, a friend's compliment on weight loss. Entrance into a new subculture is another reinforcement. Taking up a sport is a social event, either directly or indirectly. Duo or team sports are by definition social. Running can also be a social experience: many choose to work out with companions. Even if one is a solitary runner, however, running provides certain entry into conversations, social situations, and many other opportunities for interaction.

The first steps have taken a participant into new activities and a new lifestyle. If involvement continues at this level, the sport will remain a rewarding and satisfying experience. If, however, the fifth step is taken, the participant may well become unbalanced and compulsive. At this point confusion between means and ends occurs. The sport becomes one's goal rather than a route to physical and psychological well-being.

In the sixth step sports participation becomes excessive. The confusion between means and end is complete. Other activities, such as work and

TABLE 16-2

1. Has another person mentioned your spouse's running behavior?
2. Have you ever been embarrassed by your spouse's running behavior?
3. Are holidays more of a nightmare than a celebration because of your spouse's running behavior?
4. Does your spouse's running make the atmosphere in the home tense and anxious?
5. Are most of your spouses's friends running fanatics?
6. Do you find it necessary to lie to employer, relatives, or friends in order to hide your spouse's running behavior?
7. Has your spouse ever failed to remember what occurred during a period of running?
8. Has your spouse denied how far he/she has run on a given day?
9. Are you afraid of physical or verbal abuse when you confront your spouse about running?
10. Does your spouse have periods of smugness after a running occasion and criticize non-runners for their perceived torpor?

Source: Reprinted with permission from *Runner's World* Magazine, 1400 Stierlin Road, Mountain View, Ca. 94043

personal relationships, are subordinated to the sport. The participant's willingness to sacrifice other parts of his or her life is now clearly established and the addiction is in charge.

If allowed to continue, the participant moves to the seventh step, illness or injury; for example, physiological symptoms, such as cardiovascular problems or foot problems (shin splints, sprained ankles, "runner's knee"), or other manifestations, either chronic or acute.

The illness or injury leads the participant to assess his or her behavior. Here, some soul-searching begins and advice may be sought from a friend or a professional counselor. Perhaps days spent in disability will remind the practitioner of what life was like before the activity entered his or her life. At this point, the contrast between a sedentary lifestyle and one in which athletics has become all-consuming is very apparent.

After this review, the practitioner will either consider the activity totally inappropriate and give up the sport or opt for moderation. In some cases, however, the practitioner continues to confuse means and ends and will return to excessive activity.

A final variation is vacillation among termination, moderation, and excessive participation. The person may become unpredictable and erratic. In this case the exercise regimen, which for most people is a stabilizing force, becomes the unwitting source of instability.

While the preceding discussion has described the evolution of the disorder of excessive sports, the factors that cause a person to turn a beneficial, healthy activity into obsessive-compulsive behavior have not been elucidated. Glasser suggested that the first step in the etiology of addiction involves "giving up" (3). A certain subset of the society, according to Glasser, does not have the strength to deal with the inadequacies that every person experiences. (these inadequacies may be related to inability to succeed on the job or in other areas of endeavor; perceived lack of challenge in one's life; or lack of success in relating socially). By focusing more and more on their inadequacies, these people lose track of their strengths and, in an effort to relieve the miserable feelings engendered by a sense of helplessness, they give up. This helplessness frequently leads to the development of symptomatology to support the inadequacies. The individual may exhibit psychiatric (psychosis, paranoia, hallucinations) or psychosomatic symptoms like headaches, neckaches, backaches, or sinus trouble. Here the inadequacies are vested in the disease process, be it mental or physical. The result is that the person has created a syndrome that has a name, a treatment, and a specialist to deal with it.

The first two stages quite often result in addiction. Here one finds that by performing a particular act (drinking alcohol, taking medications, engaging in exercise) the symptoms can be relieved. Pain is gone for the moment—sometimes replaced by pleasurable experience. This "shot" of pleasure, which can come through exercise, temporarily relieves the symptomatology, enabling the person to sleep better, to enjoy eating more, or not to experience feelings of inadequacy and depression.

An additional factor in excessive exercises may be historical. In a highly leisured society that lacks frontiers to explore, people may be turning to risky sports such as hang-gliding, sky-diving, or mountain climbing in a quest for excitement. Extreme tests of endurance in running, swimming, and other tamer sports may serve a similar function.

Biomedical Correlates

Exercise (sport in the broad sense) is necessary for well-being and possibly for survival (16). The deleterious physiological effects of extended bed rest and extreme inactivity are well-known (17). There is presently some disagreement as to optimal exercise levels for maintaining well-being and/or reducing the risk of heart disease (18).

Stress is necessary to healthy functioning. For example, stress on the long bones of the legs prevents loss of bone minerals, as occurs with prolonged immobility. The circulatory system must be stressed by lengthy exercise in order to promote adaptations that increase the heart's efficiency. Yet excess stress from overexertion can cause problems ranging from general fatigue to organ or system failure.

The cardiovascular system is highly adaptable but unaccustomed stress can seriously disturb its normal functioning. Individuals who begin to exercise in middle age or later may manifest coronary disease that has been developing silently over years of relative inactivity (Table 16–3). Many jogging or exercise deaths (reported in the press) no doubt resulted from long-standing problems that became significant only during periods of increased demand on the heart. Also, a cardiac sudden death syndrome during exercise has been described in people without coronary blockage when cardiac electrical dysfunction caused ventricular fibrillation (19). For individuals in whom coronary disease is advanced, endurance exercise such as marathon running may slow the progression of illness, although exercise will not guarantee protection from heart attack or sudden cardiac death (20). The incidence of exercise related deaths seems to be increasing, probably in response to the growing number of persons beginning exercise programs in the middle or later years.

Even in chronically active younger individuals, excess physical activity may increase both the total mass and wall thickness of the heart and aortic blood pressure (21). In individuals engaged in chronic endurance training, electrocardiograph abnormalities such as first- and second-degree atrioventricular block, altered ventricular conduction, and repolarization alterations are not uncommon (22). These athletes frequently have sinus bradycardia and vagal tone related dysrrhythmias as well (23).

TABLE 16-3
Biomedical Effects of Excess Exercise

SOMATIC AREA	EFFECT
Cardiovascular	↑ Ventricular wall thickness ↑ Heart volume EKG abnormalities Dysrhythmias
Muscular-skeletal	Sprains, strains Stress fractures Traumatic fractures Joint stresses
Hormonal	Amenorrhea, oligomenorrhea ↓ Adrenal output
Renal	Proteinuria Hemoglobinuria Myoglobinuria
Other	Asthma Nerve trauma Dehydration Hyperthermia Gastrointestinal distress

The long-term cardiovascular consequences of excess physical activity are not known at this time. An autopsy of a famous marathon runner showed no marked cardiac abnormalities in a man who had raced for 49 years (24). Other studies have found that some adaptations disappear following cessation of training while other changes remain through later life (21, 22).

The muscular and skeletal systems are especially vulnerable to overuse in sports. Fractures and other traumatic bone injuries may occur in individuals who engage in contact or semicontact sports inappropriate for their age or physical condition. Stress fractures are common in the lower extremities of runners and joggers who run excessively on hard surfaces or increase mileage too rapidly. Bursitis and tendonitis plague tennis and racketball players and discus throwers whereas these conditions are found in the lower extremities of runners, high jumpers, and basketball players. Many such cases are aggravated by structural or functional abnormalities in the bones or joints involved. For example, congenital leg length discrepancy, which normally does not cause problems, may produce chronic pain in the hip or knee of the distance runner.

Severe endurance exercise accompanied by dehydration may produce an exhaustion syndrome resulting from adrenal deficiency: depletion of catecholamines and corticosteroids is variously described as tropical lethargy, heat sensitivity, and staleness in endurance athletes. Specific symptoms include hypotension, fatigue, apathy, depression, confusion, hypoglycemia (periodic), and ataxia.

Women engaging in chronic strenuous exercise may experience temporary suspension of menstruation (oligomenorrhea or amenorrhea); while the exact cause of these menstrual changes is not known, they tend to occur during the competitive season, when exercise is heaviest, and resolve themselves off-season.

Lengthy, heavy exercise may acutely disturb kidney function in otherwise healthy subjects. Protein and hemoglobin in the urine are often found during or after prolonged exercise. The cause of these findings is not clear, and only in rare cases does renal damage occur. These conditions normally reverse themselves within several hours to several days following a severe exercise bout. In some cases, however, cellular enzyme or electrolyte deficiencies may result in muscle damage and leakage of myoglobin into the plasma, thereby causing acute kidney dysfunction.

Numerous other types of problems may be initiated or aggravated by excessive sports participation. Sheehan's identification of gastrointestinal problems in runners could apply to other sportsmen as well (26). Exercise induced asthma and traumatic and functional nerve disorders, although less common, indicate that no body system is immune to the trauma attendant on excess activity.

Physical, Psychological, and Behavioral Correlates

As pointed out earlier, the body has a clear need for physical exertion. Such needs vary from individual to individual and change over the person's lifetime. Table 16-4 broadly summarizes the correlates of normal and excessive (which might be excessively low or excessively high) sports participation.

Biological Indications

The most obvious consequence of exercise is that the person feels good. With excessive (low or high) activity, the person more often will be sick, feel rundown, or have general physical problems.

An inappropriate exercise regimen usually is associated with a poor diet and perhaps poor attitudes toward eating. Sleeping habits are also affected by exercise level. Moderate exercise generally makes falling asleep easier and helps the participant feel rested and refreshed upon awakening. One who is sluggish from overindulgence in sports or from an overly sedentary lifestyle will feel less satisfied with any amount of sleep. Finally, par-

TABLE 16-4

Correlates of Sports Participation by Activity Level

	NORMAL	EXCESSIVE
Biological	Feels good Eats well; enjoys food Sleeps well; feels refreshed upon awakening Feels satisfied during and after usual level of sports participation	Frequently sick; feels run down, dragged out Poor diet; meals are a chore Tired in the morning; drugged feeling Lack of satisfaction associated with excessive exertion
Psychological	Feeling of integrity Peaceful after sports participation Returns to other activities refreshed from sports	Scattered feeling; unsatisfied or frustrated Often agitated that sports activity did not go well Frustrated; resentful toward next activity
Social	Relates well and evenly to significant others (spouse, children, etc.) Relates intimately with others in a predictable manner Has friends outside network of sports participation	Uneven relations with or resentment toward significant others Intimacy depends on satisfaction with sports achievement Friends exclusively among sports participants
Occupational	Interested in work Sports participation stimulates on-the-job performance Heightened ambition	Increasingly uninterested in work Sports activity causes alienation from job responsibilities Diminished ambition

ticipation in tennis, running, squash, handball, or other active sports is pleasurable to the subject, who afterward feels physically refreshed and relaxed, then the level of activity is likely to be appropriate.

Psychological Indications

Normal and appropriate physical activity will yield a feeling of bodily and mental integrity. The excessively sedentary or excessively active person will not experience such body-mind unity. Moreover, moderate exercise is followed by tranquility or peace of mind. When one is overly competitive or active in sports, agitation can remain after the exercise is over. The individual may be very concerned either with comparing his or her performances over time or with measuring his or her efforts against those of co-participants. Finally, whatever the demands of subsequent activities, the individual's ability to approach these situations refreshed, rather than frustrated and resentful, is a function of the level of sports participation. One who is excessively involved in exercise will be incapable of attending to various social, professional, or psychological needs following the sports activity.

Social Indications

A person who participates to an appropriate degree in sports should relate well to significant others. The mental well-being consequent upon physical well-being facilitates interpersonal encounters. Intimacy is very difficult, however, when physical exercise leads to frustration. Last, when an individual's social life includes only other sports participants, excessive dependence on the sport is likely.

Occupational Indications

Moderate exercise improves work performance and heightens interest in, and motivation toward, one's job. Excessive involvement in sports has opposite results, alienating the individual from the occupational context and responsibilities.

Therapy

There is no unique treatment for patients who engage to excess in sports. Indeed, many therapeutic efforts try to motivate the sedentary person to begin a regimen of physical activity, which will benefit his or her health, and correctly so.

For patients excessively involved in sports the following guidelines are offered:

1. *Recognition* that participation in the sport has become excessive in terms of time, money, or interest.
2. *Admission* of the personal and social costs thereby suffered by the addict.
3. *Understanding* of the possible biological, psychological, social, and professional consequences of continued excess.
4. *Resolution* of the problem either by the patient alone or in conjunction with an appropriate therapist.
5. *Moderation* in the activity or *substitution* of other activities that the patient is able reasonably to pursue.

Conclusion

Exercise and active sports participation have diverse benefits that disappear with overexertion. The biological and psychosocial advantages of physical exercise have been known for some time. In the skeletal muscles, exercise increases the number of myofibrils (or contractile elements) as well as the amount of stored fuel for contraction. Training also improves transmission of nerve impulses to the muscle fibers and expands the capillary network, accomplishing a better nutrient and oxygen supply and more efficient waste removal. Changes in the cardiorespiratory system that accompany exercise include the following resting adaptations: decreased heart rate, increased stroke volume, increased blood volume, increased total hemoglobin, and increased weight, volume, and capillary density of the heart.

Morgan and Hammer showed that athletes tend to be extroverted and stable, as measured by the Eysenck Personality Inventory (27). Morgan, Roberts, and Feinerman found that over 85 percent of subjects tested experienced a sense of well-being at the close of exercise whether it was aerobic or anaerobic (28). Anxiety levels consistently were diminished in the subjects after exercise periods lasting approximately 45 minutes. In fact, exercise, and jogging in particular, has become a popular therapy for depression, anxiety, and other suboptimal psychological states.

The overindulgent athlete may experience numerous muscle, bone, and joint injuries, ranging from serious fractures to minor but nagging muscle strains or joint problems, as well as cardiovascular changes whose long-term consequences are unknown. Chronic overexercisers may also exhibit renal, pulmonary, hormonal, and various other dysfunctions than can be merely uncomfortable in some cases but life threatening in others. Such problems usually cause the participant to recognize the excess and discontinue the sport or reduce the level of activity. On the other hand, excess in the direction of inactivity is equally hazardous and a middle ground must be struck to achieve the maximum benefit from exercise.

References

1. Morgan, W. P., *Influence of Acute Physical Activity on Anxiety,* University of Wisconsin Ergophysiology Laboratory, Madison, 1974.
2. Morgan, W. P., Physical fitness and emotional health: a review, *Amer. Corrective Ther. J. 23,* 124–127 (1969).
3. Glasser, W., *Positive Addiction,* Harper, New York, 1976.
4. Cooper, K. H., *The Aerobics Way,* Evans, New York, 1978.
5. Sterchi, J. M., Stresses of distance racing, *Runners World 9,* (1974).
6. Ellestad, M. H., Allen, W., Wan, M. C. K., and Kemp, G. L., Maximal treadmill stress testing for cardiovascular evaluation, *Circulation 39,* 517–521 (1969).
7. Cooper, K. H., Pollock, M. L., Martin, R. P., White, S. R., Linnerud, A. C., and Jackson, A., Physical fitness levels vs. selected coronary risk factors, *JAMA 236,* 166–169 (1976).
8. Hartung, G. H., and Farge, E. J., Personality and physiological traits in middle-aged runners and joggers, *J. Gerontology 32,* 541–548 (1977).
9. Jette, M., Habitual exercisers: a blood serum and personality profile, *J. Sports Med. 3,* 12–17 (1975).
10. Morgan, W. P., and Costill, D. L., Psychological characteristics of the marathon runner, *J. Sports Med. and Phys. Fitness 12,* 42–46 (1972).
11. Bassler, T. J., Marathon running and immunity to heart disease, *Phys. Sports Med. 3,* 77–80 (1975).
12. Bassler, T. J., Marathon running and immunity to atherosclerosis, *Ann. N.Y. Acad. Sci. 301,* 579–592 (1977).
13. Opie, L. H., Heart disease in marathon runners, *N. Eng. J. Med. 294,* 1067 (1976).
14. Noakes, T. D., Opie, L. H., Rose, A. G., and Kleynhans, P. H. T., Autopsy-proved coronary atherosclerosis in marathon runners, *N. Eng. J. Med. 301,* 86–89 (1979).
15. Hessler, D., Is running an illness? *Runners World 11,* 56–57 (1976).
16. Astrand, P.-O., and Rodahl, K., Health and fitness, in *Textbook of Work Physiology,* McGraw-Hill, New York, 1970, chap. 18.
17. Saltin, B., Blomqvist, G., Mitchell, J. H., Johnson, R. L., Jr., Wildentlal, K., and Chapman, C. B., Response to exercise after bedrest and after training, *Circulation 38* (Suppl. 7), 1–78 (1968).
18. Klumpp, T. G., How much exercise to avoid heart attacks? *Med. Times 104,* 64–74 (1976).

19. Vouri, I., Makarainen, M., and Jaaskelainen, A., Sudden death and physical activity, *Cardiology 63,* 287–304 (1978).
20. Thompson, P. D., Stern, M. P., Williams, P., Duncan, K., Haskell, W. L., and Wood, P. D., Death during jogging or running, *JAMA 242,* 1265–1267 (1979).
21. Morganroth, J., and Maron, B. J., The athlete's heart syndrome: a new perspective, *Ann. N.Y. Acad. Sci. 301,* 931–941 (1977).
22. Kichtman, J., O'Rourke, R. A., Klein, A., and Karliner, J. S., Electrocardiogram of the athlete, *Arch. Int. Med. 132,* 763–770 (1973).
23. Welton, D. E., Mokotoff, D. M., Squires, W. G., Hartung, G. H., and Miller, R. R., Relationship of vagal-related arrhythmias to aerobic capacity in middle aged joggers and marathoners, *Circulation 60,* 15 (1979) (abstract).
24. Currens, J. H., and White, P. D., Half a century of running: clinical, physiologic, and autopsy findings in the case of Clarence de Mar ("Mr. Marathon"), *N. Eng. J. Med. 265,* 988–993 (1961).
25. Sulman, F. G., Pfeifer, Y., and Superstine, E., The adrenal exhaustion syndrome: an adrenal deficiency, *Ann. N.Y. Acad. Sci. 301,* 918–930 (1977).
26. Sheehan, G. A., An overview of overuse syndromes in distance runners, *Ann. N.Y. Acad. Sci. 301,* 877–880 (1977).
27. Morgan, W. P., and Hammer, W. M., Influence of competitive wrestling upon state anxiety, *Med. and Sci. in Sports 6,* 58–61 (1974).
28. Morgan, W. P., Roberts, J. A., and Feinerman, A. D., Psychologic effect of acute physical activity, *Arch. Psy. Med. and Rehab. 52,* 422–425 (1971).

PART
THREE

17

The Environmental Generation of Excessive Behavior

John L. Falk

Classification of various behaviors as excessive depends on who is calling the behavior deviant, what standards are being applied, and whether the environmental context of the behaviors is being taken into account. A common solution to classifying excessive behavior in terms of its origins is simply to assume that the activity stems from a deranged internal process of the "sick" individual. Consequently, therapeutic intervention to correct this personal pathological state would have to be medical or quasi-medical. The danger with this approach is that anything appearing negative or troublesome to those in power can be regarded as an individual's pathologic internal process—as an illness to be cured or a demon to be cast out. Failure to conform is then, by definition, an illness.

But it can be objected that behavioral excess is neither a quality of an act nor an extreme value along some inherent yardstick of behavior. Rather, it is an assessment of the behavior in terms of rules and sanctions applied by others. By this view, excess depends on how social controlling agencies regard the behavior and what sorts of consequences they impose (1).

Behavior that is excessive in only a statistical sense may be of scant interest if it has no serious medical or social consequences. We care little if someone drinks water excessively, or rolls huge balls out of odd lengths of string, or even watches six hours of television every day. Incongruous or mildly disruptive behavior will often be tolerated provided one's immediate medical status or social functioning remains uncompromised. We become concerned, however, when excessive behavior has negative medical or social consequences. Usually the medical problems evolve into social problems because the person becomes a burden on society in terms of financial dependency or hazardous behavior. In fact, when we care enough about the consequences of excessive acts, we make formal or informal rules about them. It is the breaking of these codified laws or implied rules of comportment that we find objectionable; in a sense, such transgression defines the behavior as excessive after the fact. But to remain consistent and dispassionate as investigators our interest in behavior in excess should remain universal. Exaggerated behavior that we happen to regard as objectionable is understandably of great interest, but it may not differ fundamentally from relatively innocuous excessive behavior that lacks negative consequences. Hence, the study of how excessive behavior in general is produced, not just rule breaking behavior, is likely to illuminate the origins of those activities that society deems grossly unacceptable.

This chapter, then, assumes that there are some basic commonalities among factors that give rise to a variety of behavioral excesses. The factors operate regardless of whether society at large finds one or another excess laudable or reprehensible. Hence, to elucidate the more general problems of the roots and persistence of excessive behavior, I will describe a rather interesting way in which a particular behavior becomes exaggerated.

An Unexpected Excessive Behavior

About two decades ago I began what I thought was a straightforward animal study. The experimental arrangement was simple (2). Rats were placed in individual chambers once a day and allowed to press on a microswitch lever to earn most of their daily ration of food. They were permitted to obtain enough food each day to maintain body weight at about 80 percent of their adult, free-feeding weight. An animal remained in the chamber for a little over three hours per day, pressing a lever that delivered a small (45 mg) food pellet at variable times, averaging one pellet per minute. Technically this is called a "variable-interval one-minute schedule": the animal is free to press the lever at any time, but a lever-press pays off (is reinforced) by the delivery of a food pellet only intermittently (from a few seconds to two minutes after the last press was reinforced). This schedule produced a moderate but persistent rate of pressing throughout each session.

Water was always available freely from a drinking spout both during the daily experimental session and in the home cage. Consequently, water deprivation never occurred. Yet I soon found that this schedule produced a curious and dramatic behavioral result: each animal drank an extreme amount of water during the daily session. As each pellet was earned, the animal would quickly eat and then drink about .5 ml water before resuming lever-pressing. This postpellet consumption of water resulted in an intake of over 90 ml each session. In a three-hour period daily, these animals were drinking approximately half their body weight in water. The 24-hour water intake of these rats prior to the start of the experiment (when food was not rationed) was about 27 ml. This elevated water ingestion was all the more impressive since the usual effect of food limitation in rats (and many other animals) is a decrease in water intake (3). So, overdrinking ("polydipsia") was anomalous.

One way of measuring the excessive degree of this polydipsic phenomenon was to give animals all the food pellets they ordinarily would receive during the daily session as a single large feeding and then measure how much water they drank over the next few hours. Under this condition, rats drank about one-tenth the amount of water that they ingested when the pellets were spread out over the same period of time under the variable-interval one-minute schedule (4).

The phenomenon was easily generated, then, by a simple intermittent feeding schedule. When animals were constrained with respect to access to food and feeding opportunities were dispersed in time by permitting each small pellet only after a certain interval had elapsed since provision of the previous pellet, then water intake increased tremendously. Traditional physiological, nutritional, and behavioral considerations could not explain the origin of this persistent polydipsia, which lasted month after month, as long as the intermittent feeding schedule remained in effect (5).

What Produces Schedule Induced Polydipsia?

I was fortunate to have done my dissertation research on water balance in rats. This background made me realize that the drinking I was observing in connection with the variable-interval one-minute schedule was bizarre. And with my interest in fluid balance I was happy to pursue the factors that produced this perversely unbalanced ingestive behavior. But my suspicion concerning this phenomenon was quickly confirmed: polydipsia did not indicate homeostatic, water balance adjustments (5, 6). To make this point, I shall review briefly various factors that *failed* to explain the overdrinking.

As previously described, food limitation itself did not increase water intake. Nor did these animals show impaired renal concentrating ability or insensitivity to vasopressin (5, 7). Physiologically, the animals were normal and their bouts of drinking could not be explained by body water needs. Their disposition to drink during the session had a curious, compulsive quality. First, the pattern of behavior was highly ritualized. Unlike the drinking produced by water deprivation or increased salt intake, this polydipsia was not mitigated by presession intubation of water into the stomach (5). Furthermore, rather large amounts of solutions usually rejected (e.g., hypertonic NaCl solutions) were ingested under these conditions (8).

A classic theory of thirst and drinking holds that the drying of the mucous membranes of the mouth and throat is the immediate stimulus to drinking. This venerable, but inadequate, notion was resurrected for a time to explain schedule induced polydipsia: perhaps each food pellet dried the animal's mouth momentarily and since the rat had nothing better to do between pellets, except a little lever-pressing, it chased down the food with water. While scheduled food pellets were swallowed with alacrity whether or not water was available during a three-hour session, this theory was inappropriate for another principal reason (5). Rats trained on the variable-interval one-minute schedule using a liquid diet, rather than dry pellets, became just as polydipsic when they received 22 mg portions of this food (one-third water by weight) during daily sessions (4). Clearly, a dry mouth was not a necessary condition for the production and maintenance of this overdrinking behavior.

The rule governing when a lever-press will be reinforced by the delivery of a bit of food on a variable-interval schedule insures that the longer an animal pauses, the greater is the probability that the next press will be reinforced. If drinking occurs such that the apparatus circuitry has readied a pellet for delivery on the very next lever-press, then a superstitious chain of behavior could be built up (9). This would involve the reinforcement of drinking since it precedes very closely in time the payoff of a lever-press. Shortly after the discovery of schedule induced polydipsia, some investigators surmised that the exaggerated drinking was an instance of superstitiously maintained behavior. Again, considerable evidence militated against this interpretation (5). For example, if the apparatus were arranged so that any drinking postponed by 15 seconds the possiblity that a lever-press would be reinforced, development of polydipsia typical of a variable-interval one-minute food schedule was unimpeded. Furthermore, as described previously, the drinking episodes occurred just *after* each pellet was consumed, not just before it was earned, as would be required by the theory of superstitiously maintained drinking.

Perhaps enough evidence has been presented to convince the reader that the conditions necessary for the production of schedule induced polydipsia are simple; however, no straightforward physiological or behavioral explanation for the behavior can be offered. Given this state of affairs, one must try to determine what factors yield the phenomenon.

What aspects of their living situation made these animals different from other normal laboratory dwellers? They were subject to only two unusual constraints: the amount of daily ration and the rate at which eating was permitted during a feeding session. I noted already that a reduced food ration does not in itself produce polydipsia. But it appears that the confluence of the two constraints does. What is the relation? First, let me cut through a few years of research and do some minor violence to the facts by stating that there is nothing magical or crucial about the variable-interval one-minute schedule in generating polydipsia. Diverse food delivery schedules have produced this behavior. Some of these manipulated the passage of time between reinforced lever-presses (food delivery); others required specified numbers of presses before one would be reinforced; still other schedules used untrained animals, eliminated lever-pressing, and delivered pellets at fixed time since the last delivery. The latter schedule, in which no lever-pressing was required, is called a "fixed time" schedule. All of these schedules induced polydipsia (6). The key factor was that consummatory behavior was spread out over time.

When this time factor was explored systematically, an effective temporal range for the induction of polydipsia became evident. For example, if standard 45 mg food pellets were used and rats were allowed to press to obtain each pellet at a fixed interval since the last pellet delivery, an orderly relation was found between the interpellet time set for the session and the amount of drinking. When a few sessions were given at each of several fixed-interval (interpellet time) values, the amount of water drunk increased linearly as a function of the fixed-interval value from two seconds up to two or three minutes but fell precipitously at the five minute value (10). Several investigators have confirmed this finding (11–14). There is a range of interpellet time values, then, associated with marked polydipsia, with the effect decreasing as one moves toward smaller or larger fixed-interval values. This relation constitutes a "bitonic function": sessions with either short or long intervals between pellet consumption produce normal amounts of drinking, while intermediate values induce polydipsia.

In most of the experiments cited, food rations were adjusted so that animals were maintained at about 80 percent of their normal weight. While the limitation of food does not in itself produce an increase in fluid intake, it is nevertheless possible that reduced body weight contributes to exaggerated drinking. Perhaps the increased disposition to eat proceeding from body weight reduction is a necessary, but not a sufficient, factor in the polydipsia produced by the intermediate range of interpellet times. This possibility was explored by allowing rats to lever-press for pellets on a fixed-interval 90-second schedule at 80 percent body weight to establish a strong, daily polydipsia. Then, body weights were permitted to rise slowly over a three-week period by daily increases in postsession food rations. When body weight reached 95 percent of the preexperimental level, polydipsia began to decrease. From about 100 ml water intake each session, intake decreased linearly as weight increased, until intake was only about 20 ml when weight reached roughly 105 percent (5). Even though the animals were lever-pressing at their usual rate and eating the food pellets avidly, increases in body weight beyond the 95 percent level led to progressive decreases in polydipsia. Subsequently, postsession food supplements were eliminated and body weights were allowed to decline once again to 80 percent. Polydipsia progressively increased, returning to former levels. If we estimate the disposition to eat from the percentage of body weight value, then we can say that within a specific range increases in the disposition to eat yield a linear increase in polydipsia given an effective interpellet value.

Although the inverse correlation between body weight and degree of

polydipsia has been confirmed by other investigators (15–17), it is possible
to miss important features of the excessive drinking by placing undue stress
on this correlation. While the evidence is clear that decreases in body
weight exaggerate the polydipsia, two lines of evidence indicate that this
behavior can be acquired and maintained under conditions approximating
normal body weight. Wayner and his associates showed that even after
polydipsic rats had been returned to free-feeding for months and body
weights had normalized, again placing them daily in the session environment with food pellet delivery resulted in a modest, but clearly defined,
polydipsic pattern (18, 19). Petersen and Lyon allowed rats to live in individual chambers in which they were exposed continuously to fixed-
interval schedules (20). A lever-press delivered the standard 45 mg pellet at
the end of each interval. Over a period of a few months, the interval was
lengthened from 15 to 30 seconds and then to 60 seconds. The intervals
were subsequently decreased through the same series. When the fixed-
interval 60-second schedule was reached, marked polydipsia developed,
although animals lost at most only about 7 percent of their body weight
during this phase. Severe weight loss was not required for animals to
develop and maintain polydipsia. When the interval was progressively
shortened, daily drinking decreased in a graded fashion.

The Emergence of a Behavioral Category: Adjunctive Behavior

In physiological experimentation, the remarkable accuracy with which
amounts of water ingested equal imposed fluid deficits attests to the precise
operation of body water regulation (21). Such a gain-loss equivalence provides a normal baseline of regulatory behavior against which we can judge
schedule induced polydipsia as grossly deviant. From this perspective, at
least some kinds of behavioral excess *can* be defined as extreme values
along an inherent yardstick of behavior—one of the alternatives suggested
earlier in this chapter. Now, overindulgence with water is seldom a medical
problem and it is difficult to imagine a situation in which this behavior
would bring about negative social consequences. While exaggerated water
ingestion lacks the dramatic aspect either of rebellious, demented, or
criminal rule breaking or of medical complications, it nevertheless presents
a clear case of excessive behavior. If one can demonstrate that polydipsia is
but one example of a more general phenomenon, then perhaps this activity
could help explain how excessive behavior is generated. We need to explore, then, in what sense the conditions in schedule induced polydipsia
might represent a more general class of behavioral excess determinants.

   To show that there exist numerous kinds of excessive behavior that
belong to a class including schedule induced polydipsia, one must

demonstrate at least three things. First, it must be established that each behavior is indeed excessive when compared with an appropriate control, or baseline, level. Second, there should be a range of interpellet time values that induce the behavior excessively; perhaps the entire bitonic function should be shown. Third, an inverse correlation between the percentage of free-feeding body weight and the degree of the excessive behavior should be evident. As stated, the second and third requirements apply only to the schedule reinforcement case discussed thus far: limited food rations. Later, I shall describe experiments enabling us to generalize beyond this restricted class of reinforcing agents. But for the present purpose, a variety of food schedule induced excessive behavioral outcomes will be reviewed, along with any evidence that these patterns varied as functions of interpellet time and percentage of body weight. For if the same independent variables can produce a number of excessive behaviors, and the shapes of the resulting functions are similar, this would legitimize grouping such behavioral phenomena into a class called "adjunctive behavior." Finally, a fourth criterion, species generality, while not strictly necessary to establishing a unifying class of behavior, certainly would be persuasive. The remainder of this section describes the current status of evidence supporting all four criteria.

Studies with rats confirming both the bitonic function and the inverse correlation with body weight for schedule induced polydipsia were cited earlier. Schedule induced polydipsia also occurs in the guinea pig (22), Mongolian gerbil (23, 24), mouse (25, 26), rhesus monkey (27, 28), Java macaque (29), chimpanzee (30), and human (31). The evidence on schedule induced polydipsia in the pigeon is not yet clear; positive (32, 33) as well as negative (34–37) results have been reported. Studies on rhesus and Java macaque monkeys have confirmed the bitonic function for polydipsia in these species (28, 29).

Schedules of intermittent food delivery can induce not only polydipsia but also aggression or attack. For example, when pigeons at 80 percent of free-feeding weight earned portions of food intermittently by pecking a small plastic disc in individual chambers that also contained a semi-restrained pigeon, they attacked this pigeon repeatedly shortly after each food acquisition period (38). As was the case with schedule induced polydipsia, the level of attack was excessive when compared to baseline conditions. Several kinds of control, or baseline, conditions were used in these comparisons: no food available in the session, the entire session ration given as a single large portion, or food delivered but inaccessible (covered by a Plexiglas shield). In the squirrel monkey, too, biting attack against a fixed rubber hose occurred in conjunction with schedules of intermittent food delivery (39). In this study and in subsequent research, more attacking occurred when a greater number of lever-presses or disc-pecks were required for the delivery of each food portion (39, 40). But since actual response requirements on levers or discs were not crucial to the production of adjunctive drinking or attack (38, 41, 42), this suggests that the time between food portions was the important factor.

This hypothesis was supported by a study in which pigeons were presented with food portions after certain fixed periods of time had elapsed (43). As the interfood times were increased over many sessions—from 15 seconds through several values up to 960 seconds (16 minutes)—attack rates first increased (up to either the 60-or 120-second value) and then decreased to low rates for the longer interfood times. This was the first study that demonstrated that the bitonic function held for adjunctive attack as well as polydipsia. The bitonic function for intraspecies attack in the pigeon was confirmed by Cherek, Thompson, and Heistad, who found that the maximum attack rates occurred at either 120- or 180-second interfood times (41). Biting-attack rate in the squirrel monkey also yielded the bitonic function (44). The inverse relation between percentage body weight and adjunctive behavior was confirmed for attack in the pigeon as body weights were increased slowly from 65 to 95 percent (45). Extinction induced aggression has been studied in rats (46) and in nursery school children (47) under formats including several cycles of reinforcement and extinction conditions, and schedule induced aggression has been explored in the rat (48). However, most of the research on schedule induced attack has concentrated on the squirrel monkey and the domesticated pigeon, although a study using feral pigeons yielded results comparable to those with domesticated birds (49).

Schedule induced exaggeration in several kinds of general activity can occur. The first clear report of this phenomenon showed that rats ran excessively in activity wheels during variable-interval one-minute food sessions compared to sessions in which food was delivered for each lever-press (50). Humans reinforced by scheduled access to monetary gain, gambling opportunities, or maze solving showed greatly increased locomotor activities and body movements compared to unscheduled conditions (31, 51–55). The studies on humans did not employ scheduled access to food as the generator condition, nor were subjects food deprived; besides increases in activity, fluid intake (31, 54), eating (54), grooming (54), and smoking (52) increased.

Rats reduced in body weight by food restriction and fed a 45 mg food pellet automatically once each minute (fixed-time one-minute schedule) during daily sessions licked at a continuous airstream issuing from a tube (56). Just as in schedule induced polydipsia, protracted postpellet licking occurred and the excessive licking depended upon the scheduled delivery of the pellets (57). Further paralleling the pattern in schedule induced polydipsia, the amount of schedule induced air licking was an inverse function of the percentage of free-feeding body weight (58).

The persistent ingestion of a nonfood substance, termed "pica," has been studied in children (59, 60), women (61), and migrant families (62) and as epidemics among Australian aboriginals (63, 64). Pica in children includes the ingestion of paint flakes, paper, wood, plaster, matches, crayons, and cigarette butts; clay eating is most common in the other groups. Both family psychiatric and social pathologic factors have been implicated in the genesis of pica. The life history events and environmental dislocations that seem related to pica may parallel some of the conditions that generate adjunctive behavior. Rhesus monkeys reduced to about 80 percent body weight and given food pellets on a fixed-time 15-minute schedule ingested wood shavings after eating each pellet (65). Neither food deprivation alone nor discontinuation of the feeding schedule yielded wood shavings pica: scheduled access to food was the critical condition.

The sorts of adjunctive behavior discussed thus far, while curious and somewhat out of place, particularly in their excessive aspects, are nonetheless rather common responses. The ingestion of alternative substances and fluids when food is unavailable during semistarvation has been noted (66). Attack and hyperactivity are not entirely unexpected in frustrating situations. Behavior studies have made explicit the conditions generating and maintaining adjunctive behaviors, which are puzzling not in their occurrence but in their persistence and exaggeration. Nevertheless, schedules of reinforcement can induce behavioral outcomes that seem not to follow intuitively and are quite maladaptive: one of these is schedule induced escape.

Perhaps the last thing we would expect an animal to do in a food economy of scarcity and interruption is to make matters worse. And yet that often happens. Animals explicitly opt out of the situation, the net result being a much leaner schedule of food acquisition than that permitted by the experimental arrangement. For example, investigations done in the early sixties showed that both rats and pigeons would choose to *terminate* some schedules of reinforcement rather than fulfill the contingencies necessary for attaining food. When pigeons were required to peck a plastic disc a certain number of times ("fixed-ratio schedule") to obtain a brief feeding period, they pecked at high rates and produced many such periods during daily one-hour sessions (67). However, as the requirement was gradually lengthened from fixed-ratio 65 to 200, pigeons pecked at a second disc that terminated the fixed-ratio schedule so that pecking at the first disc would no longer deliver food. The larger the value of the fixed-ratio schedule, the greater the portion of each session spent in this time-out condition. In fact, at fixed-ratio 200 the birds spent about half the hour-long session escaping from the food schedule. Obviously, they could have paused and just not pecked if they found a fixed-ratio of 200 simply too onerous at times during the hour. Animals indeed do pause before starting comparatively large value fixed-ratios (68). But in this experiment, when given the option between just pausing or changing to stimulus conditions that signaled termination of the fixed-ratio contingency, the birds picked the time-out option more and more frequently as the fixed-ratio value increased (pecking the second disc reinstituted the fixed-ratio schedule if time-out was in effect, so the animals had complete control over how long they spent in time-out). This kind of behavior was unexpected. Birds short on food rations (they were maintained at 80 percent of normal weight) actively turned off the schedule conditions allowing them to obtain food. Not only did they not complete anywhere near as many fixed-ratios as they might have, but also they actively terminated the schedule condition permitting them to do so. Operationally, this is escape behavior. Active escape from schedules of positive reinforcement was confirmed in water deprived rats that pressed a lever resulting in time-out periods from a fixed-ratio schedule delivering small water rations (69). Again, the larger the fixed-ratio value, the greater the proportion of the session time animals chose to spend in time-out.

Why do animals engage in this seemingly maladaptive behavior, opting out of a situation that allows them to work for needed food or water? One interpretation is that the work required by large value fixed-ratios is aversive and that escape from stimulus conditions signaling a heavy work requirement is reinforcing. However, fixed-interval schedules also produce adjunctive escape and really do not require a high behavioral output (70). Furthermore, fixed- or variable-time schedules that require *no* behavior emission (food portions are delivered simply after certain intervals have elapsed) also produce adjunctive escape (71). Clearly, animals are not just escaping from work. There is a no satisfying explanation for schedule induced escape, as is the case with the other kinds of adjunctive behavior previously discussed.

Is adjunctive escape just another example of the curious behavioral excesses generated by certain schedules of reinforcement? One must proceed carefully here: there are similarities and perhaps one important difference—first, the similarities. Any amount of schedule induced escape from a food or water reinforcement schedule is excessive behavior in the sense that it is patently maladaptive; it decreases access to a physiologically required commodity that is already in short supply. So adjunctive escape is excessive behavior but somewhat different in type from exaggerated drinking, attack, or other activities previously considered. The latter activities have normal, or baseline, rates of occurrence in the situation against which their schedule induced rates are deemed excessive. But any degree of adjunctive escape from a situation allowing needed repletion of food or water can be viewed as excessive. As in the case of adjunctive polydipsia and attack, the amount of escape (number of time-outs taken) increased when percentage of body weight was allowed to decrease in connection with a food schedule (72). Here again the result was a counterintuitive one: the more important it became to stay with the situation and obtain the maximum number of reinforcements possible, the greater the number of time-outs the pigeons actually took. As body weight decreased from about 95 to 75 percent of free-feeding level, there was a linear increase in time-outs taken. Schedule induced escape has been found in a variety of species: rat, pigeon, squirrel monkey (39, 73, 74), and rhesus monkey (75).

There is a more striking way in which adjunctive escape differs from other adjunctive behavior. Although data from two out of four pigeons in one study suggested a bitonic relation between interfood time and amount of escape (70), the weight of the evidence from both fixed- and variable-time schedules indicates that the longer the time between food portions during a session, the greater the percentage of the session spent in time-out (71). No data from any rat in a study by Lydersen and colleagues yielded a bitonic function (71). This suggests that the leaner the schedule of reinforcement, the greater the amount of adjunctive escape, in contrast to the pattern with other adjunctive behavior. Such a relation is congruent with commonsense expectations: the less favorable a situation, the more it will be rejected. I shall return to this relation presently as it is a key to the phenomenon of adjunctive behavior.

In considering schedules that generate adjunctive behavior, I have stressed food schedules. Indeed, most of the research on adjunctive behavior has employed food schedules. However, schedules of reinforcement providing monetary gain, gambling opportunities, or maze solving for humans (31, 51–55) and water for rats (69) were noted. Here I wish to present further examples indicating that schedules providing commodities other than food also can induce exaggerated behavior.

Rats deprived of neither food nor water were given daily sessions allowing access to either a locked running wheel or one that was unlocked automatically for fixed periods of time during the session (76). The scheduled access to running induced an increase in a number of activities (licking, rearing, and position changes) relative to the activity levels of animals exposed to the locked-wheel condition. In further work, these investigators included a comparison between rats having access to an unlocked wheel for the entire session and those allowed scheduled access, as in the earlier experiment (77). Scheduled access again induced increased rearing and position changes when compared to the unscheduled condition.

When water was presented to water deprived rats for 7.5-second periods on a fixed-time two-minute schedule, excessive adjunctive wheel running was induced compared to a condition that allowed consumption of the entire water ration at the beginning of the session (78). Water deprived rats exposed to either fixed-time or fixed-interval one-minute schedules of water access showed schedule induced increases in eating (79).

Lever-pressing on fixed-interval schedules can be maintained not only by the delivery of such commodities as food and water but also by the presentation of noxious electric shock (80–82). This finding seems paradoxical only if one assumes that environmental events are intrinsically either positive or negative. In fact, events such as brief electric shocks can sustain behavior that results in either their continual avoidance or their repeated presentation, depending on the schedule. With a little care as to how noxious shock is scheduled, it is feasible to have animals lever-pressing both to avoid and to produce identical shocks within the same session (73). DeWeese found that schedule induced attack (hose biting) in squirrel monkeys was generated by both fixed-interval food and fixed-interval shock presentation schedules (44). Further work showed that the adjunctive attack was not directly elicited by the presentation of the food or the shocks but depended upon the schedule of presentation. The scheduling of noxious shocks under fixed-intervals, then, can lead to their repeated delivery by lever-pressing, just as in the case of fixed-interval food or water delivery. And of greater importance in the present context, fixed-interval shock schedules can induce adjunctive attack. Schedules of intermittent shock presentation can also induce adjunctive escape from the schedule (73).

Finally, while the self-administration of brief noxious shocks on fixed-interval schedules is somewhat unexpected, the intravenous self-injection of cocaine on intermittent schedules comes as no surprise. A wide range of commonly abused drugs are self-injected by animals (83). Nevertheless, squirrel monkeys self-injecting cocaine doses on a variable-interval three-minute schedule also concurrently pressed a lever that led to one-minute time-out periods according to a fixed-interval three-minute schedule (74). Hence, schedule induced escape occurs not only in connection with food and water schedules but also as an adjunct to schedules of shock or drug self-administration.

Toward an Explanation of Adjunctive Behavior

The major problem of adjunctive behavior is that it is strong and persistent but has no satisfactory explanation. Adjunctive behavior is not simply reflexive, or elicited, behavior for its form varies with the environmental opportunities available (e. g., polydipsia, pica, attack, running). Nor is it a conditioned reflex, a fixed action pattern, or complex operant behavior shaped by reinforcement contingencies of the generator schedule. That adjunctive behavior is not some sort of automatic activity entrained by the schedule conditions or an arbitrary, time filling behavior is shown by investigations demonstrating the capacity of such behavior to sustain its own reinforcement schedules. For example, if water is not freely available in a variable-interval schedule of food delivery but can be earned in small portions by completing fixed-ratios on a second lever, then polydipsia nonetheless develops and sustains large ratios on the second lever (84). Likewise, schedule induced aggression and escape can sustain performance on schedules that yield episodic opportunities to attack a restrained partner (41, 85) or to escape from the generator schedule for a time (69, 73, 74).

Recall, for a moment, the major conditions for inducing exaggerated adjunctive behavior. First, limited portions of an important commodity are delivered over time. This constraint on access to the commodity must not be too severe. If the portions are distributed on too lean a schedule, then adjunctive excesses fail to occur. Second, exigency also determines the degree of excess. For example, within limits, the greater the decrease in body weight produced by limiting daily food rations, the greater the behavioral excess induced by an effective portion delivery schedule. Food becomes an important commodity through food deprivation, and water through fluid depletion, but other commodities and activities can derive importance by other mechanisms. A running wheel can become important for a rat kept inactive. A drug such as cocaine is a strong reinforcer under many conditions. Even trivial monetary gains from gambling become important in a context of social competition among players. Once a commodity becomes important, schedule conditions constraining the rate of access to it can induce adjunctive behavior, provided the rate is not too lean. In fact, for several species the relation between the rate of access to commodity portions and the amount of polydipsia or aggression induced is bitonic. Now, recall a final, crucial observation: the leaner the schedule of reinforcement, the greater the amount of adjunctive escape. This implies a linear increasing function, rather than a bitonic one; the less favorable the situation, the more it will be rejected.

We are now in a position to see how adjunctive behavior might be generated and why the bitonic relation occurs. Access to portions of an important commodity can vary from low to high rates (see Figure 17-1). The rate of consumption of a commodity (e.g., food, water, activity, drugs, money) is directly determined by the schedule of availability (I assume that the overall schedule of access to the commodity is such that satiation is not approached). Furthermore, as rate of access to the commodity falls, escape behavior increases (see the escape gradient in Figure 17-1). These two behavioral vectors conflict so that the further they are from the midpoint, where the functions cross, the more either consummatory or escape behavior will dominate the situation. If we assume that adjunctive behavior is the inverse of the difference between these two functions, then a bitonic function for adjunctive behavior is generated (as shown). Thus, if the two vectors are equal in the situation, so that it is uncertain whether staying or escaping will occur, adjunctive behavior becomes maximal.

Why should an equivocal situation generate the most adjunctive behavior? When excessive adjunctive behavior is generated in a variety of species by similar commodity-constraint conditions, one has reason to suspect that this behavior may have adaptive significance. On the face of it,

FIGURE 17-1.
Adjunctive behavior probability as the inverse of the
difference between two functions: rate of generator
schedule consummatory behavior and probability of escape
behavior.

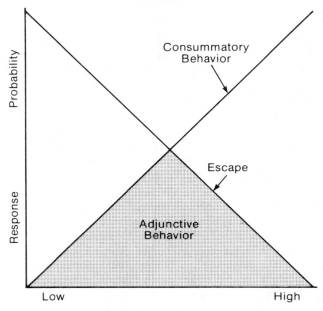

Scheduled Rate of Consummatory Events

the behavior appears wasteful, gratuitous, and without obvious adaptive value. But I have presented the case elsewhere that adjunctive behavior serves to stabilize uncertain situations in which it is unclear whether the best course is to stay or leave (86). Let us examine how this stabilization takes place and why it might be adaptive.

Animals and humans often must deal with situations that contain opposing components. Frequently there are two opposing vectors: one having to do with a major activity, such as feeding, mating, or caring for young, and the other concerned with withdrawing from the situation. For example, during territorial boundary disputes in birds, displacement activities such as feeding, sexual mounting of a nearby female, or preening are prevalent. When birds that are incubating eggs or caring for young are approached by a potential predator, they sometimes behave strangely. They may engage in seemingly irrelevant or incongruous behavior such as preening or nest building. The opposing parental and escape behaviors result in one or more "displacement activities." In a pair of stickleback fish, when their aggressive behavior intrudes upon their sexual actions, displacement egg-fanning movements occur in the male. The eggs have not yet been deposited, so the fanning is out of place and irrelevant. These and other examples may be viewed as curious intrusions of behavior into situations that contain vectors in opposition (86, 87): attack versus flight, parental versus escape behavior, or sexual activity versus aggression. These oppositions comprise one behavior of crucial adaptive significance (parental behavior, sexual activity, or territorial defense) set against behavior that is either an escape or destructive of the situation. When opposing vectors are in approximate balance, the most suitable course of action is uncertain; taking the preceding examples, is it appropriate to fight or give ground to the territorial competitor, defend the nest or flee the intruder, or continue the courtship or break it off? These are unstable equilibria, and species survival depends on which direction resolution takes. Territory must be conserved, progeny preserved, and mating consummated, but these activities must not take place if the risks are too great. The competitor may be too powerful, the predator may press the attack, and the mate may be inappropriate or flawed. These situations require either perseverance or withdrawal.

But with a balanced pair of behavioral vectors, what is the best course? It would be best to delay precipitous action in such cases since it is difficult to reverse an unstable equilibrium once it begins to take a particular course. For example, it is all but impossible to reacquire fled territory, an abandoned nest, or a forsaken mate. Perhaps the most efficacious way to delay action until the situation becomes clearer is to diversify behavior. Thus, under opposing-vector conditions, many species engage in displacement activities, which have a protective action because they maintain the status quo for a time by preventing what might be either an inappropriate continuance of the crucial behavior or an inappropriate escape. Diversification and stabilization of opposing-vector situations through pursuit of displacement activities evolved apparently because premature, and perhaps costly, resolutions are thereby prevented. It is important for a species to maintain territorial, mating, and parental behavior, unless the threat or interference is really of such a magnitude that the crucial behavior must be terminated. Displacement activities allow the opposing-vector situation time to develop and reach a point where one vector becomes dominant, defining the course of action with certainty. Arbitrary or uncertain decisions are too costly to chance their resolution to a momentary, small change in one or the other of the vectors.

The processes that produce displacement activities are precisely those responsible for adjunctive behavior. In both cases, an important activity is in progress or a crucial commodity is being acquired. These are usually territorial defense, courtship and mating sequences, and parental behavior in ethologic studies; scheduled access to food, water, activity, or money in investigations of adjunctive behavior. In one case the ongoing behavior is impeded by situational interruptions (intruders, inadequate releasing stimuli); in the other, by schedule constraints allowing only episodic access. The resulting behavior is described as incongruous or irrelevant in ethologic observations and as persistent and excessive in adjunctive behavior investigations. I suggested that displacement activities have evolved because they serve an adaptive function: allowing stabilization of an unclear situation, with a nonprecipitous resolution of competing vectors. The animal comes under the control of nearby stimuli so that it remains to feed, nest build, preen, egg-fan, or sexually mount rather than escape. In the case of scheduled feeding or drinking, there is a linear increase in escape behavior as access to the commodity decreases. Adjunctive behavior, like displacement activities, is behavior that probably serves to block premature escape from nonoptimal situations. For example, a feeding environment providing a marginal amount of food induces a variety of adjunctive activities. In a natural environment, such behavior might function to delay abandonment of a feeding range or patch that, while marginal, is nevertheless adequate.

Applications

Consider once again the prototypical adjunctive behavior situation: a variable-interval food schedule, feeding exigency (80 percent body weight), no possible escape from the situation, and freely available water; a chronic excessive drinking routine result. This kind of environment and its result may be pivotal for understanding how some excesses in humans come about and are maintained. The evolutionary reasons why such conditions foster exaggerated behavior were discussed earlier. Furthermore, I noted the continuity of generating conditions between displacement activities and adjunctive behavior. Adjunctive behavior generation is fundamentally similar to the processes underlying displacement activity induction. But adjunctive behavior is perhaps more routinized and excessive—because the conditions under which it is induced usually provide no escape from the situation, no respite from chronic deficit in the crucial commodity, or much in the way of alternative behavior. The animal is, as it were, locked into the situation. But before one rejects adjunctive behavior as the product of artificially constrained laboratory situations, it is worth asking, Are there constrained human situations that yield chronic extreme behavior? Are persistent behavioral excesses generated by combination of exigency, impeded access to a crucial commodity, and lack of either behavioral alternatives or a mode of escape from the situation? There are at least two ways to answer this question. First, we can maintain that if adjunctive behavior is indeed like the excessive activities observed clinically, then we should be able to build animal models of some of these excesses since we can manipulate the known relevant generating conditions. Second, we can ask whether any excessive behavior in humans seems to be explained by an appeal to the kinds of conditions known to generate adjunctive behavior in animals.

If animals can be induced to overdrink water persistently, what might occur if some drug solution were substituted for water? Using the schedule induction technique, we might not only get animals to self-administer large quantities of a drug but also identify the necessary and sufficient conditions for drug abuse. For the past few years this has been a growing area of investigation, and a variety of drugs have been explored. We chose to work with ethyl alcohol (ethanol) because over three decades of research had failed to coax animals to drink aqueous ethanol solutions sufficiently to become physically dependent (89). Animals had been forced to imbibe it in liquid diets or breathe it in as a vapor, but these arrangements are hardly models of elective overindulgence.

In our initial experiment we used rats housed in individual Plexiglas chambers with 5 percent ethanol solution available for drinking (90). Animals were fed automatically by attached food pellet dispensers on the following food schedule. During one-hour feeding periods, a 45 mg food pellet was dispensed to an animal every two minutes (fixed-time two-minute schedule). These one-hour feeding periods were separated by three-hour intervals. Thus, there were six feeding periods in each 24-hour cycle. Under these conditons, animals became polydipsic and overindulged in ethanol relative to a number of control group conditions (91). They ingested a daily mean of 13.1 g ethanol/kg of body weight. Serial blood samples showed that blood ethanol concentrations were greater than 100 mg/dl for most of the 24-hour cycle and often lay between 150 and 300 mg. In simpler terms, the rats were legally drunk most of the day and night.

After three months on this schedule, some of these animals, and another group in a subsequent experiment (92), were tested individually after ethanol withdrawal for the presence of physical dependence. Brief auditory stimuli elicited tonic-clonic seizures, with some animals dying, indicating the development of severe physical dependence. It was not possible to evoke in these or subsequent experiments either seizures or preconvulsive activities in various control groups (91).

Given that we could produce severe alcoholism in animals by the schedule induction technique, it then became of interest to determine whether other biomedically significant pathologic states might develop in similar generating conditions. We wondered whether such chronic situations could result in the psychosomatic production of essential hypertension. The role of environmental factors in the genesis of essential hypertension is controversial. In our experiments, we assumed that if environmental events are involved, they probably operate in concert with either genetic or physiologic predisposing factors to produce essential hypertension. Consequently, normal rats were given both a physiologic predisposition (one kidney was removed and saline drinking fluid provided) and long-term exposure to daily five-hour sessions of a fixed-time 90-second food schedule (93). Control animals received the same physiologic bias and an equivalent daily amount of food in a single ration. The only difference between the groups of animals, then, was that one received the food spread out over five hours on the fixed-time schedule while the other received the food all at once. The amount and rate of saline solution drunk were manipulated so as to be equal between the groups. A difference in mean blood pressure between the groups developed after 90 days and remained for the rest of the experiment, which lasted about six months. Water replaced saline as the drinking fluid for the last three weeks. At the termination of the experiment, direct carotid arterial blood pressure measures confirmed that the fixed-time schedule group was hypertensive (mean pressure, 170.5 mm Hg), while the control group pressure was significantly lower (142.3 mm Hg). Postmortem observations of minor pathologic changes in the kidneys and increased heart weight in the fixed-time schedule group were consistent with the maintenance of an essential hypertension of several months' duration. Hence, environmental arrangements sufficient for the induction of adjunctive behavior have an additional property: under chronic exposure conditions they generate not only various sorts of excessive behavior but also some of the untoward physiological consequences often assumed to accompany such behavior.

The creation of alcoholism and essential hypertension by schedule induction indicates that the maintenance of rather innocuous environmental circumstances can result in long-term pathologic consequences. Is it possible that similar circumstances might underlie these and other pathologic conditions in humans? The present evidence is fragmentary but promising. Studies showing schedule induced increases in drinking, eating, activity, grooming, and smoking were discussed previously (31, 51–55). Adjunctive behavior in humans has been induced by a variety of generator schedule conditions. Taken together with the extensive research on animals, the case for considering at least some excessive and persistent human behaviors as schedule induced is not unreasonable.

Drug abuse can provide an example of how this might occur. Alcohol and other drugs can function as reinforcing substances for animals and humans under many conditions. But powerful as such drugs may be for some people, the fact remains that of those exposed to a particular agent only a small percentage become habitual problem abusers. We have seen that appropriate schedules can exaggerate the reinforcing properties of alcohol or aggression so that they are administered to excess. Generator schedules transform a weak reinforcer into a powerful one. Now consider that neither natural environments nor social settings provide us with an even, uninterrupted flow of life's important commodities. Our niche in nature is seldom idyllic, nor is our social context utopian. Indeed, nature's bounty or one's socioeconomic functioning may be marginal, making either biologic survival or maintenance of an accustomed lifestyle fraught with doubt. Life in many respects is a set of complex intermittent schedules. Just what sort of adjunctive behavior might be induced by schedules of marginal supply would depend upon what alternatives for action were available to the individual. In animals, the presence of an alcohol solution, even with water or dilute glucose solutions concurrently available, makes alcohol overindulgence the probable induced behavior (94, 95). The presence of a running wheel makes hyperactivity the probable induced behavior. Likewise in humans, the alternative opportunities provided by the environment are probably critical in determining what behavioral excesses develop. In a marginal environment containing plenty of alcohol and other drugs, we can expect adjunctive drug taking, with a high incidence of drug abuse. This is the case not only because many such marginal generator schedule environments provide few reinforcing opportunities that can compete with drugs but also because those alternatives that *are* available often require previous skill to utilize them. They also may require continued social reinforcement for their maintenance. Under such conditions, the availability, immediacy of action, and schedule induced potency of a favored drug make it difficult for other potential sources of reinforcement to gain control over behavior.

In closing, let us consider situations less dramatic than drug abuse but that probably produce chronic excessive behavior. Such behavior constitutes much of our "psychopathology of everyday life" (96). Acute marginality in a situation can produce frenetic "normal" behavior. For example, at business luncheons the situation often includes scheduled bits of crucial commodities (monetary agreements, conditional promises or political alignments, valuable information) and escape vectors (presence of competitors, uncertain advantages, veiled threats). We might expect adjunctive behavior to be generated under such conditions, and the multiple martinis, heavy smoking, rapid-fire talking, and overeating yield frequent confirmation. Cocktail parties are not very different from business meetings in that many crucial social reinforcements share a crowded space with crosscurrents of loyalty and friendship and competitive jockeying for attention. Drinking, smoking, and high decibel loquacity again are prevalent. These are common acute situations. Life also presents us with ambivalent situations of a more chronic nature. Is the business really turning a profit; are the laboratory experiments going to turn out well; am I fulfilled in my present position? Such questions embody implicit escape vectors: should I sell the business and leave; terminate the experiments as unfruitful; seek a different job? Chronic situational marginality can perhaps account for what appears to be exaggerated adjunctive behavior. People facing such situations may drink, eat, talk, smoke, have sex, gamble, run, or watch television excessively. But they might also play an instrument, paint, or grow prize roses. Poised between schedules of commodity availability and situational escape components, the adjunctive behavior often functions to preserve the situation. Whether such exaggerated behavior is harmless, self-destructive, or creative (either in its intrinsic consequences or precisely because it preserves the status quo) poses varied legal, medical, and ethical questions.

Note: The author gratefully acknowledges financial support through USPHS grants DA1110 and AA00253.

References

1. Becker, H. S., *Outsiders: Studies in the Sociology of Deviance,* Free Press, New York, 1973.
2. Falk, J. L., Production of polydipsia in normal rats by an intermittent food schedule, *Science 133,* 195–196 (1961).
3. Chew, R. M., Water metabolism of mammals, in *Physiological Mammalogy, vol. 2,* W. V. Mayer and R. G. Van Gelder, eds., Academic, New York, 1965, pp. 43–178.
4. Falk, J. L., Control of schedule-induced polydipsia: type, size, and spacing of meals, *J. Exp. Anal. Beh. 10,* 199–206 (1967).
5. Falk, J. L., Conditions producing psychogenic polydipsia in animals, *Ann. N.Y. Acad. Sci. 157,* 569–593 (1969).
6. Falk, J. L., The behavioral regulation of water-electrolyte balance, in *Nebraska Symposium on Motivation,* M. R. Jones, ed., University of Nebraska Press, Lincoln, 1961, pp. 1–33.
7. Falk, J. L., Studies on schedule-induced polydipsia, in *Thirst in the Regulation of Body Water,* M. J. Wayner, ed., Pergamon, New York, 1964, pp. 95–116.
8. Falk, J. L., Analysis of water and NaCl solution acceptance by schedule-induced polydipsia, *J. Exp. Anal. Beh. 9,* 111–118 (1966).
9. Skinner, B. F., "Superstition" in the pigeon, *J. Exp. Psych. 38,* 168–172 (1948).
10. Falk, J. L., Schedule-induced polydipsia as a function of fixed interval length, *J. Exp. Anal. Beh. 9,* 37–39 (1966).
11. Flory, R. K., The control of schedule-induced polydipsia: frequency and magnitude of reinforcement, *Learn. Motiv. 2,* 215–227 (1971).
12. Keehn, J. D., and Colotla, V. A., Schedule-induced drinking as a function of interpellet interval, *Psychonom. Sci. 23,* 69–71 (1971).
13. Wayner, M. J., and Greenberg, I., Schedule dependence of schedule-induced polydipsia and lever pressing, *Physiol. Beh. 10,* 965–966 (1973).
14. Bond, N., Schedule-induced polydipsia as a function of the consummatory rate, *Psych. Rec. 23,* 377–382 (1973).

15. Freed, E. X., and Hymowitz, N., Effects of schedule, percent body weight, and magnitude of reinforcer on acquisition of schedule-induced polydipsia, *Psych. Rep. 31,* 95–101 (1972).

16. Keehn, J. D., Schedule-induced polydipsia, schedule-induced drinking, and body weight, *Bull. Psychonom. Soc'y 13,* 78–80 (1979).

17. Roper, T. J., and Nieto, J., Schedule-induced drinking and other behavior in the rat, as a function of body weight deficit, *Physiol. and Beh. 23,* 673–678 (1979).

18. Wayner, M. J., and Rondeau, D. B., Schedule dependent and schedule-induced behavior at reduced and recovered body weight, *Physiol. and Beh. 17,* 325–336 (1976).

19. Wayner, M. J., Stein, J. M., Loullis, C. C., Barone, F. C., Jolicoeur, F. B., and Rondeau, D. B., Effects of two body weight reduction regimens on schedule-dependent and schedule-induced behavior, *Physiol. and Beh. 21,* 639–645 (1978).

20. Petersen, M. R., and Lyon, D. O., Schedule-induced polydipsia in rats living in an operant environment, *J. Exp. Anal. Beh. 29,* 493–503 (1978).

21. Adolf, E. F., Regulation of body water content through water ingestion, in *Thirst in the Regulation of Body Water,* M. J. Wayner, ed., Pergamon, New York, 1964, pp. 5–17.

22. Porter, J. H., Sozer, N. N., and Moeschl, T. P., Schedule-induced polydipsia in the guinea pig, *Physiol. and Beh. 19,* 573–575 (1977).

23. Porter, J. H., and Bryant, W. E., Jr., Adjunctive behavior in the Mongolian gerbil, *Physiol. and Beh. 21,* 151–155 (1978).

24. Porter, J. H., and Bryant, W. E., Jr., Acquisition of schedule-induced polydipsia in the Mongolian gerbil, *Physiol. and Beh. 21,* 825–827 (1978).

25. Palfai, T., Kutscher, C. L., and Symons, J. P., Schedule-induced polydipsia in the mouse, *Physiol. and Beh. 6,* 461–462 (1971).

26. Symons, J. P., and Sprott, R. L., Genetic analysis of schedule-induced polydipsia, *Physiol. and Beh. 17,* 837–839 (1976).

27. Schuster, C. R., and Woods, J. H., Schedule-induced polydipsia in the rhesus monkey, *Psych. Rep. 19,* 823–828 (1966).

28. Allen, J. D., and Kenshalo, D. R., Jr., Schedule-induced drinking as a function of interreinforcement interval in the rhesus monkey, *J. Exp. Anal. Beh. 26,* 257–267 (1976).

29. Allen, J. D., and Kenshalo, D. R., Jr., Schedule-induced drinking as functions of interpellet interval and draught size in the Java macaque, *J. Exp. Anal. Beh. 30,* 139–151 (1978).

30. Byrd, L. D., Effects of d-amphetamine on schedule-controlled key pressing and drinking in the chimpanzee, *J. Pharm. Exp. Ther. 185,* 633–641 (1973).

31. Kachanoff, R., Leveille, R., McLlelland, J. P., and Wayner, M. J., Schedule-induced behavior in humans, *Physiol. and Beh. 11,* 395–398 (1973).

32. Shanab, M. E., and Peterson, J. L., Polydipsia in the pigeon, *Psychonom. Sci. 15,* 51–52 (1969).

33. Magyar, R. L., Allen, R., Sicignano, A., and Malagodi, E. F., Schedule-

induced polydipsia in the pigeon, paper presented at the meeting of the Southeastern Psychological Association, Hollywood, 1977.

34. Miller, J. S., and Gollub, L. R., Adjunctive and operant bolt pecking in the pigeon, *Psych. Rec. 24,* 203–208 (1974).

35. Whalen, T. E., and Wilkie, D. M., Failure to find schedule-induced polydipsia in the pigeon, *Bull. Psychonom. Soc'y 10,* 200–202 (1977).

36. Dale, R. H. I., Concurrent drinking by pigeons on fixed-interval reinforcement schedules, *Physiol. and Beh. 23,* 977–980 (1979).

37. Yoburn, B. C., and Cohen, P. S., Assessment of attack and drinking in White King pigeons on response-independent food schedules, *J. Exp. Anal. Beh. 31,* 91–101 (1979).

38. Azrin, N. H., Hutchinson, R. R., and Hake, D. F., Extinction-induced aggression, *J. Exp. Anal. Beh. 9,* 191–204 (1966).

39. Hutchinson, R. R., Azrin, N. H., and Hunt, G. M., Attack produced by intermittent reinforcement of a concurrent operant response, *J. Exp. Anal. Beh. 11,* 489–495 (1968).

40. Flory, R. K., Attack behavior in a multiple fixed-ratio schedule of reinforcement, *Psychonom. Sci. 16,* 156–157 (1969).

41. Cherek, D. R. Thompson, T., and Heistad, G. T., Responding maintained by the opportunity to attack during an interval food reinforcement schedule, *J. Exp. Anal. Beh. 19,* 113–123 (1973).

42. Flory, R. K., and Everist, H. D., The effect of a response requirement on schedule-induced aggression, *Bull. Psychonom. Soc'y 9,* 383–386 (1977).

43. Flory, R. K., Attack behavior as a function of minimum inter-food interval, *J. Exp. Anal. Beh. 12,* 825–828 (1969).

44. DeWeese, J., Schedule-induced biting under fixed-interval schedules of food or electric-shock presentation, *J. Exp. Anal. Beh. 27,* 419–431 (1977).

45. Dove, L. D., Relation between level of food deprivation and rate of schedule-induced attack, *J. Exp. Anal. Beh. 25,* 63–68 (1979).

46. Thompson, T., and Bloom, W., Aggressive behavior and extinction-induced response-rate increase, *Psychonom. Sci. 5,* 335–336 (1966).

47. Frederiksen, L. W., and Peterson, G. L., Schedule-induced aggression in nursery school children, *Psych. Rec. 24,* 343–351 (1974).

48. Knutson, J. F., and Schrader, S. P., A concurrent assessment of schedule-induced aggression and schedule-induced polydipsia in the rat, *Anim. Learn. Beh. 3,* 16–20 (1975).

49. Yoburn, B. C., and Cohen, P. S., Schedule-induced attack on a pictorial target in feral pigeons (*Columba livia*), *Bull. Psychonom. Soc'y 13,* 7–8 (1979).

50. Levitsky, D., and Collier, G., Schedule-induced wheel running, *Physiol. and Beh. 3,* 571–573 (1968).

51. Wallace, M., Singer, G., Wayner, M. J., and Cook, P., Adjunctive behavior in humans during game playing, *Physiol. and Beh. 14,* 651–654 (1975).

52. Wallace, M., and Singer, G., Adjunctive behavior and smoking induced by a maze solving schedule in humans, *Physiol. and Beh. 17,* 849–852 (1976).

53. Clarke, J., Gannon, M., Hughes, I., Keogh, C., Singer, G., and Wallace, M., Adjunctive behavior in humans in a group gambling situation, *Physiol. and Beh. 18,* 159–161 (1977).

54. Fallon, J. H., Jr., Allen, J. D., and Butler, J. A., Assessment of adjunctive behaviors in humans using a stringent control procedure, *Physiol. and Beh. 22,* 1089–1092 (1979).

55. Muller, P. G., Crow, R. E., and Cheney, C. D., Schedule-induced locomotor activity in humans, *J. Exp. Anal. Beh. 31,* 83–90 (1979).

56. Mendelson, J., and Chillag, D., Schedule-induced air licking in rats, *Physiol. Beh. 5,* 535–537 (1970).

57. Mendelson, J., Zec, R., and Chillag, D., Schedule dependency of schedule-induced air-licking, *Physiol. and Beh. 7,* 207–210 (1971).

58. Chillag, D., and Mendelson, J., Schedule-induced airlicking as a function of body-weight deficit in rats, *Physiol. and Beh. 6,* 603–605 (1971).

59. Millican, F. K., Lourie, R. S., and Lyman, E. M., Emotional factors in the etiology and treatment of lead poisoning, *AMA J. Dis. Child. 91,* 144–149 (1956)

60. Millican, F. K., and Lourie, R. S., The child with pica and his family, in *The Child in His Family,* in E. J. Anthony and C. Koupernik, eds., Wiley, New York, 1970, pp. 333–348.

61. Clay- and cornstarch-eating women, *Nutr. Revs. 18,* 35–38 (1960).

62. Bruhn, C. M., and Pangborn, R. M., Reported incidence of pica among migrant families, *J. Amer. Diet. Ass'n. 58,* 417–420 (1971).

63. Bateson, E. M., and Lebroy, T., Clay eating by aboriginals of the Northern Territory, *Med. J. Austral. 1* (supp.), 1–3 (1978).

64. Eastwell, H. D., A pica epidemic: a price for sedentarism among Australian ex–hunter-gatherers, *Psychiatry 42,* 264–273 (1979).

65. Villarreal, J., Schedule-induced pica, paper presented to the Eastern Psychological Association, Boston, 1967.

66. Keys, A., Brozek, J., Henschel, A., Mickelsen, O., and Taylor, H. L., *The Biology of Human Starvation,* University of Minnesota Press, Minneapolis, 1950.

67. Azrin, N. H., Time-out from positive reinforcement, *Science 133,* 382–383 (1961).

68. Ferster, C. B., and Skinner, B. F., *Schedules of Reinforcement,* Appleton-Century-Crofts, New York, 1957.

69. Thompson, D. M., Escape from S^D associated with fixed-ratio reinforcement, *J. Exp. Anal. Beh. 7,* 1–8 (1964).

70. Brown, T. G., and Flory, R. K., Schedule-induced escape from fixed-interval reinforcement, *J. Exp. Anal. Beh. 17,* 395–403 (1972).

71. Lydersen, T., Perkins, D., Thome, S., and Lowman, E., Choice of timeout during response-independent food schedules, *J. Exp. Anal. Beh. 33,* 59–76 (1980).

72. Dardano, J. F., Self-imposed timeouts under increasing response requirements, *J. Exp. Anal. Beh. 19,* 269–287 (1973).

73. Barrett, J. E., and Spealman, R. D., Behavior simultaneously maintained by both presentation and termination of noxious stimuli, *J. Exp. Anal. Beh. 29,* 375–383 (1978).

74. Spealman, R. D., Behavior maintained by termination of a schedule of self-administered cocaine, *Science 204,* 1231–1233 (1979).

75. Redd, W. H., Sidman, M., and Fletcher, F. G., Timeout as a reinforcer for errors in a serial position task, *J. Exp. Anal. Beh. 21,* 3–17 (1974).

76. Singer, G., Wayner, M. J., Stein, J., Cimino, K., and King, K., Adjunctive behavior induced by wheel running, *Physiol. and Beh. 12,* 493–495 (1974).

77. Wayner, M. J., Singer, G., Cimino, K., Stein, J., and Dwoskin, L., Adjunctive behavior induced by different conditions of wheel running, *Physiol. and Beh. 14,* 507–510 (1975).

78. King, G. D., Wheel running in the rat induced by a fixed-time presentation of water, *Anim. Learn. Beh. 2,* 325–328 (1974).

79. Bellingham, W. P., Wayner, M. J., and Barone, F. C., Schedule-induced eating in water-deprived rats, *Physiol. and Beh. 23,* 1105–1107 (1979).

80. Morse, W. H., Mead, R. N., and Kelleher, R. T., Modulation of elicited behavior by a fixed-interval schedule of shock presentation, *Science 157,* 215–217 (1967).

81. Kelleher, R. T., and Morse, W. H., Schedules using noxious stimuli III: responding maintained with response-produced electric shocks, *J. Exp. Anal. Beh. 11,* 819–838 (1968).

82. McKearney, J. W., Maintenance of responding under a fixed-interval schedule of electric shock-presentation, *Science 160,* 1249–1251 (1968).

83. Johanson, C. E., Drugs as reinforcers, in *Contemporary Research in Behavioral Pharmacology,* D. E. Blackman and D. J. Sanger, eds., Plenum, New York, 1978, pp. 325–390.

84. Falk, J. L., The motivational properties of schedule-induced polydipsia, *J. Exp. Anal. Beh. 9,* 19–25 (1966).

85. Cole, J. M., and Parker, B. K., Schedule-induced aggression: access to an attackable target bird as a positive reinforcer, *Psychonom. Sci. 22,* 33–35 (1971).

86. Falk, J. L., The origin and functions of adjunctive behavior, *Anim. Learn. Beh. 5,* 325–335 (1977)

87. Falk, J. L., The nature and determinants of adjunctive behavior, *Physiol. and Beh. 6,* 577–588 (1971).

88. Gilbert, R. M., Schedule-induced self-administration of drugs, in *Contemporary Research in Behavioral Pharmacology,* D. E. Blackman and D. J. Sanger, eds., Plenum, New York, 1978, pp. 289–323.

89. Myers, R. D., and Veale, W. L., The determinants of alcohol preference in animals, in *The Biology of Alcoholism,* vol. 2, B. Kissin and H. Begleiter, eds., Plenum, New York, 1972, pp. 131–168.

90. Falk, J. L., Samson, H. H., and Winger, G., Behavioral maintenance of high concentrations of blood ethanol and physical dependence in the rat, *Science 177,* 811–813 (1972).

91. Falk, J. L., and Tang, M., Animal model of alcoholism: critique and progress,

Alcohol Intoxication and Withdrawal, vol. 3B, M. M. Gross, ed., Plenum, New York, 1977, pp. 465–493.

92. Samson, H. H., and Falk, J. L., Schedule-induced ethanol polydipsia: enhancement by saccharin, *Pharm. Biochem. Beh. 2,* 835–838 (1974).

93. Falk, J. L., Tang, M., and Forman, S., Schedule-induced chronic hypertension, *Psychosom. Med. 39,* 252–263 (1977).

94. Samson, H. H., and Falk, J. L., Alteration of fluid preference in ethanol-dependent animals, *J. Pharm. Exp. Ther. 190,* 365–376 (1974).

95. Tang, M., and Falk, J. L., Ethanol dependence as a determinant of fluid preference, *Pharm. Biochem. Beh. 7,* 471–474 (1977).

96. Brill, A. A., *The Basic Writings of Sigmund Freud,* Random House, New York, 1938.

18

Psychodynamics of the Addictions

Leon Salzman

Addictions of various kinds, particularly to drugs and alcohol, have created sociological, theological, and moral problems from the time of the discovery that grapes, roots, and flowers have virtues beyond their nutritional value and visual interest. When mystical and dissociated states were venerated, and manic frenzies and cortical disorganizations dignified as divinely inspired, the toxic effects of these substances inspired awe and reverence. With a growing need for stability, responsibility, and cerebral clarity, on the one hand, and a more rational and less primitive concept of divinity and religious practice, on the other, excessive use of these agents came to be viewed as destructive and was criticized, restricted, or punished by the authorities. Addictions as such were unknown to the early pagan and Judaic theologies since these substances were an intrinsic part of ritual and dogma. Only in later Christian teachings against gluttony and licentiousness was unrestrained behavior of this type condemned as immoral and sinful. Until recently, and even now among large segments of the population, rich or poor, intelligent or ignorant, sophisticated or backward, the view persists that the pursuit of certain activities— overeating, drug taking, gambling, etc.—is a moral defect or a degenerative condition related to sinful, ungodly, and inhuman causes. Excessive behavior in every form is looked upon with contempt and disdain: the goal, of cultured and mature living is to restrain and control one's appetites, interests, emotions, and actions.

Accordingly, until very recently individuals who lacked such control received spiritual, moral, and theological "treatment." If these methods failed, restraint, imprisonment, or punishment was used. Whether this approach can be helpful is not the issue here. What should be noted is the underlying view of excessive behavior, which disregards centuries of studying how man functions and what devices and techniques people use to minimize discomforts and anxieties. The moralistic explanation of excessive disorders fails to recognize that certain activities go on beyond conscious control and that addictive agents, in producing physiological and/or psychological addiction, can render the individual incapable of determined and willful behavior.

Only lately have we begun to study addictive behavior in psychological terms, looking at what drives man to such activities in spite of intellectual, spiritual, and humanistic desires to abstain. The emphasis on such causes as moral degeneracy or hereditary taint overlooked individual and sociocultural factors in addiction. Reacting to this lack, psychodynamic theories have tended toward the opposite extreme, ignoring the chemical characteristics of addictive agents and the social conditions encouraging escapism while focusing exclusively on inner dynamics.

The Evolution of a Consensus on Addictions

Taking a historical view, we can spotlight the deficiencies in these formulations, as well as limit the endless controversies regarding the social value of some of the drugs, namely the hallucinogens and other stimulants, by clearly defining the addictions as socially and individually destructive conditions that are the concern of the community as well as the individual. The addictions therefore require a therapeutic program that acknowledges and encompasses these factors.

More and more, addictive behavior is being viewed as a disease related to existential, psychological, and physiological limitations. This condition develops in interaction with the cultural context, both past and present. At this point in history we know more about the external determinants of such behavior than about the inner, psychodynamic issues. I shall look at the latter area in this chapter.

Freud and his colleagues first offered psychodynamic explanations of addictive behavior. They put such behavior in the category of characterological disorders generally involving orality and overwhelming needs for reassurance and security. Addiction defined as an insatiable craving for certain substances or activities that eliminate dysphoria or induce a state of euphoria acknowledges excessive dependency and immaturity. As Savitt observed, "Object relationships are on an archaic level and the addict is unable to experience love and gratification through the usual channels of incorporation and introjection. Because of the inability to tolerate delay, he seeks an emergency measure which bypasses the oral route of incorporation in favor of a more primitive one, the intraveneous channel" (1). This perspective, which sometimes includes notions of infantile omnipotence or narcissistic mortification, defective superego, oral deprivation, and repressed homosexual tendencies, has had a widespread influence on the development of therapeutic programs even though its value is highly doubtful.

Freud, Alexander, Rado, and Schur attempted to identify specific characterological traits that related directly to particular addictions, but in general, they regarded addictions as efforts to escape from stressful situations and regressive gratifications of repressed or inhibited impulses.

Initially, Freud argued that addictions were substitutes for sexual satisfaction: "Not everyone who has occasion to take morphine, cocaine, chloral hydrate and so on, for a period acquires in this way an addiction to them. Closer inquiry usually shows that the narcotics are meant to serve directly or indirectly as a substitute for a lack of sexual satisfaction" (2). In 1897 Schur attributed all addictions to this single source: "I have gained the insight that masturbation is a 'primary addiction,' and that the other addictions, alcohol, morphine, tobacco, etc., enter into life only as a substitute for and a withdrawal [symptom] from it. This addiction plays an enormous role in hysteria. . . .The doubt of course arises whether such an addiction is curable, or whether analysis and therapy must stop short at this point and remain content with transforming a hysteria into a neurasthenia" (3). Finally, Rado postulated an "alimentary orgasm," a quasi-orgasm that involved the whole alimentary canal to account for alcoholism. He extended this notion to all addictions regardless of the route of administration (4). At a later date, Rado reformulated his theory of addiction, relating this disease to depression and elation and the ongoing attempt to deal with painful tension in individuals with a high degree of intolerance to pain.

Everybody involved in studying and treating the addictions has emphasized the escapist function of drugs and alcohol and the addict's need to deny reality. The early psychoanalytic theorists emphasized sexual issues, involving either an unwillingness to recognize a developing impotence or a repressed homosexual striving. In this connection Freud remarked, "The alcoholic will never admit to himself that he has become impotent through drink. However much alcohol he can tolerate, he cannot tolerate this piece of knowledge" (2). In recent years, the need to escape reality is viewed in much broader terms and is not necessarily considered to have psychopathic or sexual roots.

Addictions are probably not limited to specific character types, nor do certain characterological traits predispose an individual to addictive behavior. Thus, they should not be viewed as character disorders but as universal responses to internal and external pressures that the community looks upon as diseases, disorders, or antisocial acts. This implies that certain defense mechanisms may be so disruptive to the individual's social functioning that they provoke repressive or primitive responses from the community. In the addictions, the techniques of defense—denial, rationalization, projection, and many others—reflect the human desire for easy, magical solutions and man's inability and unwillingness to endure discomfort or tolerate anxiety. Accordingly, some psychiatrists see addiction not as an escape but as a search for a better life in the face of real, insuperable obstacles, an extremely helpful view in understanding drug dependence and addiction.

The methods employed in this humanistic striving for a more productive life may have disastrous consequences; nevertheless, the intent is to move toward a higher, more satisfactory mode of living (this was the principal role in ancient religious rituals of some behaviors now viewed as excessive). This view of drug use helps us understand the futility of sermonizing against "lost souls," who in fact are pursuing inappropriate means to achieve fuller lives. Of course, this issue is not universally present in drug abuse, particularly of narcotics, but is extremely common in alcoholism and addictions involving stimulants and marijuana. For other behaviors in excess—kleptomania and obesity for instance—it is more difficult to identify positive strivings. Thus, our understanding of the psychodynamics of addiction will need to include both escapist and transcendent purposes.

The Cornerstones of a Treatment Program

A comprehensive psychodynamic view of addictions must take account of physiological, psychological, and cultural determinants.

Physiological Factors

The addictive agent produces a physiological craving in spite of desire to terminate use. Prolonged drug reliance results in organ dysfunction, which requires treatment with other drugs to overcome the deficits, thereby producing a vicious cycle. This pattern is particularly apparent with substances that impair sexual potency and creative potentiality but may initially have been taken to deal with these concerns. Drug, alcohol, and food addictions cause the most physiological damage.

Psychological Factors

Character structure and underlying needs that are being dealt with in the particular addiction are vital considerations in treatment. Although dependence, orality, masochism, and passivity play a large role, obsessional devices to control and manipulate oneself and the environment are even more important in behaviors of excess. The type of addiction—to amphetamine, food, gambling, stealing, or masturbation—can be related to specific factors in the individual's psychology to account for the choice of one type of defense over another and one variety of compulsion over another. In this area psychotherapy has its greatest potential in the overall therapeutic program.

Cultural Factors

This category includes both the cultural pressures to initiate and sustain certain escapist maneuvers and social attitudes toward particular addictions. Some addictions are almost inevitably involved with criminal activities, while others are viewed as esthetically or morally distasteful. Community response in either case puts great psychological distress on the user, which tends to encourage the addictive behavior rather than the individual's effort to abandon it. The community includes not only the immediate family and the individual's life history within it but also political, religious, economic, and historical forces that impinge on the individual.

Distinguishing between Dependence and Abuse

Drug dependence causes major medical and social disruptions. Dependence may develop with nicotine, alcohol, and the fantastic assortment of pills, nostrums, dieting aids, and psychophilosophical prescriptions ranging from meditation to transcendental and transactional experiences with gurus, gestaltist leaders, prophets, and teachers. We must distinguish between drug dependence and drug abuse. Drug dependence speaks loudly and emphatically about the ills of our technological culture overburdened by political conflicts, racism, hypocrisy, and economic imbalance. But dependence is not addiction. Dependence on drugs or devices may arise for many reasons and serve many purposes, which can be classed under two headings: analgesia or stimulation. In either case, drugs are taken to alleviate painful feelings or to stimulate and enhance pleasurable affects; the individual does not suffer from the behavior but enjoys it (this seems largely to be the case with marijuana and alcohol).

General Features of Substance Abuse

The development of drug addiction is not simply a matter of character structure or interpersonal or social disturbances; this condition is related to the pleasant effects of the drug combined with the individual's capacity to deny the deleterious effects. This latter factor may explain the development and persistence of drug addictions in contrast to occasional drug use and is the key issue in other behaviors of excess, such as obesity, gambling, and compulsive masturbation. According to Bejerot, "The more potent a

dependence-producing substance and the more pleasant the psychopharmacological effects, the quicker and stronger is the development of the addiction'' (5).

Any individual can develop an addiction if certain drugs are taken
over a period of time. As Bejerot observed, "Probably everyone after only
a week's continual use of cocaine would long for the drug for the rest of his
life, so strong and pleasurable are its effects during the first phase of
abuse'' (5). In this connection, Freud, who advocated and used cocaine
quite extensively for a while, was responsible for producing an addiction in
his highly regarded teacher Ernest Fleischl von Marxow, a renowned
physiologist. Fleischl developed an addiction to morphine taken because of
severe pain in an amputation neuroma. Schur described Freud's harrowing
nightly vigils with Fleischl, who developed a cocaine addiction following
Freud's attempt to cure the morphine addiction (3). The manifestations of
the cocaine addiction were even more disastrous than those of morphine,
resulting in physical and mental deterioration.

Compulsion and Grandiosity

Addiction to drugs and alcohol has physiological effects that require continued use. In contrast, gambling and kleptomania are maintained exclusively by psychological imperatives and compulsions, bolstered by a
defensive structure that prevents realistic confrontation with the consequences of the behavior. Drug addiction and alcoholism therefore differ
essentially from other behaviors of excess in this significant regard.

Certain characteristics of the addictive process are universally
manifested: the element of compulsion and the capacity of the addicting
substance to relieve immediate anxiety even if the agent produces greater
anxiety over the long range. The addict's inability to tolerate discomfort or
to postpone gratification even briefly makes him or her appear immature.
The immediacy of the addict's demand for the addictive substance is often
described by observers as a gluttonous urge for fulfillment; in alcoholism,
obesity, or drug addiction, this urge has been called orality.

Addictive behavior involves the compulsive, ritualistic pursuit of
pharmacological agents or certain behavior patterns in an effort to deal
with intolerable anxieties. Soon, the initial phase of drug abuse or excessive
behavior rigidifies into an addiction, the dynamics and patterns of which
constitute a syndrome in their own right (5). Davidson noticed the parallel
between addiction and compulsive neurosis: "Psychologically, [addiction]
seems strikingly similar to a compulsive [neurotic] reaction. The klep-
tomaniac or pyromaniac will tell you, 'I get no pleasure out of stealing [or
setting fires] but I have a mounting unendurable tension [or anxiety] which
can be relieved in this way''' (6).

To justify continued uncontrolled drug use, users frequently either deny the physiological danger involved or insist on their ability voluntarily to terminate use. Addicts may convince themselves of the harmlessness and value of the agent through refusing to consider adverse consequences or denying their manifestation. Invariably, they insist that they can control intake. This grandiose pretension is typical of obsessive-compulsive neurosis and is crucial in maintaining addictions.

Grandiosity is the assumption of an exalted but impossible state. While this feeling is related to a sense of high esteem and worth, it is qualitatively different. Grandiosity is the negation of real self-esteem; it denies one's true assets and demands superhuman attributes to overcome one's doubts. Grandiosity is an illusory conception of strength, unjustified by actual or potential achievement; it is a defensive and adaptive mechanism that arises from certain psychological needs. The characteristic presence of this feature in the obsessional neurosis casts some light on its adaptative role in obesity, alcoholism, narcotic addiction, compulsive gambling, compulsive masturbation, and kleptomania. In all these conditions grandiosity is seen when the individual tends to assume a privileged status. In each instance the grandiose feelings are expressed in terms of being exempt from both the consequences of one's behavior and the laws of nature.

It is a commonplace that alcoholics cannot moderate their drinking. This is precisely the obsessional problem. After abandoning all controls and getting lost in alcoholic binges, the illusory superman can be revived in the grandiose fantasies of the intoxicated state. An alcoholic bout typically ends in great remorse and guilt, which produce the inevitable resolution to abandon drinking. Since the underlying compulsion is untouched, however, the resolution cannot succeed. The inabilty to abstain reinforces the alcoholic's sense of ineffectiveness, which results in more drinking. The grandiose feelings experienced while intoxicated only temporarily invoke the illusion of superhuman capacity, at the same time deceiving the person into believing that he or she can exert the necessary control at will.

Likewise, the obese individual believes that he or she can eat to the heart's content without actually overindulging. Addicted gamblers similarly insist that they can stop while they are winning even though innumerable past experiences prove otherwise. The central characteristic of the feeling of grandiose exemption from consequences is tied very closely to the immature propensity toward immediate gratification without regard for future effects. No wonder that investigators and observers at one time described a common personality structure that predisposed people to alcoholism, drug abuse, obesity, or other excessive behaviors. As noted earlier, however, they failed to recognize that external precipitating and internal predisposing factors are the key to abuse and addiction.

As Rado observed, to maintain an addiction in the face of obvious self-destructive dangers requires more than obsessive-compulsive tendencies (4). Physical dependence, relief from anxiety, and euphoria are major features of addiction, which is sustained by a distinctive use of denial supported by grandiose feelings of a special immunity from adverse consequences:

> It is impossible for the patient not to perceive what is happening. His friends and relatives deluge him with warnings to "pull himself together." At the same time the elation [following use of the drug] diminishes in intensity and the depression becomes more severe. Physical illness, unmistakably due to the use of the poison, afflicts him with pain. Then everything was in favor of the elation, whereas now the hopes set upon it have been revealed as deluding. It might be supposed that the patient would reflect on this and give up the drug—but no; he continues in his way. I must admit for many years I could not grasp the economics of the state of mind until a patient himself gave me the explanation. He said, "I know all the things that people say when they upbraid me, but mark my words, Doctor, *nothing* can happen to me." This then is the patient's position. The elation has reactivated his narcissistic belief in his invulnerability and all of his better insight and all of his sense of guilt are shattered on this bulwark.

Alleviation of Distress

While the tendency to seek immediate gratification and to feel superhuman characterizes obsessional thinking and behavior, it does not necessarily lead to addiction. Therefore, additional factors must activate the addiction process. These factors involve stress, tension, and/or social or economic conditions that have become intolerable and require magical resolution. Because stresses vary from class to class, so, too, do addictions. For example, pharmacological addictions predominant in lower socioeconomic groups; food addictions, in more affluent groups.

In highly sophisticated, technological societies the individual is conditioned to expect rapid, even magical benefits from any ameliorative prescription. Consequently, addictions may not necessarily reflect neurological or neurotic disorders but a socioeconomic context in which easy escape and comfortable release from even minimally distressing situations can be quickly achieved. Reports from China, though sparse and uncertain, tend to support the view that sociological factors are the prime determinants in drug addiction. These accounts imply that the drug problem has been markedly reduced and perhaps even eliminated in China. If this is true, we may be forced to conclude that the addictive disorders, particularly those involving drugs or alcohol, may be social diseases and not psychiatric disorders at all, which is not to rule out the role of compulsivity as a characterological prerequisite. However, this universal factor in addictions apparently can be minimized by social and economic manipulations as well as by psychotherapy.

Community Attitudes

Just as important as the social, political, and economic factors that may encourage and support the use of chemicals to deal with emotional and social dysfunctioning is the community's attitude toward the addict. Understanding of community attitudes not only influences our notion of causality but also assists our efforts to control and treat addictive disorders. The community reaction to addicts, whether it be to their need for money to support an expensive habit, their irresponsible family behavior caused by the addiction, or their physical and emotional deterioration, produces complications over and above the physiological and psychological ones initially present.

For example, the antisocial behavior of the addict in pursuit of illegal drugs may lead the psychiatrist or social scientist to view addicts as suffering from antisocial, asocial, or psychopathic character disorders. The error lies in confusing intent with consequence: antisocial behavior involving the addict in legal, as well as moral, difficulties is the result of addiction, not its cause—even when addiction is prevalent in initially antisocial individuals. This misjudgment may translate into inadequate funding of treatment programs.

Therapy

Wurmser described the interacting facets of the etiology of drug addiction by a series of concentric circles: inner problems, family, peer group, society, culture and values, and philosophical problems (7). The outer five circles relate to psychosocial factors and suggest that addictive disorders can never be resolved without the participation of nonphysicians, such as teachers, social workers, nurses, and psychotherapists. The innermost circle suggests that we reshuffle philosophical and economic resources to eliminate factors that encourage insecurities, anxieties, tensions, boredom, and alienation. A valid treatment program for the addictive disorders must address physiological, psychological, and socioeconomic factors. Some addictions—drug abuse, alcoholism, and obesity—involve all three factors. Others like kleptomania and compulsive masturbation seem to be tied primarily to psychological elements. However, no addiction can be adequately comprehended as solely a psychodynamic disorder based on some inner distortions that make the individual susceptible to addictive behavior. Though immaturity and the tendency to cope by using inappropriate, magical techniques and resources rather than by confronting and attempting rationally to resolve difficulties are prominent in addicts, these are widespread traits. They nevertheless are the inner forces that initiate and sustain the addiction and they must figure prominently in the total treatment plan.

Initially, treatment must occur on the physiological level. We must concern ourselves with the addicting agent and view the situation as an acute crisis in which the addiction must be terminated or the drug intake prevented by such techniques as substitution (methadone) or aversive conditioning designed to shift the pleasure of the addiction into pain. Though such therapeutic interventions must be viewed as only one piece of the total program, unless we quickly intercede, physiological damage to the brain and other organ systems may make the addict inaccessible to psychotherapeutic measures.

I do not propose to deal with the variety of approaches recommended for the crisis (or physiological) phase of addiction treatment or to discuss the socioeconomic issues that be addressed in a well-rounded program. Instead, I will focus on some issues that relate to psychodynamic factors.

As with all compulsions, external force, persuasion, threat, or humiliation cannot undo the addiction, which has an inner dynamic that must be exposed and understood. The addict must recognize the tendencies that foster addictive behavior—immaturity, escapism, grandiosity—as well as the true strengths of his or her personality. Equally important, the addict must learn new techniques for dealing with feelings of powerlessness and helplessness other than compulsive rituals and sham displays of power.

The contradictory nature of compulsions, most evident in drug addicts and alcoholics, emphasizes the ineffectiveness of traditional psychotherapeutic methods, which by encouraging the individual to undo his or her compulsion actually strengthen it. As Fenichel noted, "The situation, therefore, in the case of compulsion neurotics is that they must be healed with the aid of functions that are themselves affected by the illness" (8). And in fact, the addict generally comes for treatment not to terminate excessive behavior but to get help in successfully maintaining the addiction: "The patient *never* comes for relief from the repressed wish, but desires to be relieved of the exhausting drains necessary to maintain the substitution [symptom]" (9).

To abandon compulsive behavior one must acknowledge one's powerlessness vis-à-vis the compulsion and admit the need for outside help. By giving up absolute control over living through compulsive behavior, the addict can begin to exert reasonable controls without grandiose pretensions of invulnerability. This will result in the gradual abandonment of compulsive rituals and other symptomatology.

Alcoholics Anonymous recognizes this natural progression, insisting that the alcoholic accept in advance that being alcoholic means being helpless to control or alter compulsive drinking and that he or she genuinely needs help. Bateson observed that the process of "surrender" in AA involves the alcoholics' recognition of the compulsive nature of their drinking, their powerlessness in the face of this behavior, and their inability to resolve the problem by will power. The alcoholic also must agree that only a greater power can restore the former state of nondrinking; this recognition breaks the myth of self-power. According to Bateson, "The whole epistemology of self control which his friends urge upon the alcoholic is monstrous. . . . the alcoholic is right in rejecting it (10). In contrast, AA uses the technique of paradoxical intention, which initially exaggerates the excessive behavior by forcing the patient to accept the symptoms willingly and deliberately and put them under voluntary control. This process exposes the absurdity of the addiction and gives the alcoholic the opportunity to control its manifestations. Though encouraging patients to continue their addictions is obviously paradoxical, the real issue is to put the behavior under the patient's charge. As patients begin to take charge, they receive positive feedback that they are not totally powerless but, in rejecting grandiose delusions, can actually control some areas of their lives. Unfortunately, physiological changes in addictions besides alcoholism preclude general use of this technique.

Conclusion

The therapy of the addictions demands that in addition to terminating administration, addicts must be made aware of their insecurities, anxieties, and inability to deal with their anxieties. Only then can they face the consequences of their behavior and only then will we be able to mobilize their actual strengths and assets to begin the process of repair. As the addict's esteem and awareness of his or her strengths increase, he or she can slowly risk abandoning addictive patterns, becoming free to make a valid choice about the addicting agent.

Efforts to force addicts to relinquish their compulsions can be of no avail. We cannot encourage addicts to make a free choice or to exercise their will to overcome the excessive behavior when self-control is the very process that is impaired. To do so will only emphasize powerlessness and fortify the addiction. By mustering physiological, psychological, and socioeconomic support, treatment programs can help addicts recognize their strengths and their ability to undo compulsive patterns. Under such conditions the addict may be able to function without the use of chemicals. In this sense the psychodynamics of addiction is the umbrella under which all other modalities of treatment must operate in order to achieve long-term remission rather than temporary subsidence of symptoms.

References

1. Savitt, R. A., Psychoanalytic studies on ego structure in narcotic addiction, *Psychoanal. Q. 32,* 43–57 (1963).
2. Freud, S., *Standard Edition of the Complete Psychological Works of S. Freud,* vols. 1 and 3, Hogarth, London, 1966.

3. Schur, M., *Freud: Living and Dying,* International Universities Press, New York, 1972.
4. Rado, S., *Psychoanalysis of Behavior,* Grune & Stratton, New York, 1962.
5. Bejerot, N., A theory of addiction as an artificially induced drive, *Amer. J. Psychiat. 128,* 842–846 (1972).
6. Davidson, H. A., Confessions of a goof ball addict, *Amer. J. Psychiat. 120,* 750–756 (1964).
7. Wurmser, L., Drug abuse: nemesis of psychiatry, *Inter'l. J. Psychiat. 10,* 94–107 (1972).
8. Fenichel, O., *The Psychoanalytic Theory of Neurosis,* Norton, New York, 1945.
9. Kempf, E. J., *Psychopathology,* Mosby, St. Louis, 1920.
10. Bateson, G., The cybernetics of "self": a theory of alcoholism, *Psychiatry 34,* 1–18 (1971).

19

Behavior Therapy in the Treatment of Behaviors in Excess

Ronald F. Kokes

Behavior modification and therapy procedures have been applied to most of the disorders discussed in this volume. Clinically significant bodies of literature on behavioral treatment have been developed in the areas of alcoholism, anorexia, obesity, and smoking; a less extensive literature has evolved on drug addiction. This chapter first focuses on the general status of and changes in the behavioral treatments of these disorders and then reviews behavioral definitions and treatments in alcoholism, overeating and undereating, smoking, and drug addiction. The treatment programs and techniques considered are derived from behavior concepts based largely on social learning theory (1, 2). This model centers on behaviors that are operationally defined by observable phenomena. It assumes that maladaptive behaviors have been learned and shaped through experience and that they can be altered by systematic changes in that experience and through observation or instruction.

Three general sets of learning principles—respondent conditioning (3–5), operant conditioning (6), and cognitive behavior modification (7)—provide the theoretical bases for most of the techniques. In "respondent conditioning" an initially neutral stimulus (conditioned stimulus, or CS) is repeatedly paired in time and place with another stimulus (unconditioned stimulus, or UCS) that automatically elicits a specific response (unconditioned response, or UCR). When conditioning has occurred, the conditioned stimulus in the absence of the UCS will elicit a conditioned response (CR) that is similar to the UCR. In "operant conditioning" the consequences of a targeted response are systematically rearranged. Dispensing a reinforcement after performance of the targeted response increases the probability or rate of the response; withholding a previously contingent reinforcement decreases the probability or rate of the response. A punishing consequence suppresses behavior and decreases the probability of the behavior as long as the punishing consequence remains available. In avoidance learning paradigms the subject can avoid an upcoming aversive stimulus by performance of a prescribed response. For example, an alcoholic could avoid shock by discarding a drink within a designated time. In escape learning paradigms an aversive stimulus is presented and the subject terminates it by responding in a prescribed manner. For instance, a smoker extinguishes his or her cigarette to terminate a noxious level of white noise. "Cognitive behavior modification" includes the private events of cognition, thought, and self-statement in explaining the nature of maladaptive behaviors. Internal events are designated variables mediating overt behaviors or emotional states and/or are the behaviors themselves targeted for change (7).

Two of the salient features of behavior therapy are use of an experimental methodological approach to the study and treatment of behavioral disorders (8) and emphasis on the patient's personal responsibility for change. Both of these features are prominent in the literature and together they have altered the definition and treatment of the behaviors in excess.

The experimental methodological approach to studying human behavior is based on systematic observation and functional analysis of targeted behaviors to identify their specific characteristics and parameters, the cues eliciting them, and the contingencies maintaining them. In an optimal situation, therapeutic procedures derived from principles and explanations of behavior, which were formulated and tested in experimental psychology laboratories, are applied to the targeted behavior. The systematic application of various well-defined procedures to a specific behavior across different time and stimulus situations promotes understanding (9). This process has been applied somewhat systematically over the past two decades to the study of behavioral disorders. Research has proceeded from case studies to controlled single subject and group studies. The results have proven the earlier, simplistic S-R and drive reduction conditioning models of behavior (derived from learning principles) to be inadequate. The behavioral disorders continue to be viewed largely as behavior patterns that are acquired and controlled according to the same principles that govern most behaviors. However, there have been changes in understanding these disorders. They are now known to be complex and multiply determined and maintained by reinforcers from the subject's internal and external environment. These patterns of behavior are elicited by a variety of antecedent environmental, cognitive, and physiological cues, alone or in combination. They serve diverse sets of functions for specific subjects, probably associated with idiographic characteristics.

The complex interaction of social, situational, cognitive, physiological, and emotional states in the acquisition and maintenance of behavioral disorders is the major focus of current behavioral investigations (2, 8). Recognition of the complexity and robust nature of the behaviors has prompted changes in the approaches to treating them. Clearly, treatment must include more than one or two basic conditioning procedures, as in earlier studies (2). Effective treatment programs must address every aspect of the subject's system involved in the disorder. Indeed, the individual's total system—biological, physiological, metabolic, genetic, social, cultural, and familial—interacts to maintain the set of conditions that constitutes the disorder.

Ideological differences have often prevented behaviorists from engaging the total system of the patient. They have been reluctant explicitly to include potent therapy elements such as demands, expectancies, emotions of the therapist-client relationship, or anxiety reducing medications. The behavioral literature increasingly contains examples of multiple-component programs using several behavioral and traditional therapeutic procedures with each component selected for its specific relevance to a certain aspect of the disorder. Many clinical studies reveal an implicit awareness of the relevance of other models of disorder (e.g., the medical model) to treatment. For example, behavioral techniques have been used in support of medication regimens (10).

Systematic study has expanded the definitions of disordered behaviors from a single deficit, e.g., excessive drinking, to include multiple associated deficits. For example, not only may a man drink excessively but also he may have difficulties functioning in his job or family. A careful functional analysis of behavior is necessary to determine which problems cause the greatest difficulties and should have priority in treatment. A priori selection of a problem because it is most visible or most convenient to treat violates the principles on which a functional analysis of behavior is based. The way multiple deficits interact affects the priority of their treatment. A man who is depressed by a troubled marital situation may increase his excessive drinking. Attacking the depression but not the marital problems would lead to failure. Investigators have begun to respond by identifying, assessing, and treating all of a subject's significant problems (11). A combination of behavioral and/or traditional treatments, each addressing specific deficits, individualizes treatment and maximizes the benefits of therapy.

One of the major recent contributions from behavior therapy to strengthening and diversifying treatment programs has been the increased emphasis on, and explicit development of, self-control programs (12). These programs are based on the assumptions that humans have both the capacity for self-directed behavior and personal responsibility for change. They also assume that a subject's behavior is elicited by cues and maintained by contingencies in the environment whether or not he or she is aware of them. Self-control programs give instruction in monitoring and analyzing relationships among specified behaviors, their cues, and their consequences with a view toward making subjects aware of these relationships and thereby put them in a position to alter them. The subject is instructed in how functionally to analyze behavior and monitor his or her own overt, cognitive, or emotional behavior along with the associated environmental cues and consequences. Armed with these data the subject can systematically pursue guided changes in behavior. In this process not only are the person's external circumstances changed but cognitive and affective behavior also changes consequent to the experiences of success and control. When the analysis reveals skill deficits, training in the specific skill (e.g., relaxation, assertiveness) is provided. Inexpensive programs yielding promising results have been developed for almost all the behavioral disorders. These programs appear especially appropriate for subjects with circumscribed problems but without significant additional psychopathology who have good cognitive skills and are functioning adequately on their jobs and in their families.

Various problems have emerged in the application of behavioral treatment to behavioral excesses. Behavior therapy has been relatively effective in producing change in excesses when compared to traditional, nonbehavioral types of therapy. However, changes in a substantial number of cases have been statistically but not clinically significant. Furthermore, the changes have not been maintained over short-term follow-up. Evidence is mounting to indicate that behavior change and maintenance of change are related but distinct processes mediated by different mechanisms and contingencies. An effective treatment program must include provisions for both processes. Models for maintenance of change are being developed (13), and initial studies evaluating specific variables for their capacity to maintain change have been published (14).

Evaluating the relative therapeutic power of various behavioral techniques for treating excesses is a problem. Many reports present data on the effectiveness of one or a combination of techniques. Within themselves research reports generally have been methodologically sound. However, they often have failed to consider either how the results could be interpreted in light of published studies or what contribution the results could make to the systematic search for knowledge. Optimally, studies evaluating the merits of treatment should use the basic design and variables of previous studies except for the variable under examination. This variable should be changed systematically. Differences in results from such studies would then reflect the therapeutic power of the targeted treatment variable.

Finally, the general learning model is applied in substantially the same way across all the behavioral excesses without a critical examination of their specific characteristics. The human organism is made up of a variety of systems, as I noted earlier. The interaction of system components determines how and whether learning will take place. Behavioral excesses involve and affect each of these system components in different ways and in varying degrees. For example, obesity involves the metabolic system to a different and probably greater degree than does smoking. Thus, examination of the systemic and conditioning characteristics of each disorder must precede application of procedures to alter the total system. An excellent but somewhat unique example of this type of disorder examination is a recent article by Wooley, Wooley, and Dyrenforth (15). These authors studied the biological, physiological, and social aspects of eating, hunger, and weight loss, as well as the interaction between weight loss programs and these dimensions. Only such a comprehensive approach can uniquely shape a learning theory based treatment program to the special characteristics of each disorder.

Alcoholism

The behavioral treatment of alcoholism has a long history. Recent excellent reviews have presented a detailed description of this history (16–20), which will be covered only briefly here.

In the past two decades three major changes have occurred in the definition and treatment of alcoholism. First, the definition has become much more complex. Current behavioral treatments consider alcoholism a multifaceted, disordered behavioral pattern including but not limited to excessive alcohol intake. The pattern, which can be elicted by physiological and environmental cues alone or in combination, is maintained by other combinations of responses (19).

The second major change is the development and assessment of minimal treatment programs. Many previous treatment programs tended to be inpatient, with high staff to patient ratios, extensive and close personal contact, and control and responsibility for change resting largely with the therapists. Minimal treatment programs, often designated "behavioral self-control programs," require less therapist time and less patient contact time, tend to have an educational group format, and place responsibility for change on the drinker (21). Miller and his associates developed such a program, which contains an integrated set of behavioral treatment components and is directed specifically to the acquisition of controlled drinking behavior although the program will also produce abstinence (16). Miller's program includes goal setting (determination of appropriate levels of alcohol consumption based on past and current history of the effects of alcohol on the drinker); self-monitoring of drinking behavior; rate control training, designed to change the topography of drinking behavior; self-reinforcement; functional analysis of drinking behavior and training in stimulus control procedures; and training in alternative responses for use when alcohol has been consumed inappropriately. This and similar programs have yielded promising results (22, 23). Approximately 60–65 percent of drinkers will achieve and maintain controlled drinking habits. The apparent success of minimal treatment programs, plus the number of alcoholics who spontaneously stop drinking on their own, indicates that specific subgroups of alcoholics do not need intensive and extensive treatment programs. Attempts to identify the characteristics of these alcoholics are under way. Investigators suggest from available evidence that alcoholics with some or all of the following characteristics may be appropriate candidates for minimal or self-control programs: recent onset of drinking, good cognitive skills, middle- or upper-class status, and at least minimal functioning on the job and in the social environment (16).

The third major change in the behavioral treatment of excessive drinking has been the acceptance of controlled drinking as an appropriate treatment goal for at least some alcoholics. Initially, controlled drinking was merely reported in studies in which abstinence was the treatment goal. Later studies showed that controlled drinking could be attained and maintained by some alcoholics (24–26). Recent studies have been directed to designing efficient and inexpensive treatment methods for the attainment of controlled drinking and to identifying alcoholic subgroups for which controlled drinking is an appropriate goal (27, 28). Discussion of the appropriateness of controlled drinking has challenged the validity of the disease model of alcoholism and the "loss of control" hypothesis (i.e., if an alcoholic takes one drink he or she loses all control over drinking) (29). Investigators have taken issue with this model because many alcoholics terminate drinking voluntarily (30–32), former alcoholics exhibit controlled social drinking (33, 34), and a subgroup of alcoholics have become controlled drinkers after treatment (16, 24). Data from other studies in psychiatry may also support the controlled drinking position: Ritzler and colleagues reported that among first admission psychiatric patients nonalcoholic problem drinkers appeared psychologically healthier than abstainers (35). Abstinence may reflect a rigidity of response that is maladaptive in the social environment.

Most of the major alcoholic treatment programs of the past several decades have been comprehensive efforts costly in terms of staff, time, and money. This trend resulted from the general failure of single-component behavioral treatment programs and the consequent acknowledgment of the resistance to change of excessive drinking behavior. A large variety of treatments have been evaluated either singly or combined in multifaceted treatment programs, e.g. (aversion therapy, relaxation training, systematic desensitization, alcohol education, stimulus control, operant conditioning, contingency management, self-monitoring, social skills training, and cognitive retraining.) Choice of component(s) for study has often been made on the basis of theoretical conceptualization of the etiology of drinking—reduction of anxiety, classically conditioned responses, lack of appropriate alternative behaviors, and/or reinforcement from the external environment.

Sobell and Sobell described an excellent comprehensive, multiple-component program (24). Subjects were assigned to either controlled drinking or abstinence groups, with each group subdivided into behavior therapy or conventional therapy sections. Behavior therapy subjects participated in 17 sessions using the following procedures: video feedback of intoxicated behaviors to force confrontation of inappropriate behavior and to increase motivation, training in self-analysis of environmental stressors associated with excessive drinking, training in socially acceptable alternative behaviors, and aversive electrical conditioning. Conventional treatment subjects received traditional treatment procedures including group therapy, chemotherapy, Alcoholics Anonymous, physiotherapy, and other traditional services. At six-month and one-year follow-ups, behavior therapy subjects functioned significantly better than conventional therapy subjects. However, at a two-year follow-up only the controlled drinking behavioral group receiving behavior therapy continued to function better than the conventional therapy groups.

Earlier studies had used aversive therapies based on the four learning paradigms: classical conditioning, punishment, avoidance learning, and escape learning (36–38). Aversive therapies for alcoholics have been chemical, electrical, and verbal. In aversive therapy the taste, sight, or smell of alcohol is paired repeatedly with a drug (chemical), shock (electrical), or negative cognition (verbal) that elicits an aversive physiological response such as nausea, vomiting, or anxiety.

Positive results have been associated with the use of emetics like emetine, apomorphine, and ipecac (39–43). Voeghtlin and his associates reported that 51 percent of their 400 subjects were abstinent after a 13-year period (42). Despite these favorable outcomes, the relative efficacy of aversive chemical therapy remains unproven due to methodological deficiences in the studies (the larger studies of Voeghtlin and his associates did not include control groups). Aversive therapy was integrated into an intensive, multicomponent treatment program and approximately 17 percent of their subjects reported as successes in treatment had relapsed after initial treatment but were successfully re-treated. Lemere and Voeghtlin suggested that this treatment may be most productive for subjects from higher social classes who have a favorable prognosis for most types of therapy (42). Final results of attempts to condition alcoholics with paralyzing drugs like succinylcholine chloride dehydrate (anectine or scoline) have not been as positive (44, 45) as initial successes forecast (46). Miller concluded after careful review that apnea producing drugs should not be used because of their potential danger; moreover, improvement rates are generally inferior to those with nausea producing drugs (16).

Extensive studies of electrical aversion used both alone and in conjunction with other behavioral treatments have had inconclusive results, varying from high effectiveness to none. This therapy apparently does not have an effect greater than that with less aversive and more efficient methods (16, 26, 47, 48). Nor does it seem to contribute substantially to multiple-component treatment programs (16, 24).

Controlled studies have demonstrated that aversive verbal conditioning or covert sensitization (49) is effective in producing up to 40 percent abstinence rates (50–52). However, data are not sufficient to draw firm conclusions about the procedure's effectiveness (16).

Operant conditioning and contingency management programs have not been extensively applied to the treatment of alcoholics (53, 54). Such programs should theoretically include the reward of behaviors incompatible with drinking, the withdrawal of reward and the punishment of excessive drinking and behaviors associated with drinking, and the rearrangement of the drinker's environment to remove cues for drinking. Two major programs used contingency management successfully in inpatient and outpatient settings (53, 55). In both cases drinkers were able to control their imbibing level and demonstrated environmental contingency control of drinking. In a creative program for outpatients, Bigelow and his associates reinforced the taking of Antabuse by the opportunity to work each day (50). Although these approaches appear promising, their implementation may be sufficiently difficult and expensive to preclude their use. A thorough functional analysis of the disordered behavior, with consequent reengineering of the subject's environment, requires significant therapist time, effort, and patience.

Assessment of the pretreatment and outcome deficits of the behavioral excesses has lagged behind conceptualization of the problem. Investigators address interpersonal and social anxiety, depression, job related difficulties, and lack of assertiveness in their treatment programs but fail for the most part to assess pretreatment to posttreatment changes along these dimensions. Investigators have generally focused on accurately measuring alcohol consumption in the natural environment before, during, and after treatment. To increase the validity of their measures, investigators supplement the often maligned self-report (56, 57) of drinking behavior with reports from significant others who have an opportunity to observe the subject and are accordingly trained to keep accurate records. Self-reports also have been verified by periodic blood alcohol level assays (16). Finally, the drinker has been systematically observed in a natural setting.

Indirect measures of drinking level are obtained by making alcohol accessible in a treatment unit (58). In this setting, drinking behavior has been measured by amount of work performed to obtain alcohol, e.g., prescribed number of lever-presses (59), prescribed social and personal care activities (53), or amount of alcohol consumed. In a few programs, an experimental cocktail lounge, with bar, music, dim lights, and bartender, was established in a hospital unit to simulate the natural setting and cues for drinking. Alcoholics and social drinkers could mingle in the bar while being observed by staff members in the room or through closed circuit television (60). The obvious nature of such assessment situations reduces their utility. Miller and his associates creatively disguised access to alcohol by setting up a "taste test" (45). Excessive drinkers in their study were charged with rating on dimensions of taste six beverages having different amounts of alcohol. Level of drinking was assessed by total amount of alcohol consumed.

In summary, the data indicate that behavior therapy procedures have a limited but effective role in the treatment of alcoholics. Single behavioral treatment components have little effect across studies. The multicomponent programs produce a significant reduction in drinking over and above that expected from spontaneous termination. The relatively new self-control programs appear significantly to help patients with an initially good prognosis reduce or terminate drinking.

Overeating

Overeating and obesity are the disorders most extensively examined by behavioral therapy investigators. This may reflect the readily available subject population and the ease of measuring the target variable, weight (15). The springboard for the systematic evaluation of behavioral methods in treating obesity was the report by Ferster, Nurnberger, and Levitt in the early 1960s (61). Stuart's paper (62), published in the late 1960s, prompted a flood of studies on behavioral methods of weight control. He used a highly successful, individualized control program based on operant and respondent self-control procedures. The program resulted in substantial, clinically significant weight losses for the eight women completing treatment. Weight losses ranged from 26 to 47 pounds (X = 37.75) at a 12-month follow-up. The educational self-help format emphasized self-monitoring, stimulus control, alteration of the topography of eating responses, self-reinforcement, and, for some patients, covert sensitization (49). Nonspecific treatment effects were also operative in the individualized formats.

These results generated great optimism about the efficacy of behavioral methods to control eating and weight. Over 100 studies, many modeled after Stuart's multicomponent treatment program but including appropriate control groups, have evaluated the effectiveness of specific behavioral treatment components alone or in combination (63, 64). Components evaluated have included stimulus control, self-monitoring, self-reinforcement and/or punishment, therapist or external agent mediated reinforcement and/or punishment, and contingency contracting. Most multicomponent programs have been more effective than single-component programs (64, 65), although in some cases individual components have resulted in greater weight loss or change in eating behavior (66, 67).

Reviews of these studies in the mid-1970s concluded that behavioral therapy was more effective than other treatment modalities for weight loss in mild to moderate obesity (68–70). This initial optimism has been tempered by the following problems. First, the average weight loss within and across behavioral treatment groups tends not to be clinically significant (71). Second, within groups there have been large and unexplained variations in response to behavioral treatment. Some subjects lose clinically significant amounts of weight while others gain weight (63, 71). Third, in general, subjects either do not maintain weight loss over the long term (70, 72, 73) or lose no more weight after termination of the treatment contract (71, 74). Fourth, there has been a relative lack of long-term follow-up studies.

Studies in the late 1970s used component analysis of multifaceted treatment packages to determine the relative efficacy of individual elements. Inconsistent effects across studies make it difficult to determine the precise merit of individual components. However, reviews have proposed inclusion of the following elements found in many of the more successful programs (70, 75). The components, which would be presented primarily in an educational self-control format to the obese client with supplemental training for the family, include instruction in performing a complete functional analysis of eating behavior to identify cues and reinforcers for eating and the specific components of eating behavior; caloric content of foods; nutritional needs, problem solving techniques (75); stimulus control procedures to eliminate cues for overeating and to maximize cues for competitive adaptive behaviors (62); an appropriate and safe exercise program (76, 77); reprogramming and redirection of cognitive behaviors away from food associations (78); reduction of the intensity of emotional states antecedent to and concurrent with eating (79); and provision of maintenance strategies based on cue recognition to signal reinstatement of behavioral programs by the client and his or her family (80–82). Additionally, the families of obese subjects need to be trained accurately to dispense reinforcement and punishment (81, 83, 84). Armed with this knowledge, the subject should be able to implement a guided self-control–self-management program utilizing data based self-monitoring of the various aspects of daily caloric intake, including its antecedents and consequences (66).

Assessment of behavioral treatment programs for obesity and overeating has generally focused on the weight and the caloric intake of the subject. These two measures are straightforward assessments whose validity and accuracy are dependent, as in the case of alcoholism, on the absence of bias in self-reports or corroborating agent reports. In studies directed at changing the topography of eating behavior the various components of the act of eating have been monitored—number of bites, size of bites, speed of eating. These components are usually evaluated through direct observation (85, 86). Recently, skin fold measures have been developed as objective indices of obesity (87, 88). Skin fold thickness measured by calipers at designated body sites can readily be converted to percentage body fat. This measure is reliable, easily taken, and not significantly affected by loss of body fluids.

Obesity research has assumed that an imbalance in energy intake and expenditure results in the storage of fat. In this model the obese exhibit maladaptive eating habits, including eating too much food, eating faster than normal, and eating bigger bites and at shorter intervals than normal weight people (61, 89, 90). This pattern is attributed to oversensitivity to external cues (89, 91). Many of these assumptions have proven to be inaccurate generalizations: there are few differences between the eating styles of obese and normal weight subjects (85, 86, 92, 93). Additionally, there appears to be no significant relationship between changes in eating habits and weight loss. Furthermore, the expenditure side of the energy equation has been largely ignored in treatment program research even though inclusion of this element is reasonable (76). Finally, the external control model clearly is inadequate in view of the inconsistency in results across many contingency management studies (78).

The marginal success of behavioral treatment programs prompted Wilson to suggest that there had been a premature closure in explanations on which behavior therapy programs have been based (75). Relying on only these programs to change behavior implies that the current behavior therapy model is capable of offering a total explanation of behavior. In a practical sense such an attitude excludes from consideration possibly valuable data from other models of behavior. The limited success of any model in concretely explaining and predicting behavior militates against closure.

The general learning model has also been applied with a general disregard for the unique characteristics of disorders and subjects. Unique qualities of subjects can be addressed in individualized treatment programs or special programs aimed at patient subgroups for whom the procedures have been proven effective. Addressing the special characteristics of disorders demands attention to the biological, physiological, psychological, social, and possible genetic aspects of the disorder. This includes reviewing basic research in each of these areas to determine how treatment interacts with or is limited by them.

In an excellent article, Wooley, Wooley, and Dyrenforth began this process for the problem of obesity (15). They reviewed and analyzed current research data on metabolic, physiologic, and social aspects of obesity as these related to treatment. Samples of their conclusions from this analysis demonstrate the necessity of adjusting behavior treatment programs to specific disorders. For example, the obese do not eat more food than the nonobese, nor do they have different eating styles. Normal weight subjects appear to have the ability to dispose of excess calories much more easily than the obese. Another example is that human bodies adapt to food reduction by a lowered metabolic rate and decreased energy expenditure. This adaptation occurs more rapidly with successive fasting diets. Also, after fasting the lowered metabolic rate may readjust slowly to normal levels so that weight lost through dieting is rapidly regained. Clearly, dieting is not a neutral event. In prolonged periods of caloric restriction, hunger is directly related to the amount eaten during a given interval; that is, when eating is severely curtailed hunger is not as pronounced as under conditions of moderate eating. Hunger appears to be suppressed when there are unambiguous signals that food is unavailable. This article not only provides relevant data for the study and treatment of obesity but also stands as an example of study needed for other behavioral excesses.

In summary, the behavioral treatment of obesity has been only moderately effective. Some multicomponent programs providing individualized treatment have produced clinically significant weight losses that were maintained. In general, group programs are not successful: weight losses are regained by a short-term follow-up.

Anorexia Nervosa

Behavioral treatment of anorexia nervosa began in the mid-1960s. Aside from a few early studies (94, 95), all behavioral treatments of anorexia nervosa have utilized some variation of contingency management. Bachrach, Erwin, and Mohr reported the first contingency management treatment program (96). In their program the subject was placed initially in a stimulus-free room and not permitted social or recreational activities. The investigators supplied reinforcement for eating. Later, other privileges were made contingent on the amount of food eaten. The client gained 17 pounds in two months and was discharged. Subsequent studies have focused on other aspects of eating—number of mouthfuls eaten (97, 98), calories consumed (97), and weight gain (98). Reinforcing contingencies have varied from verbal reinforcement (98), to access to exercise (99), to having communication with visitors (100).

Currently, it is generally accepted that anorexics will gain weight and reestablish normal eating habits on an inpatient unit when treated with a sound contingency management program (101). Follow-up studies of anorexics have indicated that for a significant number of the treatment successes there is poor maintenance of weight and poor adjustment to the outside environment. Brady and Rieger reported the condition of 15 anorexics at a mean duration of 23 months after successful weight gain in an operant inpatient program (102). Two had died, five had made a good adjustment, five had made a fair adjustment, and three had made a poor adjustment physically and psychologically. In a follow-up of seven anorexics by Bhanji and Thompson at a mean of 32 months after discharge only one patient was given a good adjustment rating (103). Other investigators have reported similar results (104).

These findings suggest that disordered eating is only one aspect of anorexia nervosa. The inpatient operant conditioning weight gain program must be supplemented by therapy directed to personal and social adjustment (105). Investigators hypothesize that the anorexic performs a function for a disordered family. The patient is reinforced for performing this role by attention from parents and family members.

In a classic paper Leibman, Minuchin, and Baker presented a complete therapy program based on operant principles (106). The four patients described were anorexics hospitalized for weight gain. After initiation of the operant conditioning weight gain program a family therapy lunch session was scheduled for the patient, her family, and her doctors. This session allowed the patient to eat in the presence of the family without the development of family difficulties. At this session, the role of the family in the syndrome was also redefined in terms of family conflict. Upon discharge but within two weeks of the first family meeting, another such meeting was held to outline the outpatient program. This part of the treatment, designed by the doctors but maintained by the parents, followed an operant conditioning model. For prescribed weight gain the anorexic earned time out of the house with her friends. If she did not gain weight she had to remain at home with another family member. The family program was designed to withdraw the anorexic from the family difficulties and to increase the stress on the family to expedite changes in familial structure, organization, and functioning. At an average follow-up of 7.2 months all subjects exhibited normal weight and eating patterns.

In summary, anorexics achieve weight gain in inpatient contingency management programs. This approach can also be used as a component of family treatment to help restructure family interactions (106).

Smoking

Smoking has been the target of numerous behavioral treatment programs. Recent excellent reviews have critically evaluated these programs (107–111). In general, cigarette smoking is defined as an overlearned, highly practiced behavior pattern with immediate physiological and social reinforcement. This activity is acceptable in social settings and most of its negative consequences are remote. Reviews suggest that most treatment programs can produce a significant reduction—up to 40 percent of baseline—but there is regression to 75 percent of baseline after a relatively short time (three to six months). Less than one-third of subjects who achieve abstinence by the end of treatment remain so after three to six months (112).

Behavioral treatment programs for smoking may use contingency contracting, relaxation, self-reward or self-punishment, self-monitoring, systematic desensitization, hypnosis, instructions, stimulus control, behavioral rehearsal, covert sensitization, rapid smoking, aversive conditioning, nicotine fading, electric shock, and satiation. The techniques can be assigned to three categories: contracting, self-management, and aversion techniques (107). Single-component treatments of the first two types have fared little (if at all) better than other types of treatment in long-term results. Some aversive techniques, and multiple-component treatment programs composed of techniques from all three areas, show promise of success.

Rapid smoking is the most effective single-component treatment (113), although several studies identified negative aspects of this technique. Danaher noted that the negative results have been produced by significant deviations from the original design (113). Hall, Sachs, and Hall replicated the finding of 60 percent abstinence at a six-month follow-up in a study using the procedure as originally designed (114). In the procedure a smoker takes a puff and inhales the smoke from a cigarette every six seconds until he or she feels unable to continue. The smoker is to stop short of loss of consciousness or vomiting. After a brief rest the subject resumes rapid smoking until reaching the above level again. The subject continues this process until he or she cannot take another puff. There are six to eight such sessions (115). Several investigators emphasized the high level of stress this procedure puts on the cardiovascular system (116). Recent data suggest that healthy subjects are not in serious danger but they should be carefully screened prior to joining programs employing rapid smoking (116).

The failure of single-component therapies led investigators to try increasing the efficacy of treatment by combining techniques that address different facets of smoking behavior. Lichtenstein and Brown selected a group of techniques because each was suited for a specific stage of treatment and for severity of the problem (107). A review of earlier multiple-component programs concluded that their effectiveness was not greater than that of single-component approaches. However, data from most recent studies counter this claim. Foxx and Brown reported a 40 percent abstinence rate 18 months after treatment with a combination of nicotine fading and self-monitoring (117). Smokers reduced daily nicotine and tar intake to 61 percent and 70 percent of baseline, respectively. Likewise, Lando and associates found satiation plus self-control procedures effective at follow-up (118). Elliott and Denney presented an eight-component instructional treatment package including rapid smoking (119). Subjects designed their own treatment by selecting from various techniques. Forty-five percent were abstinent six months after treatment and all participants were smoking at an average of 41 percent of baseline rate. As expected, these multiple-component programs appear to have greater (but still limited) power because they address more aspects of the subject's internal and external environment. Multiple-component program development is progressing systematically but slowly. Conclusions about the effectiveness of these programs are not yet possible.

Earlier smoking programs aimed at abstinence. Investigators recently have accepted a significantly lower consumption of nicotine and tar as a reasonable goal (119, 120). Impetus for this change came from a report that smokers of low tar and nicotine cigarettes are less likely to develop lung cancer and coronary heart disease than smokers of high nicotine and tar cigarettes (121). Indeed, abstinence or reduction below a certain level may be inhibited by withdrawal symptoms associated with physiological addiction (122). Almost every study now reflects this goal adjustment by reporting results in terms of abstinence rates and reductions in levels of tar and nicotine consumption.

Assessment of smoking levels includes measurement of the harmful constituents of tobacco smoke. The smoking level is determined by three variables: levels of carbon monoxide, tar, and nicotine, rate of smoking and topography of smoking (i.e., total tobacco smoked, inhaling level, etc.) (123). The most common measurement method has been to count the number of cigarettes in which carbon monoxide yield and levels of tar and nicotine are known and to compute the amount of these substances inhaled in a specific time period. Recently, Danaher, Lichtenstein, and Sullivan described a reliable method of assessing carbon monoxide levels by analyzing exhaled air (124). This physiological correlate of smoking can be used to verify smoking self-reports.

Because recidivism is a major problem in smoking programs, recent reviews have stressed the importance of ways to maintain abstinence. Booster sessions have not proven helpful (119, 125). Continued telephone contact with therapists (113, 115) and instruction in management skills have been included in treatment programs, but their efficacy for maintenance is unknown. Results are beginning to be reported from studies comparing the power of specific techniques to maintain change. Colletti and Stern found a self-monitoring group maintained reduced smoking levels significantly better than did either a modeling group or subjects observing a treatment group (14). At a two-year follow-up the self-monitoring group was smoking at 37.5 percent of baseline and 38.5 percent were abstinent—only slightly better than would be expected from natural remission.

In summary, behavioral treatments are useful to a limited degree in reducing smoking. High rates of recidivism accompany moderately acceptable reductions in smoking.

Drug Addiction

Behavior therapy procedures have been applied to a limited but increasing extent in the treatment of drug addiction during the past 15 years. The increase is probably associated with the present accelerated and widespread use of drugs. Early studies had defined drug addiction as a behavioral excess to be eliminated (126). This notion was soon altered. Drug addiction investigators seem to have benefited from the experiences of researchers in other areas of behavior excess. They recognize the complexity of drug addiction and appreciate the difficulties involved in changing a behavioral disorder such as drug abuse. Currently, the drug addict is defined as a person who consumes and is physiologically and/or psychologically addicted to excessive amounts of illegal substances. The addict with poor prognosis also lacks social and interpersonal skills and job performance abilities. Treatment programs generally focus on eliminating illegal substance abuse, maintaining prescribed drug substitutes or antagonists, and establishing skills related to social and job functions. Internal reactions of addicts—anxiety (127) and depression (125–130)—are also addressed.

Behavioral research on drug addiction has generally yielded negative results because of high levels of attrition. A mean dropout rate greater than 50 percent probably skews previously randomized groups in an unknown direction, virtually eliminating the possibility of meaningful assessing treatment effects.

Contingency management, the behavior therapy technique most frequently applied to drug addicts, has been used principally in support of medication regimens in inpatient (128, 131–133) and outpatient programs (134). A few programs have emphasized drug ingestion (i.e., reduction in heroin use and increase in methadone) (129, 130, 135). Contingency management has also been used clinically to aid in the adjustment of methadone levels. Most studies, however, have applied contingencies in medication programs to increase socially acceptable behaviors, decrease specific behavior problems (129, 10), improve counseling attendance among methadone maintenance clients (136), decrease supplemental drug use by addicts (130), increase social, personal, and job performance skills, and maintain addicts in a narcotic antagonist clinic (137, 138). Reinforcing contingencies have included money, the privilege of taking methadone at home, opportunity for self-regulating methadone use, and reduced frequency of urinalysis.

Kurland, McCabe, and Hanlon were able to maintain significantly more subjects (paroled felons with histories of narcotic abuse) in treatment by dispensing a narcotic antagonist contingently (139). Opiate antagonists theoretically occupy receptor sites and block the euphoric effects of heroin (140). Antagonists are typically used for maintenance when subjects are opiate-free. The antagonist was administered on an increasing schedule as long as the addict produced "dirty" urine. It was discontinued when "clean" urine was produced. Sixty-three percent of 108 subjects remained in a program for six months, compared to 39 percent of a non-chemotherapy group. During follow-up 8 percent of the treatment group were reinstitutionalized versus 37 percent of the control group.

Two major projects have utilized contingency management as one treatment component. The Drug Project at the University of Florida integrated contingency management into a therapist controlled highly structured program based on intensive relationships with clients (141). Long-term follow-up data indicated clinically significant positive results in measures of time gainfully spent and reduced illegitimate drug use. Study results are hard to interpret because of the use of an all-white population not representative of the addict world, the lack of control groups, and the presence of nonspecific treatment effects that cannot be separated from effects of contingency management. The Heroin Antagonist and Learning Therapy Project (HALT), in Ventura County, California, was a comparative study of treatments (12). The behavioral therapy group received a contingency management program plus relaxation training, desensitization, covert sensitization, and self-control procedures as needed. The group had intensive involvement with staff members and received instruction in life management skills. The narcotic antagonist group received naltrexone plus vocational preparation and job placement aid. A third group received a combination of the other two treatments. The group receiving a combination of drug and behavior therapy and the group receiving naltrexone gave significantly fewer opiate-positive urines than did subjects in the behavior therapy group. Furthermore, clients in behavior therapy stayed in treatment a significantly shorter length of time (remaining in the program was one criterion of success).

Data from behavior therapy studies suggest that behavior therapy does not have a significant effect when divorced from medication or intensive group therapy. However, this approach is useful for developing and increasing behaviors necessary for continued participation in treatment and for managing life outside the treatment setting.

Conclusion

Behavior therapy applied in a well-designed multiple-component program produces significant, although inconsistent, positive clinical changes in alcoholism, overeating, anorexia, smoking, and drug addiction. Programs are most effective when they include an integrated set of the hypothetically most powerful procedures from the behavioral and traditional therapy models and when the program is applied to a population characterized by good prognostic features (e.g., adequate cognitive skills, satisfactory functioning on the job and in the family, and no evidence of chronic psychopathology). However, changes are generally not maintained. Behavioral change and maintenance of change are obviously related but different processes. Models of relapse and maintenance are currently being developed and refined; initial assessments of the force of specific variables in maintaining behavior change are now being published.

The discouraging results of behavioral treatment programs have caused adjustments in the boundaries of the gereral behavioral model. The adjustments reflect a slow but consistent movement toward accepting a systems model of behavior such as Engel's biopsychosocial scheme (143). The systems model assumes that behavior is determined by an interaction of multiple subsystems of the human organism. Variables previously rejected—cognitive and affective behavior—are now commonly accepted as necessary aspects of treatment programs. Also, the family's critical role in behavioral disorders is recognized (families reinforce and maintain certain behavior patterns of their members because the behaviors maintain homeostasis in the family).

Though we now recognize the usefulness of other models, this does not signal the demise of behavior therapy. Models can secure certain data as a function of their unique observational perspective. Use of such data can aid in developing a more effective behavioral model; for example, a thorough understanding of developmental or psychoanalytic parameters may help a behavioral therapist choose more appropriate reinforcing contingencies.

Finally, there has been growing recognition of the need to shape treatment to the special characteristics of the individual. Behavior therapy has recognized the unique learning history of each individual but has often failed to relate treatment programs to this dimension. Recent failures in treatment have underlined the need for individualized therapy.

References

1. Bandura, A., *Social Learning Theory,* Prentice-Hall, Englewood Cliffs, 1977.
2. Franks, C. M., Introduction: behavior therapy and its Pavlovian origins: review and perspectives, in *Behavior Therapy: Appraisal and Status,* C. M. Franks, ed., McGraw-Hill, New York, 1969, pp. 1–28.
3. Pavlov, I. P., *Conditioned Reflexes: An Investigation of the Physiological Activity of the Cerebral Cortex,* Oxford University Press, New York, 1927.
4. Pavlov, I. P., *Lectures on Conditioned Reflexes,* vol. 1, Lawrence & Wishart, London, 1928.
5. Wolpe, J., *Psychotherapy by Reciprocal Inhibition,* Stanford University Press, Stanford, 1958.
6. Skinner, B. F., *Science and Human Behavior,* Macmillan, New York, 1953.

7. Meichenbaum, D., *Cognitive Behavior Modification,* Plenum, New York, 1977.

8. Stolz, S. B., Wienckowski, L. A., and Brown, B. S., Behavior modification: perspective on critical issues, *Amer. Psych. 30,* 1027–1048 (1975).

9. Kazdin, A. E., Fictions, factions, and functions of behavior therapy, *Beh. Ther. 10,* 629–654 (1979).

10. Bigelow, G., Stitzer, M., Lawrence, L., Krasnegor, N., D'Lugoff, B., and Hawthorne, J., Narcotics addiction treatment: behavioral methods concurrent with methadone maintenance, *Inter'l. J. Addict.* (in press).

11. Rawson, R. A., Glazer, M., Callahan, E. J., and Liberman, R. P., Naltrexone and behavior therapy for heroin addiction, in *Behavioral Analysis and Treatment of Substance Abuse* (NIDA Research Monograph No. 25), N. A. Krasnegor, ed., GPO, Washington, D. C., 1979, pp. 26–43.

12. Golddiamond, I., A diary of self-modification, *Psych. Today 7,* 95–102 (1973).

13. Marlatt, G. A., A cognitive-behavioral model of the relapse process, in *Behavioral Analysis and Treatment of Substance Abuse* (NIDA Research Monograph No. 25), N. A. Krasnegor, ed., GPO, Washington, D.C., 1979, pp. 191–199.

14. Colletti, C., and Stern, L., Two-year follow-up of a nonaversive treatment for cigarette smoking, *J. Consult. and Clin. Psych. 48,* 292–293 (1980).

15. Wooley, S. C., Wooley, O. W., and Dyrenforth, S. R., Theoretical, practical, and social issues in behavioral treatments of obesity, *J. Appl. Beh. Anal. 12,* 3–25 (1979).

16. Miller, W. R., and Hester, R. K., Treating the problem drinker: modern approaches, in *The Addictive Behaviors: Treatment of Alcoholism, Drug Abuse, Smoking, and Obesity,* W. R. Miller, ed., Pergamon, New York, 1980, pp. 3–141.

17. Lovibond, S. H., Behavioral control of excessive drinking, in *Progress in Behavior Modification,* vol. 5, M. Hersen, R. M. Eisler, and P. M. Miller, eds., Academic, New York, 1977, pp. 63–109.

18. Sobell, L., Critique of alcohol treatment evaluation, in *Behavioral Approach to Alcoholism,* G. Marlatt and P. Nathan, eds., Rutgers Center of Alcohol Studies, New Brunswick, 1978, pp. 166–182.

19. Miller, P. M., *Behavioral Treatment of Alcoholism,* Pergamon, New York, 1976.

20. Briddell, D. W., and Nathan, P. E., Behavior assessment and modification with alcoholics: current status and future trends, in *Progress in Behavior Modification,* vol. 2, M. Hersen, R. M. Eisler, and P. M. Miller, eds., 1976, pp. 2–52.

21. Goldfried, M. R., and Merbaum, M., *Behavior Change through Self-control,* Holt, New York, 1973.

22. Caddy, G. R., and Lovibond, S. H., Self-regulation and discriminated aversive conditioning in the modification of alcoholics' drinking behavior, *Beh. Ther. 7,* 223–230 (1976).

23. Pomerleau, O., Pertschuk, M., Adkins, D., and d'Aguili, E., Treatment for

middle income drinkers, in *Alcoholism: New Directions in Behavioral Research and Treatment,* P. E. Nathan, G. A. Marlatt, and T. Loberg, eds., Plenum, New York, 1978, pp. 143–160.

24. Sobell, M. B., and Sobell, L. C., Alcoholics treated by individualized behavior therapy: one-year treatment outcome, *Beh. Res. and Ther. 11,* 599–618 (1973).

25. Bigelow, G., Cohen, M., Liebson, I., and Faillace, L. A., Abstinence or moderation? choices by alcoholics, *Beh. Res. and Ther. 10,* 209–214 (1972).

26. Lovibond, S. H., and Caddy, G., Discriminated aversive control in the moderation of alcoholics' drinking behavior, *Beh. Ther. 1,* 437–444 (1970).

27. Miller, W. R., and Joyce, M. A., Prediction of abstinence, controlled drinking, and heavy drinking outcome following behavioral self-control training, *J. Consult. and Clin. Psych. 47,* 773–775 (1979).

28. Pattison, E. M., Sobell, M. B., and Sobell, L. C., *Emerging Concepts of Alcohol Dependence,* Springer, New York, 1977.

29. Sobell, L. C., Sobell, M. B., and Christelman, W. C., The myth of "one drink," *Beh. Res. and Ther. 10,* 119–123 (1972).

30. Smart, R., Spontaneous recovery in alcoholics: a review and analysis of the available research, *Drug and Alc. Depend. 1,* 277–285 (1976).

31. McNamee, H. B., Mello, N. K., and Mendelson, J. H., Experimental analyses of drinking patterns of alcoholics: concurrent psychiatric observations, *Amer. J. Psychiat. 124,* 1063–1069 (1968).

32. Nathan, P. E., and O'Brien, J. S., An experimental analysis of the behavior of alcoholics and nonalcoholics during prolonged experimental drinking, *Beh. Ther. 2,* 455–476 (1971).

33. Lemere, F., What happens to alcoholics, *Amer. J. Psychiat. 109,* 674–676 (1953).

34. Selzer, M. L., and Holloway, W. H., A follow-up of alcoholics committed to a state hospital, *Q. J. Stud. Alc. 18,* 98–120 (1957).

35. Ritzler, B. A., Strauss, J. S., Vanord, A., and Kokes, R. F., Prognostic implications of various drinking patterns in psychiatric patients, *Amer. J. Psychiat. 134,* 546–549 (1977).

36. Franks, C. M., Alcoholism, in *Symptoms of Psychopathology,* C. G. Costello, ed., Wiley, New York, 1970, pp. 448–480.

37. Lovibond, S. H., Aversive control of behavior, *Beh. Ther. 1,* 80–91 (1970).

38. Barlow, D. H., Aversive procedures, in *Behavior Modification: Principles and Clinical Applications,* W. S. Agras, ed., Little, Brown, Boston, 1972, pp. 87–126.

39. Voegtlin, W. L., and Broz, W. R., The conditioned reflex treatment of chronic alcoholism X: an analysis of 3,125 admissions over a period of ten and a half years, *Ann. Int. Med. 30,* 580–597 (1949).

40. Raymond, M. J., The treatment of addiction by aversion conditioning with apomorphine, *Beh. Res. and Ther. 1,* 287–291 (1964).

41. Voegtlin, W. L., Lemere, F., Broz, W. R., and O'Hollaren, P., Conditioned reflex therapy of alcoholic addiction VI: follow-up report of 1,042 cases, *Amer. J. Med. Sci. 203,* 525–528 (1942).

42. Lemere, F., and Voegtlin, W. L., An evaluation of the aversion treatment of alcoholism, *Q. J. Stud. Alc. 11,* 199–204 (1950).

43. Thimann, J., Conditioned reflex treatment of alcoholics II: the risks of its application, its indications, contraindications, and psychotherapeutic aspects, *N. Eng. J. Med. 241,* 406–410 (1949).

44. Clancy, J., Vanderhoff, E., and Campbell, P., Evaluation of an aversive technique as a treatment of alcoholism: controlled trial with succinylcholine-induced apnea, *Q. J. Stud. Alc. 28,* 476–485 (1967).

45. Madill, M. F., Campbell, D., Laverty, S. G., Sanderson, R. E., and Vanderwater, S. J., Aversion treatment of alcoholism by succinylcholine-induced apneic paralysis, *Q. J. Stud. Alc. 27,* 483–509 (1966).

46. Sanderson, R. E., Campbell, D., and Laverty, S. G., An investigation of a new aversive conditioning treatment for alcoholism, *Q. J. Stud. Alc. 24,* 261–275 (1963).

47. Miller, P. M., Hersen, M., Eisler, R. M., and Hemphill, D. P., Electrical aversion therapy with alcoholics: an analogue study, *Beh. Res. and Ther. 11,* 491–498 (1973).

48. Vogler, R. E., Lunde, S. E., Johnson, G. R., and Martin, P. L., Electrical aversion conditioning with chronic alcoholics, *J. Consult. and Clin. Psych. 34,* 302–307 (1970).

49. Cautela, J. R., Covert sensitization, *Psych. Rep. 20,* 459–468 (1967).

50. Cautela, J. R., The treatment of alcoholism by covert sensitization, *Psychotherapy 7,* 86–90 (1970).

51. Anant, S. S., A note on the treatment of alcoholics by a verbal aversion technique, *Can. Psych. 8,* 19–22 (1967).

52. Anant, S. S., Treatment of alcoholics and drug addicts by verbal aversion techniques, *Inter'l. J. Addict. 3,* 381–388 (1968).

53. Cohen, M., Liebson, I. A., and Faillace, L. A., The modification of drinking in chronic alcoholics, in *Recent Advances in Studies of Alcoholism: An Interdisciplinary Approach,* N. R. Mello and J. H. Mendelson, eds., GPO, Pub. No. HSM 71–9045, Washington, D. C., 1970, pp. 745–766.

54. Pomerleau, O., and Adkins, D., Evaluating behavioral and traditional treatment for problem drinkers, in *Evaluating Alcohol and Drug Abuse Treatment Effectiveness: Recent Advances,* L. C. Sobell, M. B. Sobell, and E. Ward, eds., Pergamon, New York, 1980, pp. 93–108.

55. Alterman, A. I., Gottheil, E., Gellens, H. K., and Thornton, C. C., Relationship between drinking behavior of alcoholics in a drinking-decisions treatment program and treatment outcome, in *Alcoholism: New Directions in Behavioral Research and Treatment,* P. E. Nathan, G. A. Marlatt, and T. Loberg, eds., Plenum, New York, 1978, pp. 211–233.

56. Sobell, M. B., and Sobell, L. C., Second-year treatment outcome of alcoholics treated by individualized behavior therapy: results, *Beh. Res. and Ther. 14,* 195–215 (1976).

57. Sobell, M. B., Sobell, L. C., and VanderSpek, R., Relationships among clinical judgment, self-report, and breath analysis measure of intoxication in alcoholics, *J. Consult. and Clin. Psych. 47,* 204–206 (1979).

58. Miller, P. M., Behavioral Assessment in alcoholism research and treatment: current techniques, *Inter'l. J. Addict. 8,* 825–833 (1973).

59. Mello, N. R., and Mendelson, J. H., Operant analysis of drinking patterns of chronic alcoholics, *Nature 206,* 43–46 (1965).

60. Mills, K. C., Sobell, M. B., and Schaefer, H. H., Training social drinking as an alternative to abstinence for alcoholics, *Beh. Ther. 2,* 18–27 (1971).

61. Ferster, C. B., Nurnberger, J. I., and Levitt, E. B., The control of eating, *J. Math. 1,* 87–109 (1962).

62. Stuart, R. B., Behavioral control of overeating, *Beh. Res. and Ther. 5,* 357–365 (1967).

63. Penick, S. B., Filion, R., Fox, S., and Stunkard, A. J., Behavior modification in the treatment of obesity, *Psychosom. Med. 33,* 49–55 (1971).

64. Bellack, A. S., A comparison of self-reinforcement and self-monitoring in a weight reduction program, *Beh. Ther. 7,* 68–75 (1976).

65. Kazdin, A. E., and Wilson, G. T., *Evaluation of Behavior Therapy: Issues, Evidence, and Research Strategies,* Ballinger, Cambridge, 1978.

66. Romanczyk, R. G., Tracey, D. A., Wilson, G. T., and Thorpe, G. L., Behavioral techniques in the treatment of obesity: a comparative analysis, *Beh. Res. and Ther. 11,* 629–640 (1973).

67. McReynolds, W. T., and Paulsen, B. K., Stimulus control as the behavioral basis of weight loss procedures, in *Obesity: Behavioral Approaches to Dietary Management,* G. J. Williams, S. Martin, and J. Foreyt, eds., Brunner/Mazel, New York, 1976, pp. 43–64.

68. Chlouverakis, C., Dietary and medical treatments of obesity: an evaluative review, *Addict. Beh. 1,* 3–21 (1975).

69. Abramson, E. E., A review of behavioral approaches to weight control, *Beh. Res. and Ther. 11,* 547–556 (1973).

70. Stunkard, A. J., and Mahoney, M. J., Behavioral treatment of the eating disorders, in *Handbook of Behavior Modification and Behavior Therapy,* H. Leitenberg, ed., Prentice-Hall, Englewood Cliffs, 1976, pp. 45–73.

71. Jeffery, R. W., Wing, R. R., and Stunkard, A. J., Behavioral treatment of obesity: the state of the art 1976, *Beh. Ther. 9,* 189–199 (1978).

72. Abramson, E. E., Behavioral approaches to weight control: an updated review, *Beh. Res. and Ther. 15,* 355–363 (1977).

73. Stunkard, A. J., *The Pain of Obesity,* Bull, Palo Alto, 1976.

74. Levitz, L. S., and Stunkard, A. J., A therapeutic coalition for obesity: behavior modification and patient self-help, *Amer. J. Psychiat. 131,* 423–427 (1974).

75. Wilson, G. T., Behavior therapy and the treatment of obesity, in *The Addictive Behaviors: Treatment of Alcoholism, Drug Abuse, Smoking, and Obesity,* W. R. Miller, ed., Pergamon, New York, 1980, pp. 207–237.

76. Stalonas, P. M., Johnson, W. G., and Christ, M., Behavior modification for obesity: the evaluation of exercise, contingency management, and program adherence, *J. Consult. and Clin. Psych. 46,* 463–469 (1978).

77. LeBow, M. D., Can lighter become thinner? *Addict. Beh. 3,* 116–120 (1977).

78. Rodin, J., Cognitive-behavioral strategies for the control of obesity, in *Cognitive Behavior Therapy,* E. Meichenbaum, ed., Eddie Audio Cassette, Guilford, New York, 1978.

79. Hodgson, R., Rankin, H., and Stockwell, T., Craving and loss of control, in *Alcoholism: New Directions in Behavioral Research and Treatment,* P. E. Nathan, G. A. Marlatt, and T. Loberg, eds., Plenum, New York, 1978, pp. 341–350.

80. Marlatt, G. A., and Gordon, J. R., Determinants of relapse: implications for the maintenance of behavior change, in *Behavioral Medicine: Changing Health Life Styles,* P. Davidson, ed., Brunner/Mazel, New York, 1979, pp. 410–452.

81. Brownell, K. D., Heckerman, C. L., Westlake, R. J., Hayes, S. C., and Monti, P. M., The effect of couples training and partner cooperativeness in the behavioral treatment of obesity, *Beh. Res. and Ther. 16,* 323–333 (1978).

82. Pearce, J. W., LeBow, M. D. and Orchard, J., The role of spouse involvement in the behavioral treatment of obese women, paper presented to the Canadian Psychological Association, Quebec City, 1979.

83. Saccone, A. J., and Israel, A. C., Effects of experimenter versus significant other controlled reinforcement and choice of target behavior on weight loss, *Beh. Ther. 9,* 271–278 (1978).

84. Mahoney, M. J., Moura, N. G., and Wade, T. C., Relative efficacy of self-reward, self-punishment, and self-monitoring techniques for weight loss, *J. Consult. and Clin. Psych. 40,* 404–407 (1973).

85. Stunkard, A. J., and Kaplan, D., Eating in public places: a review of reports of the direct observation of eating behavior, *Inter'l. J. Obes. 1,* 89–101 (1977).

86. Warner, K., and Balagura, S., Intrameal eating patterns of obese and nonobese humans, *J. Comp. and Physiol. Psych. 7,* 778–783 (1975).

87. Franzini, L. R., and Grimes, W. B., Skinfold measures as the criterion of change in weight control studies, *Beh. Ther. 7,* 256–260 (1976).

88. Grimes, W. B., and Franzini, L. R., Skinfold measurement techniques for estimating percentage body fat, *J. Beh. Ther. and Exp. Psychiat. 8,* 65–69 (1977).

89. Schachter, S., and Rodin, J., *Obese Humans and Rats,* Erlbaum, Potomac, 1974.

90. Mahoney, M. J., Self-reward and self-monitoring techniques for weight control, *Beh. Ther. 5,* 48–57 (1974).

91. Schachter, S., Some extraordinary facts about obese humans and rats, *Amer. Psych. 25,* 129–144 (1971).

92. Coll, M., Meyers, A., and Stunkard, A. J., Obesity and food choices in public places, *Arch. Gen. Psychiat. 36,* 795–797 (1979).

93. Cooke, C. J., and Meyers, A., The role of predictor variables in the behavioral treatment of obesity, *Beh. Assess. 2,* 59–69 (1980).

94. Lang, P. J., Behavior therapy with a case of nervous anorexia, in *Case Studies in Behavior Modification,* L. P. Ullman and L. Krasner, eds., Holt, New York, 1965, pp. 217–221.

95. Hallsten, E. A., Adolescent anorexia nervosa treated by desensitization, *Beh. Res. and Ther. 3,* 87–91 (1965).

96. Bachrach, A. J., Erwin, W. J., and Mohr, J. P., The control of eating behavior in an anorexic by operant conditioning techniques, in *Case Studies in Behavior Modification*, L. P. Ullman and L. Krasner, eds., Holt, New York, 1965, pp. 153–163.

97. Agras, W. S., Barlow, D. H., Chapin, H. N., Abel, G. G., and Leitenberg, H., Behavior modification of anorexia nervosa, *Arch. Gen. Psychiat. 30*, 279–286 (1974).

98. Leitenberg, H., Agras, W. S., and Thomson, L. E., A sequential analysis of the effect of selective positive reinforcement in modifying anorexia nervosa, *Beh. Res. and Ther. 6*, 211–218 (1968).

99. Blinder, B. J., Freeman, D. M. A., and Stunkard, A. J., Behavioral therapy of anorexia nervosa: effectiveness of activity as a reinforcer of weight gain, *Amer. J. Psychiat. 126*, 1093–1098 (1970).

100. Halmi, K. A., Powers, P., and Cunningham, S., Treatment of anorexia nervosa with behavior modification, *Arch. Gen. Psychiat. 32*, 93–95 (1975).

101. Vandereycken, W., and Pierloot, R., A learning theory approach to anorexia nervosa, *Psych. Belg. 17*, 71–85 (1977).

102. Brady, J. P., and Rieger, W., Behavioral treatment of anorexia nervosa, in *Applications of Behavior Modification: International Symposium on Behavior Modification at Minneapolis 1972*, T. Thompson and W. S. Dockens, eds., Academic, New York, 1975, pp. 45–63.

103. Bhanji, S., and Thompson, J., Operant conditioning in the treatment of anorexia nervosa: a review and retrospective study of 11 cases, *Brit. J. Psychiat. 124*, 166–172 (1974).

104. Pertschuk, M. J., Behavior therapy: extended follow-up, in *Anorexia Nervosa*, R. A. Vigersky, ed., Raven, New York, 1977, pp. 305–313.

105. Bhanji, S., Operant conditioning in anorexia nervosa, in *Current Psychiatric Therapies, vol. 15*, H. Masserman, ed., Grune & Stratton, New York, 1975, pp. 59–64.

106. Liebman, R., Minuchin, S., and Baker, L., An integrated treatment program for anorexia nervosa, *Amer. J. Psychiat. 131*, 432–436 (1974).

107. Lichtenstein, E., and Brown, R. A., Smoking cessation methods: review and recommendations, in *The Addictive Behaviors: Treatment of Alcoholism, Drug Abuse, Smoking, and Obesity*, W. R. Miller, ed., Pergamon, New York, 1980, pp. 169–206.

108. Bernstein, D. A., and Glasgow, R. E., The modification of smoking behavior, in *Behavioral Medicine: Theory and Practice*, O. F. Pomerleau and J. P. Brady, eds., Williams & Wilkens, Baltimore, 1979, pp. 233–254.

109. Frederiksen, L. W., and Simon, S. J., Modification of smoking behavior, in *Modification of Pathological Behavior*, R. S. Davidson, ed., Gardner, New York, 1979, pp. 477–556.

110. Schwartz, J. L., Smoking cures: ways to kick an unhealthy habit, in *Research on Smoking Behavior* (NIDA Research Monograph No. 17), GPO, Washington, D. C., 1977, pp. 308–335.

111. Lichtenstein, E., and Danaher, B. G., Modification of smoking behavior: a critical analysis of theory, research, and practice, in *Progress in Behavior*

Modification, vol. 3, M. Hersen, R. M. Eisler, and P. M. Miller, eds., Academic, New York, 1976, pp. 79–124.

112. Hunt, W. A. and Bespalec, D. A., An evaluation of current methods of modifying smoking behavior, *J. Clin. Psych. 30,* 431–438 (1974).

113. Danaher, B. G., Rapid smoking and self-control in the modification of smoking behavior, *J. Consult. and Clin. Psych. 45,* 1068–1075 (1977).

114. Hall, R. G., Sachs, D. P. L., and Hall, S. M., Medical risk and therapeutic effectiveness of rapid smoking, *Beh. Ther. 10,* 249–259 (1979).

115. Schmahl, D. P., Lichtenstein, E., and Harris, D. E., Successful treatment of habitual smokers with warm smoky air and rapid smoking, *J. Consult. and Clin. Psych. 38,* 105–111 (1972).

116. Lichtenstein, E., and Glasgow, R. E., Rapid smoking: side effects and safeguards, *J. Consult. and Clin. Psych. 45,* 815–821 (1977).

117. Foxx, R. M., and Brown, R. A., Nicotine fading and self-monitoring for cigarette abstinence or controlled smoking, *J. Appl. Beh. Anal. 12,* 111–125 (1979).

118. Lando, H., Successful treatment of smokers with a broad-spectrum behavioral approach, *J. Consult. and Clin. Psych. 45,* 361–366 (1977).

119. Elliott, C. H., and Denney, D. R., A multiple-component treatment approach to smoking reduction, *J. Consult. and Clin. Psych. 46,* 1330–1339 (1978).

120. Frederiksen, L. W., Peterson, G. L., and Murphy, W. D., Controlled smoking: development and maintenance, *Addict. Beh. 1,* 193–196 (1976).

121. Hammond, E. C., Garfinkel, L., Siedman, H., and Lew, E. A., "Tar" and nicotine content of cigarette smoke in relation to death rates, *Environ. Res. 12,* 263–274 (1976).

122. Levinson, B. L., Shapiro, D., Schwartz, G. E., and Tursky, B., Smoking elimination by gradual reduction, *Beh. Ther. 2,* 477–487 (1971).

123. Frederiksen, L. W., Controlled smoking, in *Behavioral Analysis and Treatment of Substance Abuse* (NIDA Research Monograph No. 25), N. A. Krasnegor, ed., GPO, Washington, D. C., 1979, pp. 128–139.

124. Danaher, B. G., Lichtenstein, E., and Sullivan, J. M., Comparative effects of rapid and normal smoking on heart rate and carboxyhemoglobin, *J. Consult. and Clin. Psych. 44,* 556–563 (1976).

125. Kopel, S. A., The effects of self-control, booster sessions, and cognitive factors on the maintenance of smoking reduction, Ph.D. dissertation, University of Oregon, 1974.

126. Callahan, E. J., Alternative strategies in the treatment of narcotic addiction: a review, in *The Addictive Behaviors: Treatment of Alcoholism, Drug Abuse, Smoking, and Obesity,* W. R. Miller, ed., Pergamon, New York, 1980, pp. 143–167.

127. Hall, S. M., Bass, A., Hargreaves, W. A., and Loeb, P., Contingency management and information feedback in outpatient heroin detoxification, *Beh. Ther. 10,* 443–451 (1979).

128. Pickens, R., A behavioral program for treatment of drug dependence, in *Behavioral Analysis and Treatment of Substance Abuse* (NIDA Research

Monograph No. 25), N. A. Krasnegor, ed., GPO, Washington, D. C., 1979, pp. 44–53.

129. Hall, S. M., Cooper, J. L., Burmaster, S., and Polk, A., Contingency contracting as a therapeutic tool with methadone maintenance clients: six single subject studies, *Beh. Res. and Ther. 15,* 438–441 (1977).

130. Stitzer, M. L., Bigelow, G. E., and Liebson, I., Reinforcement of drug abstinence: a behavioral approach to drug abuse treatment, in *Behavioral Analysis and Treatment of Substance Abuse* (NIDA Research Monograph No. 25), N. A. Krasnegor, ed., GPO, Washington, D. C., 1979, pp. 68–90.

131. Glicksman, M., Ottomanelli, G., and Cutler, R., The earn-your-way credit system: use of a token economy in narcotic rehabilitation, *Inter'l. J. Addict. 6,* 525–531 (1971).

132. Melin, L., Anderson, B. E., and Götestam, K. G., Contingency management in a methadone maintenance treatment program, *Addict. Beh. 1,* 155–158 (1975).

133. Eriksson, J. H., Götestam, K. G. Melin, L., and Öst, L. G., A token economy treatment of drug addiction, *Beh. Res. and Ther. 13,* 113–125 (1975).

134. Boudin, H. M., Valentine, V. E., III, Inghram, R. D., Jr., Brantley, J. M., Ruiz, M. R., Smith, G. G., Catlin, R. P., III, and Regan, E. J., Jr., Contingency contracting with drug abusers in the natural environment, *Inter'l. J. Addict. 12,* 1–16 (1977).

135. Stitzer, M. L., and Bigelow, G. E., Drug abuse research in outpatient clinics, in *Self-administration of Abused Substances: Methods for Study* (NIDA Research Monograph No. 20), N. A. Krasnegor, ed., GPO, Washington, D. C., 1978, pp. 59–67.

136. Stitzer, M., Bigelow, G., Lawrence, C., Cohen, J., D'Lugoff, and Hawthorne, J., Methadone take-home as a reinforcer in a methadone maintenance program, *Addict. Beh. 2,* 9–14 (1977).

137. Callahan, E. J., Rawson, R. A., Glazer, M., McCleave, B. A., and Arias, R., Comparison of two naltrexone treatment programs: naltrexone alone versus naltrexone plus behavior therapy, in *Narcotic Antagonists: Naltrexone* (NIDA Research Monograph No. 9), D. A. Julius and P. F. Renault, eds., GPO, Washington, D. C., 1976, pp. 150–157.

138. Callahan, E. J., Rawson, R. A., McCleave, B. A., Arias, R. J., Glazer, M. A., and Liberman, R. R., The treatment of heroin addiction: naltrexone alone and with behavior therapy, unpublished manuscript, West Virginia University, 1977.

139. Kurland, A. A., McCabe, L., and Hanlon, T., Contingent naloxone treatment of the narcotic addict: a pilot study, *Inter'l. J. Addict. 11,* 131–142 (1976).

140. Julius, D. A., and Renault, P. F., *Narcotics Antagonists: Naltrexone* (NIDA Research Monograph No. 9), GPO, Washington, D. C., 1976.

141. Boudin, H. M., Contingency contracting with drug abusers in the natural environment: treatment evaluation, in *Evaluating Alcohol and Drug Abuse Treatment Effectiveness,* L. C. Sobell, M. B. Sobell, and E. Ward, eds., Pergamon, New York, 1980, pp. 108–128.

142. Garmezy, N., Observation on high-risk research and premorbid development in schizophrenia, in *The Nature of Schizophrenia: New Approaches to Research and Treatment,* L. C. Wynne, R. L. Cromwell, and S. Matthysse, eds., Wiley, New York, 1978, pp. 460–472.

143. Engel, G. L., The need for a new medical model: a challenge for biomedicine, *Science 196,* 129–136 (1977).

INDEX

Index

Oral gratification, smoking tobacco and, 156
Outpatient treatment, anorexia nervosa, 240
Overdrinking: *see* Polydipsia
Overeaters Anonymous, 203
Overeating: *see* Obesity
Overexertion, 298; *see also* Sports, excess
Oxymorphone, as reinforcer, 5; *see also* Opiates

Palatability, obesity and, 196
Paradoxical therapy, gambling and, 279
Paranoia:
  caffeine and, 173
  psychomotor stimulants and, 75–76
Passive immunization, blocking reinforcing action of opiate drugs by, 18–19
PCP, 97, 108–109
Peer group therapy, Alcoholics Anonymous and, 58
Pentazocine, as negative reinforcers, 6
Personality:
  alcoholism and, 124
  anorexia nervosa and, 223
  caffeinism and, 179–180
  gambling and, 275–278
  LSD and change in, 106
  work addiction and, 268, 269
Pharmacotherapy, tobacco smoking cessation and, 161–162
Phencyclidine (PCP), 97, 108–109
Phenobarbital, LSD treatment, 104
Phenoxybenzamine, anorexia nervosa and, 237
Phenylethylamines, 98
  mescaline, 96, 98–99
  myristicin, 98, 101
  STP, 97, 98, 100–101

see also Amphetamines; Marijuana
4-Phosphoryloxy-N,N-dimethoxy-tryptamine, 101, 102–103
Physical dependence, on opiates, 12–14
Pica, schedule induced ingestion of, 321–322
Pimozide, 87
1-Piperidinocyclohexane-carbonitrile, 108
Pleasure codes, 283
Polydipsia (schedule induced overdrinking), 314–315
  production of, 315–319
  bitonic function for, 317, 319
Positive reinforcement, 3
  sedatives, hypnotics, and minor tranquilizers:
    immediate nature of, 46–47
    probability of, 47–48
  tobacco smoking cessation and, 162
  tolerance to opiates as, 11–12
Pregnancy:
  alcoholism and, 124, 129
  marijuana, 143
Preintoxication condition, 43
Process codes, 283
Progressive-ratio procedure, reinforcing efficacy of drugs and, 8–9
Propanolol, caffeinism and, 184
Propiram, as negative reinforcers, 6
Propoxyphene, dosage, 7
d-Propoxyphene (hydrochloride), as reinforcer, 5; *see also* Opiates
d-Propoxyphene (napsylate), as reinforcer, 5; *see also* Opiates
Pseudomourning, tobacco smoking cessation and, 155

DATE DUE

DEC 0 3 2001			
GAYLORD			PRINTED IN U.S.A.